# Urban Governance Practices in China

Since the reform and opening-up, China has experienced the largest and fastest urbanization process in the history of the world. In the process of urbanization, due to unbalanced and inadequate development, we are experiencing urban diseases, including environmental pollution, traffic congestion, resource shortages, lack of security, the deep gap between the rich and the poor.

To achieve the goal of "Better City, Better Life", some cities in China has been carried out some new practices of good urban governance. This book series aims to summary and promote the advanced experience of urban governance in different regions of China, which can provide excellent experience for the cities in other countries.

The key words in UGPC include but are not limited to:

- China
- Urban Governance
- Practice & Experience

More information about this series at http://www.springer.com/series/16301

Xueqing Jing
Editor

# Development of the Yangtze River Economic Belt in China

上海交通大學出版社
SHANGHAI JIAO TONG UNIVERSITY PRESS

Springer

*Editor*
Xueqing Jing
Institute of Applied Economics
Shanghai Academy of Social Sciences
Shanghai, China

This book is sponsored by “B&R” Book Program

ISSN 2661-8796 ISSN 2661-880X (electronic)
Urban Governance Practices in China
ISBN 978-981-16-1577-1 ISBN 978-981-16-1578-8 (eBook)
https://doi.org/10.1007/978-981-16-1578-8

Jointly published with Shanghai Jiao Tong University Press
The print edition is not for sale in China (Mainland). Customers from China (Mainland) please order the print book from: Shanghai Jiao Tong University Press.



This Springer imprint is published by the registered company Springer Nature Singapore Pte Ltd.
The registered company address is: 152 Beach Road, #21-01/04 Gateway East, Singapore 189721, Singapore

# Preface

The State Council issued the *Guidelines for Promoting the Development of the Yangtze River Economic Belt by Relying on Golden Waterways (Guidelines)* on September 12, 2014, which is a major initiative for China to enter the "New Normal" and another important layout of China's regional economic development strategy following the development strategy of coastal areas, strategy of West China development, the strategy of Northeast Revitalization, and the strategy of the Rise of Central China. The Yangtze River Economic Belt involves 11 provinces and cities including Shanghai city, Jiangsu province, Zhejiang province, Anhui province, Jiangxi province, Hubei province, Hunan province, Chongqing city, Sichuan province, Guizhou province, and Yunnan province, stretching over the east, middle, and west three belts and connecting the south and the north. The geographical location is very important. The further development of the Yangtze River Economic Belt is of great significance to bring along the economy of China to maintain the medium-high rate of growth and the coordinated regional economic development under the New Normal.

The Yangtze River is the longest river in China. The main stream and tributaries of the Yangtze River are crisscrossed and with abundant water yield. The waterway transportation on the Yangtze River plays an important role in china, and the Yangtze River Economic Belt is connected by the Yangtze River "golden waterways". The "*Guidelines*" issued by the State Council is accompanied with the *Comprehensive Multiple-Dimensional Traffic Corridor Planning of the Yangtze River Economic Belt* (2014–2020), which has made strategic arrangements to coordinate the construction of transportation infrastructure of waterway transportation, railway transportation, road transportation, air transportation, oil and gas pipeline network transportation, and urban transportation in the Yangtze River Economic Belt, to strengthen the organic connection of various transportation modes, and to improve the comprehensive transportation system within the planning period. Therefore, we believe that how the Yangtze River Economic Belt can achieve coordinated development, joint development, cooperative development, and integrated development in the region with the help of the convenient transportation network is a proposition that is worthy of our attention. This book is just to present the observation and study of this proposition.

The book is divided into seven chapters and discusses the coordinated development of the Yangtze River Economic Belt from different levels, mainly focusing on the industrial collaboration. Specifically speaking: the chapter "Linkage Development of Manufacturing Industry and Logistics Industry of the Yangtze River Economic Belt" is about the joint development of manufacturing industry and logistics industry in the Yangtze River Economic Belt, the chapter "Coordinated Development of Information Industry in Yangtze River Economic Belt" is about the coordinated development of the information industry in the Yangtze River Economic Belt, the chapter "Coordination and Deepening of Agricultural Development in Yangtze River Economic Belt" is about the coordination and deepening of the agricultural development of the Yangtze River Economic Belt, and the chapter "Coordinated Development of Ecological Environment in Yangtze River Economic Belt" is about the coordinated development of the ecological environment in Yangtze River Economic Belt, the chapter "Integrated Development of Regional Finance in the Yangtze River Economic Belt" is about the financial integration development of the Yangtze River Economic Belt, the chapter "Coordinated Development of Ports in the Yangtze River Economic Belt" is about the coordinated development of ports in the Yangtze River Economic Belt, and the chapter "Industrial Division of Work and Cooperation in the Yangtze River Economic Belt" is about the industrial division and cooperation in the Yangtze River Economic Belt.

This book is a collective creation of all researchers working in the Research Office of Regional Economic and Urban-Rural Development of the Department of Economic Research Institute, Shanghai Academy of Social Sciences. The chief editor is Jing Xueqing and the specific division of work is as follows: chapter "Linkage Development of Manufacturing Industry and Logistics Industry of the Yangtze River Economic Belt" is edited by Jing Xueqing, chapter "Coordinated Development of Information Industry in Yangtze River Economic Belt" by Xu Limei, chapter "Coordination and Deepening of Agricultural Development in Yangtze River Economic Belt" by Wang Xiuzhi chapter "Coordinated Development of Ecological Environment in Yangtze River Economic Belt" by Sun Lin, chapter "Integrated Development of Regional Finance in the Yangtze River Economic Belt" by Zhang Yan, chapter "Coordinated Development of Ports in the Yangtze River Economic Belt" by Wang Xiaojuan, and chapter "Industrial Division of Work and Cooperation in the Yangtze River Economic Belt" by Fan Fuzhuo.

The creation and publication of this book have been encouraged and supported by Director Sun Fuqing of the Department of Economic Research Institute, Shanghai Academy of Social Sciences. The publication of this book is funded by the Project of "Innovation Economy and Shanghai Transformation and Development" for Shanghai Academy of Social Sciences. Colleagues who have worked together for this work have made their unremitting efforts. We would like to extend our appreciation to all the people here!

Some inadequacies and mistakes in the book are inevitable and all kinds of criticism and correction from readers are welcomed.

Shanghai, China Xueqing Jing
November 2015

# Contents

**Linkage Development of Manufacturing Industry and Logistics Industry of the Yangtze River Economic Belt** ........................ 1
Xueqing Jing

**Coordinated Development of Information Industry in Yangtze River Economic Belt** ........................ 37
Limei Xu

**Coordination and Deepening of Agricultural Development in Yangtze River Economic Belt** ........................ 75
Xiuzhi Wang

**Coordinated Development of Ecological Environment in Yangtze River Economic Belt** ........................ 107
Lin Sun

**Integrated Development of Regional Finance in the Yangtze River Economic Belt** ........................ 147
Yan Zhang

**Coordinated Development of Ports in the Yangtze River Economic Belt** ........................ 183
Xiaojuan Wang

**Industrial Division of Work and Cooperation in the Yangtze River Economic Belt** ........................ 211
Fuzhuo Fan

**References** ........................ 249

# Linkage Development of Manufacturing Industry and Logistics Industry of the Yangtze River Economic Belt

**Xueqing Jing**

## 1 Introduction

All industrial sectors of regional economy is interrelated and interacted with each other, and the difference lies only in the way of interrelation and the intensity of interaction. Manufacturing industry is one of the most important sectors to meet the material needs of human beings and various economic entities, and is also the main driving force and important pillar of the regional economic development. The development of manufacturing industry is inseparable from the support of service industry. Producer service industry in the service industry and then the logistics industry in producer service industry are the most direct basic supporting industrial sectors of manufacturing industry. From the international point of view, logistics industry is regarded as the artery and basic industry for national economic development, and its level of development has become one of the important symbols to measure the modernization degree and comprehensive national strength of one state. It is known as the "accelerator" and "the third source of profit" to promote economic growth. Therein, the development of logistics industry is most closely related to the manufacturing industry.

The original meaning of LINKAGE refers to a number of related things. When one of them moves or changes, others will follow the movement or change, that is, joint action. The linkage between manufacturing industry and logistics industry means that manufacturing industry and logistics industry rely on, integrate with, support each other and develop together. The linkage between manufacturing industry and logistics industry is the deep penetration and cooperation between the two industries.

The linkage development of manufacturing industry and logistics industry can promote manufacturing enterprises to focus on the core business, improve the

X. Jing (✉)
Institute of Applied Economics, Shanghai Academy of Social Sciences, Shanghai, China
e-mail: jxq@sass.org.cn



X. Jing (ed.), *Development of the Yangtze River Economic Belt in China*, Urban Governance Practices in China,
https://doi.org/10.1007/978-981-16-1578-8_1

competitiveness of manufacturing enterprises, meanwhile to reduce logistics costs and improve customer logistics satisfaction. On the one hand, outsourcing logistics business that is not in the proficiency of manufacturing enterprises can make enterprises to concentrate the largest resources to develop the main business, improve the competitiveness of their core business, and continuously strengthen their competitive advantages in the market competition. On the other hand, outsourcing part or all of the logistics business to competent logistics enterprises can optimize their own logistics processes, reduce logistics costs, and provide satisfactory logistics services to the customers of manufacturing enterprises through professional logistics services, so as to improve the satisfaction of customers to the manufacturing enterprises.

The linkage development of manufacturing industry and logistics industry can promote logistics enterprises to improve their service level and expand their living space. In the process of linkage between manufacturing industry and logistics industry, logistics enterprises and manufacturing enterprises are bound with closer partnership. Pitching in the production process of manufacturing enterprises and strengthening the control power over the whole logistics process of manufacturing enterprises require the logistics enterprises to continuously improve their level of logistics services and enhance the ability to serve. One the other, in the interconnecting process of manufacturing industry and logistics industry, the breadth and depth of logistics services provided by logistics enterprises for manufacturing enterprises have been greatly improved, which increases the profit point of logistics enterprises and expands the survival space of logistics enterprises.

In the *Logistics Industry Adjustment and Revitalization Plan* as issued by the Chinese government, the linkage development of manufacturing industry and logistics industry is one of the "Nine Major Projects". The plan emphasizes that "production and trade enterprises shall be encouraged to separate or outsource logistics functions according to the principle of division and cooperation". Therefore, it is of great practical significance to build an exchange platform for regional manufacturing and logistics industry, create cooperation opportunities, and promote coordinated and linkage development.

The Yangtze River Economic Belt includes Shanghai City, Jiangsu Province, Zhejiang Province, Anhui Province, Jiangxi Province, Hubei Province, Hunan Province, Chongqing City, Sichuan Province, Guizhou Province and Yunnan Province, with a total of 11 provinces and cities, spanning the eastern, central and western three major regions where the development difference of manufacturing industry is very obvious, and the logistics development in each region has its own characteristics. Therefore, that how to explore the development of manufacturing industry and logistics industry, especially the situation of linkage development based on the characteristics of the Yangtze River Economic Belt will be taken as the emphasis and main content of this chapter.

## 2 Development and Characteristics of Manufacturing Industry and Logistics Industry in the Yangtze River Economic Belt

The analysis of industrial development status and its characteristics is rooted at the convincing data, but the availability of data is subject to limitations. Since it is difficult to collect comparatively comprehensive and systematic data of manufacturing industry, the industrial data have to be adopted. Although the scope of industrial data is relatively large, it includes the mining industry as well as the production and supply industry of electric power, heat, gas and water in addition to the manufacturing industry, however, the manufacturing is the main body of the industry, accounting for the vast majority of the industry. Herein, four indicators including number of enterprises, total assets, revenue from main business and total profit in four typical years of 2000, 2004, 2007 and 2013 are selected to calculate the proportion of manufacturing enterprises above designated scale to industrial enterprises above designated scale. It is found that: the number of manufacturing enterprises accounts for more than 90% of the number of industrial enterprises, the revenue from main business accounts for more than 80%, and the total assets and total profits account more than 70% (refer to Table 1). Although the situations of the Yangtze River Economic Belt and its 11 provinces and cities are not copying that of the whole state, the basic situations are broadly in line. Therefore, the data of industrial enterprises above the scale are adopted to replace the data of manufacturing industry to analyze the development status and characteristics of manufacturing industry, and the same method is also used in the analysis of the linkage development process of manufacturing industry and logistics industry.

**Table 1** Proportion of manufacturing enterprises above designated scale in industrial enterprises above designated scale of typical years in China (%)

| | Number of enterprises | Total assets | Revenue from main business | Total profit |
|---|---|---|---|---|
| Year 2000 | 93.01 | 75.75 | 86.55 | 79.99 |
| Year 2004 | 92.72 | 76.94 | 86.87 | 73.20 |
| Year 2007 | 92.76 | 75.13 | 86.86 | 72.17 |
| Year 2013 | 92.75 | 76.56 | 87.64 | 80.70 |

*Note* The basic data sourced from *China Statistical Yearbook* of corresponding years

## 2.1 *Development Status and Characteristics of Manufacturing Industry*

(I) **The development status of manufacturing industry in the Yangtze River Economic Belt and its nationwide comparison**

This paper takes 2000 as the base period and 2013 as the report period, and takes the sum of the representative indicators of 11 provinces and cities as the representative indicator of the whole Yangtze River Economic Belt to discuss the development status of manufacturing industry in the whole Yangtze River Economic Belt.

1. The manufacturing industry in the Yangtze River Economic Belt developed faster than the national average

Since 2000, the statistical data of indicators of industrial enterprises above the designated scale in each provincial area have been published by the state every year, where the number of enterprises, the total assets, the revenue from main business and the total profit are the four indicators with representativeness and time consistency. In 2000, the values of these four indicators of the Yangtze River Economic Belt were 70,422 enterprises, 5,025.2 billion yuan, 3,459.3 billion yuan and 147.6 billion yuan respectively and increased to 167,473 enterprises, 34,618.8 billion yuan, 42,515.1 billion yuan and 248.9 billion yuan respectively in 2013 (refer to Table 2) with annual average growth rates of 6.66%, 14.84%, 19.30% and 21.73%[1] respectively, while the average annual growth rates of these four indicators of the state in the same period were 5.94%, 14.68%, 19.26% and 20.46% respectively. It can be seen that the scale expansion of manufacturing industry in the Yangtze River Economic Belt is faster than the national average.

2. The manufacturing industry in the Yangtze River Economic Belt is playing an important role for the whole state, and presenting the tendency of rising in stability.

In 2013, the four indicators, i.e. number of industrial enterprises above designated scale, total assets, revenue from main business and total profit accounted for 47.50%, 40.69%, 41.31% and 39.61% of those for the state respectively (refer to Table 3). In general, the manufacturing scale of the Yangtze River Economic Belt accounts for about 40% of the state, so it occupies an important position in the whole state. In terms of dynamic changes, the proportion of the four indicators of industrial enterprises above designated scale in the Yangtze River Economic Belt in the whole state was increased by certain degrees from 2000 to 2013, namely 4.27%, 0.87%, 0.20% and 6.02%, respectively. The increase of amplitude is not particularly large, but is presenting the tendency of rising in stability.

[1]In order to reduce the influence of price factors, the average growth rate is calculated by the formula as follows: $100 \times (\text{Ln}a_n - \text{Ln}a_0)/n$, where $a_0$ and $a_n$ are the indicators at the beginning and the end of the period respectively, n is the number of years from the beginning to the end of the period, and Ln is the natural logarithm sign and same for the below.

**Table 2** Main indicators of the Yangtze River Economic Belt and industrial enterprises above designated scale in typical years

| | | Number of enterprises (enterprises) | Total assets (one hundred million) | Revenue from main business (one hundred million) | Total profit (one hundred million) |
|---|---|---|---|---|---|
| Yangtze River Economic Belt | Year 2000 | 70 422 | 50 252 | 34 593 | 1 476 |
| | Year 2002 | 83 151 | 58 693 | 45 832 | 2 328 |
| | Year 2006 | 150 631 | 123 811 | 133 884 | 6 972 |
| Yangtze River Economic Belt | Year 2008 | 212 160 | 180 346 | 203 882 | 10 907 |
| | Year 2011 | 152 016 | 277 835 | 346 951 | 23 181 |
| | Year 2013 | 167 473 | 346 138 | 425 151 | 24 890 |
| Nationwide | Year 2000 | 162 885 | 126 211 | 84 152 | 4 394 |
| | Year 2002 | 181 557 | 146 218 | 109 486 | 5 785 |
| | Year 2006 | 301 961 | 291 215 | 313 593 | 19 504 |
| | Year 2008 | 426 113 | 431 306 | 500 020 | 30 562 |
| | Year 2011 | 325 609 | 675 797 | 841 830 | 61 396 |
| | Year 2013 | 352 546 | 850 626 | 1 029 150 | 62 831 |

*Note* ① Since the state did not publish the revenue from the main business of industrial enterprises above designated scale in 2000 and 2002, therefore, the revenue for product sales revenue is used here instead
② The data sourced from *China Statistical Yearbook* of corresponding years

**Table 3** Proportion of major indexes of industrial enterprises above designated scale in China in typical years (%)

| | Number of enterprises | Total assets | Revenue from main business | Total profit |
|---|---|---|---|---|
| Year 2000 | 43.23 | 39.82 | 41.11 | 33.59 |
| Year 2002 | 45.80 | 40.14 | 41.86 | 40.24 |
| Year 2006 | 49.88 | 42.52 | 42.69 | 35.75 |
| Year 2008 | 49.79 | 41.81 | 40.77 | 35.69 |
| Year 2011 | 46.69 | 41.11 | 41.21 | 37.76 |
| Year 2013 | 47.50 | 40.69 | 41.31 | 39.61 |

*Note* ① Refer to the note ① in Table 2
② The basic data sourced from *China Statistical Yearbook* of corresponding years

3. The average scale of manufacturing enterprises in the Yangtze River Economic Belt was smaller than the national average, but the expansion of scale was faster.

The average scale of each industrial enterprise can be obtained when the total assets, revenue from main business and total profit are divided by the number of industrial enterprises above the scale in the Yangtze River Economic Belt. Table 4 shows the average scale of the Yangtze River Economic Belt and the whole state in six typical

**Table 4** Average scale of industrial enterprises above designated scale in Yangtze River Economic Belt and China in typical years

| | | Average assets (10 thousand Yuan/enterprise) | Average revenue from main business (10 thousand Yuan/enterprise) | Average profit (10 thousand Yuan/enterprise) |
|---|---|---|---|---|
| Yangtze River Economic Belt | Year 2000 | 7 136 | 4 912 | 210 |
| | Year 2002 | 7 059 | 5 512 | 280 |
| | Year 2006 | 8 220 | 8 888 | 463 |
| | Year 2008 | 8 500 | 9 610 | 514 |
| | Year 2011 | 18 277 | 22 823 | 1 525 |
| | Year 2013 | 20 668 | 25 386 | 1 486 |
| Whole state | Year 2000 | 7 748 | 5 166 | 270 |
| | Year 2002 | 8 054 | 6 030 | 319 |
| | Year 2006 | 9 644 | 10 385 | 646 |
| | Year 2008 | 10 122 | 11 734 | 717 |
| | Year 2011 | 20 755 | 25 854 | 1 886 |
| | Year 2013 | 24 128 | 29 192 | 1 782 |

*Note* Same as Table 3

years from 2000 to 2013. It can be seen from Table 4 that from 2000 to 2013, the average total assets, revenue from main business and total profit of each enterprise above the designated scale in the Yangtze River Economic Belt were increased from 71.36 million Yuan, 49.12 million yuan and 2.1 million yuan to 206.68 million yuan, 253.86 million Yuan and 14.86 million yuan respectively, with an average annual growth rate of 8.18%, 12.63% and 15.07% respectively. It demonstrated that the expansion of enterprise scale was relatively fast, but the average enterprise scale was smaller than the national average. In several typical years in Table 4, the total assets, revenue from main business and total profit of each industrial enterprise above the scale in the Yangtze River Economic Belt were lower than those of the whole state.

4. The operation efficiency of manufacturing enterprises in the Yangtze River Economic Belt was lower than the national average, but the increasing rate was higher than that of the whole state.

In 2013, the asset profit margin and sales margin of industrial enterprises in the Yangtze River Economic Belt were 7.19 yuan/100 yuan and 5.85 yuan/100 yuan, respectively, with a weighted average of 6.39 yuan/100 yuan (according to the importance of indicators, the weights of asset profit margin and sales margin were taken as 0.4 and 0.6 respectively), all of which were lower than the national average of 7.39 yuan/100 yuan, 6.11 yuan/100 yuan and 6.62 yuan/100 yuan in the same period. The same is true for other typical years (refer to Table 5). It can be seen that the operation efficiency of manufacturing enterprises in the Yangtze River Economic Belt was lower than the national average.

**Table 5** Operation efficiency of Yangtze River Economic Belt and industrial enterprises above designated scale in typical years

| | Yangtze River Economic Belt | | | Whole state | | |
|---|---|---|---|---|---|---|
| | Asset profit margin (Yuan/100 Yuan) | Sales margin (Yuan/100 Yuan) | Weighted average (Yuan/100 Yuan) | Asset profit margin (Yuan/100 Yuan) | Sales margin (Yuan/100 Yuan) | Weighted average (Yuan/100 Yuan) |
| Year 2000 | 2.94 | 4.27 | 3.74 | 3.48 | 5.22 | 4.52 |
| Year 2002 | 3.97 | 5.08 | 4.64 | 3.96 | 5.28 | 4.75 |
| Year 2006 | 5.63 | 5.21 | 5.38 | 6.70 | 6.22 | 6.41 |
| Year 2008 | 6.05 | 5.35 | 5.63 | 7.09 | 6.11 | 6.50 |
| Year 2011 | 8.34 | 6.68 | 7.34 | 9.09 | 7.29 | 8.01 |
| Year 2013 | 7.19 | 5.85 | 6.39 | 7.39 | 6.11 | 6.62 |
| 2000–2013 average annual growth rate (%) | 6.88 | 2.42 | 4.12 | 5.79 | 1.21 | 2.93 |

*Note* ① The asset profit margin equals to the total profit divided by the total assets, the sales margin equals to the total profit divided by the revenue from the main business, and the average value equals to the arithmetic average value of the asset profit margin and the sales margin
② The basic data sourced from *China Statistical Yearbook* of corresponding years

However, from the perspective of dynamic changes, the growth of operation efficiency in the Yangtze River Economic Belt was better than the national average. From 2000 to 2013, the average annual growth rates of asset profit margin and sales margin in the Yangtze River Economic Belt were 6.88% and 2.42%, respectively. The weighted average annual growth rate of these two indicators was 4.12% and all three indicators were higher than the national average of 5.79, 1.21 and 2.93% in the same period. It can be seen that the operation efficiency of manufacturing enterprises in the Yangtze River Economic Belt was increased faster than the national average.

(II) **The development status and comparison of manufacturing industry in provinces and cities belong to Yangtze River Economic Belt**

1. The scale of manufacturing industry varies greatly among provinces and cities, and the extreme value ratio of comprehensive indicator was more than 16 times.

In 2013, the number of industrial enterprises above designated scale, total assets, revenue from main business and total profit of Jiangsu Province were 46387 enterprises, 9208.2 billion yuan, 13227 billion yuan and 783.41 billion yuan respectively, all of which were the highest among the 11 provinces and cities in the Yangtze River Economic Belt, while those of Guizhou Province were the lowest (as seen in Table 6). The four indicators of Jiangsu Province were 15 times, 9 times, 19 times and 16 times of those of Guizhou Province, while those of Guizhou Province were only 6.8%, 10.5%, 5.2% and 6.1% of those of Jiangsu Province respectively.

**Table 6** Main indexes of industrial enterprises above designated scale in provinces and cities in Yangtze River Economic Belt

| | Number of enterprises (enterprises) | Total assets (one hundred million) | Revenue from main business (one hundred million) | Total profit (one hundred million) |
|---|---|---|---|---|
| Shanghai City | 9 782 | 33 538 | 34 534 | 2 415.2 |
| Jiangsu Province | 46 387 | 92 082 | 132 270 | 7 834.1 |
| Zhejiang Province | 36 904 | 59 633 | 61 765 | 3 385.9 |
| Anhui Province | 15 114 | 25 168 | 33 079 | 1 758.8 |
| Jiangxi Province | 7 601 | 13 640 | 26 700 | 1 756.7 |
| Hubei Province | 13 441 | 30 132 | 37 865 | 2 080.7 |
| Hunan Province | 13 323 | 19 032 | 31 617 | 1 585.1 |
| Chongqing City | 5 237 | 13 136 | 15 417 | 878.4 |
| Sichuan Province | 13 163 | 34 729 | 35 252 | 2 168.4 |
| Guizhou Province | 3 139 | 9 704 | 6 878 | 477.3 |
| Yunnan Province | 3 382 | 15 344 | 9 773 | 549.1 |

*Note* The data sourced from *China Statistical Yearbook* of 2014

In order to comprehensively reflect and compare the scale of manufacturing industry among regions, the following calculation and processing have been made: firstly, the corresponding indicators of 11 provinces and cities in the Yangtze River Economic Belt were divided by the number of industrial enterprises above designated scale, total assets, revenue from main business and total profit in Guizhou Province in 2013, and then the index of four indicators of 11 provinces and cities were obtained. According to the importance degree, the weights of 0.1, 0.2, 0.5 and 0.2 were assigned respectively, and the indexes of the four indicators of each province and city were summed up to obtain the composite index of industrial scale of each province. Finally, the composite index of industrial scale of each province was sequenced from large to small, and the chart is prepared as shown in Fig. 1.

According to the composite index of industrial scale of 11 provinces and cities in Fig. 1, the scale of manufacturing industry in Jiangsu Province was the largest and was more than 16 times of Guizhou Province, and followed by that of Zhejiang Province, which was more than 8 times of Guizhou Province. The next ones were

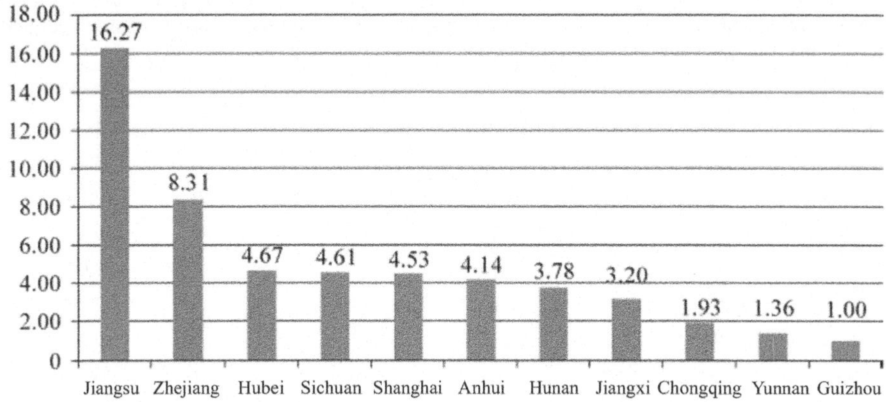


**Fig. 1** Industrial scale composite index of 11 provinces and cities in the Yangtze River Economic Belt in 2013

Hubei Province, Sichuan Province, Shanghai City and Anhui Province with the manufacturing scale more than 4 times of Guizhou Province. The scale of manufacturing industry in Hunan Province and Jiangxi Province was 3–4 times of Guizhou Province, and that of Chongqing city was about twice of Guizhou Province. The scale of manufacturing industry in Yunnan Province was similar to that of Guizhou Province and was only 36% larger than Guizhou Province. The scale of manufacturing industry in Shanghai was about one fourth of Jiangsu Province, one half of Zhejiang Province and was roughly the same as that of Hubei Province and Sichuan Province.

2. There were significant differences in the growth rate of manufacturing industry among provinces and cities, and the extreme value ratio of composite indicators was more than twice.

From 2000 to 2013, the average annual growth rate of the number of industrial enterprises above designated scale in Anhui Province reached 10.9% while that of Shanghai was only 1%, presenting quite remarkable disparity; From the perspective of total assets, the average annual growth rate of Zhejiang Province reached 16.5%, while that of Shanghai was only 9.7%, presenting quite large difference; From the perspective of revenue from main business, the average annual growth rate of Jiangxi Province was 26.1%, while that of Shanghai was only 12.9%, presenting quite large difference. From the perspective of total profit, the average annual growth rate of Jiangxi Province was up to 38.9%, while that of Shanghai was only 14%, also presenting quite large difference (as seen in Table 7).

Here, we assign 0.1, 0.2, 0.5 and 0.2 weights to the four indicators of the number of enterprises, total assets, revenue from main business and total profit respectively to calculate the weighted average growth rate of industries in each region (see Fig. 2). This indicator combines the above four indicators and is a composite indicator reflecting the industrial growth rate. Among the 11 provinces and cities in the Yangtze River Economic Belt, the weighted average growth rate of industry in

**Table 7** Average annual growth rate of main indicators of industrial enterprises in provinces and cities in the Yangtze River Economic Belt from 2000 to 2013 (%)

| | Number of enterprises | Total assets | Revenue from main business | Total profit |
|---|---|---|---|---|
| Shanghai | 1.01 | 9.75 | 12.93 | 14.00 |
| Jiangsu | 7.15 | 16.28 | 19.89 | 23.48 |
| Zhejiang | 7.15 | 16.47 | 17.33 | 17.38 |
| Anhui | 10.87 | 16.42 | 22.89 | 29.45 |
| Jiangxi | 5.86 | 15.43 | 26.10 | 38.09 |
| Hubei | 5.85 | 14.17 | 19.84 | 22.87 |
| Hunan | 7.84 | 14.83 | 23.13 | 29.45 |
| Chongqing | 7.25 | 14.69 | 2136 | 30.98 |
| Sichuan | 8.44 | 15.57 | 2180 | 26.27 |
| Guizhou | 3.14 | 14.27 | 18.84 | 27.98 |
| Yunnan | 3.58 | 14.56 | 17.10 | 15.87 |

*Note* The basic data sourced from *China Statistical Yearbook* of 2001 and 2014

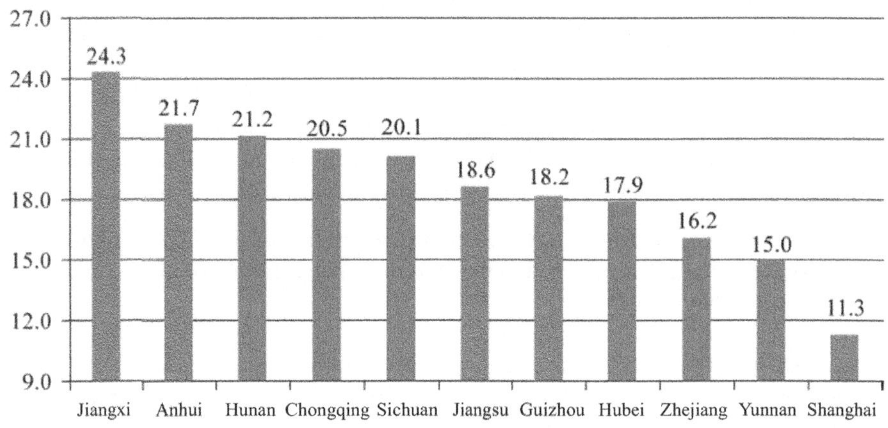


**Fig. 2** Weighted annual average growth rate of industries of provinces and cities in the Yangtze River Economic Belt in 2013 (%)

Jiangxi Province was the largest and up to 24.3%. Those for Anhui Province, Hunan Province, Chongqing city and Sichuan Province were all between 20 and 22% which meant the growth rate of manufacturing industry was relatively high. The weighted average growth rates of industry in Jiangsu Province, Zhejiang Province, Hubei Province and Guizhou Province were all about 16–19%, which meant the growth rate of manufacturing industry was medium, while that of Yunnan Province was rather slow with the weighted growth rate of industry only about 15%. The growth rate of manufacturing industry in Shanghai was the lowest, and the weighted growth rate of industry was about 11.3%. The growth rate of Jiangxi Province was 2.15 times as much as that of Shanghai.

3. There was a significant difference in the average scale of manufacturing enterprises among provinces and cities, and the extreme value ratio of the composite index was more than 2 times

In 2013, in terms of total assets, the average scale of industrial enterprises in Yunnan Province was the largest, with an average asset of about 454 million yuan, while that of Hunan Province was the smallest, with an average asset of about 143 million yuan (refer to Table 8), and the former was 3.2 times as much as the latter; from the perspective of the revenue from main business and total profit, the average scale of industrial enterprises in Shanghai was largest and the average revenue from main business and total profit of each industrial enterprise were about 353 million yuan and 24.7 million yuan respectively, and the average scale of Zhejiang Province was the smallest and the average revenue from main business and total profit of each industrial enterprise were about 167 million yuan and 9.2 million yuan respectively, and the former was 2.1 times and 2.7 times as much as the latter. It can be seen that there was a big difference in the average scale of manufacturing industry among the 11 provinces and cities in the Yangtze River Economic Belt.

In order to combine the three indicators, one composite indicator was used to reflect the relative scale of manufacturing industry in 11 provinces and cities, and the comparison was carried out. Here, the weighted average index in 2013 was calculated. The specific operation methods are as follows: firstly, the corresponding values of 11 provinces and cities were divided by the average assets, average revenue

**Table 8** Average scale of industrial enterprises above designated scale in provinces and cities of Yangtze River Economic Belt in 2013

| | Total assets (100 million yuan/each) | Revenue from main business (100 million yuan/each) | Total profit (100 million yuan/each) |
|---|---|---|---|
| Shanghai | 3.428 6 | 3.530 3 | 0.246 9 |
| Jiangsu | 1.985 1 | 2.851 5 | 0.168 9 |
| Zhejiang | 1.615 9 | 1.673 7 | 0.091 7 |
| Anhui | 1.665 2 | 2.188 7 | 0.116 4 |
| Jiangxi | 1.794 5 | 3.512 7 | 0.231 1 |
| Hubei | 2.241 8 | 2.817 1 | 0.154 8 |
| Hunan | 1.428 5 | 2.373 1 | 0.119 0 |
| Chongqing | 2.508 3 | 2.943 9 | 0.167 7 |
| Sichuan | 2.638 4 | 2.678 1 | 0.164 7 |
| Guizhou | 3.091 3 | 2.191 3 | 0.152 1 |
| Yunnan | 4.537 1 | 2.889 8 | 0.162 4 |

*Note* The basic data sourced from *China Statistical Yearbook* of 2014

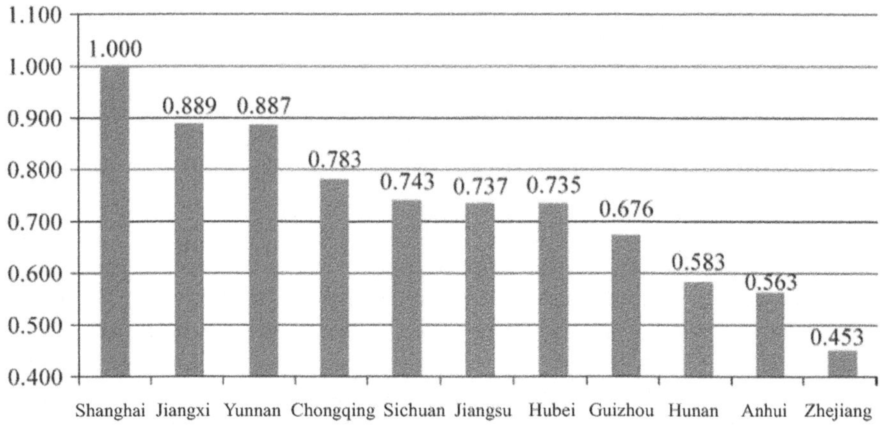


**Fig. 3** Weighted index of average scale of industrial enterprises in provinces and cities of Yangtze River Economic Belt in 2013

from main business and average total profit of each industrial enterprise above the scale in Shanghai to get the index of the two indicators of each province relative to Shanghai, and then the three indicators with weights of 0.2, 0.6, and 0.2 were assigned to calculate the weighted average index of the average scale of industrial enterprises in each province, and finally the same were sequenced in order from large to small and made into chart, as shown in Fig. 3.

According to the weighted average index in 2013, the average scale of manufacturing enterprises in Shanghai was the largest, with the weighted average index of 1, while the average size of manufacturing enterprises in Zhejiang Province was the smallest, with the weighted average index of 0.453, which meant the average scale of manufacturing enterprises in Zhejiang Province was only about 45% as much as that of Shanghai City, and that of Shanghai city was more than twice of Zhejiang Province; the average scale of manufacturing enterprises in Jiangxi Province and Yunnan Province was relatively large with the weighted average index close to 0.9. The average scale of manufacturing enterprises in Anhui and Hunan provinces was small, with the weighted average index between 0.5 and 0.6. The average scale of manufacturing enterprises in Jiangsu, Hubei, Chongqing, Sichuan and Guizhou Provinces was medium with the weighted average index between 0.65 and 0.8.

4. There was a big difference in the operation efficiency of manufacturing enterprises between provinces and cities, and the extreme value ratio of comprehensive index was close to 2 times

In 2013, among the 11 provinces and cities in the Yangtze River Economic Belt, Jiangxi Province had the largest asset profit margin which was up to about 12.88 yuan/100yuan, while Yunnan Province had the smallest profit margin of 3.58 yuan/100 yuan (refer to Table 9). The former was more than 3.5 times of the latter, presenting significant difference between the two. From the perspective of sales

**Table 9** Operation efficiency of industrial enterprises in provinces and cities of Yangtze River Economic Belt in 2013

| | Asset profit margin (yuan/100 yuan) | Sales margin (yuan/100 yuan) | Weighted average |
|---|---|---|---|
| Shanghai | 7.201 | 6.994 | 7.077 |
| Jiangsu | 8.508 | 5.923 | 6.957 |
| Zhejiang | 5.678 | 5.482 | 5.560 |
| Anhui | 6.988 | 5.317 | 5.985 |
| Jiangxi | 12.879 | 6.579 | 9.099 |
| Hubei | 6.905 | 5.495 | 6.059 |
| Hunan | 8.329 | 5.013 | 6.339 |
| Chongqing | 6.687 | 5.698 | 6.094 |
| Sichuan | 6.244 | 6.151 | 6.188 |
| Guizhou | 4.919 | 6.940 | 6.131 |
| Yunnan | 3.578 | 5.618 | 4.802 |

*Note* ① The asset profit margin equals to the total profit divided by total assets, the sales margin equals to the revenue from main business divided by total profit, and the average value equals to the arithmetic average value of the asset profit margin and the sales margin
② The basic data sourced from the *China Statistical Yearbook* of 2014

margin, the index of Shanghai city was the largest and up to 6.99 yuan/100 yuan, while that of Hunan Province was the smallest and about 5.01 yuan/100 yuan. The former was about 1.4 times of the latter, and the difference between the two was relatively small.

According to the importance of the indicators, the asset profit margin and sales margin are assigned with the weights of 0.4 and 0.6 respectively, and the weighted average of these two indicators of 11 provinces and cities in the Yangtze River Economic Belt were calculated, as shown in Table 9. Among them, the weighted average of Jiangxi Province was the largest with the value up to about 9.1, whist that of Yunnan Province was the smallest with the weighted average about 4.8 which meant the former was about 1.9 times of the latter. It can be seen that the difference in the efficiency of manufacturing enterprises in the 11 provinces and cities of the Yangtze River Economic Belt was relatively large.

## 2.2 *Development Status and Characteristics of Logistics Industry*

Simply speaking, logistics industry is a kind of service industry which makes the goods displacement so as to realize the purpose of living and production. There are many indicators to measure the logistics industry. According to the principle of comprehensiveness and data availability, four indicators are selected here: employees and added value of transportation, warehousing and postal service, freight volume and freight turnover. Transportation, warehousing and postal service are hereinafter referred to as transportation industry. Like the manufacturing industry, this paper takes 2000 as the base period and 2013 as the report period, and takes the sum of the representative indicators of 11 provinces and cities as the representative values of the whole Yangtze River Economic Belt to discuss the development status of logistics industry in the whole Yangtze River Economic Belt.

(I) **The development of logistics industry in Yangtze River Economic Belt and its comparison with the whole state**

1. The logistics industry in the Yangtze River Economic Belt had grown rapidly, with an average annual growth rate of about 10% since 2000

From 2000 to 2013, the freight volume and freight turnover of the Yangtze River Economic Belt were increased from 511.84 million tons and 1458.7 billion tons per kilometer to 17.33888 billion tons and 6497.2 billion tons kilometers, respectively (refer to Table 10). The annual average growth rates were 9.39% and 11.49%, respectively, which were higher than 8.49% and 10.25% of the national average. The number of employees and added value of the transportation industry were increased from 2.455 million and 274.2 billion yuan in 2000 to 3.2352 million and 1081 billion yuan in 2013, respectively, with an average annual growth rate of 2.12% and 10.55%, both less than the national growth rate of 2.37% and 11.45%. It can be seen that the growth rate of freight volume and freight turnover in the Yangtze River Economic

**Table 10** Main indicators of Yangtze River Economic Belt and national logistics industry in typical years

| | | Employees of transportation industry (10 thousand yuan) | Added value of transportation industry (100 million yuan) | Freight volume (10 thousand tons) | Freight turnover (100 million tons kilometer) |
|---|---|---|---|---|---|
| Yangtze River Economic Belt | Year 2000 | 245.50 | 2 742 | 511 584 | 14 587 |
| | Year 2004 | 240.36 | 4 650 | 660 317 | 22 940 |
| | Year 2006 | 235.01 | 4 817 | 791 809 | 30 798 |
| | Year 2008 | 240.78 | 6 135 | 1 068 225 | 43 006 |
| | Year 2011 | 284.62 | 9 022 | 1 494 700 | 61 133 |
| | Year 2013 | 323.52 | 10 810 | 1 733 888 | 64 972 |
| Whole state | Year 2000 | 622.20 | 6 161 | 1 358 682 | 44 321 |
| | Year 2004 | 650.90 | 12 081 | 1 706 412 | 69 445 |
| | Year 2006 | 650.89 | 12 183 | 2 037 060 | 88 840 |
| | Year 2008 | 658.79 | 16 362 | 2 585 937 | 110 300 |
| | Year 2011 | 779.52 | 22 433 | 3 696 961 | 159 324 |
| | Year 2013 | 846.22 | 27 283 | 4 098 900 | 168 014 |

*Note* The data sourced from *China Statistical Yearbook* of corresponding years

**Table 11** Proportion of logistics industry in Yangtze River Economic Belt in China in typical years (%)

| Year | Employees of transportation industry | Added value of transportation industry | Freight volume | Freight turnover |
|---|---|---|---|---|
| 2000 | 39.46 | 44.51 | 37.65 | 32.91 |
| 2002 | 36.93 | 46.74 | 37.74 | 33.28 |
| 2006 | 36.11 | 39.54 | 38.87 | 34.67 |
| 2008 | 36.55 | 37.50 | 41.31 | 38.99 |
| 2011 | 36.51 | 40.22 | 40.43 | 38.37 |
| 2013 | 38.23 | 39.62 | 42.30 | 38.67 |

Belt was higher than the national average, but the growth rates of employees and added value of transportation industry were lower than those of the whole state.

2. The logistics industry in the Yangtze River Economic Belt plays an important role in China, accounting for about 40% of the whole state.

In 2013, the proportion of employees and the added value, freight volume and freight turnover in the transportation industry of the Yangtze River Economic Belt accounted for 38.23%, 39.62%, 42.30% and 38.67% of the state respectively (as seen in Table 11). It can be seen that the logistics industry of the Yangtze River Economic Belt accounted for 40% of the whole state on the whole.

In terms of dynamic changes and from several typical years since 2000, the proportion of freight volume and freight turnover in the Yangtze River Economic Belt in the whole state has been rising in fluctuation, while the proportion of employees and added value of transportation industry has been declining in fluctuation.

3. The operation efficiency of the logistics industry in the Yangtze River Economic Belt was better than the national average by and large

In 2013, the added value of each employee in the transportation industry of the Yangtze River Economic Belt was 334,100 yuan, higher than the 322,400 yuan of the whole state in the same period (refer to Table 12). The added value of the transportation industry in the Yangtze River Economic Belt per 100 ton kilometer turnover was 16.64 yuan, which was also higher than the national level of 16.24 yuan in the same period. The added value of the transportation industry of the Yangtze River Economic Belt per ton of freight volume was 62.25 yuan, less than the national level of 66.56 yuan in the same period. The added value of transportation industry per unit freight volume and added value per unit freight turnover volume of transportation industry belong to the same kind of indicator, but the latter is obviously of more importance. Therefore, on the whole, the operation efficiency of the logistics industry in the Yangtze River Economic Belt was better than the national average.

Since 2000, among the three indicators reflecting the operational efficiency of the logistics industry, the per capita added value of the transportation industry in

**Table 12** Operation efficiency of Yangtze River Economic Belt and national logistics industry in typical years

| | | Added value per person for transportation industry (10 thousand yuan per capita) | Added value per unit freight volume for transportation industry (yuan/ton) | Added value per unit freight turnover for transportation industry (yuan/100 ton kilometer) |
|---|---|---|---|---|
| Yangtze River Economic Belt | Year 2000 | 11.17 | 53.60 | 18.80 |
| | Year 2004 | 19.35 | 70.42 | 20.27 |
| | Year 2006 | 20.50 | 60.84 | 15.64 |
| | | Added value per capita for transportation industry (10 thousand yuan/person) | Added value per unit freight volume for transportation industry (yuan/ton) | Added value per unit freight turnover for transportation industry (yuan/100 ton kilometer) |
| Yangtze River Economic Belt | Year 2008 | 25.48 | 57.43 | 14.27 |
| | Year 2011 | 31.70 | 60.36 | 14.76 |
| | Year 2013 | 33.41 | 62.35 | 16.64 |
| Whole state | Year 2000 | 9.90 | 45.35 | 13.90 |
| | Year 2004 | 18.56 | 70.80 | 17.40 |
| | Year 2006 | 18.72 | 59.81 | 13.71 |
| | Year 2008 | 24.84 | 63.27 | 14.83 |
| | Year 2011 | 28.78 | 60.68 | 14.08 |
| | Year 2013 | 32.24 | 66.56 | 16.24 |

*Note* "The per capita added value of transportation industry" is equal to the added value of transportation industry divided by the employees of transportation industry, "the added value per unit freight volume of transportation industry" is equal to the added value of transportation industry divided by freight volume, and "the added value per unit freight turnover of transportation industry" is equal to the average value of transportation industry divided by freight turnover

the Yangtze River Economic Belt and the added value of the transportation industry per unit freight volume in the Yangtze River Economic Belt have been rising in fluctuation. Since 2008, the added value of the transportation industry per unit freight turnover has also been rising. Therefore, as for the dynamic change, the operation efficiency of the logistics industry in the Yangtze River Economic Belt has been improved in fluctuation.

**Table 13** Main indicators of logistics industry of provinces and cities in Yangtze River Economic Belt in 2013

| | Employees of transportation industry (10 thousand person) | Added value of transportation industry (100 million yuan) | Freight volume (10 thousand tons) | Freight turnover (100 million tons kilometer) |
|---|---|---|---|---|
| Shanghai | 49.16 | 935.1 | 84 305 | 14 333 |
| Jiangsu | 48.41 | 2 530.0 | 181 775 | 9 925 |
| Zhejiang | 31.37 | 1 326.0 | 188 679 | 8 951 |
| Anhui | 22.01 | 707.1 | 396 391 | 12 335 |
| Jiangxi | 21.24 | 678.6 | 135 172 | 3 640 |
| Hubei | 33.19 | 1 078.1 | 131 000 | 4 752 |
| Hunan | 24.53 | 1 174.3 | 184 535 | 3 832 |
| Chongqing | 26.09 | 580.9 | 87 241 | 2 299 |
| Sichuan | 39.38 | 751.6 | 167 759 | 2 249 |
| Guizhou | 11.34 | 775.1 | 72 703 | 1 295 |
| Yunnan | 16.80 | 273.5 | 104 329 | 1 362 |

(II) **The development status and comparison of logistics industry in provinces and cities in Yangtze River Economic Belt**

1. The scale of logistics industry varied greatly among provinces and cities, and the extreme value ratio of composite index approached 7 times

In 2013, the number of employees in Shanghai transportation industry was the largest in 11 provinces and cities and up to 491,600, and that in Guizhou Province was as low as 113,400 (refer to Table 13), which meant the former was more than four times of the latter; in terms of the added value of transportation industry, it was largest in Jiangsu Province up to 253 billion yuan, and it was the lowest in Yunnan Province to 27.35 billion yuan, which meant the former was more than nine times of the latter; in terms of freight volume, it was the largest in Anhui Province up to 3,963.91 million tons and the lowest in Guizhou Province to 7,270.3 billion yuan which meant the former was about 5.5 times of the latter. In terms of freight turnover, it was the largest in Shanghai up to 1,433.3 billion tons kilometer, whilst it was the lowest in Guizhou to 129.5 billion tons kilometer, which meant the former was more than 11 times of the latter.

Here, the following method is used to calculate the weighted index of the above four indicators to comprehensively reflect the regional logistics industry scale: the corresponding index values of each province and city was divided by the employees of transportation industry, added value of transportation industry, freight volume and freight turnover volume of Guizhou Province to get the index of four indicators of 11 provinces and cities. Then, according to the contribution of the indicators, the weights of 0.2, 0.5, 0.1 and 0.2 are assigned to these four indicators respectively,

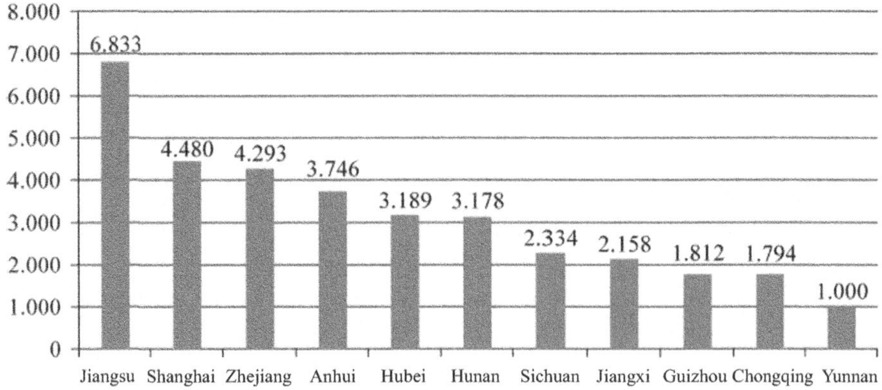


**Fig. 4** Weighted index of logistics industry scale of provinces and cities in Yangtze River Economic Belt

and the weighted index of logistics industry of each province and city is calculated, sequenced from large to small and made into chart, as shown in Fig. 4.

It can be seen from Fig. 4 that the weighted index of logistics industry scale in Jiangsu Province was the largest, about 6.83 times that of Yunnan Province, that of Shanghai and Zhejiang Province was more than 4 times of Yunnan Province, that of Anhui Province and Hubei Province was more than 3 times of Yunnan Province, that of Sichuan Province and Jiangxi Province was more than 2 times of Yunnan Province, and that of Guizhou Province and Chongqing city was about 1.8 times of Yunnan Province.

2. There were significant differences in the growth rate of logistics industry among provinces and cities, and the extreme value ratio of composite index was more than 2.4 times

From 2000 to 2013, the average annual growth rate of employees for transportation industry in Shanghai reached 6.77%, while that in Hubei Province and Hunan Province was negative, with an average annual growth rate of −0.09% and −0.79% (as seen in Table 14); In terms of added value of transportation industry, the growth rate of Guizhou Province was the highest and up to 19.11%, while that of Yunnan Province was the slowest and only 6.35%, which meant the former was more than three times of the latter; in terms of freight volume and freight turnover, the growth rate of Anhui Province was the highest and up to 16.92% and 18.94% respectively, while that of Shanghai was the lowest and only 4.53% and 6.34%, which meant the former was 3.7 times and 3 times respectively of the latter. Therefore, it can be concluded that the differences of the growth rates of these four indicators among provinces and cities in the Yangtze River Economic Belt were significant.

From the perspective of composite indicators, 0.2, 0.5, 0.1, 0.2 weights are also assigned to the employees of transportation industry, added value of transportation

**Table 14** Average annual growth rate of logistics industry of provinces and cities in the Yangtze River Economic Belt from year 2000 to 2013 (%)

| | Employees of transportation industry | Added value of transportation industry | Freight volume | Freight turnover |
|---|---|---|---|---|
| Shanghai | 6.77 | 8.36 | 4.53 | 6.34 |
| Jiangsu | 1.28 | 11.64 | 5.73 | 14.75 |
| Zhejiang | 3.27 | 8.69 | 7.07 | 15.46 |
| Anhui | 0.47 | 10.53 | 16.92 | 18.94 |
| Jiangxi | 1.67 | 9.59 | 13.46 | 13.31 |
| Hubei | −0.09 | 11.03 | 9.32 | 11.39 |
| Hunan | −0.79 | 11.09 | 9.90 | 9.84 |
| Chongqing | 4.31 | 13.67 | 9.10 | 15.95 |
| Sichuan | 3.53 | 8.49 | 9.09 | 9.87 |
| Guizhou | 2.04 | 19.11 | 11.83 | 8.96 |
| Yunnan | 0.14 | 6.35 | 5.35 | 7.99 |

industry, freight volume and freight turnover to calculate their weighted growth rate, then sequenced from large to small, and made into chart, as shown in Fig. 5.

In Fig. 5, the weighted average annual growth rate of logistics industry in Guizhou Province was the highest up to 12.94%, while that of Yunnan Province was only 5.34%, which meant the former was more than 2.4 times of the latter; the weighted average annual growth rate of Chongqing city and Anhui Province were 11.8% and 10.84% respectively, which were more than twice of Yunnan Province. The weighted average annual growth rates of Jiangsu Province, Jiangxi Province, Zhejiang Province and Hubei Province were 1.6–1.8 times of Yunnan Province, and

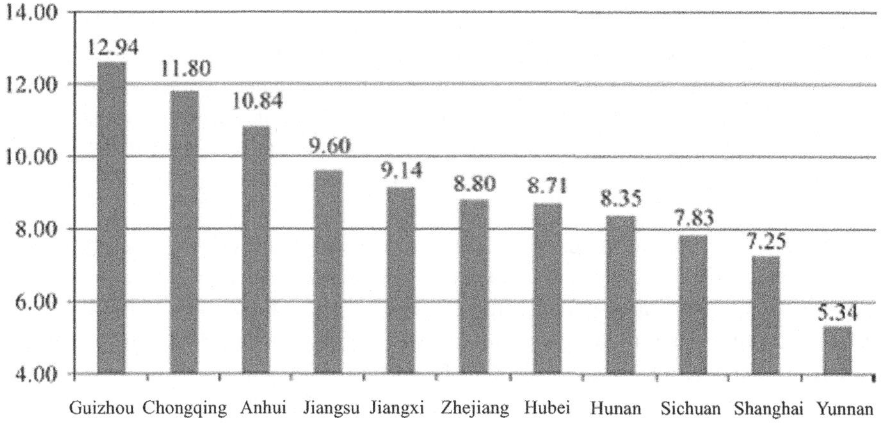


**Fig. 5** Weighted average annual growth rate of logistics industry of provinces and cities in the Yangtze River Economic Belt from year 2000 to 2013 (%)

**Table 15** Operation efficiency of logistics industry in provinces and cities of Yangtze River Economic Belt in year 2013

| | Per capita added value of transportation industry (10 thousand per capita) | Added value per unit freight volume for transportation industry (yuan/ton) | Added value per unit freight turnover for transportation industry (yuan/100 ton kilometer) |
|---|---|---|---|
| Shanghai | 19.02 | 110.91 | 6.52 |
| Jiangsu | 52.26 | 139.18 | 25.49 |
| Zhejiang | 42.27 | 70.28 | 14.81 |
| Anhui | 32.13 | 17.84 | 5.73 |
| Jiangxi | 31.95 | 50.20 | 18.64 |
| Hubei | 32.48 | 82.30 | 22.69 |
| Hunan | 47.87 | 63.64 | 30.64 |
| Chongqing | 22.27 | 66.59 | 25.27 |
| Sichuan | 19.08 | 44.80 | 33.42 |
| Guizhou | 68.35 | 106.61 | 59.87 |
| Yunnan | 16.28 | 26.22 | 20.08 |

those of Hunan Province, Sichuan Province and Shanghai city were 1.3–1.6 times of Yunnan Province.

3. The operation efficiency of logistics industry varied greatly among provinces and cities, and the extreme value ratio of composite index was about 8 times

In 2013, the per capita added value of transportation industry in Guizhou Province was 683,500 yuan, which was the largest among 11 provinces and cities, and the smallest was 162,800 yuan in Yunnan Province (as seen in Table 15), which meant the former was 4.2 times of the latter; the added value per ton of freight volume of transportation industry in Jiangsu Province was 139.2 yuan, which was the largest among 11 provinces and cities, and that of Anhui Province was the lowest to 17.8 yuan, which meant the former was 7.9 times of the latter; The added value per 100 ton kilometer of transportation industry in Guizhou Province was the highest about 60 yuan, which was the largest among 11 provinces and cities, and that of Anhui Province was the lowest about 5.7%, which meant the former was 10.4 times of the latter.

The following method is used to calculate the weighted index of the above four indicators herein to comprehensively reflect the operation efficiency of regional logistics industry: the per capita added value of transportation industry in Anhui Province, the added value per unit freight volume of transportation industry, and the added value of transportation industry per unit freight turnover volume of Anhui Province are used to divide the corresponding index values of each province and city, and then the indexes of four indicators in 11 provinces and cities can be obtained, and then according to the contribution of the indicators, the three indicators are assigned with weights of 0.2, 0.2 and 0.6 respectively, and the weighted indexes of logistics

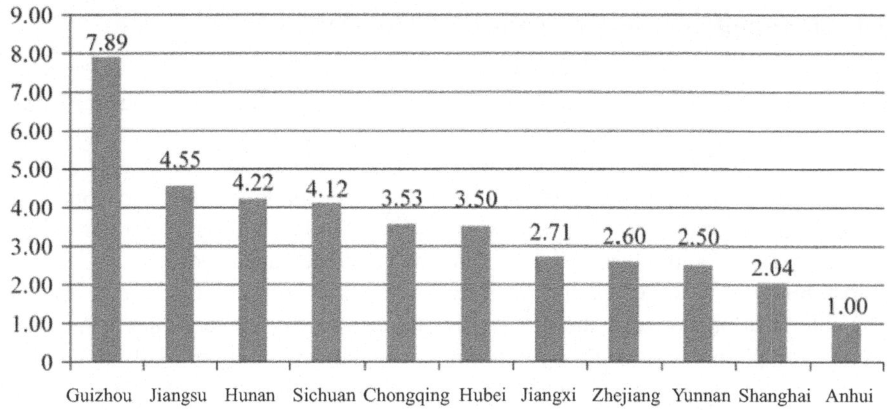


**Fig. 6** Weighted index of logistics industry operation efficiency of provinces and cities in Yangtze River Economic Belt in year 2013

industry in each province and city are calculated. Finally, they are sequenced from large to small, and are made into chart as shown in Fig. 6.

It can be seen from Fig. 6 that the weighted index of logistics industry operation efficiency in Guizhou Province was the largest, about 7.9 times of Anhui Province; those of Jiangsu Province, Hunan Province and Sichuan Province were more than 4 times of Anhui Province, those of Chongqing and Hubei Province were more than 3 times of Anhui Province, those of Jiangxi Province, Zhejiang Province, Yunnan Province and Shanghai city were more than 2 times of Anhui Province. It can be seen that the operational efficiencies of logistics industry in the provinces and cities of the Yangtze River Economic Belt presented great disparity.

## 3 Introduction of Analysis Method

Now, the method of grey correlation analysis will be used to discuss the linkage development of manufacturing industry and logistics industry in the Yangtze River Economic Belt, since the grey correlation analysis has the following advantages compared with the regression analysis, variance analysis, principal component analysis and other systematic analysis methods in mathematical statistics: firstly, a satisfactory score analysis of the results can be obtained only by short time series data without requiring a large amount of data. Secondly the calculation load is low and the calculation process is simple, so it is not necessary to make a complex calculation program for calculation on the computer. Thirdly, it is not required to satisfy the strict conditions such as the probability distribution with sample obeying a model and the linear relationship between the factor data and the system characteristic data.

## 3.1 Principle of Grey Correlation Theory

The grey system theory was founded by Professor Deng Julong, a famous scholar in China, in the early 1980s. This theory has attracted the attention of many scholars and practical workers both at home and abroad. It has been widely and deeply applied in the correlation analysis, modeling, prediction, decision-making and control of many disciplines such as society, economy, science and technology, geosciences and medical science, and a series of achievements have been achieved.

All kinds of systems in the objective world are composed of many factors. The interrelation between these systems and factors is very complex, especially the surface phenomena and the randomness of changes are more likely to confuse people's intuition and cover up the essence of things, which makes it difficult for people to get comprehensive and sufficient information and form a clear concept when they are trying to understand, analyze, predict and make decisions. The condition that the real appearance of the relationship between systems and factors is half hidden and half exposed is called "grey". It is under a state of neither "white" nor "black", that is, the real appearance is neither completely exposed nor completely submerged. This kind of system in "grey" makes it difficult for people to grasp the major conflicts and find its main features and main relationships.

Grey correlation theory is a part of grey system theory. Grey correlation analysis is an effective method to analyze the relation among the above grey systems. The basic idea of grey correlation analysis is to judge whether the relationship is close according to the similarity of geometric shapes of time series curves of some grey systems. The closer the curves are, the greater the correlation degree between corresponding systems or factors will be, and vice versa. The relational degree between grey systems is identified by calculating its grey correlation degree, which includes absolute grey correlation degree, relative grey correlation degree and comprehensive grey relational degree. The calculation methods and properties of these grey correlation degree are introduced in the following sections.

## 3.2 Calculation Method and Properties of Absolute Grey Correlation Degree

### (I) Calculation method

Let $X_0$, $X_i$ two systematic factors, and the observed data on the serial number $k$ are $x_0(k)$ and $x_i(k)$, where $k = 1, 2, \ldots, n$, so the followings

$$X_0 = (x_0(1), x_0(2), x_0(3), \ldots, x_0(n))$$

$$X_i = (x_i(1), x_i(2), x_i(3), \ldots, x_i(n))$$

are called the behavior sequence of factor $X_0$ and $X_i$.

Firstly, calculate the initial point zeroized image $X_0^0$ and $X_i^0$ of sequence $X_0$ and $X_i$ with the same and equal time interval.

Set:

$$\begin{gathered}X_0^0(1) = x_0(1) - x_0(1)\\ X_0^0(2) = x_0(2) - x_0(1)\\ X_0^0(3) = x_0(3) - x_0(1)\\ \cdots\\ X_0^0(n) = x_0(n) - x_0(1)\end{gathered}$$

Then: $X_0^0 = \left(X_0^0(1), X_0^0(2), X_0^0(3), \ldots, X_0^0(n)\right)$

Set:

$$\begin{gathered}X_i^0(1) = x_i(1) - x_i(1)\\ X_i^0(2) = x_i(2) - x_i(1)\\ X_i^0(3) = x_i(3) - x_i(1)\\ \cdots\\ X_i^0(n) = x_i(n) - x_i(1)\end{gathered}$$

Then: $X_i^0 = \left(X_i^0(1), X_i^0(2), X_i^0(3), \ldots, X_i^0(n)\right)$

And then, solve $|s_0|$, $|s_i|$, $|s_i - s_0|$

$$|s_0| = \left|\sum_{k=2}^{n-1} x_0^0(k) + \frac{1}{2}x_0^0(n)\right| \tag{1}$$

$$|s_i| = \left|\sum_{k=2}^{n-1} x_i^0(k) + \frac{1}{2}x_i^0(n)\right| \tag{2}$$

$$|s_i - s_0| = \left|\sum_{k=2}^{n-1}\left(x_i^0(k) - x_0^0(k)\right) + \frac{1}{2}\left(x_i^0(n) - x_0^0(n)\right)\right| \tag{3}$$

Finally, the absolute grey correlation degree is calculated.

$$\varepsilon_{0i} = \frac{1 + |s_0| + |s_i|}{1 + |s_0| + |s_i| + |s_i - s_0|} \tag{4}$$

## (II) **Properties**

Firstly, $0 < \varepsilon_{0i} \le 1$.

Secondly, $\varepsilon_{0i}$ is only related to the geometry of $X_0$ and $X_i$, but not to its relative spatial position, or translation does not change the value of absolute correlation degree.

Thirdly, any two sequences are not absolutely independent, that is, $\varepsilon_{0i}$ is never to be zero.

Fourthly, the greater the geometric similarity between $X_0$ and $X_i$, the greater the $\varepsilon_{0i}$ will be.

Fifthly, $\varepsilon_{00} = 1$, $\varepsilon_{ii} = 1$, $\varepsilon_{0i} = \varepsilon_{i0}$.

## 3.3 *Calculation Method and Properties of Grey Correlation Degree*

(I) **Calculation method**

If the length of the sequence $X_0$ and $X_i$ is the same, and the initial value is not zero, and $X_0^{'}$ and $X_i^{'}$ are the initial value images of $X_0$ and $X_i$ respectively, then the absolute grey correlation degree of $X_0^{'}$ and $X_i^{'}$ is called the relative grey correlation degree of $X_0$ and $X_i$, which is denoted as $r_{0i}$.

Firstly, the initial value image $X_0^{'}$ and $X_i^{'}$ of $X_0$ and $X_i$ are calculated.

Set:

$$\begin{aligned} X_0^{'}(1) &= x_0(1)/x_0(1) \\ X_0^{'}(2) &= x_0(2)/x_0(1) \\ X_0^{'}(3) &= x_0(3)/x_0(1) \\ &\cdots \\ X_0^{'}(n) &= x_0(n)/x_0(1) \end{aligned}$$

Then: $X_0^{'} = \left(X_0^{'}(1), X_0^{'}(2), X_0^{'}(3), \ldots, X_0^{'}(n)\right)$

Set:

$$\begin{aligned} X_i^{'}(1) &= x_i(1)/x_i(1) \\ X_i^{'}(2) &= x_i(2)/x_i(1) \\ X_i^{'}(3) &= x_i(3)/x_i(1) \\ &\cdots \\ X_i^{'}(n) &= x_i(n)/x_i(1) \end{aligned}$$

Then: $X_i^{'} = \left(X_i^{'}(1), X_i^{'}(2), X_i^{'}(3), \ldots, X_i^{'}(n)\right)$

Then, according to the steps of calculating the grey relative correlation degree, the absolute grey correlation degree $X_0^{'}$ of $X_0^{'}$ and $X_i^{'}$ is calculated, which is the grey relative correlation degree $\varepsilon'_{0i}$ of $X'$ $X$, i.e. the grey relative correlation degree $r_{0i}$ of $X_0$ and $X_i$.

$$r_{0i} = \varepsilon_{0i}^{'} = \frac{1 + \left|s_0^{'}\right| + \left|s_i^{'}\right|}{1 + \left|s_0^{'}\right| + \left|s_i^{'}\right| + \left|s_i^{'} - s_0^{'}\right|} \tag{5}$$

(II) **Properties**

Firstly, $0 < r_{0i} \leq 1$.

Secondly, $r_{0i}$ is only related to the variation rate of the sequence $X_0$ and $X_{\mathrm{i}}$ relative to the starting point, but has nothing to do with the scale of the observation data, or we can say that the scalar multiplication of the observation data does not change the grey relative correlation degree

Thirdly, the variation rate of any two sequences is not unrelated, that is, $r_{0i}$ is never to be zero.

Fourthly, the more consistent the variation rate of $X_0$ and $X_i$ relative to the starting point, the greater $r_{0i}$ will be.

Fifthly, when the variation rate of $X_0$ and $X_i$ relative to the starting point is the same, that is, $X_0 = aX_{\mathrm{i}}$, then $r_{0i} = 1$.

Fifthly, $r_{00} = 1$, $r_{ii} = 1$, $r_{0i} = r_{i0}$.

## 3.4 *Calculation Method and Properties of Grey Comprehensive Correlation Degree*

(I) **Calculation method**

Let $X_0$ and $X_i$ have the same length, and the initial values are different from zero, $\varepsilon_{0i}$ and $r_{0i}$ are the absolute grey correlation degree and relative grey correlation degree of $X_0$ and $X_i$, respectively, and $\theta \in [0,1]$, then

$$\rho_{0\mathrm{i}} = \theta\varepsilon_{0i} + (1 - \theta)r_{0i} \tag{6}$$

is the comprehensive grey correlation degree of $X_0$ and $X_{\mathrm{i}}$.

The comprehensive grey correlation degree not only reflects the similarity degree of the broken line $X_0$ and $X_{\mathrm{i}}$, but also reflects the proximity of the variation rate of $X_0$ and $X_{\mathrm{i}}$ relative to the starting point. It is a quantitative index that comprehensively characterizes the proximate relationship between sequences. If the importance of the absolute magnitude is considered to be same as that of variation rate, $\theta$ can be taken as 0.5. If more attention is paid to the relationship between absolute magnitudes, $\theta$ can be larger; if the variation rate is emphasized, smaller $\theta$ can be taken.

(II) **Properties**

Firstly, $0 < \rho_{0i} \leq 1$.

Secondly, $\rho_{0i}$ is not only related to the scale of the observation data of the sequence $X_0$ and $X_i$, but also to the variation rate of various data relative to the starting point.

Thirdly, $\rho_{0i}$ is never to be zero.

Fourthly, $\theta$ depends on the value of $\rho_{0i}$.

Fifthly, $\rho_{00} = 1$, $\rho_{ii} = 1$, $\rho_{0i} = \rho_{i0}$.

# 4 Empirical Analysis of the Linkage Development of Manufacturing Industry and Logistics Industry in the Yangtze River Economic Belt

## *4.1 Data Description*

In the grey correlation analysis of manufacturing industry and logistics industry in the Yangtze River Economic Belt, the total assets, revenue from main business and total profit of industrial enterprises above the scale are selected as the characterization indicators of manufacturing industry, and the added value, freight volume and freight turnover of transportation, warehousing and postal industry are selected as the characterization indicators of the logistics industry.

The data sample interval is the continuous annual data from 2000 to 2013.

The data of these indicators are all from the *China Statistical Yearbook*. Although there are some missing data in some years, in order to maintain the consistency of data sources, no other datum is used to supplement these missing data, instead to use the original data for make up through reasonable methods. For example, the data of total assets, revenue from main business and total profits of industrial enterprises above designated scale in 2003 and 2005 were not available in *China Statistical Yearbook*. The remedy here is to calculate the arithmetic average of these indicators in 2002 and 2004 as the indicators in 2003, and calculate the arithmetic average of 2004 and 2006 as the indicators of 2005.

The statistical caliber of some indicators in the sample time interval is not the same. For example, the marketing revenue index of industrial enterprises above designated scale in 2000–2002 and 2004 was "product sales revenue", while the marketing revenue index of 2006–2013 was "revenue from main business". The statistical caliber of the two indicators was slightly different, but there was little difference in numerical value. Therefore, these data are used here and unified as revenue from main business.

The values of the three indicators of manufacturing industry and logistics industry in the whole Yangtze River Economic Belt are the sum of corresponding indicators of 11 provinces and cities.

## *4.2 Construction and Calculation of Composite Index for Manufacturing and Logistics Industries*

Assets, revenue from main business and profit represent the overall scale of regional industrial enterprises from different aspects. It is unable to fully represent the total scale of industrial enterprises in the region by any of them and thus it is better to combine these three indicators to form a composite index, which can, to the comparatively maximum extent, reflect the overall scale of regional industrial enterprises.

The added value, freight volume and freight turnover of the transportation, warehousing and postal industry also have the same problems in presenting the overall scale of the logistics industry.

Next, to take the construction and calculation of the industrial composite index of the whole Yangtze River Economic Belt as an example, the structure and calculation method are introduced. The 11 provinces and cities of the Yangtze River Economic Belt and the national industrial composite index are calculated by the same method. The calculation method of composite index of logistics industry is the same as that of this kind.

Firstly, the total assets, revenue from main business and total profit of industrial enterprises above the designated scale in 11 provinces and cities are added up each year to get the values of the three indicators of the Yangtze River Economic Belt from 2000 to 2013, as shown in Table 16.

Then, the average of the three indicators from 2000 to 2013 are calculated respectively, which were 16,166.8 billion yuan, 18,130.6 billion yuan and 1,081.33 billion yuan respectively, and the values of the corresponding indicators in each year are divided by the average, so as to obtain the average index of the three indicators from 2000 to 2013, as shown in Table 17.

Finally, according to the importance of these three indicators, the total assets, revenue from main business and total profit are assigned with the weights of 0.2, 0.6 and 0.2 respectively, and the weighted average of these three indicators in each year is calculated, so as to obtain the annual industrial composite index from 2000 to

**Table 16** Main indicators of industrial enterprises above designated scale in Yangtze River Economic Belt (2000–2013)

| | Total assets (100 Million yuan) | Revenue from main business (100 Million yuan) | Total profit (100 Million yuan) |
|---|---|---|---|
| Year 2000 | 50 252 | 34 593 | 1 475.8 |
| Year 2001 | 54 269 | 38 909 | 1 800.8 |
| Year 2002 | 58 693 | 45 832 | 2 327.6 |
| Year 2003 | 70 714 | 62 457 | 3 316.0 |
| Year 2004 | 82 735 | 79 082 | 4 304.4 |
| Year 2005 | 103 273 | 106 483 | 5 638.3 |
| Year 2006 | 123 811 | 133 884 | 6 972.3 |
| Year 2007 | 151 678 | 170 402 | 9 745.6 |
| Year 2008 | 180 346 | 203 882 | 10 906.9 |
| Year 2009 | 204 256 | 220 465 | 12 891.1 |
| Year 2010 | 245 709 | 288 318 | 20 017.7 |
| Year 2011 | 277 835 | 346 951 | 23 181.2 |
| Year 2012 | 313 648 | 381 870 | 23 919.0 |
| Year 2013 | 346 138 | 425 151 | 24 889.5 |

**Table 17** Average index and composite index of industrial enterprises in Yangtze River Economic Belt (2000–2013)

| | Total assets | Revenue from main business | Total profit |
|---|---|---|---|
| Year 2000 | 0.310 8 | 0.190 8 | 0.136 5 |
| Year 2001 | 0.335 7 | 0.214 6 | 0.166 5 |
| Year 2002 | 0.363 0 | 0.252 8 | 0.215 3 |
| Year 2003 | 0.437 4 | 0.344 5 | 0.306 7 |
| Year 2004 | 0.511 8 | 0.436 2 | 0.398 1 |
| Year 2005 | 0.638 8 | 0.587 3 | 0.521 4 |
| Year 2006 | 0.765 8 | 0.738 4 | 0.644 8 |
| Year 2007 | 0.938 2 | 0.939 9 | 0.901 3 |
| Year 2008 | 1.115 5 | 1.124 5 | 1.008 7 |
| Year 2009 | 1.263 4 | 1.216 0 | 1.192 2 |
| Year 2010 | 1.519 8 | 1.590 2 | 1.851 2 |
| Year 2011 | 1.718 5 | 1.913 6 | 2.143 8 |
| Year 2012 | 1.940 1 | 2.106 2 | 2.212 0 |
| Year 2013 | 2.141 0 | 2.344 9 | 2.301 7 |

2013, as shown in Fig. 7. In the same way, we can calculate the industrial composite index of 11 provinces and cities of the Yangtze River Economic Belt and the whole state.

The process of constructing and calculating the composite index of logistics industry is basically the same. The difference is that the weights of added value, freight volume and freight turnover of transportation industry are assigned as 0.5, 0.2 and 0.3 respectively in actual operation. The composite index of logistics industry

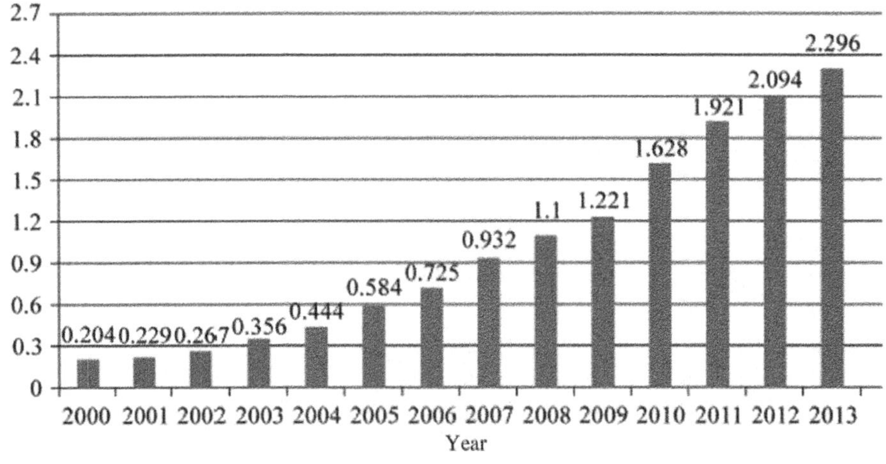


**Fig. 7** Industrial composite index of Yangtze River Economic Belt (2000–2013)

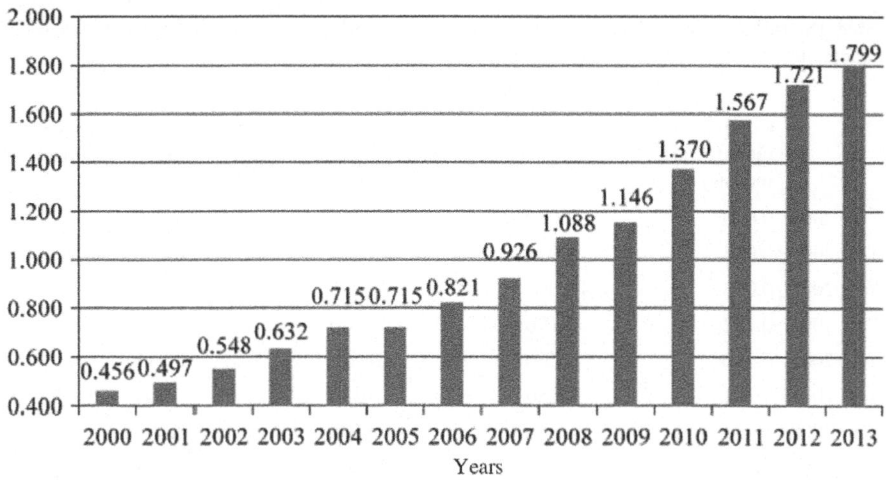


**Fig. 8** Comprehensive index of logistics industry in Yangtze River Economic Belt (2000–2013)

in Yangtze River Economic Belt can be obtained by calculation, as shown in Fig. 8. In the same way, we can calculate the composite index of logistics industry of 11 provinces and cities of the Yangtze River Economic Belt and the whole state.

Due to the limitation of space, the composite index of industry and logistics industry of 11 provinces and cities of the Yangtze River Economic Belt and the whole state are not listed, but are directly used in the calculation of grey correlation degree below.

## *4.3 Grey Correlation Between Manufacturing Industry and Logistics Industry in Yangtze River Economic Belt and Its Comparison with that of the Whole State*

### (I) Grey correlation degree of Yangtze River Economic Belt in the study period and its comparison with the whole state

The calculation process of absolute grey correlation degree is as follows.

First of all, according to the method described above, calculate the initial point zeroized image of the Yangtze River Economic Belt and the national manufacturing industry composite index and logistics industry composite index, as shown in Table 18.

Then, on this basis, according to formula (1), formula (2) and formula (3), calculate $|s_0|$, $|s_i|$ and $|s_0 - s_i|$, as shown in Table 19.

According to the formula (4) and with the data in Table 19, we can calculate the absolute grey correlation degree of the manufacturing and logistics industries in the

**Table 18** Initial point zeroized image of the Yangtze River Economic Belt and the national manufacturing and logistics composite index

| | Yangtze River Economic Belt | | Whole state | |
|---|---|---|---|---|
| | Composite index of manufacturing industry | Composite index of logistics industry | Composite index of manufacturing industry | Composite index of logistics industry |
| Year 2000 | 0.000 | 0.000 | 0.000 | 0.000 |
| Year 2001 | 0.025 | 0.041 | 0.020 | 0.038 |
| Year 2002 | 0.063 | 0.093 | 0.055 | 0.075 |
| Year 2003 | 0.152 | 0.176 | 0.140 | 0.106 |
| Year 2004 | 0.240 | 0.260 | 0.226 | 0.212 |
| Year 2005 | 0.381 | 0.259 | 0.365 | 0.304 |
| Year 2006 | 0.521 | 0.365 | 0.504 | 0.397 |
| Year 2007 | 0.728 | 0.471 | 0.707 | 0.538 |
| Year 2008 | 0.896 | 0.633 | 0.909 | 0.651 |
| Year 2009 | 1.017 | 0.691 | 1.027 | 0.718 |
| Year 2010 | 1.424 | 0.914 | 1.419 | 0.894 |
| Year 2011 | 1.717 | 1.112 | 1.717 | 1.098 |
| Year 2012 | 1.890 | 1.265 | 1.888 | 1.251 |
| Year 2013 | 2.092 | 1.343 | 2.074 | 1.325 |

**Table 19** $|s_0|$, $|s_i|$, and$|s_0 - s_i|$ of absolute grey correlation

| | $\|s_0\|$ | $\|s_i\|$ | $\|s_0 - s_i\|$ |
|---|---|---|---|
| Yangtze River Economic Belt | 10.099 3 | 6.950 0 | 3.149 3 |
| Whole state | 10.014 8 | 6.944 0 | 3.070 9 |

Yangtze River Economic Belt and the whole state, as shown in the second column of Table 20.

Similarly, according to the calculation method and formula (5) as introduced above, the relative grey correlation degree of manufacturing and logistics industries in the Yangtze River Economic Belt and the whole state can be calculated, as shown in the third column of Table 20.

**Table 20** Grey correlation of the manufacturing and logistics industries between Yangtze River Economic Belt and the whole state

| | Absolute grey correlation degree | Relative grey correlation degree | Composite grey correlation degree |
|---|---|---|---|
| Yangtze River Economic Belt | 0.851 44 | 0.657 45 | 0.735 05 |
| Whole state | 0.853 97 | 0.663 41 | 0.739 63 |

**Table 21** Grey correlation between manufacturing industry and logistics industry in Yangtze River Economic Belt and the whole state in two periods

| | Absolute grey correlation degree | | Relative grey correlation degree | | Composite grey correlation degree | |
|---|---|---|---|---|---|---|
| Time period | 2000–2006 | 2007–2013 | 2000–2006 | 2007–2013 | 2000–2006 | 2007–2013 |
| Yangtze River Economic Belt | 0.816 69 | 0.911 97 | 0.720 00 | 0.857 95 | 0.758 68 | 0.879 56 |
| Whole state | 0.815 02 | 0.855 98 | 0.725 03 | 0.785 15 | 0.761 03 | 0.813 48 |

According to the calculation method and its formula (6) as introduced above, the composite grey correlation degree of manufacturing and logistics industries in Yangtze River Economic Belt and the whole state can be calculated, as shown in the fourth column of Table 20 (herein, $\theta = 0.4$).

It can be seen from Table 20 that the composite grey correlation degree of the Yangtze River Economic Belt is 0.735 05, which is up to a "higher" level, but slightly lower than the national average, and the national composite grey correlation degree is 0.739 63. Therefore, we can draw a conclusion: on the whole, the linkage between the development of manufacturing industry and logistics industry in the Yangtze River Economic Belt is relatively high, but it is still slightly lower than the national average.

(II) **Dynamic change of grey correlation degree of Yangtze River Economic Belt in two periods of study and its comparison with that of whole state**

In order to investigate the dynamic changes of the linkage development of manufacturing industry and logistics industry in the Yangtze River Economic Belt, the year 2000–2013 is separated into two equal periods, namely, 2000–2006 and 2007–2013. According to the calculation method as introduced above, the absolute grey correlation degree, relative grey correlation degree and composite grey correlation degree ($\theta = 0.4$) of the Yangtze River Economic Belt and the whole state are calculated respectively, as shown in Table 21.

It can be seen from Table 21 that the composite grey correlation degree of manufacturing industry and logistics industry in the Yangtze River Economic Belt in 2000–2006 and 2007–2013 were 0.758 68 and 0.879 56 respectively, and the latter was greater than the former, which indicated that the linkage development of manufacturing industry and logistics industry in the Yangtze River Economic Belt had been improved. From the perspective of the improved linkage development, the magnitude in second period of the Yangtze River Economic Belt was increased by about 15.9% compared with that of the first time period and far greater than the national increase of 6.9%. Moreover, it led to the fact that the composite grey correlation degree of the Yangtze River Economic Belt from 2007 to 2013 surpassed the national average. It is shown that, from the perspective of dynamic development trend, the linkage development of manufacturing and logistics industries in the Yangtze River Economic Belt has been significantly improved, and the increased magnitude was greater than the national average, which led to the fact that the degree of linkage development of the Yangtze River Economic Belt in 2007–2013 surpassed that of the whole state.

## *4.4 Grey Correlation Degree and Comparison Between Manufacturing Industry and Logistics Industry in Provinces and Cities of Yangtze River Economic Belt*

(I) **Grey correlation degree and its comparison among 11 provinces and cities in Yangtze River Economic Belt in the study period**

According to the calculation method as described above, the absolute grey correlation degree and the relative grey correlation degree are calculated one by one by the composite indexes of manufacturing industry and logistics industry of 11 provinces and cities. On this basis, the composite grey correlation degree ($\theta = 0.4$) can be further calculated, as shown in Table 22.

It can be seen from Table 22 that among the 11 provinces and cities, composite grey correlation degree of Chongqing City was the largest about 0.805, followed by Guizhou Province of about 0.801, and Shanghai, which is in the third place, was about 0.799. The composite correlation degree of these three provinces and cities was around 0.8, which meant that the manufacturing and logistics industries in these regions were in the process of fast linkage development. The composite grey correlation degree of Yunnan Province was the smallest about 0.651, which meant the degree of linkage development of logistics industry is relatively low, while the composite grey correlation degree of other seven provinces was between 0.69 and

**Table 22** Grey correlation degree between manufacturing industry and logistics industry in provinces and cities of Yangtze River Economic Belt

| | Absolute grey correlation degree | Relative grey correlation degree | Composite grey correlation degree |
|---|---|---|---|
| Shanghai City | 0.876 95 | 0.746 76 | 0.798 84 |
| Jiangsu Province | 0.841 26 | 0.637 41 | 0.718 95 |
| Zhejiang Province | 0.859 20 | 0.670 09 | 0.745 73 |
| Anhui Province | 0.897 98 | 0.683 46 | 0.769 27 |
| Jiangxi Province | 0.832 09 | 0.597 44 | 0.691 30 |
| Hubei Province | 0.837 16 | 0.652 26 | 0.726 22 |
| Hunan Province | 0.820 81 | 0.606 23 | 0.692 06 |
| Chongqing City | 0.920 18 | 0.728 34 | 0.805 08 |
| Sichuan Province | 0.815 30 | 0.606 98 | 0.690 31 |
| Guizhou Province | 0.901 41 | 0.733 30 | 0.800 54 |
| Yunnan Province | 0.737 87 | 0.593 17 | 0.651 05 |

0.77, and the linkage development degree of manufacturing industry and logistics industry were medium among 11 provinces and cities; Thereinto, the composite grey correlation degrees of Anhui Province, Zhejiang Province, Hubei Province and Jiangsu Province were 0.77–0.72, showing a stepwise downward distribution. The composite grey correlation degrees of Hunan Province, Jiangxi Province and Sichuan Province were relatively close and slightly higher than 0.69.

### (II) Dynamic change and comparison of grey correlation degree of Yangtze River Economic Belt in two study periods

The section from year 2000 to 2013 is separated into two equal time periods, that is, 2000–2006 and 2007–2013. According to the calculation method as described above, the absolute grey correlation degree, relative grey correlation degree and composite grey correlation degree of 11 provinces and cities of the Yangtze River Economic Belt in these two periods are calculated respectively (taking $\theta = 0.4$), as shown in Table 23.

**Table 23** Grey correlation degree of manufacturing industry and logistics industry in provinces and cities of Yangtze River Economic Belt in two time periods

| | Absolute grey correlation degree | | Relative grey correlation degree | | Composite grey correlation degree | |
|---|---|---|---|---|---|---|
| Time periods | 2000–2006 | 2007–2013 | 2000–2006 | 2007–2013 | 2000–2006 | 2007–2013 |
| Shanghai City | 0.874 82 | 0.771 46 | 0.810 06 | 0.730 81 | 0.835 96 | 0.747 07 |
| Jiangsu Province | 0.788 57 | 0.911 97 | 0.686 63 | 0.857 11 | 0.727 41 | 0.879 05 |
| Zhejiang Province | 0.857 64 | 0.945 39 | 0.749 23 | 0.921 41 | 0.792 59 | 0.931 00 |
| Anhui Province | 0.826 95 | 0.868 90 | 0.735 75 | 0.755 90 | 0.772 23 | 0.801 10 |
| Jiangxi Province | 0.762 05 | 0.908 21 | 0.654 90 | 0.808 54 | 0.697 76 | 0.848 41 |
| Hubei Province | 0.782 59 | 0.900 79 | 0.710 61 | 0.814 36 | 0.739 40 | 0.848 93 |
| Hunan Province | 0.766 14 | 0.861 85 | 0.670 18 | 0.759 11 | 0.708 56 | 0.800 21 |
| Chongqing City | 0.867 22 | 0.895 37 | 0.785 43 | 0.805 61 | 0.818 15 | 0.841 51 |
| Sichuan Province | 0.825 11 | 0.798 41 | 0.729 97 | 0.695 94 | 0.768 03 | 0.736 93 |
| Guizhou Province | 0.828 57 | 0.969 54 | 0.737 57 | 0.941 63 | 0.773 97 | 0.952 79 |
| Yunnan Province | 0.810 62 | 0.673 36 | 0.728 05 | 0.627 53 | 0.761 08 | 0.645 86 |

It can be seen from Table 23 that compared with the two periods of 2007–2013 with year 2000–2006, only Shanghai, Sichuan and Yunnan had a lower composite grey correlation degree in 2007–2013 than that in 2000–2006, while eight provinces and cities of Jiangsu, Zhejiang, Anhui, Jiangxi, Hubei, Hunan, Chongqing, and Guizhou had higher composite correlation degree in 2007–2013 than that in 2000–2006, that is to say, the number of regions with composite correlation degree in 2007–2013 being lower than that in 2000–2006 accounted for about 1/4 of the total, while the number of regions with composite correlation degree being higher than that of 2000–2006 accounted about 3/4 of the total. This shows that, from the perspective of dynamic changes, in the development process of the Yangtze River Economic Belt in recent 14 years, the linkage development of manufacturing industry and logistics industry in most provinces and cities (about 3/4) has been improved, and the coordination of the development of the two industrial sectors has been enhanced. From the view of composite indexes of manufacturing industry and logistics industry, the main reason for the decline of linkage development of these two industries in Shanghai, Sichuan and Yunnan was that the development of logistics industry was lagged far behind that of manufacturing industry during the period of 2007–2013.

From the absolute value of composite grey correlation degree from 2007 to 2013, the composite correlation degree of Zhejiang Province and Guizhou Province reached 0.9 above, and the linkage development of the two industries reached the "high" level. The composite correlation degree of six provinces, i.e. Jiangsu Province, Anhui Province, Jiangxi Province, Hubei Province, Hunan Province, and Chongqing City reached 0.8–0.9 and the linkage development of two industries reached "higher" level with the composite correlation degree of Shanghai, Sichuan Province and Yunnan Province less than 0.8, and that of Yunnan Province was only 0.646, which meant the linkage development degree of the two industries was relatively low.

## 5 Conclusion

Firstly, in terms of the development of manufacturing industry, the manufacturing industry in the Yangtze River Economic Belt developed fast and played an important role in the whole state. The average scale of enterprises was smaller than the national average, but the expansion was faster. The industry operation efficiency was lower than the national average, but the growth was faster. There were significant differences among the 11 provinces and cities of the Yangtze River Economic Belt in terms of regional scale, growth rate, average scale of enterprises, operation efficiency etc.

Secondly, in terms of the development of logistics industry, the logistics industry in the Yangtze River Economic Belt grew fast and played an important role in the whole state, and the operation efficiency of the industry was sound. In terms of regional scale, growth rate and industrial operation efficiency of the logistics industry, there were significant differences among the 11 provinces and cities in the Yangtze River Economic Belt.

Thirdly, based on the introduction of grey correlation analysis method, the linkage development of manufacturing industry and logistics industry in the Yangtze River Economic Belt was analyzed and intuitive and clear conclusions were obtained. On the whole, from 2000 to 2013, the linkage degree of manufacturing and logistics industry in the Yangtze River Economic Belt was relatively high, but slightly lower than the national average. From the perspective of dynamic changes, the degree of linkage development of manufacturing and logistics industry in the Yangtze River Economic Belt was obviously improved from 2007 to 2013 compared with the period of 2000–2006, and the magnitude of improvement was greater than the national average, which led to the fact that the degree of linkage development of the Yangtze River Economic Belt in 2007–2013 surpassed that of the whole state.

Fourthly, from the comparison of provinces and cities in the Yangtze River Economic Belt, the linkage development of manufacturing industry and logistics industry in Chongqing, Guizhou and Shanghai was higher, while that of Yunnan Province was lower and that of Jiangsu Province, Zhejiang Province, Anhui Province, Jiangxi Province, Hubei Province, Hunan Province and Sichuan Province was at intermediate level. In terms of dynamic changes, in the development process of the last 14 years and compared with the time period 2000–2006, the linkage development of manufacturing industry and logistics industry in most provinces and cities of the Yangtze River Economic Belt (about 3/4) showed an upward trend from 2007 to 2013, and there were 8 provinces and cities with "high" and "higher" level of interconnected industrial development, accounting for the vast majority of the total (about 73%).

# Coordinated Development of Information Industry in Yangtze River Economic Belt

**Limei Xu**

## 1 Concept and Characteristics of Information Industry

### *1.1 International Definition of Information Industry*

Today's concept of "Information Industry" is produced and developed on the basis of knowledge industry study. Professor F. Machlup, an American economist, first proposed the concept similar to information industry. In his book *Knowledge and Distribution in the United States* published in 1962, he put forward the concept of "Knowledge Industry" for the first time. Although Professor F. Machlup did not use the term "Information Industry" definitely, and its scope was different from that of the current information industry, it is undeniable that it basically reflects the main characteristics of the information industry.

In 1977, on the basis of Machlup's research on information industry, M. U. Porat published the book *Information Economy: Definition and Measurement*, which extended knowledge industry to information industry, and pioneered the quartering method, i.e., the social economy was divided into four categories: agriculture, industry, service industry and information industry, and the information industry was divided into the so-called primary and secondary information sectors. This provides an operational method for the study of information industry structure.

As an emerging industrial sector, the connotation and extension of information industry will be extended and changed with the continuous expansion and maturity

In the context, the "coordination" and "linkage" are synonymous, which refer to the mutual dependence, mutual influence, reasonable division of work and common development of the information industry of provinces and cities in the Yangtze River Economic Belt.

L. Xu (✉)
Institute of Applied Economics, Shanghai Academy of Social Sciences, Shanghai, China
e-mail: xlm@sass.org.cn



X. Jing (ed.), *Development of the Yangtze River Economic Belt in China*, Urban Governance Practices in China,
https://doi.org/10.1007/978-981-16-1578-8_2

of the industry. Since F. Machlup first proposed the concept of knowledge industry, scholars from all over the world have carried out extensive research and discussion on the concept and scope of information industry. But so far, there is still no unified and standard definition of "information industry". In order to meet the actual needs of industrial development, governments or departments of various countries have defined "information industry". The main definitions are exampled as follows.

According to the 1987 *Standard Industry Classification* of the United States, the definition of information industry in *Digital Economy 2000* issued by the U.S. Department of Commerce is that the information industry shall be composed of four parts: hardware industry, software and service industry, communication equipment manufacturing industry and communication service industry.

The definition of information industry defined by AIIA is that information industry is a means of innovation depending upon the new information technology and information processing and a combination of production activities that make and provide information products and services.

In the North American Free Trade Area (NAFTA), the United States, Canada and Mexico jointly formulated the *North American Industrial Classification System (NAICS)* in 1997, the information industry was defined as an independent industry sector for the first time. The system stipulated that the information industry, as an independent and complete sector, should include the following units: units producing and publishing information and cultural products; units providing methods and means to transmit and release these products; and units of information services and data processing. It included four industries in specific: publishing industry, film and audio-visual industry, radio and television and telecommunication industry, information and data processing service industry.

It was defined by the European Information Provider Association (EURIPA) that the information industry is the electronic information industry that provides information products and services.

The Association of Science, Technology and Economy of Japan holds the opinion that information industry is an industrial group composed of information technology industry and information commercialization industry, which is formed by improving human information processing ability and promoting social circulation, including information technology industry and information productization. The content of information industry is relatively concentrated, mainly including software industry, database industry, communication industry and corresponding information service industry.

## *1.2 Definition and Scope Division of Information Industry in China*

Many Chinese scholars (Wu Jiapei, Qu Weizhi, Zhang Shouyi, etc.) have done relevant research on "information industry", and put forward their own views on its concept and scope. Professor Wu Jiapei, a quantitative economist and an information economist, believes that the information industry is an industry to serve the industry, and it is the general name of enterprises and institutions and relevant internal organizations engaged in the production of information products and services, the construction of information systems, the manufacturing of information technology equipment, etc. These studies of these scholars play a certain role in promoting the development of information industry.

The definition of the information industry by the Ministry of Industry and Information Technology of China is that the information industry belongs to the fourth category of industry, which includes the traditional information sectors such as telecommunications, telephone, printing, publishing, news, radio and television, and the emerging information sectors such as electronic computer, laser, optical fiber and communication satellite. It is mainly based on electronic computers and engaged in the production, transmission, storage, processing and handling of information. In addition, the information industry refers to the industry that transforms information into commodities. It includes not only software, database, various wireless communication services and online information services, but also traditional newspapers, books and periodicals, films and audio-visual products.

From the statistical caliber, China's Industry Classification of National Economy (GB/T 4754-2011) classified the information industry into information manufacturing industry and information service industry, as shown in Table 1.

### *1.3 Characteristics of Information Industry*

Compared with the traditional industry, the information industry has the following characteristics:

(1) Information industry is a knowledge and technology intensive industry. Information industry is mainly based on knowledge and technology. Knowledge and technology are the key factors to promote the development of information industry. In the process of production, the information industry relies more on intelligence and technology than on other factors of production. In the production process of information industry, the investment of capital and labor is one aspect, but the more important is the input of knowledge, intelligence and technology. Therefore, in the information industry enterprises, scientific and technological personnel often take a large proportion, and the labor productivity of enterprises is relatively high. Especially the development of information technology has been changing with each passing day and the vitality of information industry innovation also comes from the high investment in technology research and development. The high degree of innovation and rapid renewal have become the important features for the development of global electronic information industry by taking the scientific and technological research and development as a guide.

**Table 1** Classification of national economy of information industry

| Information industry | Industry code | Industry classification |
|---|---|---|
| Manufacturing industry of computer, communication and other electronic equipment | 391 | Manufacturing of computer |
| | 392 | Manufacturing of communication equipment |
| | 393 | Manufacturing of radio and television equipment |
| | 394 | Manufacturing of radar and supporting equipment |
| | 395 | Manufacturing of audio visual equipment |
| | 396 | Manufacturing of electronic device |
| | 397 | Manufacturing of electronic component |
| | 399 | Manufacturing of other electronic equipment |
| Information transmission, software and information technology services | 63 | Telecommunications, radio & television and satellite transmission services |
| | 64 | Internet and related services |
| | 65 | Software and information technology services |

① The fourth industry is a general term for the knowledge, technology and information intensive industrial sectors which are differentiated from the third industry. It shall include: design and production of electronic computer software and its service department, consulting department, application of microcomputer, optical fiber, laser, genetic engineering new technology department, high automation, electrification department, etc. Information industry is the independent fourth industry.

(2) Information industry is the industry involving high-risk but high-revenue. First of all, the research and development of the information industry requires a large amount of investment, including human resources, capital and technology. Moreover, due to the uncertainty of the success rate of invention and creation, the huge investment may get nothing back, so the research and development of information industry is also full of uncertainties. Secondly, even if some research projects are successful, not every item of technology can be successfully commercialized. If the products can not meet the market demand, the technology and industry will be eliminated soon. Thirdly, the information industry is to pursue the speed of technological renewal. If the technological renewal is slow or the strategy of technological innovation is improper, it may be eliminated. All of these are the high risk embodiment of information industry.

The high profitability of the information industry is mainly manifested in that once the enterprise carries out technology investment and development, and the market is successful, it will bring huge benefits. According to the *Statistical Annual Report of Electronic Information Industry in 2014*, China's top 100 electronic information enterprises include Huawei Company, Haier Group, China electronic information industry group, etc. The top 100 enterprises have implemented the strategy of large companies, and their scale and efficiency have increased steadily. In 2014, the main business revenue had reached 2.3 trillion yuan, which presented obvious and high profitability.

(3) The information industry is the industry with high driving force and high permeability. Information industry is closely related to various industries with high driving force. The development of information industry has driven the development of microelectronics, semiconductor, laser and other industries within the industry. At the same time, with the help of information technology, software engineering technology, database technology, network technology and other industries have been produced. The information industry has driven the development of many industries, such as new material, new energy, machine manufacturing, military science, and so beyond the information industry. Meanwhile, it catalyzed the edge industries, such as optical electronics, avionics, automotive electronics and other industries. Because of the high relevance and high driving force of information technology, information industry has become the largest industry in developed countries and the pillar industry of moderately developed countries and emerging developing countries.

At the same time, the information industry has a high permeability to other industries. At present, the further development of all walks of life is inseparable from the application of electronic information technology and electronic information products. The integration of information industry and traditional industry provides comprehensive technical support for traditional industry and vests new connotation to traditional industry. For example, information technology has been fully used in industrial design, production, control and other fields; computer control technology, computer aided design and analysis are widely used in machinery, electronics, aviation, aerospace and other fields. Through the application and integration of information technology, the development of other industries has been directly affected and the competitiveness of traditional industries has been improved.

(4) Information industry can provide more opportunities of work. It is believed with traditional ideas that with the continuous progress of science and technology, technology will replace the labor and then to cause further unemployment. However, some people believe that with the continuous innovation and progress of technology, the development of emerging industries will create more employment opportunities. Relevant research showed that the information industry is the high-tech industry, but also a high employment industry. With the development of information industry, the relevant jobs opportunities

will be created. For example, according to the practical research on the development of the information industry in the United States, the employment of information related industries is increasing rather than declining. From 1990 to 1997, the average annual employment growth rate of information related industries in the United States reached 2.69%, and a total of 5.9 million jobs opportunities were increased. It is precisely because of the rapid growth of employment in the information industry and information related industries, the low unemployment rate can be maintained in the United States. In addition, according to the statistics of U.S. Department of Labor, the jobs of information industry in Silicon Valley have been increased by 25% since 2007. All these indicated that the development of information industry has brought more jobs opportunities. At present, the rapid development of information industry has become an important channel to ease the employment pressure in China.

## 2 Motivation and Evolution of Information Industry Collaborative Development

### *2.1 The Motivation of Coordinated Development of Information Industry*

The coordinated development of information industry in a certain region will be beneficial to the optimization of regional industrial structure and ultimately promote the development of regional economy. The main motivations for the coordinated development of information industry include factor mobility, industrial transfer, industrial alliance and industrial linkage.

(I) **Factor mobility**

The factor mobility means the mobility of production factor which refers to the spatial transfer of production factors such as raw material, labor, technology, capital, information and so on. The mobility of production factors is one of the basic conditions for the linkage of all industries, and also one of the motivations for the coordinated development of information industry.

First of all, in a certain region, the mobility of production factors promotes closer connection and linkage among industries. At the same time, the breadth and depth of the mobility of production factors determine the strength and level of industrial connection and linkage in the region. For example, in the lower reaches of the Yangtze River, the famous Yangtze River Delta Region in China, thanks to the rapid process of economic integration, there are relatively few barriers among the administrative regions, which promotes the extensive mobility of talents, technology and capital. The deep mobility of these elements promotes the strong linkage among industries in the region, and meanwhile various industries will have deeper linkage in the process of development and upgrading.

Secondly, between different regions, such as the coastal and inland areas in China, and the upper, middle and lower reaches of the Yangtze River, production factors always flow from the areas with low price to those with high price, or from underdeveloped areas to relatively developed areas. In this way, the mobility of production factors promotes the industrial linkage within the region. As the information industry itself is a knowledge, technology, capital intensive industry, when the technical elements, human resources and industrial investment are available in the region, the information industry will be first developed. The Yangtze River Delta Region is one of the earliest and fast developing areas of information industry in China, which is inseparable from the abundant and high-quality production factors in this region.

When the industry develops to a certain stage and when the economic, technological and human resource conditions in other regions reach a certain level, some traditional elements will flow from developed areas to developing areas. With the mobility of factors in developed areas, other newly developed areas will attract the aggregation of production factors, thus to promote the revitalization of industry in this region. For example, the industrial policies and resource conditions of Chongqing continuously attract the launching of multinational information enterprises, thus to promote the vigorous development of information industry in the region in recent years.

(II) **Industrial transfer**

Industrial transfer refers to the economic behavior and process that some industries transfer from one country or region to another due to changes in resource supply or product demand conditions (Lewis 1984). Industrial transfer is a phenomenon of regional industrial linkage, which appears at a certain stage of economic development to make full use of regional comparative advantages. In China, industrial transfer is an important factor in the formation of industrial division among different regions, and is also an important way to adjust and upgrade the industrial structure in the areas where industries move out and those where industries move in.

There are two main motivations for industrial transfer. The first is the need of industrial division of work. Specialized production is an important motivation of industrial transfer. With the development of industry globalization, the advantages of specialized production in specific areas have been formed in some regions. This advantage has been further strengthened with the enhancement of industrial aggregation-the production cost is relatively low, but the production technology is relatively mature. In this case, these production links with comparative advantages in some industries will be transferred to specific regions to enhance their core competitiveness. This situation is obvious in the global transfer of information industry. Like the Sichuan Province in the upper reaches of the Yangtze River, it has become a new cluster place of global electronic information industry through actively undertaking global industrial transfer when the sales of traditional PC declined and the sales of Tablet are under the new trend of ascendant. At present, the electronic information capacity undertaken by Sichuan mainly focuses on mobile internet terminal products, for which its own advantages of professional production have been gradually formed.

According to the statistics of Chengdu Customs, 34 million portable computers were exported under the supervision of Chengdu Customs in 2012, a significant increase of 80.7% compared with 2011; the value of sales was 12.85 billion US dollars, with the year-on-year increase of 71.4%.

The second is the demand of market expansion, which is one of the most important motivations for industrial transfer. Due to the continuous aggregation of industries towards the same region, the resources, land and environment in these areas will get into a tense situation, and even certain constraints, which will encourage them to transfer some relatively low-end industries out. For example, in the Yangtze River Delta Region of China and due to the limitations of resources and environment and the rapid updating of technology, some relatively matured products are gradually replaced by new and better products. In recent years, the Yangtze River Delta Region has gradually shifted from the original computer manufacturing and NoteBook manufacturing to the development of Internet of things, big data, cloud computing and Internet finance. As a relatively low-end industry, in order to continue to obtain profits, the information manufacturing industry has gradually turned to the Midwest regions of China to seek the new room for market development.

### (III) **Industrial alliance**

Industrial alliance is a long-term cooperation mode of complementary advantages and shared risks formed by enterprises focusing on some common strategic interests through various equity, agreements or contracts when the cooperation between enterprises steps to a certain stage. Industrial alliance is the main linkage mode of regional industrial linkage development to the advanced stage. With the help of the virtual organization of industrial alliance, resources and information can be shared in a certain range, so that the optimal allocation of labor, finance, material and information can be realized in an extensive range, and more competitive advantages can be obtained.

According to the different motivations, industrial alliance can be classified into two types: type of intrinsic factor and type of external factor. The intrinsic industry alliance is when the industry is developed to a certain extent, there will be fierce competition among enterprises and enterprises will compete to reduce costs and enhance innovation, but the result is the competition among enterprises, especially price competition, often leads to destruction of both sides. At the same time, the innovation achievements after large amount of investment by the enterprise will be quickly replaced by imitation of other enterprises, however, it is also hard for a single enterprise to bear the large amount of capital and labor required by innovation. In this case, the intrinsic industry alliance will come into being.

External industrial alliance is when the development of one industry encounters external pressure, such as technical development barriers which are difficult to be broken through or vicious competition between regions or when one single enterprise is too weak to complete technological innovation or to compete with strong competitors. In this case, multiple enterprises will actively form alliances under the organization and coordination of Chamber of Commerce or leading enterprises to jointly fight against the external pressure. At present, in the development of the information industry, many technology alliances have been formed under the leadership of the government. For example, with the approval of Jiangsu Provincial Economic and Information Commission, Jiangsu International Institute of Industrial Technology and Jiangsu Sailian Information Industry Research Institute jointly initiated the establishment of "Jiangsu Province Information Industry Collaborative Innovation Alliance" in March 2014. The alliance aims to focus on the major innovation needs of the information industry, jointly carry out major industrial innovation and technology research activities, promote the realization of industrial technology breakthroughs, and enhance the overall competitiveness of the information industry.

### (IV) **Industry Linkage**

Industrial linkage is an industrial cooperation activity between enterprises in the same or different links of the industrial chain and is based on industrial association. The principal of industrial linkage is the enterprises, but the government policies have an important impact on the industrial linkage. According to the direction of regional industrial linkage, industrial linkage can be classified into vertical linkage and horizontal linkage.

Vertical industrial linkage refers to the process of industrial linkage based on the vertical connection of industrial chain. The basis of industrial vertical linkage is intra-industry vertical division of work (Yi Ming 1999). Industrial division of work and upstream and downstream cooperation of industrial chains are the causes of regional linkage (Weintraub 2002). Intra industry vertical division of work refers to the linkage between economic entities in different links of value chain and production chain, and its basis is the regional division of work. The vertical linkage of industry usually shows the global and regional industrial transfer activities. For example, in the value chain of information industry, semiconductor materials have become a kind of raw materials and primary products. The United States has just transferred such a product with high investment and low product rate to Korea, China and other places, but focuses its attention on the development of software industry, network industry and e-commerce.

Horizontal industrial linkage refers to the cooperation and linkage at horizontal level in technology development, information exchange and market development based on trust or contract between enterprises. In the horizontal industrial linkage, the cooperative competition and diffusion and sharing of technology among regions based on trust are remained as the main characteristics of this type of linkage (Wang Lei 2007) although the complementarity of industries still can be revealed. Horizontal linkage is mainly based on the interests of long-term development of enterprises, to achieve efficient interaction and cooperation in industrial investment, technology development, marketing, export and other aspects, so as to compete with stronger competitors. Technology linkage is a typical horizontal industrial linkage. In the development of information industry, technology is the most important driving factor, so technical linkage or technology alliance is quite common. For instance, in order to promote the development of information industry, an information technology industry alliance has been formed in Guizhou Province. The alliance aims to build a cross industry innovation platform combining industry, university and research, create industrial standards, patented technologies and proprietary technologies with independent intellectual property rights, and enhance the overall competitiveness of the information industry. Technology alliance is the advanced development direction of industrial alliance, and also the outstanding performance of regional industrial linkage development towards the advanced stage.

## 2.2 Evolution of Spatial Linkage of Information Industry

The linkage development process of information industry constantly shapes the spatial pattern of regional information industry, and the spatial pattern of information industry in turn affects the spatial behavior of information industry linkage development. According to Friedman (1966) spatial organization theory, the evolution of spatial linkage of information industry can be divided into the following stages.

(I) **Low level dispersion stage**

This stage is characterized by the scattered, isolated and closed cycle of information economy in a small region, and there is barely spatial aggregation effect, instead, there are only a few small nodes formed in history, and the scope of aggregation and diffusion is relatively small. At this stage, information manufacturing enterprises appear in some areas with good industrial foundation and high level of science and technology, such as Shanghai, Jiangsu, etc., but the enterprises are decentralized, the scope of products and services is rather limited, and the organization and management functions of enterprises are also very simple. It reflects the characteristics of the pre-industrial society, when the economic level is not developed enough, all kinds of business activities are basically in a spontaneous state, the production scale of enterprises is limited, the scope of economic activities and influence is relatively small, and the enterprises are not closely linked. It can be said that the impact of enterprise development in this stage is balanced in space and is under a relatively stable initial state.

The development of information industry in China began with the founding of new China. At the beginning of the founding of the People's Republic of China, there were only three or four small factories relying on imported parts for repair and maintenance, with a total of 4000 employees. In 1949, the total output value of the whole industry was 4.956 million yuan. By 1957, the state had established 40 central-governmental enterprises and 337 local factories with total 85,400 employees. Through technical refurbishment, the embryonic form of electronic information industry base has been formed in Nanjing, Beijing, Chengdu and Shanghai. From the early days of the founding of the People's Republic of China to the period before the reform and opening up, the distribution of enterprises in the information industry is basically independent and decentralized. No certain scale and aggregation has been formed, so it is named as "low level dispersion stage".

### (II) Aggregation development stage

Since the basic natural conditions and resource endowment in various places are different, the development of information industry in different regions begins to show differences. As the information industry with high scientific and technological content, it always begins to develop and expand in some places where the economy is more developed, the advantages of talents and science and technology are more prominent, and the transportation infrastructure is relatively convenient, as a result, cluster place of economic activity information industry presenting in dots has emerged and is characterized by aggregation development in space. The Yangtze River Delta, the Pearl River Delta and the Bohai Rim are the three earliest aggregation areas of information industry in China. The advantages of enterprise aggregation development lie in that, on the one hand, the low-cost competitive advantage can be obtained through its own economies of scale, scope economy and external economy; on the other hand, its competitiveness can be further enhanced through such factors as low cost of labor, land, and loose taxation policy and low cost for environmental protection. Due to the developed economy and convenient transportation, it has attracted the capital, talents, goods and other elements of the surrounding areas and the low-end links of the industrial chain to be continuously gathered in the center, so that it will become the growth pole to drive and coordinate the regional industrial development.

Reform and opening up has brought infinite vigor and vitality to the development of information industry in China. A series of policies and guidelines of the government to promote the development of the information industry have greatly accelerated the development pace of the information industry. In the 1980s, Deng Xiaoping proposed that the electronic information industry shall be united to form business group. The Yangtze River Delta and the Pearl River Delta regions in China took the advantages of good natural and technological conditions, coupled with the promotion of the government support for the development of information industry policy, manufacturing industry development cluster was formed at first and the information manufacturing enterprises were gradually increased, as well as the relationship was getting closer. In 1998, the total annual output of China's electronic information industry reached 480 billion yuan, 59 times that of 1979, and the export volume reached 25.7 billion US dollars, 2,570 times that of 1979. Therefore, the period from the reform and opening up to the beginning of the 21st century can be regarded as the initial stage of the regional linkage development of information industry in China, and its corresponding spatial structure is aggregated.

### (III) The development stage of radiation expansion

This stage can be regarded as the growth stage of regional linkage development of information industry. Along the Yangtze River Economic Belt and with the deep exploitation of the Yangtze River Delta, Chengdu-Chongqing and other areas with developed economy and industry and convenient transportation, the scale of the information industry has been expanded, and the space has been enlarged, thus forming an increasing number of information industry nodes. When the number of these nodes increases in geometric multiples, the aggregation scope of regional information industry continues to be enlarged and the industrial spatial structure develops to multiple levels to form different hierarchical system. In this stage, it is just the development of industrial nodes and routes that promotes the network development of spatial linkage of regional information industry and the evolution of external specific patterns.

Since the 21st century up to now, the electronic information industry in China has walked into a new stage of global development. During this period, some information industry clusters have gradually grown, showing a trend of expansion in both spatial distribution and industrial output. In 2014, the added value of electronic information industry in Yangtze River Delta was 826 billion yuan, accounting for nearly 10% of GDP in Yangtze River Delta. In recent years, the scale of electronic information industry in Chengdu has been expanding, the industrial structure has been constantly optimized, and the information products have become more and more abundant. At present, the scale effect of the electronic information industry cluster mode in Chengdu comprehensive bonded area is quite obvious, and an industrial chain from the packaging and testing of computer core components to the production of terminal products has been formed. The information industry in Chongqing is also developing with fast pace. In 2014, 64 million sets of computers were produced here, including 61 million NoteBooks, making it the world's largest production base for NoteBooks. It can be seen that several information industry aggregation areas along the Yangtze River are developing in a trend of radiation expansion.

### (IV) High level equilibrium development stage

This is the mature stage of the linkage development of information industry. It is characterized by network, equilibrium, multi-center and multi domain surface, and the corresponding spatial structure develops in equilibrium. When entering this stage, the mobility of elements is liberalized and equilibrated, the transfer of enterprises and industries has entered a relatively stable state; industrial aggregation has been formed and entered into a relatively matured state; the division of work in the industrial chain has been improved; the information industry and other industries are related and interacted closer and the influences are getting deeper. In this stage, the information industry cluster center, industrial development node and spatial structure of industrial hinterland suggest a dynamic equilibrium of homogenization, presenting a network layer and special structure with multi-center and in crisscross pattern. The information industry has entered a high level of equilibrium development.

At present, the information industry in China has not entered this stage of development yet.

# 3 Current Situation and Problems of the Coordinated Development of Information Industry in the Yangtze River Economic Belt

## *3.1 Spatial Distribution Characteristics of the Information Industry*

There is information industry in all 11 provinces and cities in the Yangtze River Economic Belt, but the development levels vary from each other. At present, the lower reaches of the Yangtze River, namely, the Yangtze River Delta, Sichuan, Chongqing and other obvious industrial aggregation areas have been formed. The information industry cluster focusing on IC design and manufacturing and communication equipment manufacturing has been formed in the Yangtze River Delta region. In recent two years, e-commerce, Internet and other information service industries have developed rapidly. In the middle reaches of the Yangtze River, it gives the priority to the flat panel display, communication equipment, optoelectronics and other information manufacturing industries. In the upper reaches of the Yangtze River, an information industry cluster with military electronics, communication equipment, optical communication and software has been structured.

Moreover, in the development of information industry in the Yangtze River Economic Belt, the difference of regional information industry generally presents the trend of "strong in the lower part and weak in the upper part", that is, the development of the information industry in the lower reaches is much higher than that of the middle and upper reaches, and the regional information industry presents a trend of polarization. Of course, this is closely related to the level of economic development and the foundation of information resource in various regions.

In addition, there are also spatial differences in the growth of regional information industry in the Yangtze River Economic Belt. The growth of information industry in the lower reaches of the Yangtze River tends to be stable, while that of Anhui, Chongqing, Sichuan and other post developing provinces and cities is growing faster; the information industry in the lower reaches is transforming to the "service" and more attentions are turned to Internet, e-commerce, software and other industries, while the "post developing provinces" such as Anhui and Chongqing have undertaken the characteristics of information manufacturing, that is, for the production of NoteBook, mobile equipment and corresponding spare parts.

(I) **The information manufacturing enterprises are marked by the aggregation in lower reaches**

In terms of the number of enterprises, according to the data of Wind Information, in 2013, there were 9,025 information manufacturing enterprises above designated scale in 11 provinces and cities in the Yangtze River Economic Belt, including 7,047 in the lower reaches, accounting for 78.08% of the total enterprises, 1,319 in the middle reaches, accounting for 14.61% of the total enterprises, and 659 in the upper

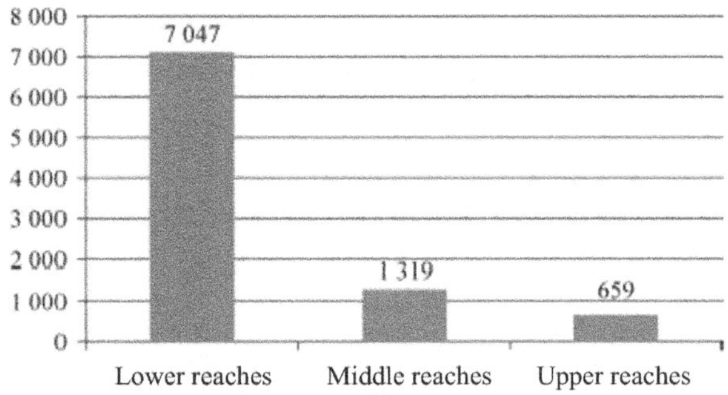


**Fig. 1** Number of electronic information manufacturing enterprises above designated scale in the upper, middle and lower reaches of the Yangtze River Economic Belt in 2013. *Source* Wind Information

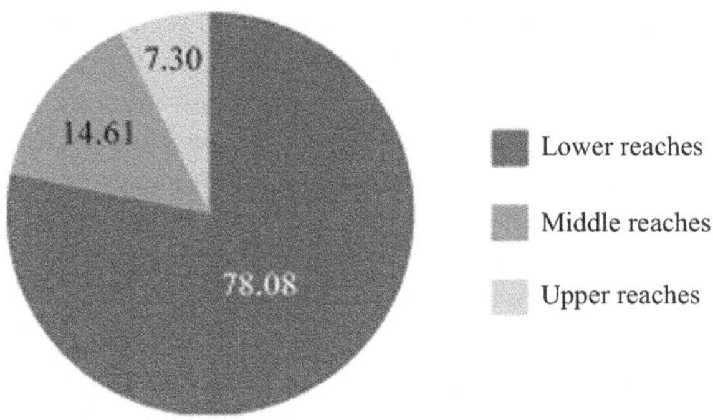


**Fig. 2** Proportion of electronic information manufacturing enterprises above designated scale in the upper, middle and lower reaches of the Yangtze River Economic Belt in 2013. *Source* Wind Information

reaches, accounting for 7.30% of the total enterprises (refer to Figs. 1 and 2). It can be seen that information manufacturing enterprises are mainly concentrated in the lower reaches of the Yangtze River Economic Belt, while the number of enterprises in the middle and upper reaches is relatively less.

In terms of the fixed assets investment of enterprises, in 2013, the total investment completed in the lower reaches was 218.452 million yuan, accounting for 59.47% of the total accumulated investment in the information industry of the Yangtze River Economic Belt; the cumulative completed investment in the middle reaches was 98.134 million yuan, accounting for 26.71% of the total investment in the information industry of the Yangtze River Economic Belt; the total investment in the lower reaches was 50.075 million yuan, accounting for 13.82% of the total investment in information industry in the Yangtze River Economic Belt (refer to Figs. 3 and 4). As can be seen from Fig. 3, the total amount of investment in information manufacturing industry in the lower reaches of the Yangtze River Economic Belt is relatively

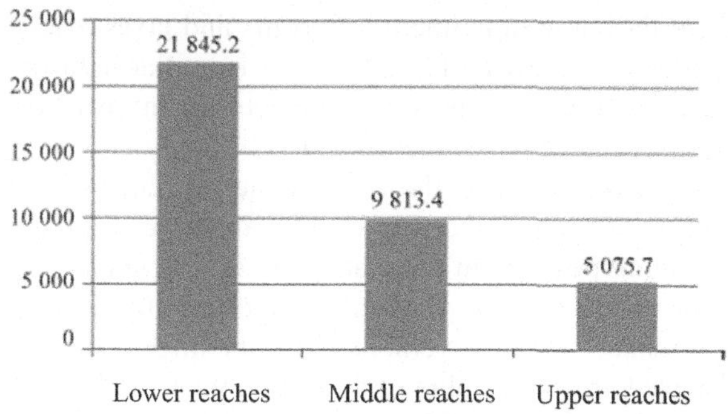


**Fig. 3** Investment in fixed assets of information industry in upper, middle and lower reaches of Yangtze River Economic Belt in 2013 (unit: 10,000 yuan). *Source* Wind Information

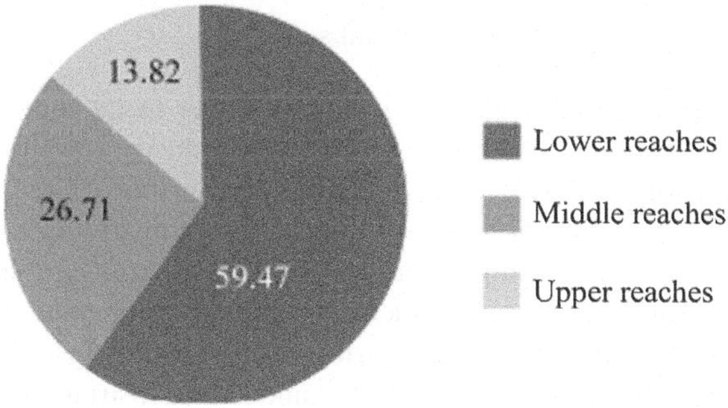


**Fig. 4** Proportion of completed fixed assets investment in information industry of upper, middle and lower reaches of Yangtze River Economic Belt in 2013. *Source* Wind Information

large, and the scale of information industry also exceeds that in the middle and upper reaches.

**Column 1: Development of Information Industry in Yangtze River Delta in 2014**[1]

1. Outstanding economic contribution

In recent years, the information industry in the Yangtze River Delta has been maintaining a leading position in the national economy, and its contribution to economic growth has become increasingly prominent. In 2014, the added value of information industry in Shanghai reached 246.01 billion yuan, accounting for 10.4% of GDP. The information industry has become the pillar industry of the national economy. The electronic information industry in Zhejiang Province has achieved an added-value of 254 billion yuan with a year-on-year increase of 14.6%, accounting for 6.3% of the

[1]Source: *Economic Development Report of the Yangtze River Delta in 2015*, Shanghai Academy of Social Sciences Press.

provincial GDP; at the same time, the total profits and taxes reached 139.7 billion yuan, with a year-on-year growth of 17.9%, it is also pillar industry of the national economy. The revenue from main business in electronic information manufacturing industry in Jiangsu Province has achieved 2,920 billion yuan, an increase of 6.4% over the same period of last year; the accumulated revenue of software business reached 643.9 billion yuan, with the year-on-year increase of 24.4%, and continued to maintain the leading position in the state. The development of electronic information industry in Anhui Province caught up and got ahead of others with more outstanding performance. As of November 2014, the information industry in Anhui Province has achieved an added value of 41 billion yuan, an increase of 44.8% and a growth rate of 51.2%. The growth rate and contribution rate both ranked first in 40 industries, and its growth trend exceeded that of Shanghai, Zhejiang Province and Jiangsu Province. The electronic information industry has become the fastest growing economic field in Anhui Province.[2]

2. Continuous expansion of the industrial scale

The scale of information industry in the Yangtze River Delta continues to expand. In 2014, the added value of Shanghai's information industry was increased by 9.6% compared with that of the previous year, 0.8% higher than that of GDP, and accounting for more than 10% of GDP; the scale of information industry in Zhejiang Province accounted for 6.3% of GDP with an increase of 0.4% point over the previous year; the output value of information manufacturing industry (computer, communication and other electronic equipment manufacturing industry) in Jiangsu Province reached 1,805.59 billion yuan, an increase of 4.1%, and the industrial scale continued to expand; the growth of information industry in Anhui Province was more prominent, and the added value was increased by 44.8% from January to November 2014, which was 32.6% point higher than that of all industries above designated scale. It can be seen that the total amount of information industry in each region of the Yangtze River Delta expanded and the scale of the industry grew in the continuous manner.[3]

In addition, from the perspective of software industry, the software industry in the Yangtze River Delta region developed with robust in 2014. No matter the revenue from software service industry, software product or information system integration service, the growth rate was relatively high. Except that the growth rate of these three indicators in Shanghai was slightly lower than the national average, the growth of Jiangsu Province, Zhejiang Province and Anhui Province exceeded the national average. In particular, the revenue from software services in Anhui Province was increased by 43.8% and the revenue from software products was increased by 53.8% (as seen in Table 2).

Jiangsu, Shanghai and Zhejiang, after entering the top 10 of the national software industry in 2013, respectively entered the top 10 provinces and cities with the fastest

[2]Source: *Statistical Bulletin of National Economic and Social Development of Each Province or City in 2014.*

[3]Source: *Statistical Bulletin of All Provinces and Cities in 2014 and Report* issued by Economic and Information Commission.

**Table 2** Software enterprises and their revenue in Yangtze River Delta from January to November 2014

| Region | Number of enterprise (enterprise) | Revenue from software services (10,000 yuan) | |
|---|---|---|---|
| | | Accumulated in current period | Year on year increase or decrease (%) |
| Whole state | 36 459 | 329 949 122 | 20.1 |
| Shanghai City | 2 500 | 23 990 800 | 15.5 |
| Jiangsu Province | 5 925 | 58 023 233 | 21.3 |
| Zhejiang Province | 2 032 | 20 790 450 | 28.4 |
| Anhui Province | 292 | 1 066 995 | 43.8 |
| Total of Yangtze River Delta | 10 749 | 103 871 478 | |

| Revenue from software product (10,000 yuan) | | Revenue from information system integration services | |
|---|---|---|---|
| Accumulated in current period | Year on year increase or decrease (%) | Accumulated in current period | Year on year increase or decrease (%) |
| 101 510 821 | 18.4 | 67 411 234 | 18.8 |
| 8 578 700 | 15.6 | 5 105 900 | 14.5 |
| 16 238 756 | 22.8 | 9 679 661 | 21.9 |
| 5 283 557 | 27.3 | 2 457 237 | 21.2 |
| 504 379 | 53.8 | 323 160 | 27.6 |
| 30 605 392 | | 17 565 958 | |

*Source* Ministry of Industry and Information Technology of China, http://www.miit.gov.cn/nl1293472/index.html

growth rate of software industry in China in 2014 (from January to November). All cumulative growth rates of software business revenue of these three provinces and cities exceeded 15% (Fig. 5).

3. Declined growth rate of industrial investment

In recent years, the growth rate of investment in information industry in the Yangtze River Delta has declined. In terms of the total amount of industrial fixed assets investment in 2014, the investment in various regions ranked top in China, but the growth rate of investment was all decreasing. For example, compared with 2013, the total investment in Jiangsu Province still ranked the first in China, Shanghai was still outside the top 10, while Zhejiang Province ranked No. 10 in 2013 but was not in the top 10 in 2014; Anhui Province dropped from the fifth place in 2013 to the sixth in 2014; however, the growth rate of investment in Jiangsu, Zhejiang and Anhui provinces was lower than 5%, and they are all lower than 11% of the state, and much lower than 30% of Hebei Province and 77.7% of Chongqing city, as shown in Fig. 6.

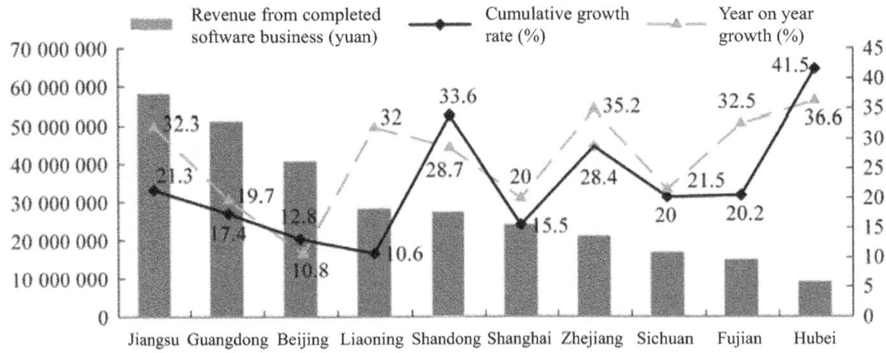


**Fig. 5** Growth of software industry in China's top ten provinces and cities from January to November 2014. *Source* Ministry of Industry and Information Technology of China, https://www.miit.gov.cn/jgsj/yxj/xxfb/art/2020/art_80be4ee609594c4b980352fd987b0b91.html

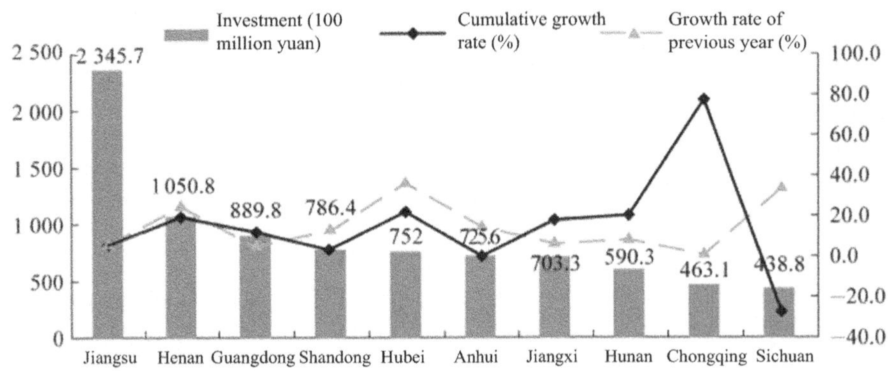


**Fig. 6** Investment in fixed assets of China's top ten provinces and cities in 2014. *Source* Ministry of Industry and Information Technology, "investment in fixed assets of electronic information industry in 2014"

4. Continuous optimization of industrial structure

In 2014, the structure of information industry in Yangtze River Delta continued to be optimized. Firstly, one was reflected in the optimization of industrial structure and the growth of information service industry was faster than that of information manufacturing industry. For example, the electronic information products manufacturing industry of Shanghai achieved an output value of 625.234 billion yuan in 2014, an increase of −2.3% over the previous year, while the software industry in Shanghai exceeded 300 billion yuan for the first time, with a year-on-year growth of 21.7%. The electronic information manufacturing industry in Zhejiang Province realized an added value of 113.4 billion yuan, an increase of 8.2% over the previous year, while the revenue of software service industry in Zhejiang Province reached 20.79 billion yuan, an increase of 28.4% over the previous year.

**Table 3** Output of partial information products in the Yangtze River Delta in 2014

| Province or city | Product name | Unit | Output | Increase over the previous year (%) |
|---|---|---|---|---|
| Shanghai | Mobile communication handset (mobile phone) | 10,000 unit | 5 484.75 | 11.1 |
| | Integrated circuit | 100 million pcs | 223.33 | 13.3 |
| Jiangsu | Integrated circuit | 100 million pcs | 328.9 | 11.3 |
| | SPC exchanges | 10,000 lines | 1.9 | −18.4 |
| Zhejiang | Integrated circuit | 100 million pcs | 60.9 | 11.4 |
| | electronic component | 100 million pcs | 1 018.3 | 2.7 |
| | Microcomputer | 10,000 unit | 191.0 | 16.3 |

*Source Statistical Bulletin of National Economic and Social Development of Provinces and Cities in 2014*; relevant data of Anhui Province have not been released yet

The other one was reflected in constant adjustment of the product structure of electronic information industry. Traditional products such as Desktop grew slowly, while emerging high-tech products grew fast. For example, in Jiangsu Province, the output of integrated circuits in 2014 was 32.89 billion pieces, an increase of 11.3% over the previous year; the output of SPC exchanges was 19,000 lines, 18.4% below the previous year; the output of integrated circuits in Zhejiang Province was 6.09 billion pieces, an increase of 11.4% over the previous year, and the output of electronic components was 101.83 billion pieces, only 2.7% higher than the previous year (as seen in Table 3). In general, the smart terminals based on mobile phones were growing fast, while the growth of computer peripherals and electronic components was quite slow.[4]

5. Import and export of products was either increased or decreased

In 2014, the export of information products in the Yangtze River Delta was either increased or decreased with different performances. In terms of export, Jiangsu Province, Shanghai city and Zhejiang Province ranked the second, third and fifth place in the export of electronic information products in China, with the export volume of 143.9 billion, 93.4 billion and 27.6 billion US dollars; At the same time, the year-on-year growth of Shanghai continued the trend of 2013 and remained negative and that of Jiangsu Province was increased from negative in 2013 to 2.0% in 2014; the export of Zhejiang Province continued to grow, from 4.5% in 2013 to 9.0% in 2014, far higher than the national average of 1.2% (as seen in Fig. 7).

In terms of import, Jiangsu Province and Shanghai city are outstanding in terms of total volume, ranking the second and third in China respectively. Their export volumes were 91.2 billion US dollars and 71.3 billion US dollars respectively, but their growth rates were both negative, namely −2.6% and −1.0%. However, the

[4]Source: *Statistical Bulletin of National Economic and Social Development of Provinces and Cities in 2014.*

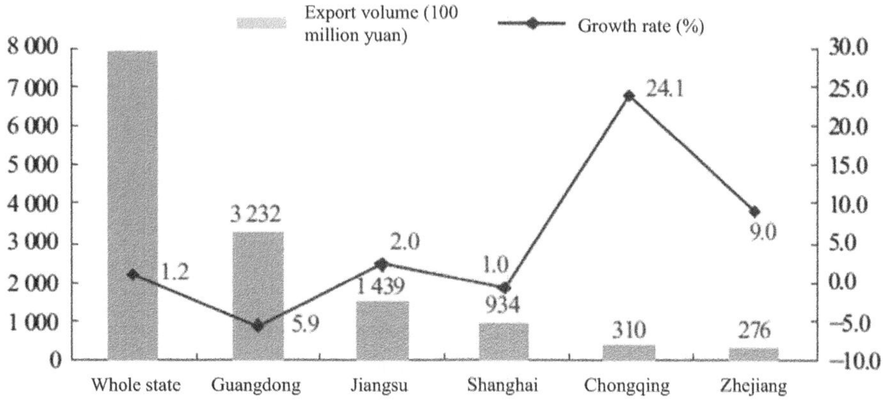


**Fig. 7** Top five provinces and cities of export volume for electronic information products from January to December 2014. *Source* Import and export of electronic information products from January to December 2014, website of the Ministry of Industry and Information Technology of the People's Republic of China

import of Ningxia, Guizhou, Guangxi and other provinces was increased rapidly, with the growth rate of more than 100%.

### (II) The foundation of information industry in lower reaches is good, and the middle and upper reaches catch up fast

From the perspective of provinces and cities, the number of information manufacturing enterprises in the four provinces in the upper reaches came out in front and entered the first lineup, especially the Jiangsu Province with the largest number of enterprises; the second lineup included Hunan, Hubei, and Jiangxi in the middle reaches, ranking the fifth, seventh and eighth respectively; Sichuan Province in the upper reaches has stepped away from the "third lineup" but run into the second lineup and ranked the sixth (refer to Fig. 8).

In terms of the total industrial output value of each province, it was the highest in Jiangsu Province and Shanghai city, ranking the first and second place respectively; Sichuan and Chongqing in the upper reaches also had higher industrial output value, ranking the third and fifth respectively; Anhui Province in the lower reaches and Jiangxi Province in the middle reaches had lower industrial output value, ranking the eighth and ninth respectively (as seen in Fig. 9).

In terms of the completion of fixed assets investment of enterprises, Jiangsu Province still ranked the first for the accumulated fixed assets investment in 2013, far more than the followed provinces; followed by Anhui Province, which ranked the second after Jiangsu Province; while the information industry in the middle reaches, like Hubei Province and Jiangxi Province developed rapidly because of their large investment scale. In addition, Zhejiang Province and Shanghai city had lower ranking at the seventh and ninth respectively (as seen in Fig. 10). It can be seen that the speed

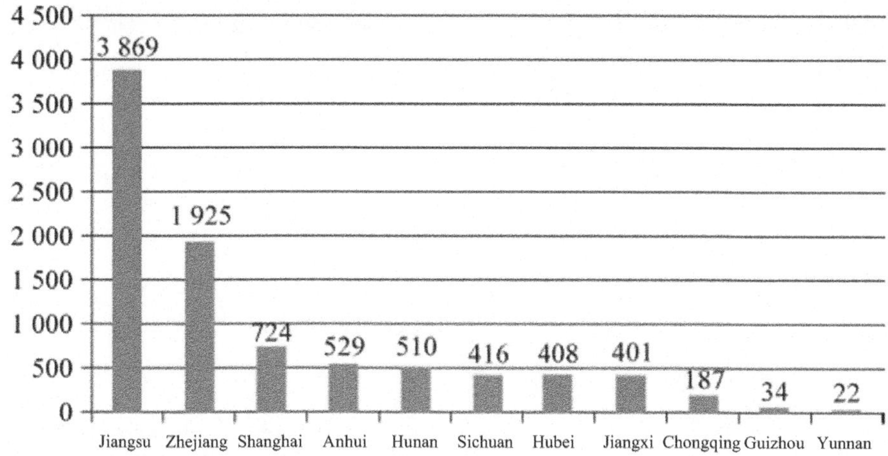


**Fig. 8** Number of electronic information manufacturing enterprises above designated scale in provinces and cities of Yangtze River Economic Belt in 2013. *Source* Wind Information

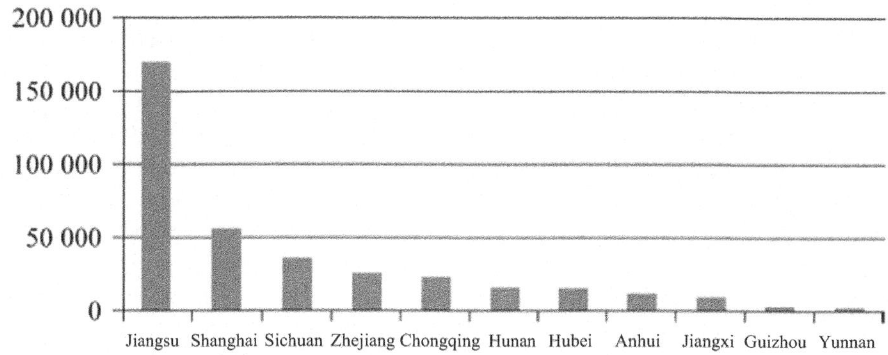


**Fig. 9** Total industrial output value of information manufacturing industry in provinces of Yangtze River Economic Belt in 2013 (unit: 10,000 yuan). *Source* China Industrial Database

of fixed asset investment in information industry of Zhejiang Province and Shanghai city was slowed down in 2013.

**Column 2: Development of Electronic Information Industry in Hubei Province in 2014**[5]

In 2014, the electronic information industry in Hubei Province showed a good development trend of high-level operation and high-speed growth.

1. Remarkable achievements in industrial development
(1) High level operation of industrial growth

[5]Source: website of Hubei Provincial Commission of Economy and Information Technology.

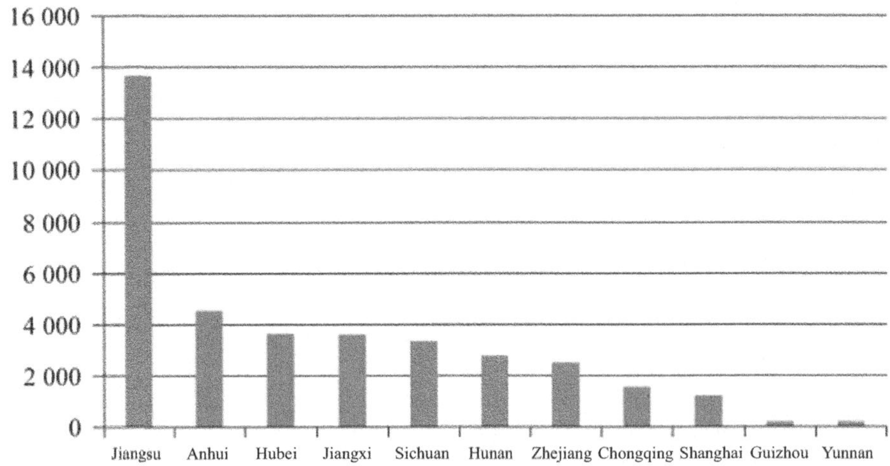


**Fig. 10** Fixed assets investment in electronic information industry of provinces and cities in the Yangtze River Economic Belt in 2013 (unit: 10,000 yuan). *Source* Wind Information

In 2014, the electronic information industry in Hubei Province realized the revenue from main business of 417.7 billion yuan, the industrial added value of 128.4 billion yuan, the total profit of 21.5 billion yuan, the total profit and taxes of 32.8 billion yuan, respectively, an increase of 23.57%, 22.75%, 12.57% and 15.9% over the previous year. Among them, the revenue from main business of electronic information manufacturing industry was 318.4 billion yuan, an increase of 16.1%, and that of software business was 95.3 billion yuan, an increase of 33.8%. The development of the whole industry showed a rapid growth trend, and the monthly growth rate of main business revenue was maintained at more than 20%. The growth rate of industrial added value was 10.5% and 14.8% higher than that of the electronic information manufacturing industry above the national scale and the industry above the provincial scale respectively. The electronic information industry has become the pillar industry with fastest development rate. The output of key products was increased rapidly and the growth rate of smart phones, Tablet, integrated circuits and other products exceeded 54%. The comprehensive industrial strength ranked the 13th in China and second in central China.

(2) Obvious leading role of backbone enterprises

Key backbone enterprises shall give full play to the leading role to support and drive the development. The newly introduced large and medium-sized enterprises and the original backbone enterprises are playing an important role in the industrial growth. Wuhan Institute of Posts, Changfei and Camel Group have been awarded as one of the top 100 electronic enterprises in China in successive years; Wuhan Lenovo has grown rapidly since its operation, and its revenue from main business reached nearly 30 billion yuan in 2014; the newly introduced enterprise projects such as Xiangyang Shimainuo have driven the rapid growth of the consumer electronics market in Xiangyang, with an annual output value of 5.079 billion yuan, an increase of 27.98% over the same period of the previous year. A number of newly introduced enterprises, such as Huaxun Fangzhou, Jingmen GEM, Suizhou Meiyad and Xiantao Jianding, etc. have played an important role in driving the industrial growth. By the end of December, there were two more enterprises above 10 billion yuan in the province compared with the previous year. There were total five enterprises, namely Hongfujin at 32.7 billion yuan, Lenovo at 29.6 billion yuan, Wuhan Institute of Posts and Technology at 23.5 billion yuan, Camel Group at 11.1 billion yuan and TPV at 10 billion yuan.

(3) Continuous and rapid development of software industry

The software industry shows a rapid development trend. From January to December, the year-on-year growth rate of software business revenue had been maintained above 32.42%. The total revenue from software business in the whole year was 95.3 billion yuan, with a year-on-year growth of 33.8%. Among them, 39.4 billion yuan was from software products, 19 billion yuan from information system integration services, 9.2 billion yuan from information technology consulting services, 17.7 billion yuan from data processing and storage services, and 10 billion yuan from embedded system software and integrated circuit design. The industrial added value was 33.8 billion yuan, a year on year increase of 33.1%. Profits and taxes were increased significantly over the same period of the previous year, with a total profit of 7.9 billion yuan and taxes of 3.7 billion yuan. There were 183,300 software employees, an increase of 5.5% compared with 173,800 in the same period of the previous year. The software industry has entered high speed development and has made great contribution to the rapid growth of electronic information industry in Hubei Province.

(4) Speedup of major construction projects

With the acceleration of industrial transfer, Hubei Province has increased the efforts to attract the investment, actively undertaken industrial transfer, and further expanded the scale of industrial investment. In 2014, the fixed assets investment in electronic information industry in Hubei Province was significantly accelerated. The total investment of the whole industry was 75.2 billion yuan, with a year-on-year growth of 22.7%. The value of newly added fixed assets was RMB 40.45 billion, with a year-on-year increase of 66.8%. The scale of fixed assets investment is currently ranked the fifth in China. The rapid growth of investment added the momentum for the development of electronic information industry in Hubei Province.

(5) Enhanced export-oriented characteristics

From January to December, there were nine electronic information enterprises being ranked among the top 20 import enterprises in the province, with an accumulative import worth of 3.934 billion US dollars and an increase of 1.574 billion yuan compared with that of the top 20 electronic information enterprises in 2013. The year-on-year increase was 66.69% and it accounted for 23.96% of the total foreign trade import of the province with an increase of 6.6% points over 2013.

From January to December, there were eight electronic information enterprises being ranked among the top 20 export enterprises in the province, with a cumulative export of 4.802 billion US dollars and an increase of 944 million yuan compared with the top 20 electronic information enterprises in 2013. The year-on-year increase was 24.47% and it accounted for 8.02% of the total export volume of the province with an increase of 1.1% over 2013. The electronic products exported from Hubei Province mainly include Desktop and Tablet, smart phones, integrated circuits, liquid crystal displays, etc.

(6) Competitive development of industries in all cities and provinces.

The electronic information industry of Wuhan played an important role in supporting the industrial development of the whole province. The revenue from main business of electronic information manufacturing industry accounted for 70.25% of the provincial total, and the software business revenue accounted for 98.4% of the provincial total. From January to December, the revenue from main business of electronic information manufacturing industry in seven cities was increased by more than 21% on year-on-year basis. The revenue from main business of Huangshi, Shiyan, Xianning and other cities was increased by more than 27.2%. The revenue from main business of Xiangyang electronic information manufacturing industry exceeded 37 billion yuan, and that of Yichang City and Jingzhou City reached 18 billion yuan and 14 billion yuan respectively. In the past year, the industry development of 16 cities in Hubei Province where the electronic information industry statistics has been carried out has maintained the sound momentum of steady growth.

2. Main problems in industrial development
(1) The industrial profit space has been continuously compressed

On the one hand, the output value of enterprises increases and the scale expands; on the other hand, some enterprises are facing numbers of unexpected challenges, leading to the decline of profits. The factors such as operators' centralized purchasing make the price of products declined continuously, and the continuous increase of human resources cost leads to the weak growth of product profit. A variety of adverse effects lead to the obvious decline of profits of some key enterprises. As of December 2014, the revenue from main business of Wuhan Lenovo was increased by 68.94% on year-on-year basis, but its total profit was decreased by 13.15%; it happens that there is a similar case that the revenue from main business of Wuhan Tianma was increased by 6.87% year-on-year, but the total profit was decreased significantly, say 359.19%; the profits of Changfei, HGTECH, Wuhan Xinxin and Tianyu Information also showed negative growth of profit whist with increasing revenue. The total profit was decreased by 1.2%, 28%, 29.79% and 48.23% year-on-year respectively.

(2) The output and sales volume of some products decreased significantly.

From January to December 2014, the output and sales volume of polycrystalline silicon battery modules, liquid crystal displays and semiconductor light-emitting diodes were all declined, showing a negative growth year-on-year. The output of polycrystalline silicon battery modules was increased by −1.9% and sales volume by −0.8%; while the output of LCD and semiconductor light-emitting diodes (LED) was decreased significantly, with the increase rate of −33.2% and −61.6% respectively, and the sales increase rate of −34.3% and −9.3%, respectively.

### (III) High location quotient of Shanghai, Chongqing, Jiangsu and Sichuan

As a quantitative tool for the efficiency and benefit analysis of an industry, location quotient is a common cluster identification method, which is often used to measure the relative concentration of an industry in a specific region. Therefore, applying the location quotient to analyze the information industry of Yangtze River Economic Belt can systematically understand the relative aggregation degree and spatial distribution pattern of information industry development.

Location quotient, also known as specialization rate, is the ratio between the proportion of a certain industrial sector in the whole state and the proportion of the whole industry in the whole state. The commonly used measurement indicators can be output value, output, number of employment, fixed assets, etc. The calculation formula is given as follows:

$$LQ_{ij} = \frac{L_{ij}}{L_i} \bigg/ \frac{L_j}{L} = \frac{L_{ij}}{L_j} \bigg/ \frac{L_i}{L} \quad (1)$$

where, $LQ_{ij}$ is the location quotient or specialization rate, $L_{ij}$ is the number of employment of $j$ department in region $i$, $L_i$ is the total number of employment in region $i$, $L_j$ is the number of employment of $j$ department in the whole state, and $L$ is the total number of employment of the whole state.

Taking the total industrial output value as the calculation factor, the location entropies of the lower, middle and upper reaches of the Yangtze River are shown in Table 4.

It can be seen from Table 4 that the location quotient of the lower reaches of the Yangtze River was the highest and up to 1.2775, which was far greater than 1, that is to say, the aggregation degree of information industry in the lower reaches of the Yangtze River was the highest; the location quotient of the upper reaches of the Yangtze River was 1.0857, which was also greater than 1, indicating that the aggregation of information industry in the upper reaches was higher; while the location quotient in the middle reaches was 0.5233, which is far less than 1, indicating that the degree of aggregation in the lower reaches was relatively low.

**Table 4** Location quotient of information manufacturing industry in upper, middle and lower reaches of Yangtze River Economic Belt

| Region | Location quotient |
|---|---|
| Lower reaches | 1.277 5 |
| Middle reaches | 0.523 3 |
| Upper reaches | 1.085 7 |

*Source* China Industry Database

**Table 5** Location quotient of information manufacturing industry of provinces and cities in the Yangtze River Economic Belt

| Provinces and cities | Location quotient | Cities and provinces | Location quotient |
|---|---|---|---|
| Shanghai | 2.206 3 | Hubei | 0.472 4 |
| Chongqing | 1.759 4 | Jiangxi | 0.462 6 |
| Jiangsu | 1.635 2 | Anhui | 0.405 7 |
| Sichuan | 1.292 3 | Guizhou | 0.104 5 |
| Hunan | 0.632 6 | Yunnan | 0.024 7 |
| Zhejiang | 0.514 6 | | |

From the perspective of 11 provinces and cities, the calculation of location quotient is shown in Table 5. Among them, the location quotient of Shanghai was the highest and up to 2.2063, followed by Chongqing, Jiangsu and Sichuan, which were 1.7594, 1.6352 and 1.2923, respectively. The location quotient all exceeded 1, which indicated that the aggregation degree of information manufacturing industry in these provinces and cities was relatively high. The location quotient of Hunan, Zhejiang, Hubei, Jiangxi, Anhui, Guizhou and Yunnan were all lower than 1, which indicated that the aggregation degree of information manufacturing industry in these areas was low.

### (IV) The software industry in the lower reaches is relatively developed

As one kind of information industry, software industry belongs to information service industry. Its development is related to and different from the information manufacturing industry. As can be seen from Fig. 11, the regions with the most developed software industry are basically those with more developed information manufacturing industry. The provinces and cities in top rank in terms of software industry revenue are Jiangsu, Zhejiang, Shanghai, Sichuan, Hubei and Chongqing, while revenues of software industry in Anhui, Jiangxi, Guizhou and Yunnan are relatively low.

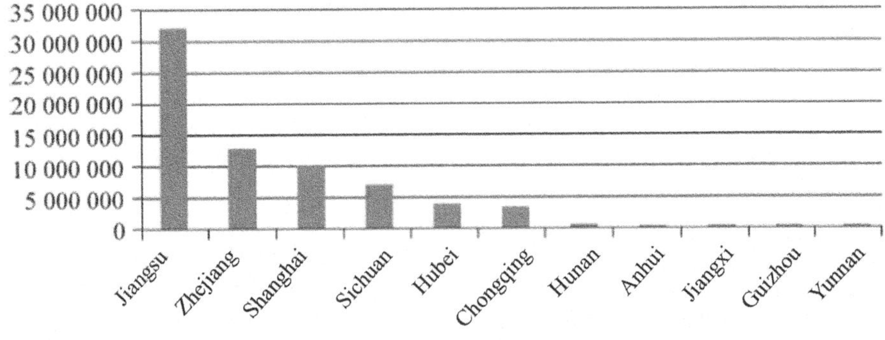


**Fig. 11** Software industry revenue of provinces and cities from January to November 2014 (unit: 100 million yuan). *Source* Website of Ministry of Industry and Information Technology of China

Software industry includes information technology consulting service industry, data processing and operation service industry, embedded system software industry and IC design industry. The development of software industry in the Yangtze River Economic Belt is very different. The specific data are shown in Table 6. In addition to data processing and operation services, Jiangsu Province ranked the first in terms of software industry revenue; Shanghai ranked the second to fourth for various items of revenue; the revenue of data processing and operation services in Zhejiang Province was the highest, ranking the first among 11 provinces and cities, followed by embedded system software industry; Zhejiang Province ranked the second, while its information technology consulting service industry only ranked the sixth; all revenues of software industry in Guizhou Province and Yunnan Province basically ranked at the bottom of the list.

**Column 3: 2013 Guizhou Software and Information Technology Service Industry Development Analysis Report of Guizhou Province in 2013**[6]

1. Development status of software and information technology service industry in Guizhou Province

In 2013, the software and information technology service industry in Guizhou Province showed the development characteristics of "continuous growth of main business revenue, gradual enhancement of enterprise strength, continuous expansion of business scope, promotion of industrial aggregation trend and gradual appearance of brand effect".

The revenue from main business continued to grow. The income from main business of software and information technology service industry in the whole province reached 7.073 billion yuan, with a year-on-year increase of 16.27%. Where, the revenue from software development reached 2.867 billion yuan, that from system integration service reached 3.807 billion yuan, and that from information technology consulting service reached 207 million yuan.

However, the industrial structure is still unbalanced. In 2013, the revenue from software products and system integration accounted for more than 94% of the total. The total revenue from information technology consulting services, embedded software and IC design was about 400 million yuan, accounting for 6% of the total. It ranked at the bottom list in China, and the disequilibrium of revenue structure was still apparent.

The strength of enterprises has gradually enhanced. There are more than 300 software and information technology service enterprises in Guizhou Province, and 210 enterprises are included in the statistics in 2013. As of 2013, there were 62 enterprises with system integration qualification. Among them, there are 2 enterprises qualified at Grade II, 23 qualified at Grade III, and 6 qualified at Grade IV, as well as 31 qualified with temporary provincial Grade III; 6 enterprises were qualified with information system engineering supervision; 73 enterprises passed the software

[6]Source: Website of Guizhou Economic and Information Commission.

**Table 6** Development data of software industry in provinces and cities of Yangtze River Economic Belt in 2014

| Provinces and cities | Information technology consulting service revenue (10,000 yuan) | | Data processing and operational services revenue (10,000 yuan) | | Embedded system software revenue (10,000 yuan) | | IC design revenue (10,000 yuan) | |
|---|---|---|---|---|---|---|---|---|
| | Accumulated in current period | Year on year increase or decrease (%) | Accumulated in current period | Year on year increase or decrease (%) | Accumulated in current period | Year on year increase or decrease (%) | Accumulated in current period | Year on year increase or decrease (%) |
| Shanghai | 2 996 700 | 17.1 | 4 328 500 | 16.7 | 1 001 000 | 11.2 | 1 980 000 | 15.1 |
| Jiangsu | 4 061 143 | 22.1 | 6 294 898 | 21.4 | 19 254 890 | 19.1 | 2 493 885 | 25 |
| Zhejiang | 451 332 | 39.2 | 7 362 176 | 38.5 | 4 972 182 | 20.3 | 263 966 | 8.7 |
| Anhui | 52 932 | 39 | 51 008 | 30.6 | 92 233 | 11 | 43 283 | 11 956.6 |
| Jiangxi | 72 093 | 25.6 | 22 826 | 6.8 | 20 113 | 27.6 | 47 471 | 27.4 |
| Hubei | 891 343 | 40.1 | 1 733 934 | 42.7 | 908 335 | 41.5 | 54 334 | 37.9 |
| Hunan | 132 027 | 31.7 | 352 072 | 40.5 | 308 062 | 22.9 | | |
| Chongqing | 1 275 833 | 27.3 | 1 056 230 | 28.7 | 1 187 647 | 13.7 | 18 935 | 25 |
| Sichuan | 2 013 012 | 19.9 | 3 911 220 | 20 | 142 622 | 23.5 | 668 816 | 0.3 |
| Guizhou | 23 743 | 20.8 | 7 517 | 13.4 | 14 372 | 25.3 | 527 | 23.4 |
| Yunnan | 15 430 | 9.1 lePara> | 25 706 | −26.3 | 2 516 | −28.2 | 573 | |

enterprise identification and annual review, and 1 key software enterprise entered the national planning layout.

Business domains are expanding continuously. In the whole year, there were 130 registered software products in Guizhou Province, with accumulated 592 software products being registered. A number of business domains have been initially formed, including embedded system, industry application software development, system integration, Internet and telecom value-added services, smart grid, energy-saving system, digital security, digital content and multimedia. The products covered e-government, food and medicine, public health, and equipment manufacturing and so on.

The trend of industrial aggregation has been increased. Since 2013, the development trend of software and information technology service industry in Guizhou Province has been prominent, and the aggregation benefits have begun to appear. With the rapid development of the Industrial Park represented by Gui'an New District Electronic Information Industrial Park, the infrastructure construction has been gradually improved and a large number of excellent enterprises and talents have been attracted. Gui'an Electronic Information Industrial Park has successfully introduced large information industry projects such as China Telecom Southern Data Center and Foxconn Green Tunnel Data Center. The promotion of industrial park infrastructure and the introduction and cultivation of large enterprises will effectively promote the development of software and information technology service industry in Guizhou Province.

Brand effect is gradually emerging. A number of indigenous enterprises with independent intellectual property rights and with leading technology in some fields have been gradually formed in Guizhou Province. Such as Zhenxing aluminum and magnesium embedded system and control software, Langma Internet and telecom value-added service software, Wanhua digital security integrated management system and other products have been established with certain reputations in China.

More supports are required for the project. In 2013, Guizhou Economic and Information Commission supported 12 software and information technology service projects, including 11 software projects and 1 animation project. The total investment of the 12 projects was 124.74 million yuan including self-owned funds of 98.68 million yuan and the external funds of 5 million yuan. The proportion of external funds is only 4.0%, and the proportion is low and the scope of funding is rather limited. The product development and promotion of software enterprises will take very long time and will have large initial investment. The software enterprises in Guizhou Province are generally small in scale and poor in profitability, it is more than urgent to have more support.

2. Challenges of the development of software and information technology services

(1) The industrial scale is still small.

The software and information technology service industry in Guizhou Province is still characterized by small industrial scale, low contribution and widening gap with surrounding provinces. In 2013, the software and information technology service industry of Guizhou achieved the revenue of 7.073 billion yuan from its main business. During the same period, the revenue scale of Chongqing and Sichuan were 68.3 billion yuan and 138.6 billion yuan, respectively, which were 10 times and 20 times of that for Guizhou Province. However, it was only 2 times and 5 times in 2002. In 11 years, Guizhou Province was left far behind. The proportion of revenue from software and information technology service industry in Guizhou Province accounted for 10.6%, which was lower than the proportion of 20.4% (value in 2012) of the whole state. The software industry has not made enough contribution to the information industry.

(2) The enterprise is less competitive.

The number of software leading enterprises in Guizhou Province is rather limited, the scale is small and the average qualification level is rather low. The certification above CMM/CMMI Grade IV and system integration Grade I qualification are still in blank. The average income of software enterprises in Guizhou Province was 33.68 million yuan, which was only 25% of Chongqing and Sichuan Province (data in November 2013). The enterprise is less competitive and it is difficult to expand the market.

(3) The shortage of supporting funds restricts the industrial development.

With the implementation of large-scale projects and the rapid maturity of new technologies, the industrial development will enter a new round of rapid growth stage, and the competition between provinces and cities will be further intensified, however the limited support funds of Guizhou Province will become the constraint for project introduction and industry development.

## *3.2 Problems in Spatial Distribution of Information Industry*

(I) **Regional cooperation mechanism has not yet formed**

The regional cooperation mechanism has not been formed yet in 11 provinces and cities along the Yangtze River, which seriously affected the equilibrium development of regional information industry. From the present point of view, the local protectionism is serious, the cooperation between governments and enterprises is relatively weak, and there is no effective coordination and cooperation mechanism and clear division of work and positioning relationship among provinces and cities. Specific to the development of the industry, there is a lack of unified planning and deployment. Blind comparison and ineffective competition among regions have replaced scientific cooperation among regions, leading to duplication of key industries and low efficiency development. There are information manufacturing industries in the upper, middle and lower reaches of the Yangtze River, but there is no division of work among different regions, as a result, there are multiple industrial duplications. The information industry in the lower reaches of the Yangtze River is relatively developed, with abundant human resources and scientific and technological resources. However, due to the lack of regional cooperation mechanism and motivation for resource mobility, it is rarely able to provide effective help to the development of the information industry in the middle and upper reaches. In view of the weak economic foundation, low degree of industrialization and inadequate conditions for the development of information industry in the middle and upper reaches of the Yangtze River, it is more necessary for the government to plan from a commanding view, to make unified consultation among government authorities and to provide strong support by the lower reaches.

### (II) **Similar regional structure of information industry**

At present, although there are some differences in the development of information industry along the Yangtze River, the problem of similar industrial structure is still prominent. In addition to the rapid development of the information industry in the lower reaches, and more attention has been paid to the "service", the information industry in Anhui, Jiangxi, Sichuan, Chongqing, Guizhou and other places is still dominated by the low-end information manufacturing industry. It's ubiquitous everywhere that the funds, talents, and investment are in shortage, the technological innovation is weak, the system is not adapted to the policy environment, and information infrastructure construction lags behind. Moreover, due to the lack of effective guidance and planning in the process of industrial development, provinces and cities are making the development strategy of local information industry in great blindness. For example, many provinces and cities propose to develop cloud computing, big data and other new generation information technology industries, and take the same field as the development focus, but their own development conditions and market environment are being ignored. They just jumped on the bandwagon and made investment in blindness, which led to waste of resources, vicious competition and a series of low-level repeated and redundant construction.

### (III) **Disequilibrium development of information industry space**

First of all, it is reflected in the disequilibrium of key resource elements and economic development. There are obvious differences between the economically developed areas and the underdeveloped areas along the Yangtze River. Economically developed areas such as Shanghai and Zhejiang are well rooted with basic conditions for the development of information technology industry, especially they have the congenital advantages in the development of a new generation of information technology industry. In the process of vigorously developing the new generation of information technology industry, all kinds of production factors, such as funds and talents, will inevitably accelerate the flow to economically developed areas, thus further to spread the gap between regions. Secondly, the scale, structure and energy grade of the information industry are not in equilibrium. As the key resource elements tend to flow to the developed areas, it will result the small scale, the unreasonable structure, and the low energy grade in the underdeveloped areas, and further it will be more difficult for the information industry in this area to keep pace with the developed areas. Finally, the policies and government support to promote the development of information industry are so different that the further disequilibrium of industrial development grade is caused.

(IV) **The spatial distribution of information talents is unbalanced**

Information industry is a knowledge, technology and intelligence intensive industry, and talent is the key element in the development of information industry. As an important part of the information industry, information production and information service are highly dependent on talents. Without high-quality talents, it is impossible for the information industry to obtain unprecedented development. However, the mobility and aggregation of information talents are affected by natural environment, economic development level, social infrastructure and other conditions. The lower reaches of the Yangtze River Economic Belt and some key cities in the middle and upper reaches of the Yangtze River attract more high-tech talents because of their high living standards and sound social facilities. However, due to the limitations of economic development and living standards, there are only few high-tech and high-quality talents in most of the middle and upper reaches of the Yangtze River Economic Belt, which imposes a negative constraint on the development of local information industry. Chongqing, for example, is also a key city in the Yangtze River Economic Belt. However, according to the data released by Chongqing Economic Information Commission in 2011, there were nearly 200,000 employees in various types of electronic information industry in Chongqing, including 160,000 in electronic manufacturing industry and 40,000 in software and service industry. In the next five years, there will be a shortage of 800,000 talents in the electronic information industry, including 700,000 in the electronic manufacturing industry and 100,000 in the software and service industry.

# 4 Strategies and Measures for Coordinated Development of Information Industry in the Yangtze River Economic Belt

## *4.1 Significance of Coordinated Development of Information Industry in Yangtze River Economic Belt*

In order to realize regional integration and industrial layout integration, the coordinated development of information industry is of great significance.

### (I) In line with the development trend of regional economic integration

The coordinated development of industry is an advanced form of regional economic integration and the deepening of the traditional theory of regional coordinated development. Promoting the coordinated development of information industry is an important part of the coordinated development of the Yangtze River Economic Belt, which is in line with the development trend of regional economic integration. At present, the regional economic belt and metropolis circles have become the main driving force to promote the regional economic development in China and "multi-level parallel development" is the general trend of regional economic development of China in the future. Promoting the coordinated development of information industry in provinces and cities along the Yangtze River is not only conducive to the integration of regional advantageous information resources to promote the free and reasonable flow of industrial elements, but also the information industries in various regions can learn from others and overcome its own weakness to realize competitive and cooperative development. In addition, promoting the coordinated development of information industry along the Yangtze River will certainly accelerate the regional division of work and cooperation, drive the coordinated development of regional economy, and be conducive to form a new pattern of interaction and coordinated development of the east, the middle and the west.

### (II) It can promote the rational aggregation and sound development of information industry

The provinces and cities in the Yangtze River Economic Belt are close to each other and the transportations are convenient, but there are great differences in resource endowment and economic development. Promoting the linkage and coordinated development of information industry among various city clusters, provinces and cities can further take the advantages of regional industrial integration. The advantages of talents, science and technology in the lower reaches of the Yangtze River shall be fully used, and the human resources and land advantages of the upper and middle reaches of the Yangtze River shall be utilized so as to give full play to the complementary advantages of the resource endowment and industrial foundation of various regions, form a higher degree of correlation between the upstream and downstream of the information industry and even between different industries, and establish a certain level of industrial gradient; The cross regional freedom of production factors such as funds, technology, labor force, etc. shall be enhanced to establish a unified, open, competitive and well-ordered market; information industry enterprises shall carry out cross regional investment and management activities, jointly carry out information technology breakthrough and market development, and establish a regional information industry chain with strong international competitiveness. Some competent information enterprises can carry out cross regional mergers and acquisitions to constitute large-scale enterprise groups or establish industrial alliances, so as to promote the rational aggregation of enterprises and then to give full play to the convenience and benefits brought out by industrial aggregation.

(III) **It is conducive to promote the development of the Yangtze River Economic Belt and the industrial belt along the Yangtze River**

The Yangtze River Economic Belt strides across 11 provinces and cities including Shanghai, Jiangsu, Yunnan and Guizhou, covering an area of about 2.05 million square kilometers, and both its population and GDP exceed 40% of the national total. Along the Yangtze River Basin, there have been formed "steel industry corridor", "automobile industry corridor", "petrochemical industry corridor", "power industry corridor" and "electronic information industry cluster", all of which are playing the important roles in the development of national economy. Promoting the linkage and coordinated development of the information industry in the Yangtze River Economic Belt will be helpful to promote the rational mobility of all the resources of elements, facilitate the development of "Internet plus", and promote the integration and development of traditional industries and emerging industries; It will be beneficial to facilitate informatization, and lead industrialization with information technology, and speed up the construction of a modern industrial system with the advanced development of modern manufacturing, modern service and modern agriculture. It is also conducive to optimizing the industrial structure and upgrading the industrial grade of the Yangtze River Economic Belt as well as promoting the economic development along the Yangtze River.

## 4.2 Strategies and Measures to Promote Coordinated Development of Information Industry in Yangtze River Economic Belt

The foundation of the coordinated development of industries in the Yangtze River Economic Belt lies in the "three links", that is, smooth traffic, circulated material and accommodated funds (Xu Changle 1998). At the same time, it is necessary to establish a multi-level operation mechanism with complementary advantages and common development, including the cooperation promotion mechanism at the government level, enterprise alliance at the regional level, technical cooperation, cooperation promotion mechanism at the enterprise level, service mechanism at the social level and compensation mechanism at the interests level to jointly promote the coordinated and linkage development of information industry along the Yangtze River.

(I) **Establish cooperation promotion mechanism at the government level**

Although governments at all levels are paying more and more attention to the coordinated development of regional industries, the Yangtze River Economic Belt is a new national strategy, and provinces and cities along the Yangtze River still need to make considerable efforts to strengthen inter regional administrative cooperation and industrial integration. The cooperation between governments shall not only break through the shackles of administrative regions and create external conditions for the coordinated development of industries, such as enhancing the accessibility of infrastructure and eliminating the obstacles of free circulation of industrial factors, but also and more importantly, it is necessary to establish regional cooperation mechanism at the government level, give full play to the positive guidance of the government, and form reasonable division of work among regions as well as to improve the overall industrial energy level through unified industrial planning and policies.

At present, in the process of coordinated development of information industry in the Yangtze River Economic Belt, the government needs to play the following functions. One is to establish the information industry development cooperation organization which is trans-regional, guided by government and combined with the enterprise operation. As the industrial linkage across 11 provinces and cities across the Yangtze River, it is necessary to form an integrated coordination mechanism and strengthen the high-level consultation and discussion among provinces and cities, so as to coordinate the cooperation and linkage of information industry among different regions, and promote the development of information industry integration along the Yangtze River. Second is to continuously break the administrative barriers between regions, build various platforms for economic belt cooperation, enhance the accessibility of regional systems, and promote the free circulation of products and elements. The third is to realize the coordination and unification of the information industry development planning in various regions. While carrying out the industrial planning, the overall development of the Economic Belt shall be considered as a whole. Not only shall a relatively unified and standardized industrial planning be prepared according to the actual situation of various regions, but also the characteristics of resources and elements in each region shall be fully considered. Priority shall be laid on some particular fields and industries shall complement each other.

### (II) Promote the interregional alliance of enterprise and industry

As an information industry belt across 11 provinces and cities, the Yangtze River information industry belt involves alliances and cooperation between enterprises in information manufacturing industry and software industry. The work can be carried out in various ways including:

One is to strengthen the alliance among the enterprises in the upper, middle and lower reaches. Many information enterprises in the Yangtze River Economic Belt have certain similarities and complementarities, especially in the lower reaches of the economic belt, namely the Yangtze River Delta, is an important cluster area of information industry in China. In order to avoid fierce competition, share existing resources, and further exert the advantages of scale economy, industrial restructuring and cross regional alliance can be appropriately carried out to form leading enterprises with larger scale and higher competitiveness. Then through the upstream and downstream supporting enterprises in the region with joint holding by leading enterprises to shape a number of large enterprise groups based on the Yangtze River Economic Belt and even transnational development to drive the cross regional development of information industry.

The second is to cultivate the alliance between foreign enterprises and local enterprises to promote the upgrading of regional information technology level. At present, the developed countries have mastered the key technologies of the information industry, while the technology in China is far behind the developed countries. According to the 2014 *Global Information Technology Report* released by the world economic forum, the development of information and communication technology in developed economies is relatively fast, in high rank, while China only ranked at 62nd. Therefore, it is necessary to encourage local enterprises to strengthen technology alliance with foreign enterprises, encourage cross regional and transnational merger activities, actively cooperate with multinational enterprises, and share the ownership of core technology and the initiatives of development and progress in related fields in developed countries.

The third is to strengthen the cooperation between industrial parks along the Yangtze River. In recent years, many coastal and riverside development zones are facing the challenge of rising costs of land, energy, labor, etc. In the face of this situation, some development zones choose to "go out" and allocate elements in a broader space as guided by resources, costs and markets. The cooperation between the many development zones and parks along the Yangtze River can be carried out through project docking, capital cooperation and co-construction. The interactive development of investment in development zones and industrial parks can be promoted through joint efforts to increase investment attraction, jointly organize investment promotion activities, share investment project information, and jointly publicize investment environment. Mutual benefit and win-win results can be achieved by jointly building development zones in different places to constitute a group of investment carriers of information industry with strong radiation and driving force.

### (III) Strengthening regional cooperation in technological innovation

The overall energy level of China's information industry is not high, and it lies in the middle and lower reaches of the global value chain, so is the development of information industry along the Yangtze River Economic Belt. Of course, this is mainly due to the low level of industrial technology and weak overall innovation in China, but there are also reasons for the weak technical linkage caused by lacking the industrial linkage development in various regions; Look on the other side, the low industrial energy level also restricts the further development of regional industrial linkage. Therefore, strengthening the linkage development of information industry and upgrading and transformation of industrial structure, enhancing the innovation driving force of regional industry and improving the overall energy level of regional industry have become one of the most important targets of the development of information industry in the Yangtze River Economic Belt.

In order to improve the overall energy level of regional industry, technological innovation cooperation is the most critical link. The abundant human resources and technological advantages are available in the lower reaches of the Yangtze River, while those in the middle and upper reaches are relatively deficient. Therefore, through the agreement and division of work between regions, we can strengthen the joint tackling of information technology between the upstream and downstream, improve the information technology transfer mechanism, and optimize the allocation of innovation resources in the free cross regional flow; the regional scientific research forces can be integrated and scientific research cooperation can be carried out in view of the key technologies and common technologies that restrict the construction and development of information industry chain; The information technology research and development institution can be jointly set up to establish industrial technology innovation alliance and carry out cross regional cooperation of industry, university and research. The technology trading platform shall be improved in the cooperative manner and jointly carry out information technology trading activities as well as promote the transformation and application of scientific research achievements.

### (IV) Strengthening the industrial undertaking and transfer among regions

In order to realize the coordinated development of information industry along the economic belt, industrial transfer is an important aspect since the development of information industry in the Yangtze River Economic Belt is out of equilibrium. Through industrial transfer, resources and production elements flow from the developed areas of the Yangtze River Economic Belt to the less developed areas, so as to promote the coordinated development of the electronic information industry in the whole region. Therefore, full play shall be given to local advantages and industrial transfer or further undertaking shall be arranged in order. The development level of information industry in the lower reaches of the Yangtze River is relatively high. We should take the opportunity of international industrial transfer to further improve the ability of independent innovation, promote technological progress and product upgrading, and actively develop from the low end of the industrial chain to the high end of the industrial chain. At the same time, some basic industries shall be gradually transferred to the middle and upper reaches of the Yangtze River.

For the middle and upper reaches of the economic belt, it is necessary to undertake the transfer of electronic information industry from lower reaches in order. When undertaking the transfer of information industry, we should stick to the principle of high starting point and high quality, take the initiative to undertake those industries that have less environmental pollution and low energy consumption and those of great significance to the upgrading and transformation of local industries. The dislocation development shall be realized in the process of undertaking the transfer of external industry and homogeneous competition with other regions shall be avoided to achieve a reasonable division of work and coordinated development of information industry along the Yangtze River Economic Belt. Of course, as the electronic information is a high-tech industry, it requires the coexistence of industrial environment and technological environment, therefore, not every place needs to have the information industry and the regional layout of the industry shall be rationalized.

### (V) Establishing the mechanism of social service and benefit compensation

First of all, to give full play to the role of industrial self-government organizations in promoting regional industrial linkage, guide the establishment of regional information industry autonomous organizations or cross basin information industry associations, carry out investigation and research on the development of information industry along the Yangtze River, and scientifically discuss the theory and practice of information industry development, exchange experience and information, and find out the correct direction of information industry linkage development to provide decision-making reference for the government to formulate corresponding policies and regulations. In addition, it is also possible to formulate industrial standards and norms through intra industry consultation to form a unified and efficient institutional supply, so as to promote the coordinated and balanced development of regional industries.

Secondly, it is necessary to establish an interregional interest compensation mechanism. The regional economic cooperation and benefit sharing of the western developed countries are mainly realized through the market policy, market mechanism and market system with the market power playing the leading role. However, due to the special administrative division system and the imperfect market economy in China, it is difficult to realize cross administrative regional economic cooperation and benefit sharing through market channels. Therefore, under the existing system, we need to comply with the existing administrative framework, at the same time break through the institutional barriers, establish the interest compensation mechanism of regional economic cooperation, and find a new path of regional economic cooperation. For example, we can establish a community of interests for the coordinated development of information industry along the Yangtze River. All provinces and cities can give full play to the basic function of market allocation of resources, and to the comparative advantages of all parties so that a community of interests for the linkage development of information industry can be established to jointly build the "information industry corridor" in the Yangtze River Basin.

# Coordination and Deepening of Agricultural Development in Yangtze River Economic Belt

**Xiuzhi Wang**

The "new normal" of economic development needs to find more development impetus from "endogenous" factors, and one of the so-called "endogenous" development logic is cooperation. It is the fundamental demand and objective of the development of the Yangtze River Economic Belt to form mutual dynamic development interaction with the help of certain resource dependence. It was agreed by most experts that it is the right time to vigorously promote the construction of the Yangtze River Economic Belt under the background of the "new normal". In terms of regional cooperation, all provinces and cities shall carry out scientific industry positioning and establish economic cooperation mechanism with common interests as the link; in terms of development path, the construction of the Yangtze River Economic Belt shall be jointly promoted from the aspects of urban-rural integration, innovation driven, modern logistics, and river basin development; in terms of exploration and innovation, provinces and cities shall formulate targeted development policies according to the actual situation to realize the regional overall promotion in the exploration of differentiation path; in the aspect of development drive, the national level shall give active policy support to provide reliable institutional guarantee for the construction of the Yangtze River Economic Belt. In this process, agriculture is the top priority. The natural environment and agricultural development level with large internal differences are not only one of the short boards of agricultural coordinated development, but also an important space for future development. The development of agriculture in the Yangtze River Economic Belt is confronting both challenges and opportunities.

According to the law of agricultural development, the modernization of China is the process of industrialization and modernization of agricultural countries. That how an economically backward or underdeveloped agricultural country can be transformed into an economically developed industrial country with advanced technology

X. Wang (✉)
Institute of Applied Economics, Shanghai Academy of Social Sciences, Shanghai, China
e-mail: wxz@sass.org.cn



X. Jing (ed.), *Development of the Yangtze River Economic Belt in China*, Urban Governance Practices in China,
https://doi.org/10.1007/978-981-16-1578-8_3

and management system will be the topic of this paper. The self-characteristics of the natural endowment and the complicated process of modernization endowed China with its own characteristics. It not only lies in the path of institutional change based on historical development, but also exists in the induced institutional innovation based on changes. The Yangtze River Economic Belt is not only the advantageous region of agricultural development in China, but also the concentrated area of agricultural system innovation since the reform and opening up. The great changes in the past 30 years also revealed the problems of agricultural development in this region. In this region, the reform impetus represented by household responsibility contract, joint-stock cooperatives and returning right and endowing power has been formed, but also the agricultural development dilemma with coordination of agricultural development, ecological sustainable recovery, and food security being intermingled with each other. Therefore, it is not only the need of reform and development, but also the necessary measure to realize the overall well-off in the region to consider the agricultural development plan from the overall height and to discuss the way of regional agricultural development from the perspective of cooperation.

This chapter will be divided into three sections. We will introduce the basic features of agricultural development in the Yangtze River Economic Belt in the first section. After understanding the advantages and disadvantages of the region, we need to grasp the difficulties of agricultural development in the region at this stage. In particular, considering the weakness and multiplicity of agriculture, the agricultural cooperation must be well targeted. The second section will focus on the exploration of agricultural cooperative development with problem oriented. The last section will be the further exploration and some suggestions based on the above analysis.

## 1 General Overview of Agricultural Development in the Yangtze River Economic Belt

The Yangtze River which has long been known as the “golden waterway”, flows through the region with city clusters, developed economy, rich resources and large population. The Yangtze River Economic Belt is an important first-class development axis in the “T” shaped spatial structure strategy of land exploitation and economic layout in China, and constitutes the golden corridor of economic development with the coastal economic belt. On the whole, the Yangtze River Economic Belt covers an area of about 400,000 $km^2$, the regional population accounted for 42.74% of the nation (2014), and the output value of the primary industry accounted for about 40.57% of the national total, which is basically equivalent to its economic position in the state (both the population and GDP of the Yangtze River Economic Belt exceed 40% of the national total). However, the provinces and cities within the Yangtze River Economic Belt varied greatly. In addition, since the reform is quite dependent on the mobility, the disequilibrium is further widened. In the agricultural development of this region, there are not only modern urban agriculture driven by big cities, but also plateau agriculture and mountain agriculture with regional characteristics. The resource endowment of agricultural development also varies from capital intensive, market-oriented, and export-oriented agriculture to the labor-intensive and survival oriented agriculture. Therefore, only by further understanding the characteristics of agricultural development in the Yangtze River Economic Belt can we straighten out the path of coordinated development within the belt.

## *1.1 Natural Environment Characteristics of Agricultural Development in Yangtze River Economic Belt*

Because of the dual characteristics of agricultural production, the laws of nature and market must be followed to realize its value. The dual characteristics are associated with double risks, so there will be certain complexity and particularity for the agriculture to be an industry. The natural force and productivity of nature are the foundation for social productive forces, and in particular for the agricultural production. The function of all agricultural technologies can be attributed to the development and utilization of natural productivity. In the history of China, there were developed traditional agriculture and traditional agronomy, which effectively supported the uninterrupted development of Chinese civilization. One of its important manifestations was that the understanding and utilization of natural productivity reached a higher level. Therefore, it is necessary to understand the characteristics of the natural environment at first in order to understand the agricultural development of this region. From the traditional element utilization to the environmental protection of agricultural development, the role of natural characteristics in agricultural development is constantly changing and strengthening.

### (I) **Natural characteristics of agriculture in social changes**

Natural resources are not only the support for agriculture, but also the basis for the sustainable development of agriculture. Traditionally, from the single exploitation of natural resources by agriculture to the multi-dimensional interaction of nature, human and development, great changes have taken place for the natural characteristics of agricultural development. It was revealed once in Marx's view of productivity that labor productivity not only intrinsically contains natural productivity, but also roots in natural productivity. The production process is a bilateral interaction between human beings and nature. Therefore, Marx said: "all productivities were attributed to natural forces" and "all productivities were attributed to nature". This does not mean that human being melts into nature. On the contrary, in the process of development, utilization and recreation of natural productivity, the subjective initiative of human can be really carried forward.

From agriculture in the era of slash-and-burn cultivation to the petroleum agriculture in the era of industrialization, natural resources, as passive participants, have been integrated into the trend of modernization. However, with the "quiet revolution", people began to understand nature from the perspective of initiative and life. Especially while facing the survival challenge under the pressure of environmental damage, the agricultural development has entered the sustainable development stage of "symbiosis with nature". In addition to that concluded by Simon Kuznet "agriculture has made the contribution to the economic development in four forms (product contribution, element contribution, market contribution and foreign exchange contribution)", people start to pay more and more attention to the ecological contribution and green contribution of agriculture. In recent years, the attention to the climate change has given people a fresh understanding of the natural characteristics of agriculture. The research shows that the impacts of climate change on natural ecosystems, natural resources, tertiary industries, social systems and natural disasters include: climate change has a profound impact on the structure and function of natural ecosystems. For example, the productivity of vegetation in the permafrost region of Northeast China was decreased, while that of Qinghai Tibet Plateau was increased; climate change led to the decrease of precipitation in most areas of North China and Northeast China and the decrease of runoff of many rivers in the north; because of climate change, people's demand for energy in production and life has changed; extreme events caused by climate change (including frequency and intensity), water shortage and other issues under the background of climate change, the improvement of heat resources will help to prolong the growth period of crops, but the increase of extreme events will also cause instability of agricultural production; climate change can not only indirectly affect the secondary and tertiary industries through the impact of agriculture and natural resources, but also the mitigation measures of climate change(such as carbon tax, carbon tariff, carbon trading, etc.) will also impose a broad and profound impact on the social economy.

It can be said that natural resources for agricultural development has completed a huge turn in the development of more than 30 years. Natural resources have changed from the original resource development to the protection of natural resources at present. Such a change has named a new proposition for agricultural development. Under the new resource constraints, what kind of road agriculture needs to seek will be the first challenge of agricultural development in the Yangtze River Economic Belt.

### (II) Natural risk characteristics of agricultural development in the Yangtze River

In addition to the inherent topography and water temperature that will normally remain stable in agricultural development, natural disaster is also an important factor affecting agricultural development in a region. The natural disasters in the East and West of the Yangtze River Economic Belt are not only the main shapers of regional agricultural development characteristics, but also the destroyers of regional agricultural production. "The law of solving agricultural difficulties"—"social rescue law of agricultural congenital dilemma" is an objective economic law. Its essential is: agriculture is strictly restricted by four factors: season of crops growth, outdoor large-area operation, constantly changing climate, and product storage difficulty. Natural disasters are frequent, and the ineffective consumption of human and material resources is serious, so its input-output rate is obviously lower than that of the industry, and its value form expansion and reproduction is trapped in a congenital dilemma. Only by the comprehensive and sustained rescue of the society can we realize the expansion and reproduction of the value form and really play its role as the foundation of the national economy; at the same time, as equal members of the society, farmers can also get more income and gradually maintain the same level with the income of the urban citizens. Therefore, as far as natural disasters are concerned, agricultural modernization must respond positively in order to solve the fetters of its development. The frequent occurrence of natural disasters in China is the result of the joint efforts of natural factors and human factors. It is closely related to climate, season, region, natural environment and risk management capacity, and also to the lack of risk management system. At the same time, natural disasters have a strong correlation with economic and social development, and even directly affect economic development and social stability. Therefore, the analysis of regional natural disasters plays an important role in the development of regional agricultural economy.

Under monsoon climate, agriculture in the Yangtze River Economic Belt is facing either drought or waterlogging. Therefore, it is an important step to realize regional agricultural modernization to pay attention to natural disasters effectively, adjust agricultural industrial layout timely and strengthen agricultural disaster resistance ability. Based on the existing data, the statistical data in 2013 showed that drought is the main disaster, and the affected area of drought is related to the cultivated land area of the province. Among the 11 provinces and cities in the Yangtze River Economic Belt, the affected area in Hubei and Hunan are relatively large (refer to Fig. 1).

From another view of disasters, the agricultural natural disasters in the Yangtze River Economic Belt have obvious regional characteristics. The coastal areas are greatly affected by typhoons. For example, in the agricultural statistics of Zhejiang

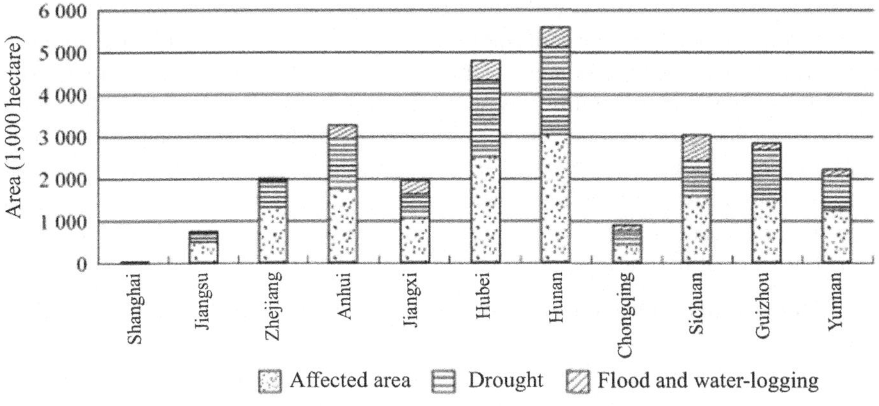


**Fig. 1** Structure of disaster area types of provinces and cities in the Yangtze River Economic Belt (Agricultural Statistical Yearbook of 2014)

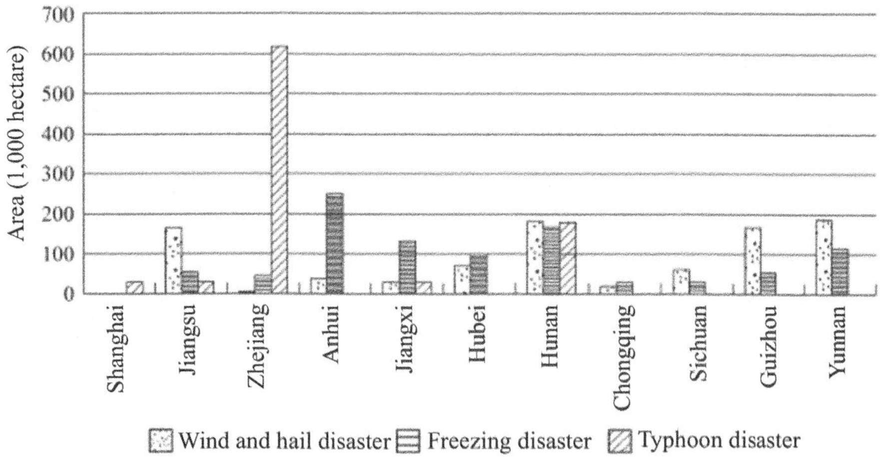


**Fig. 2** Seasonal disaster structure of provinces and cities in the Yangtze River Economic Belt (Agricultural Statistical Yearbook of 2014)

Province in 2013, the affected area by typhoon accounted for the most part. The freezing disaster is more prominent in Anhui Province. Compared with this, Yunnan and Guizhou Provinces are mainly suffering from wind and hail (refer to Fig. 2).

## *1.2 Social Characteristics of Agricultural Development in the Yangtze River Economic Belt*

In addition to the natural characteristics of agriculture, agriculture also has certain social characteristics. The agricultural social culture related to the mode of agricultural production is bound to change in the process of modernization. For modern agriculture, the output of agricultural products makes the constitution and spread of agricultural culture to be depended on the product medium. The social characteristics of agriculture no longer simply stay in the self-emerge of culture within the region, but more are based on the interaction of products. With the pushing and pulling interaction to the rural areas by modernization, agricultural elements begin to circulate. Land denaturation and function transformation, labor inflow and outflow, and the continuous extension of product value chain have become the social characteristics related to agricultural development.

### (I) **Uncertainty characteristics in the process of agricultural modernization**

On one hand, agricultural uncertainty is based on the external impact on agricultural development, on the other hand, it is based on the impact of agriculture itself on the external world. According to Ulrich Beck's risk society theory, some unpredictable risks such as industrial pollution, climate change, and nuclear war and so on have the potential impact on every social individual although science and technology have made progress in the post-industrial era. In this context, agricultural development will be also endowed with such risk characteristics, and we can say food safety is the performance of uncertainty in agricultural development. Of course, what we mean by food safety is not moral accusation and responsibility based on food quality, but more about the impact brought by food safety.

In the process of China's rapid development, food safety crisis, as a kind of social risk, has a profound impact on Chinese society. In the past 20 years, domestic accidents for food safety occurred frequently; the use of pesticides and insecticides ranked the first in the whole world; food export was often rejected due to additives, and the food safety situation was still worrisome. In the current Chinese society, the three levels of risks caused by food safety problems are mixed with each other, forming a mixture of risks, which poses an urgent and complex challenge to the Chinese people, society and country. What can not be ignored behind this are the trust crisis, political stability and social justice which need to be solved urgently in the period of social modernization and transformation. Professor Yan Yunxiang classified the social risks caused by food safety problems from three aspects.

The first category is food hygiene problems and traditional risks. After the reform and opening up, with the increase of consumer demand and the improvement of food processing technology, Chinese consumers increasingly rely on convenience food, fast food and semi-finished products. However, consumers know little about the raw materials and actual processing process of these types of food, and this isolation relationship is easy to induce worries and doubts about food safety. Many surveys have pointed out that small family workshops accounted for more than 70% of the market share in the food processing industry, which posed great challenges to public health, quality management and food processing and transportation industries. A survey showed that production license or business license was not available for 80% small food processing workshops in Hunan Province. It can be seen that the traditional risks caused by food hygiene problems are mainly concentrated in the field of public health, but they can be improved and managed through education activities, regulation of market and strengthening supervision.

The second is unsafe food and post-industrial risks. This kind of unsafe food mainly comes from excessive use of pesticides, fertilizers, insecticides, hormones, etc., which is closely related to the background of environmental pollution. Chemical pollution and the development of modern agricultural technology is a global phenomenon. It is not only a technical problem, but also related to the unexpected consequences caused by modernization. The surge of consumer demand and large-scale production has led to various unsafe potentials. For example, the use of antibiotics and feed additives, although international standards are revised be to more strict every year, it is still difficult for specific producers to comply with the rules in China. Due to the lack of safety knowledge of some farmers, nearly half of the fruits and vegetables planted in China contain the residual pesticide exceeding the official standard. On average, more than 100000 people will be poisoned by pesticides remained in their food every year.

The last aspect is toxic food and trust risk. Toxic food is devastating. A small number of producers, processors and sellers will add prohibited toxins to food for human or animals even they knew it perfectly well. The most morally disturbing ones are those large-scale and well-organized toxic food production and distribution chains. Under some circumstances, even government management authorities are involved. Down to the workers on the assembly line, to entrepreneurs and officials from quality supervisors, they are all involved in this type of industry. Compared with small family workshops, this kind of large-scale production destruction is extremely serious and susceptible to social panic.

### (II) The characteristics of integration in the process of agricultural modernization

As one link in the national economic structure, agriculture is not only the supply element of modernization, but also the demand element in the process of modernization. The circulation among elements forms the way of exerting comparative advantage in the process of modernization. As far as agriculture is concerned, a large number of land, human and even capital elements flow into cities and other industries, and the element structure of agriculture itself has been changed, which provides an effective opportunity for agricultural to move forward from traditional structure to modern mode. At the same time, as the other economic entities and space in the agricultural periphery, the market function of agricultural development have been formed, and the same will constantly constitute impact and claim on the agriculture. Capital, human resources and other elements flow into the countryside again with new roles to reshape the development of rural economy and construct the relationship between urban and rural areas.

Agricultural development will inevitably bring about the mobility of elements, among which labor force is the most active one. It can be said that the mobility of urban and rural labor force is the only way which must be taken for all industrialized countries. The adjustment and optimization of industrial structure and urban-rural structure are also inseparable from the mobility of labor. With the reform and opening up and the relaxation of the household registration system, a large number of labor mobility has occurred in China. The migration of a large number of labors will inevitably form the trend of integration, but in reality, it is still in the "migratory birds" style. Discrimination and institutional problems seize the bottleneck of further labor mobility. The Yangtze River Economic Belt is not only a densely populated area in China, but also a region with large population mobility. The mobility of element resources assigned agricultural development with the transformation characteristics of integration. On the one hand, the outflow of labor force provides opportunities for the transformation of agricultural endowment in the outflow area; on the other hand, the inflow of labor force accumulates human resources for the place of acceptance. Combined with the data of the sixth census of population, it can be found that all regions are all provinces with net population outflow except Shanghai, Jiangsu and Zhejiang (Fig. 3).

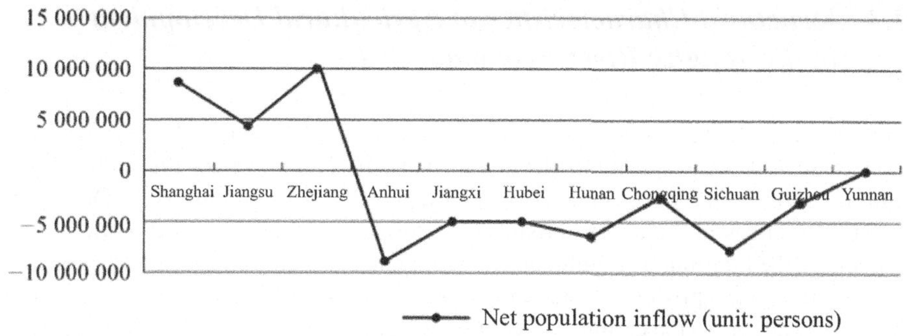


**Fig. 3** Net inflow of population in the Yangtze River Economic Belt. Date source: China Sixth Nationwide Population Census, http://www.stats.gov.cn/tjsj/pcsj/rkpc/6rp/indexch.htm

The integration of the Yangtze River Economic Belt is not only the integration between elements, but also that based on "network". In recent years, there is not only a large trend of integration in the real economy, but also a strong development momentum in the virtual economy due to the better radiation capacity of science and technology, the advantages of transportation resources and the strong market pushing and pulling force in the economic belt. Therefore, after the agriculture is characterized with integration, the path of agricultural development needs to take the innovative road of collaborative development. Only by actively responding to this integration can we create a new way out for agricultural development. Therefore, agricultural development shall not only deal with endogenous problems, but also give full play to the exogenous driving capacity of industrialization and urbanization. It is necessary to strengthen technical efficiency and scale efficiency, continue to expand the openness of regional economy, build urban and rural Internet, logistics network and Internet of things, break the situation of urban-rural segmentation by infrastructure construction and information construction, share the information between urban and rural areas, promote the spillover effect of regional economic stock on agricultural TFP by frequent exchange and cooperation, and break the element barrier and institutional barrier that restrain the improvement of agricultural TFP to establish appropriate agricultural production, management and marketing system, then to enhance the spatial correlation effect. The way out for China's agriculture lies in speeding up the improvement of the system and mechanism for the integration of urban and rural development, focusing on promoting the integration of urban and rural planning, infrastructure and public services, promoting the equal exchange of urban and rural elements and the balanced allocation of public resources, forming a new type of relationship between industry and agriculture, urban-rural integration, and accelerating the process of agricultural modernization.

### *1.3 Structural Characteristics of Agricultural Development in the Yangtze River Economic Belt*

Further grasping the characteristics of agricultural development in the Yangtze River Economic Belt from the micro level can make it clear to select the path of agricultural coordinated development of the Yangtze River Economic Belt. Due to the great differences in the characteristics of natural and social structure in the region, especially the continuous combination of elements caused by continuous impact on the industry in the process of marketization, the structural adjustment of agriculture constantly adapts to the changes of economic and social situation. Understanding its internal structural characteristics is not only an accurate grasp of the current situation, but also a prerequisite for further optimization.

(I) **Industrial structure characteristics of agricultural development in Yangtze River Economic Belt**

The industrial structure is the industrial composition of a country or region, including the allocation of resources among industries, development level and technical and economic ties. Many factors such as social consumption level, investment level, natural endowment and science and technology level will affect the rationalization and development of industrial structure. Agriculture is an important industry related to the national economy and people's livelihood. The adjustment and optimization of agricultural industrial structure is also an important part of adjustment for economic structure. Vigorously promoting the adjustment and upgrading of agricultural industrial structure is one of the important ways to solve the "three rural issues: agriculture, rural areas and farmers". As an important feature of industrial structure, agricultural product structure can reflect the optimization of regional agricultural structure, on the other hand, it can also reflect the regional natural conditions and consumption structure. As an important agricultural industrial belt in China, the Yangtze River Economic Belt is also a region with great changes in agricultural landforms. Therefore, the diversification of agricultural industrial structure is not only the advantage but also the direction of regional agricultural development.

According to the agricultural statistics in 2013 (refer to Fig. 4), the industrial structure of agriculture in the Yangtze River Economic Belt is diversified with obvious characteristics of large-scale agriculture. In addition to the dominant planting industry, all forestry, fishery and animal husbandry occupied a large share. Moreover, this structure is influenced by regional natural endowment and external environment. With the inland extension of the region, the constraints of agricultural development have been relaxed. The share of animal husbandry and forestry is increasing. On the contrary, the share of fishery with strong constraints decreases from east to west due to the distribution of freshwater resources.

The diversified industrial structure, on the one hand, adjusts the agricultural industry, makes the agricultural products diversified, enriches the market supply, and enhances the farmers' ability to become rich; on the other hand, it is conducive to the improvement of agricultural ecology, especially the development of forestry,

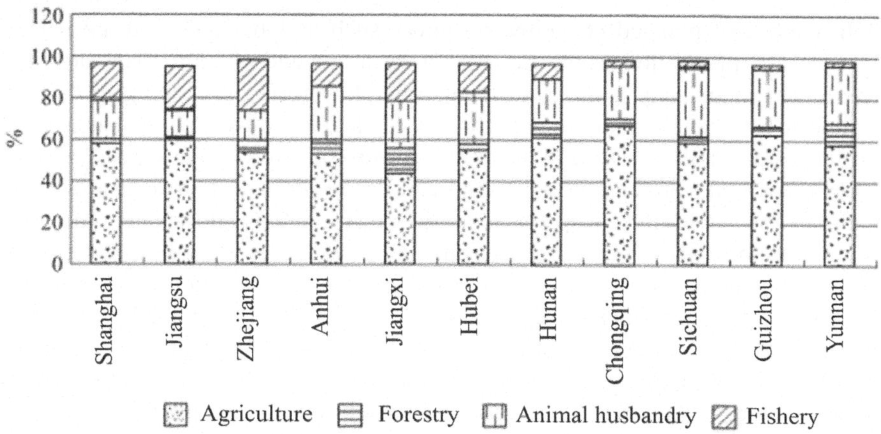


**Fig. 4** Structure of agricultural output value of provinces in the Yangtze River Economic Belt (Agricultural Statistical Yearbook of 2014)

which plays a key role in the improvement of agricultural ecological environment. The forest, wetland and desert are the three major systems in the terrestrial ecosystem of the earth, and the three systems have strong externality in terms of function. Especially in the context of regional openness and increasingly active resource mobility, coordinating the positive effect of flow and reducing the negative effect are the basic proposition of ecological development. The construction of ecological civilization and striving to build a beautiful China as proposed by the 18th National Congress of the Communist Party of China is just based on this background. The functional characteristics of agricultural development are no longer limited to the development and stability of agriculture itself, but a global concept. Taking forestry as an example, it characterizes with foundation, public welfare, livelihood and inclusiveness. Forestry is of great importance and comprehensive complexity to the development of nature, society and economy. It must be brave enough for the forestry to take on new historical mission and effectively play the all the roles of engine, converter and regulator.

### (II) Income structure characteristics of agricultural development in Yangtze River Economic Belt

Behind the industry, it is a feature of income structure, while that based on the income is the structure of consumption. Such a linkage link constitutes the external demand environment for agricultural development. In the external world, the most critical is the change and innovation of agricultural demand brought along by the change of income structure. According to theory of hierarchy needs by Maslow, human needs can be divided into physiological needs, security needs, love and belonging, respect and self-realization. The demands in different stages have built different product structure and action logic, and such a demand structure also deeply affected the development of agriculture.

In the era of planned economy, resources such as labor and land are held in the hands of production teams and collective farms, and planting plans are often determined collectively by the social teams; after the reform and opening up, the right to allocate labor and for planting plans has been delegated to every peasant household, but the land is still not allowed to be transferred privately. In this case, peasants become the main production units, and can freely arrange their own production activities, but also shall be responsible for their own economic decisions; at the same time, the reform also liberated the surplus labor, which can turn to other fields to earn wages. In this case, the income of rural families has been generally increased. With the development of urbanization and the new industrial planning, land elements are involved in the process of modernization. The dividend brought by the system at the beginning of the reform has gradually formed diversified sources of income, of which property income is the most crucial demonstration. Although the income from family operating is still an important source, the source of income growth of peasants has undergone essential changes: from the growth of family operating income in the past to the growth mainly relying on labor remuneration, at the same time, the source of growth has been simplified. These changes mean that the nature of the problem of income has changed. It is no longer a simple agricultural problem, nor can it be covered by the "three rural issues: agriculture, rural areas and farmers", instead it is a problem more and more associated with non-agricultural employment. The core of increasing the income of peasants has changed to the problem that how to solve the non-agricultural employment.

According to the agricultural statistics in 2013 (refer to Fig. 5), the income sources of peasants in 11 provinces and cities in the Yangtze River Economic Belt mainly included four parts: wages, net family operating income, transfer income and property income. Since the regional resource endowment and the degree of marketization are

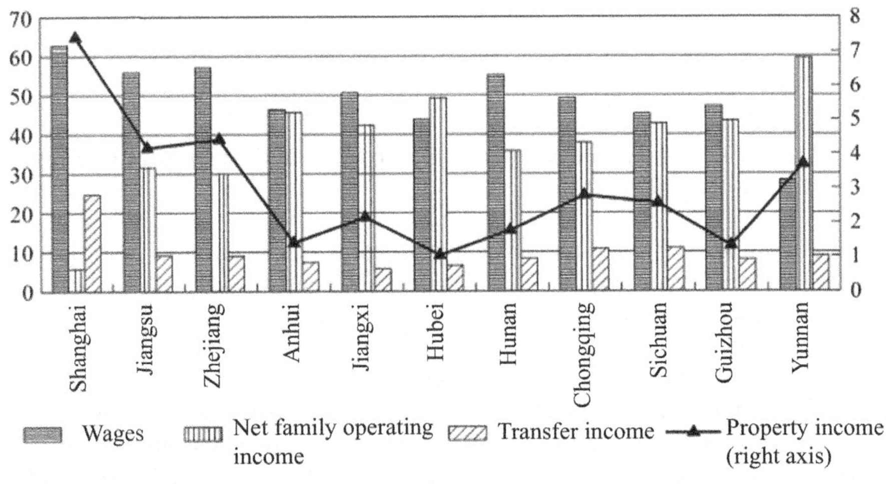


**Fig. 5** Income structure of provinces and cities in the Yangtze River Economic Belt (Agricultural Statistical Yearbook of 2014)

different, the income structure of peasants also varies greatly. For example, property income ranked first in Shanghai among 11 provinces and cities. However, in the relatively backward central and western regions such as Hubei and Guizhou, the property income was relatively low. At the same time, the net operating income of household in 11 provinces and cities was the highest in Yunnan Province, which showed that the income diversification mechanism in the western region has not been improved. As one of the most important solutions to the three rural issues: agriculture, rural areas and farmers in recent years, transfer payment has become one of the sources of peasants income in recent years. However, the performance of transfer payment still needs to match the fiscal and tax capacity of local government.

The change of income structure is the following of consumption structure. The research shows that the insufficient income is the primary factor restricting the consumption of rural residents, and the consumption of rural residents in most provinces is still for living necessities. At present, the income of rural residents in China remains sustainable growth, the total consumption is higher, the structure is optimized, and the propensity to consume is higher than that of urban residents. However, the gap between urban and rural areas, regions and people clusters is widening, and the contribution rate of consumption is declining. Education cost, infrastructure and credit constraints restrict both the increase of peasant income and the expansion of rural consumption. At the same time, the increase of peasant income is confronting the test of external environment changes, and rural consumption is also indirectly restricted by rural social security and population structure.

Among the 11 provinces and cities in the Yangtze River Economic Belt, the added value of the primary industry only in four provinces and cities accounted for less than 10% of the GDP. There is still a large space for the optimization of industrial structure. The proportion of retail sales of consumer goods of towns and villages against the retail sales of the whole society was higher in provinces with high agriculture proportion (refer to Fig. 6).

## 2 Orientation and Dilemma of Agricultural Development of Provinces and Cities in the Yangtze River Economic Belt

From the above analysis of the current situation of agricultural development in the Yangtze River Economic Belt, the whole Yangtze River Economic Belt needs to structure the chain mode of "large scale market + large scale logistics + large scale production". In this way, we can effectively realize the complementarity of short board and long board in the region and realize the effective optimization of existing resources. The division of work shall be deepened within the region and the industrial chain of agricultural products shall be enhanced while realizing the coordinated development. This section focuses on the analysis of regional orientation

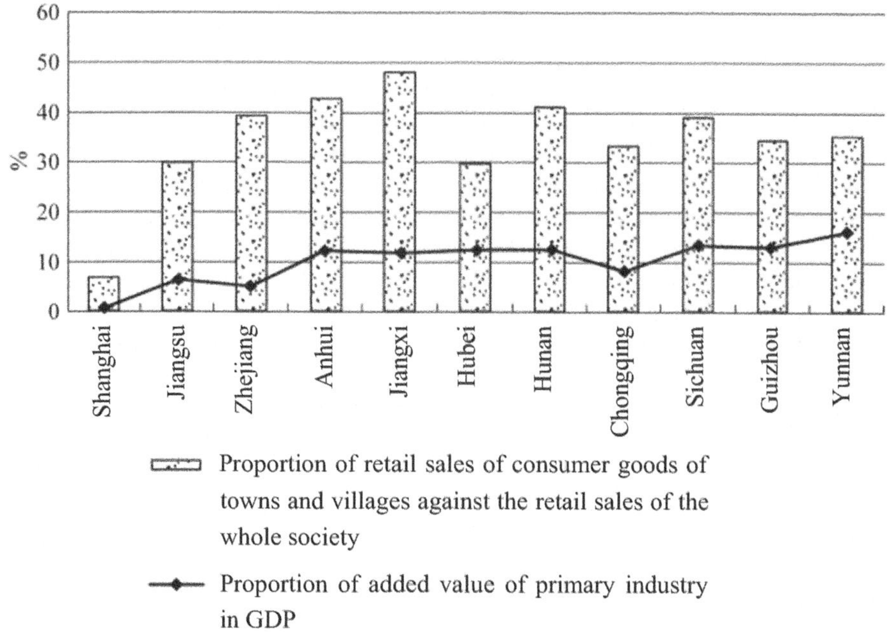


**Fig. 6** Agricultural consumption and expense structure of provinces and cities along the Yangtze River (Agricultural Statistics Yearbook of 2014)

and dilemma, viewing the policy-oriented issue from the perspective of orientation and understanding the trend of future from the perspective of difficulties.

## *2.1 Regional Orientation of Agricultural Development in Yangtze River Economic Belt*

The weakness of agricultural industry and protection policy has attracted the attention of disputes for agricultural development. Of course, the agricultural protection policy is not only limited to the market strategy in terms of price, but also includes guidance at the planning aspect. In fact, in the past ten years of new rural construction, we have made great progress on agricultural planning in China. Taking the work report of provincial and municipal governments in the Yangtze River Economic Belt in 2015 as an example, each region has a clear understanding of its own internal tasks of agricultural development and a clear description of its orientation (refer to Table 1).

From the positioning of the above provinces and cities, more attention is attracted to the characteristics and problems of their agricultural development. However, on the whole, the preparation of all regions for agricultural cooperation in the Yangtze River Economic Belt is obviously deficient, and the top-level design is inadequate.

**Table 1** Orientation and deployment of agricultural development reported by provincial and municipal governments in the Yangtze River Economic Belt in 2015

| Provinces and cities | Agricultural positioning and deployment |
|---|---|
| Shanghai | The national modern agriculture demonstration area was established in the organization system. Actively develop ecological and sightseeing agriculture. Vigorously cultivate new professional peasants. Strengthen the construction of irrigation and water conservancy facilities and forest network, promote the construction of vegetable production core bases, and ensure the production, supply and quality safety of real-estate agricultural products |
| Zhejiang | Strengthen the construction of local talent team and the training of peasants, and practically carry out the protection and inheritance of intangible cultural heritage and traditional skills; effectively implement the transformation of "Zhejiang Style Houses" in thousands of villages, sewage treatment and environment improvement, protection of 1000 ancient villages and 10,000 ancient dwellings, and conservation of ancient roads, bridges and wells; speed up the construction of beautiful villages |
| Jiangsu | Vigorously develop efficient agriculture, ecological agriculture and export-oriented agriculture, and push the construction of modern agriculture to a new stage; vigorously develop family farms, strengthen professional skills training, and improve the effectiveness of training; improve the development quality of peasants' cooperatives and give full play to the leading role of agricultural enterprises; encourage and guide industrial and commercial capital to develop modern planting and breeding industry suitable for enterprise in rural areas |
| Anhui | Further promote the construction of grain production capacity and the adjustment of agricultural structure; continue to carry out the construction of high-yield and grain production functional areas, thoroughly implement the action plan for the transformation and upgrading of small-scale water conservancy projects, make efforts in supporting the renovation of large-scale vegetable stations and the continued construction of large and medium-sized irrigation districts, promote agricultural standardized and clean production, promote water-saving, fertilizer saving and pesticides saving, and explore to develop multi-functional large-scale recycling agriculture |
| Jiangxi | Improve the efficiency of agricultural production; focus on the development of grassland animal husbandry, special fruit industry, special aquatic products, facility cultivated vegetables, tea, oil tea, flowers and seedlings, etc., which have good market prospect and high added values; build the brand of ecological agriculture. Implement the agricultural brand development strategy with the theme of "ecological Poyang Lake and green agricultural products", and cultivate a number of influential agricultural product brands in China |

(continued)

**Table 1** (continued)

| Provinces and cities | Agricultural positioning and deployment |
|---|---|
| Hubei | Strengthen the construction of rural infrastructure. Highlight the weak links such as farmland and water conservancy. Accelerate the implementation of the grain safety project, stabilize grain production, and improve the ability to guarantee grain and major agricultural products; speed up the construction of a rural comprehensive property rights trading market system under the unified provincial networking with Wuhan Rural Comprehensive Property Rights Exchange as the leader, and trading platforms in county (city, district) as the foundation |
| Hunan | Accelerate the transformation of agricultural development mode; stabilize the production of primary agricultural products and ensure that the total grain production remains at about 30 billion kilograms. Optimize the agricultural industrial structure, focus on building three hundred billion industries of grain, livestock and poultry, fruits and vegetables, strengthen and optimize the oil, tea, bamboo and wood industries with special advantages, and cultivate and expand 100 leading enterprises in agricultural industrialization; develop ecological circular agriculture, promote agricultural standardization and clean production, and improve the incentive and restraint mechanism of water saving, fertilizer saving and pesticide saving |
| Chongqing | Continue to do a good job in the follow-up work of "three rural issues: agriculture, rural areas and farmers" and the Three Gorges Project; change the agricultural development mode; promote the transformation of agriculture from "production oriented" to "consumption oriented", and accelerate the formation of a pattern of acting to local circumstances, large-scale production and specialized supporting facilities; complete the annual task of the follow-up work of the Three Gorges Project |
| Sichuan | Accelerate the development of modern agriculture and ensure the supply of high-quality and safe agricultural products; speed up the construction of a number of high-quality agricultural products distribution center, such as livestock, poultry, fruits, vegetables and tea, and support the creation of "Sichuan Brand" for agricultural products<br>Continue to deepen rural reform, solidly promote the registration and certification of land contractual management rights, innovate the agricultural management system, develop operation in moderate scale, and develop various new types of agricultural management entities |
| Guizhou | Exert the efforts in the work of "three rural issues: agriculture, rural areas and farmers" and poverty alleviation and development. Take the advantages of "mountains" and "trees", vigorously promote the adjustment of agricultural structure, and accelerate the cultivation of new growth points of "agriculture, rural areas and peasantry". To achieve "one after another". Actively promote the moderate scale operation of agriculture. Made efforts to cultivate new types of agricultural business entities, such as large-specialized-households of crop and animal productions, family farms, farmers' cooperatives, enterprises and farmers, and accelerate the reform and development of supply and marketing cooperatives |

(continued)

**Table 1** (continued)

| Provinces and cities | Agricultural positioning and deployment |
|---|---|
| Yunnan | Improve the quality and efficiency of plateau featured agriculture; speed up the construction of granaries on the plateau; actively develop diversified agriculture, enhance the benefits of characteristic cash crops, and promote the development of mountain animal husbandry, freshwater fisheries and efficient forestry; make solid efforts to promote poverty alleviation and development; further promote poverty alleviation and development in the four major areas, old revolutionary base areas and ethnic minorities with a small population, and continue to carry out poverty alleviation efforts for the whole village, township, county, prefecture and ethnic groups |

The development of agriculture in the Yangtze River Economic Belt is only limited to the import and export of labor force and the circulation of products within the region. At a higher level, such as the regional resource coordination under the concept of low-carbon economy is obviously insufficient. In recent years, the land index replacement and carbon emission trading market construction proposed by most scholars have not yet entered the construction at policy level. At the same time, large-scale environmental pollution, especially the haze problem in recent years, has been gradually approaching the provinces and cities in the Yangtze River Economic Belt, and all levels of the region have been affected. Therefore, only by constituting a higher level of cooperation concept, going out of the perspective of agricultural resources, and further deepening the understanding of environmental protection function are the new requirements of agricultural development in the Yangtze River Economic Belt. Since the 18th National Congress of the Communist Party of China, the new normal has become the new background of economic development: from high-speed growth to medium-high speed growth with optimization and upgrading of economic structure and from element driven and investment driven to innovation driven. Han Changfu, Minister of Agriculture, said: as China's economy has entered the new normal, reform into deep-water area, and economic and social development into a new stage, profound changes are taking place in both internal and external environment of agricultural development, and it is more urgent to speed up the construction of modern agriculture. We shall deeply realize that only by actively adapting to the new normal, can the agricultural and rural economy achieve sustainable and healthy development. Only by deeply understanding the new background of agricultural development can we better adapt to the new normal, whereas the environment is the first background of agricultural development.

## 2.2 Dilemma in Deepening Agricultural Cooperation in the Yangtze River Economic Belt

The problems in agricultural development are not only the problems to be overcome in agricultural development itself, but also the premise of agricultural cooperation. The current situation of agricultural development will basically usher in the "large scale market + large scale network + large scale production" mode. The so-called "large scale market" refers to the existence of several provincial capital cities and national cities in the Yangtze River Economic Belt. These regions feature at large population and large demand for agricultural products, therefore, the huge market will directly promote the transformation of agricultural production. However, only by using the network can we construct an effective market. From information network, logistics network to sales network and the supporting safety network, it will be a new channel for agricultural development in the future. At the same time, the construction of the network expands and deepens the external market of agriculture and integrates the essential resources of agricultural production. Agricultural production in many areas has been extended because of the network. However, on the other hand, the expansion of the market puts forward new requirements for agricultural production. The focus of agricultural "mass production" in the new period is the quality and diversification rather than the scale and quantity of production. It can be said that under the support of the network, agriculture has really entered the era of mass production. However, we still need to see that the coming of this mode needs to integrate resources with a new attitude. Therefore, it is an important perspective to understand the current regional agricultural development dilemma.

(I) **The deterioration of natural environment and ecological pollution have brought great challenges to the agricultural development of the Yangtze River Economic Belt**

From the perspective of the core resources of agricultural development, one is the land, the other is the water. According to the *National Soil Pollution Survey Status Bulletin* published in April 2014, the overall situation of the national soil environment is not optimistic. The soil pollution in some areas is serious, the soil environmental quality of cultivated land was worth of serious consideration and the soil environmental problems of industrial and mining wasteland are prominent. In terms of pollution distribution, the soil pollution in the south is more serious than that in the north; the soil pollution in the Yangtze River Delta, the Pearl River Delta and the northeast old industrial base is more worrisome, and the heavy metals in soil in the southwest and central south regions is quite excessive than the standard; the contents of cadmium, mercury, arsenic and lead gradually increase from northwest to southeast and from northeast to southwest. As the concentrated area of China's industrial development, although there are internal differences in the degree of soil pollution within the Yangtze River Economic Belt, it still remains a concern compared with other regions.

From the perspective of water resources, available water resources on the earth are scarce. From the perspective of changing relationship between supply and demand, the scarcity of this type of resource is more serious than that of oil. The increase of population, the acceleration of urbanization, the rise of per capita demand, and various extreme weathers caused by global climate change highlight the tension of water resources. The Yangtze River Economic Belt is an area with earlier agricultural development and faster industrial development in China. Although there are internal differences among 11 provinces and cities, compared with northwest and northeast China, the industrialization in this region is high. Among them, the secondary industry accounted for about 40.91% of the national total, and the industrial output value was 40.52% (2014 statistical data). The implementation of early industrialization resulted in great challenges for the environment. In 2013, four of the eight provinces (Guangdong, Jiangsu, Shandong, Zhejiang, Henan, Hebei, Sichuan and Hunan) with wastewater discharge of more than 3 billion tons were included in the region. The industrial and agricultural production of the Yangtze River Economic Belt mainly depends on the water source of the Yangtze River. Especially in agricultural production, due to the large demand of agricultural water resources in this region, the polluted water sources will directly affect the sustainability of agricultural development.

Along with China's relatively rapid industrialization process, the urbanization speed of China's economic frontier is also gradually improving. However, with the deepening of development, industrialization, agricultural modernization, urbanization and informatization are confronting some dilemmas and being trapped in the development bottleneck. These bottlenecks and dilemmas not only restrict the deepening of "four modernizations", but also hinder the transformation of economic development mode. To break through these dilemmas and bottlenecks, we must adhere to the strategic principle of synchronized "four modernizations". The synchronization of "four modernizations" and the new normal of economy are to seek a sustainable way of agricultural development and coordinated growth with economic society under the pressure of ecological environment. In China, the constraints of tight agricultural resources and deterioration of ecological environment have become increasingly prominent. For many years, resource conditions have been strained, and agricultural non-point source pollution, farmland quality decline, groundwater overdraft and other issues have become increasingly prominent. Especially after the problem of food and clothing is solved, the public have imposed higher requirements on the ecological environment and the quality and safety of agricultural products, therefore it is urgent to speed up the transformation of agricultural development mode.

As a densely populated area in China, the Yangtze River Economic Belt concentrated 42.75% of China's population. The higher level of urbanization and the large urban population in this region not only brought a larger external market capacity to agricultural development, but also became an important challenge to guarantee the urban consumption in this region. The Yangtze River Economic Belt, with the good background of industrialization and urbanization, provided a well and sound space for agricultural development.

### (II) The system and mechanism of the coordinated development of agriculture in the Yangtze River Economic Belt is still lagging behind

For now, although the Yangtze River Economic Belt has been put forward on the agenda, it is still difficult to form an effective platform for cooperation due to institutional problems. It can be said that the Yangtze River Economic Belt has been mentioned by scholars as early as the 1980s. "Yangtze River Economic Belt" was first put forward by the Chinese Society of Productive Forces Economics in 1984–1985. The concept used at that time was "Yangtze River Industrial Intensive Belt", which refers to the large scale economic zone by taking the several large cities in Yangtze River Basin as the center and driving the medium-sized cities and rural areas in their surroundings through radiation and attraction. The Fourteenth National Congress of the Communist Party of China proposed that we should take the opportunity of Pudong Development in Shanghai as an opportunity to further open cities along the Yangtze River, build Shanghai into an economic growth pole in the Yangtze River Basin, and drive the Yangtze River Basin to achieve great leap forward development. The Fifth Plenary Session of the Fourteenth Central Committee of the Communist Party of China further clarified that it is necessary to "build the Yangtze River Delta and the economic belt along the Yangtze River with Shanghai as the leader". In the new century, regional cooperative governance and coordinated development have become an important national strategy. It happens that "Golden waterway" is one of the important strategic deployments.

According to the monitoring data of the Yangtze River Water Conservancy Commission of the Ministry of Water Resources, the annual wastewater discharge in the Yangtze River Basin has exceeded 30 billion tons since 2007 and reached 34.74 billion tons in 2012, which presented a sustained growth. Under the background of the increasingly serious ecological environment crisis, it is intended to speed up the construction of cross provincial ecological compensation mechanism of Yangtze River Economic Belt from the perspectives of organization and coordination, capital investment, industrial support, technical support and supervision and management. Under the current operating mechanism of administrative centralization and fiscal decentralization, cross regional cooperation between local governments will inevitably encounter the contradiction between administrative division barriers and cross-border market resources allocation. In order to maximize the regional interests, most local governments are prone to be trapped into a vicious circle of local protectionism, which pursues "local interests" unilaterally but ignores the "overall interests" of river basin.

From the perspective of the overall economic and social development, the following problems still exist in the industrial division and cooperation of the Yangtze River Economic Belt: the development of regional marketization is relatively low, and the market system of regional integration is far from being structured; the economy in the administrative region still seriously restricts the trans-regional industrial cooperation and the free circulation of elements; the industrial level of the central city is low, which restricts the cooperation with due division of work and optimization and upgrading of regional industries; regional industrial innovation ability and motivation are insufficient, and the industrial chain level is generally low. Faced with such a cooperation dilemma, it shall be attributed to the existing system on the one hand and more efforts are needed in deepening the reform; on the other hand, it shall be attributed to the particularity of the agricultural industry. From the agricultural point of view, because of its strong externality and difficulty to operate the division of property rights, it is difficult to establish an effective incentive mechanism. Taking the ecological compensation mechanism as an example, the development system formed under the existing mode has gone far beyond the spatial layout relying on administrative division. However, the effective transaction mechanism and compensation mechanism stopped abruptly on the administrative boundary. On the one hand, the objective of deepening reform needs strong top-level design, but also needs to introduce more effective incentive mechanism. To get rid of the obstacles in the system and mechanism, we need to rely on the system and innovation. It is an important way out for agricultural development to form "radiation cooperation" thinking in replace of the traditional "resource input-output" concept.

## 3 Selection of Mode for the Agricultural Cooperative Development in the Yangtze River Economic Belt

Taking the rise and completion of industrialization as the boundary, there are three kinds of agricultural growth patterns: traditional agriculture, industrialized agriculture and modern agriculture. The size of per capita land scale and the contribution of labor-intensive technology constitute the growth source of traditional agriculture, while the per capita physical scale and physical capital intensive technology, the per capita generalized capital equipment ratio and generalized capital intensive technology are the main drives for the income growth of industrialized agriculture and modern agriculture respectively. Different drives result in different options for agricultural development, but for agricultural development mode, we not only need to understand the path dependence of historical dimension, but also need to pay attention to the modernization trap of realistic dimension. In a sense, agricultural development mode is how the agricultural production in the region is carrying on. As for the selection of agricultural production mode, there are significant differences among the three academic traditions of classicism, Marxism and populism, which are not only related to their different academic concerns, but also to the differences in the times, regions and cultural backgrounds of their emergence and development. Under the current political, economic and social background of China, it is the best way for the development of agriculture, rural areas and peasants to allow and promote the diversified development of agricultural production structure and agricultural production mode. The agricultural development road with Chinese characteristics shall be constructed by taking this opportunity.

The path of agricultural modernization of diversified development is reflected in two dimensions in the practice of agricultural development in the Yangtze River Economic Belt. The first is to form the development characteristics relying on its own development, optimize its own agricultural development structure and form the core power of agricultural development; the second is to form an effective trading and interactive mode at the perspective of cooperation and taking comparative advantage as the guidance. Therefore, the cooperation mode of the Yangtze River Economic Belt is unfolded based on these two dimensions. Since the different development background, different element endowments and different game forces in regional linkage, the mode selection for agricultural development in Yangtze River Economic Belt has formed its own characteristics. From the perspective of geographical differences, it holds the opinion that there are two different modes of agricultural development in the Yangtze River Economic Belt:

(1) The Yangtze River Economic Belt has formed three agricultural core circles from east to west: the market-oriented agricultural circle with the Yangtze River Delta as the center, the granary agricultural circle with Hunan, Hubei and Jiangxi as the center, and the characteristic agricultural circle with Sichuan as the center in the upper reaches of the Yangtze River.
(2) The Yangtze River Economic Belt has formed an agricultural economic belt with "market + characteristics" and with the Yangtze River as the center.

Furthermore, the development of the agricultural mode of the Yangtze River Economic Belt can be described as: the agricultural development mode with the combination of the circle and belt, with market as orientation and with the characteristics as the support.

## *3.1 The Agricultural Development Mode of the Yangtze River with the Combination of Economic Circle and Belt*

The limited resources shall be invested in the regions and industries with higher efficiency, so as to obtain the rapid growth of regional economy and drive the development of other regions and industries. Due to the differences of natural resources endowment and the non-uniformity of social resources allocation in different countries and regions, there are regional and spatial differences in economic development. The disequilibrium of regional economic development is the general law of economic development. In the process of disequilibrium development, there are two crucial ideas. One is that disequilibrium is only based on the result of the resource consideration. When pattern is observed from multiple perspectives, disequilibrium is no longer a state, but a sink of resources based on technology, institution and other restrictive factors; secondly, disequilibrium is a kind of space to be optimized urgently rather than a trap of development. Disequilibrium is just a prerequisite for diversification in the age of technology and network.

China's regional development strategy has gone through three periods: the balanced development strategic layout focusing on the mainland in the early days after founding the People's Republic of China, the unbalanced development strategic layout emphasizing on the coastal areas in the early stage of reform and opening up, and the relatively coordinated development spatial layout since the early 1990s. From then on, more attention has been paid to the equality of spatial development, so as to narrow the regional development gap and promote regional coordinated development. The change of regional development strategy pattern corresponded to the change of regional policy and regional control measures, and also led to the emergence of regional problems, which was manifested in the long-term existence of regional gap, which is narrowing though; the regional comparative advantage has not been brought into full play, thus the overall performance of regional strategy was reduced; the "concentration" effect is strong while the "decentralization" effect is relatively weak. The core driving of the core-edge structure needs to be strengthened.

Since the reform and opening up, China has taken the lead in implementing the coastal economic development strategy. The Yangtze River Delta, the Pearl River Delta and the Bohai Rim Region, which are located in the coastal economic belt of China, have achieved extraordinary development and have led to the prosperity of the national economy. However, the regional development strategy and related policies in Yangtze River coastal area, another major development axis in China, was proposed relatively late. Since the 18th National Congress of the Communist Party of China, top-level design and deepening reform have become an important focus for China's development. From the traditional unbalanced regional pattern to the coordinated development of linkage, we need to take the advantage of the traditional unbalanced advantages on the one hand, and also need to plant the balanced development concept into the process of collaborative development. The agricultural development mode of the Yangtze River Economic Belt is to further deepen the division of work and form the capacity of circuitous production on the basis of own advantages and then to realize the repeated deepening on the basis of non-equilibrium. In addition, the mode of combination of circle and belt is not to eliminate the status of circle, nor to homogenize the development of the belt, but to combine characteristics with division of work, combine the division of work with growth, and growth with equilibrium. The three characteristic circles in the Yangtze River Economic Belt are combined with the characteristic agricultural circle based on the Yangtze River Basin. Modern logistics and information flow technology are used in the belt to form interactive and coordinated development. Therefore, the agriculture of the Yangtze River Economic Belt is to take an agricultural development mode based on characteristics, division of work, growth and equilibrium.

### 3.2 Comparison of Agricultural Development Modes of Three Core Circles

Based on its own resource advantages, the large core circle has formed three different development modes (refer to Table 2). There are some differences among these three modes. Due to the different development modes selected, their development demands, approaches and value chain are also differentiated. The market advantage of the Yangtze River Delta provides agricultural development with large market capacity. The demand market is so large that the agricultural development must find a high value-added path. In the second agricultural circle with grain as its main feature, the grain, as the development direction of agriculture, needs to seek a breakthrough in

**Table 2** Scope and characteristics of agriculture in Yangtze River Economic Belt

| Region | Scope | Characteristics |
|---|---|---|
| Market oriented agricultural circle centered on Yangtze River Delta | Shanghai, Zhejiang, Jiangsu, and Anhui | Export oriented mode is an important direction of agricultural development<br>Be available with a large market demand capacity<br>Leisure agriculture and urban agriculture are the future growth points<br>The ecological significance of agriculture has been extensively concerned |
| The granary agricultural circle with Hunan, Hubei and Jiangxi as the center | Hunan, Hubei, and Jiangxi | The main grain producing area is an important feature of the region<br>Biotechnology is the focus of agricultural science and technology in this region<br>Speed up the land circulation and cooperative construction, and improve the scale operation<br>Promoting the construction of Regional Marketization and urbanization |
| Characteristic agricultural circle in the upper reaches of the Yangtze River with Sichuan as the center | Sichuan, Chongqing, Yunnan, and Guizhou | Characteristic agriculture is the center of the regional agricultural development<br>Overall coordination of poverty alleviation and development<br>Promote regional urbanization and market-oriented construction<br>Develop characteristic agricultural industry chain |

technology on the one hand, and to seek sustainable power in the system on the other. In order to improve the low added value of grain production and form the motive force of grain industry, we shall develop the cooperative, speed up the circulation of agricultural land and form large-scale family farms.

## *3.3 Policy Suggestions on the Coordinated Development of Agriculture in the Yangtze River Economic Belt*

From the perspective of industrial economy, the basic driving force to push the evolution of industrial clusters lies in the stability and symbiosis of cooperation among enterprises within the cluster. In the chaotic state of cluster evolution, the direction and mode of cluster evolution will be determined by the symbiosis and cooperation stability among enterprises within the cluster and the influence from external environment. As far as the development of industrial clusters in China is concerned, it is necessary to guide the formation and development of industrial clusters conditionally and selectively; to cultivate and strengthen the symbiotic mechanism within clusters; and to choose adaptive industrial cluster development strategies based on the principle of coordinated development of regional industrial clusters and regional economy. The development of agriculture in the Yangtze River Economic Belt, characterized by the combination of circle and belt, is the favorable condition for agricultural coordination. On the one hand, it strengthens the radiation ability of "circle structure", on the other hand, it strengthens the coordination ability of "belt structure".

If we say that the agricultural development in the traditional sense has inherent natural constraints, there is less possibility of mobility. Then the development of modern logistics industry and the high implantation of information for other industries have made an important change in the endowment and development mode of agriculture. Therefore, collaborative development has become one of the options of agricultural development in the future. From the perspective of elements, the two major elements of agricultural development have undergone significant changes since the reform and opening up. The high mobility of population but the lack of effective security mechanism, the rapid development of land but the lack of efficient utilization mode, which exacerbated the problem of agricultural development to a certain extent, "three rural issues: agriculture, rural areas and farmers" is just the response to such a trend. In essence, the issue of agriculture, rural areas and peasants is the precursor of agricultural coordinated development.

The development of industrialization, urbanization and informatization provides better conditions for agricultural coordination. Agriculture has become an important support for coordination with other industries, and other industries have become a bridge for agricultural development. Taking producer services as an example, producer services and their internal industries play an important role in promoting the agricultural development. Producer services and agricultural development in the whole state present a coordinated effect of mutual influence, interaction and common development in space. Producer services in central cities and agricultural development in surrounding areas have a coordinated effect in space. The producer services in Beijing, Shanghai and Guangzhou play an important role in promoting, radiating and supporting agricultural development in the Bohai Rim, Yangtze River Delta and Pearl River Delta. Therefore, the coordination is the inevitable trend for the agriculture development in the Yangtze River Economic Belt.

Mode optimization is an important issue in the economic development. It can be said that, the mode optimization in a certain sense is the process of expanding the constraints, comprehensively considering the coordination among various elements, sharing the development interests and expanding the development achievements. The optimization of agricultural development has a long history. From the traditional technology promotion, efficiency improvement and system innovation centered on yield, to ecological construction and low-carbon construction centered on environmental sustainability, it can be said that the road of agricultural development is a course of continuous optimization of agriculture. In the process of agricultural optimization, it shall be based on certain national conditions, which is also the diversity difficulty in the process of agricultural optimization. However, there are still some similar characteristics among the optimization paths. The experience of agricultural development since the reform and opening up is an important support for path optimization. As early as the beginning of the reform and opening up, when the agricultural reform had just made fruits, in October 1982, Deng Xiaoping put forward that "the development of agriculture depends on both policies and science". With the deepening of agricultural reform and development, the experience of agricultural development has been sublimated. We will try to understand the optimization of agricultural development mode in the Yangtze River Economic Belt based on the perspective of agricultural development experience.

### (I) Strengthen the top-level design of regional coordination to form the institutional basis for the coordinated development of agriculture in the Yangtze River Economic Belt

From the administrative division of regional agriculture to the belt agriculture, a more effective coordination mechanism is needed. As far as agriculture is concerned, due to the wide radius of external radiation, more institutional construction and integration are needed in terms of institutional guarantee. Therefore, it is suggested that the State Council take the lead to set up the Yangtze River Basin Cooperation and Development Committee with the participation of the central agricultural ministries and commissions as well as relevant provinces and cities in the Yangtze River Economic Belt to exercise the rights of planning, construction and management of the Yangtze River Economic Belt on behalf of the state. We shall abandon the narrow regional mode of traditional agricultural development, and strengthen the regional coordination of agriculture especially in terms of ecological function. The development of agriculture in the Yangtze River Economic Belt is not only a problem to output value among the three major industrial sectors, but also a problem to ecological environment protection in the Yangtze River Basin.

Therefore, strengthening the top-level design is to strengthen the negative externalities in agricultural development. China's agricultural development has been resulted in the extrusion and mutual interference of development in the specific basin due to the long term dependence. The main stream system is destroyed since there is no planning for the tributary water system, and as a result the tributary system is damaged by the excessive use of the main stream system. It is difficult to guarantee the rights of each other, and the vicious use makes agricultural production and ecological environment extremely fragile. The construction of strong top-level design has to be the institutional guarantee for the coordinated development of agriculture in the Yangtze River Economic Belt in the future.

### (II) Strengthen the support of regional agricultural policy and form the policy guarantee of agricultural coordinated development in the Yangtze River Economic Belt

It can be said that agricultural policy is not only a kind of support, but also a type of correction. To straighten out the macro basis of agricultural development from the perspective of top-level design is both the starting point and destination of agricultural policy. In the process of making agricultural policies, policy makers have to find a balance between agricultural pollution control, food security and farmers income. We shall improve the institutional arrangements, strengthen the provisions related to the use of agricultural inputs, provide consulting and promotion services, modify the provisions related to product standards, implement environmental cost sharing, and strengthen monitoring and research activities and meanwhile we shall learn the practice of developed countries to reduce pollution and improve the quality of rural environment under the condition that farmers' income is not affected or slightly reduced for some of them but the overall income of farmers is increased.

As for the agricultural policy of the Yangtze River Economic Belt, the main bottleneck of agricultural development in the region lies in the effective sharing of environmental governance issues and the social public goods of population mobility in the region. Environmental problems can be said to be the key issues to the governance of modernization in China. As the Yangtze River Economic Belt is linked by the Yangtze River, the environmental pollution associated with the Yangtze River is not only the key dilemma for the regional agricultural development, but also for the regional urbanization. In the top-level design, it is an important step to strengthen the environmental remediation and reasonably layout the industrial structure in the Yangtze River Industrial Belt. Agriculture is also facing such an issue. Rational distribution of agricultural structure and formation of an agricultural belt interconnected with the ecological environment of the Yangtze River is the development objective of this region. Such a layout planning needs to start from the perspective of policy, and the top-level design is required to break down the constraints of regional thinking and separation of departments.

At the same time, as an important population inflow and outflow area of economic belt in China, land circulation and human urbanization has become a key problem in the future regional agricultural development. The outflow of population along with urbanization not only provides a relaxed environment for agricultural development, but also provides impetus for urbanization. However, the equalization of public services in this process is a difficult problem in the regional agricultural development and urban development. The welfare problem needs to be solved after population migration from the perspective of top-level design. As an area with good industrial foundation and better agricultural development in China, the Yangtze River Economic Belt shall be the pioneer to explore the institutional innovation of public service equalization, which is not only an effective opportunity to win institutional dividend for this region, but also an experience spillover for other regions.

As a weak industry, agriculture also needs policies to protect it. The continuity and stability of the agricultural subsidy policy shall be maintained to gradually expand the scale and scope of the "Green Box" support policy, adjust and improve the "Yellow Box" support policy, and give full play to the effect of benefiting agriculture and increasing income. We will continue to implement policies such as direct subsidies for grain farmers, subsidies for improved varieties, subsidies for purchasing agricultural machinery and tools, and comprehensive subsidies for agricultural materials. Select some regions to carry out reform pilot projects to improve the guidance and effectiveness of subsidies. Improve the subsidy policy for the purchase of agricultural machinery and tools, give preference to major production areas and new agricultural operators, and expand the scope of subsidies for the purchase of water-saving irrigation equipment. Implement the subsidy policy to promote the major technical measures for agricultural production. Implement financial incentive and subsidy policies for major counties in grain and oil production, grain crop seed production, pig supply and cattle and sheep breeding counties. Expand the scope of awards and subsidies for modern agricultural demonstration areas. Improve the system for interest compensation, farmland protection compensation and ecological compensation in major grain producing areas.

### (III) Actively explore the mode of institutional innovation to constitute the incentive mechanism for the coordinated development of agriculture in the Yangtze River Economic Belt

Compared with policy support, institutional innovation has certain micro characteristics. Activating agricultural development from the micro level can mobilize the enthusiasm of micro individuals and lay a good foundation for macro policies. Modern agricultural system is the management system of modern agriculture, which provides strong support to the modernization of agricultural technology and equipment. The establishment of modern agricultural system shall be started with the reform and innovation of rural economic and social services so that it can become a systematic system to boost modern agriculture and new rural construction. And the management system of agriculture is constantly innovated because of technical differences. As for the agricultural development of the Yangtze River Economic Belt, diversified agricultural development is not only its development advantage, but also its promotion resistance due to its large regional span. Therefore, the promotion of agricultural development with the help of modern agricultural management system is an effective choice for regional agricultural coordinated development.

For a period of time, the Yangtze River Economic Belt is an important area of agricultural system innovation in China. From the household contract responsibility system originated in Anhui at the beginning of the reform to the cooperative system innovation represented by Zhejiang, Shanghai and Jiangsu since the 21st century, and the land centered reform of property rights which was carried out in Sichuan and Chongqing, it can be said that the Yangtze River Economic Belt are prepared with good tradition and conditions of institutional innovation, which has formed the institutional dividend for the agricultural development of the region and provided demonstration for the agricultural development in other regions.

The construction of macro economy needs a better micro foundation. A dynamic micro environment can not only provide a good source of information but also a good feedback mechanism for the macro-economy. To rediscover the micro basis of macro-economy, on the one hand, is to understand the basis of macro policies, and to activate micro links to build a good order for macro-economy on the other. To further encourage all regions in the Yangtze River Economic Belt to actively explore agricultural mode innovation is to make efforts on the standardized and orderly circulation of land management rights, land circulation and scale operation mode on the basis of adhering to and improving the basic rural management system and on the basis of the dominant position of family operation, so as to realize various forms of moderate scale operation and improve the organization degree of farmers.

In addition, in the downstream links of agricultural production, it is supposed to actively use modern logistics technology to innovate agricultural sales mode, improve the backbone network of agricultural products circulation in the region, and strengthen the construction of warehousing and logistics facilities for important agricultural products. We need to strengthen the construction of production site and market for agricultural products, accelerate the construction of trans-regional cold chain logistics system, and promote the docking of cooperatives with supermarkets, schools, enterprises and communities. Clean up and rectify the problem of arbitrary charges for the transportation and marketing of agricultural products; develop the futures trading of agricultural products and develop new varieties of futures trading of agricultural products. Support e-commerce, logistics, commerce, finance and other enterprises to participate in the construction of agricultural e-commerce platform.

### (IV) Explore the adaptive technology of regional development, and form the technical support for the coordinated development of agriculture in the Yangtze River Economic Belt

Schumacher put forward the concept of intermediate technology in his book *Small Is Beautiful*, which brought new thinking to economics. He put forward the basic concept of compact work unit and regional workplace using local human resources. In the course to develop the economics, a unique mode of thinking has been formed. In agricultural development, we shall not only understand the advantages brought by technology itself, but also straighten out the new constraints formed by technology selection. The subsequent adaptive technology just has such characteristics. Adaptive technology is not as extreme as diversity technology centrism. It claims that as long as individuals think and act in a friendly way, free market will create positive effects on the environment. Therefore, the green consumer groups, investors, citizens and employees are very powerful for a green economy. From this point of view, although the market plays an important role in environmental economics, some environmental restrictions must be strictly observed in order to achieve the broader sustainable development objectives (even if some development activities are ignored).

The idea of adaptive technology is to seek a road of "technology—environment—development" in the process of technology implantation while developing the regional economy. The Yangtze River Economic Belt is not only an area rich in agricultural resources, but also an area with fragile ecological environment. Only by making use of the scientific and technological achievements in the region and realizing better transformation, can we finally create the sustained driving force for development. Therefore, we need to improve the incentive mechanism of agricultural science and technology innovation in this region, improve the human resources circulation and part-time system of scientific research institute, universities and enterprises, and promote the reform pilot of scientific research achievements, disposal, income management and equity incentive of scientific and technological personnel, and stimulate the enthusiasm for innovation and entrepreneurship of scientific and technological personnel. Establish a mechanism to optimize and integrate the agricultural science and technology program, planning and coordination of scientific and technological resources, and improve the mechanism of national major scientific research infrastructure and large scientific research instruments to the public. Strengthen the guidance and support for enterprises to carry out agricultural science and technology research and development, so that enterprises can become the principal of technological innovation and application. Accelerate agricultural science and technology innovation and make major breakthroughs in the fields of biological breeding, intelligent agriculture, agricultural machinery and equipment, and ecological and environmental protection. Establish agricultural science and technology collaborative innovation alliance and build agricultural science and technology financing, information, brand service platform relying on the national agricultural science and technology park. Explore the establishment of a trading center for agricultural scientific and technological achievements. Give full play to the role of scientific research institutes, universities and their new rural development research institutes, colleges, and the science and technology commissioners in the transformation of scientific research achievements.

### (V) Coordinate the regional public services and form the social foundation for the coordinated development of agriculture in the Yangtze River Economic Belt

Compared with other industries, agriculture has strong social characteristics. The agriculture, countryside and farmers on the road of modernization can be called the last step to modernization. Only by realizing its complete transformation, can we ensure the common ownership and sharing of the achievements of modernization. Therefore, the equalization of public services proposed in recent years is just with such logic, and the social foundation of agricultural development can be realized on this basis. Basic public service is the basic condition for the survival and development of people in the society and is the basic welfare that can be effectively met and fully guaranteed only when it is provided by the government. Equal access to basic public services is the basic rights of the people. At present, there is obvious non equalization of basic public services in China, the most prominent manifestation of which is the uneven possession of resources, the uneven level of consumption and the imbalance of dualistic system as well as rights and interests of public services. The equalization of basic public services does not only mean that everyone can enjoy basic public services, but also can enjoy them on an equal footing. Therefore, we must further increase the financial investment in public services, reasonably share the responsibility of basic public services, establish the financial input mechanism with service equilibrium oriented, deepen the reform of public service departments and institutions, build the basic public service system covering all people and integrating the urban and rural areas, and realize the equalization of basic public services.

In the Yangtze River Economic Belt, it is necessary to ensure that migrant workers and their accompanying families can enjoy urban basic public services equally, expand the coverage of urban social insurance for migrant workers, take prevention and assistance measures for occupational diseases of migrant workers, improve the relevant policies for migrant workers' children to receive compulsory education and participate in the entrance examination for senior high middle school and universities, and explore specific methods for migrant workers to enjoy urban security housing. We shall speed up the reform of household registration system, establish the residence permit system, and promote the transferred agricultural population in categories to settle in cities and towns and enjoy the same treatment as the local residents. At the same time, it is supposed to support the construction of public and inclusive private kindergartens in rural areas. Accelerate the development of high school education, focus on junior high school and senior high school graduates who failed for further studies, promote the full coverage of secondary vocational education and vocational skills training, and gradually realize secondary vocational education for free. Carry out serious illness insurance for urban and rural residents and strengthen the capacity of basic medical care and public health in rural areas and the construction of rural doctor team. Promote the interconnection between designated medical institutions at all levels and the provincial new rural cooperative medical information system and actively develop remote consultation system benefiting rural areas. Expand major cultural projects to serve the "three rural issues: agriculture, rural areas and farmers". Strengthen the standard management of rural minimum living security system, establish a comprehensive temporary assistance system, and improve rural social assistance. Implement the unified basic endowment insurance system for urban and rural residents. Support the construction of a variety of rural pension services and cultural and sports facilities. Integrate and utilize the existing facilities, sites and resources to build a rural primary comprehensive public service platform.

# Coordinated Development of Ecological Environment in Yangtze River Economic Belt

**Lin Sun**

## 1 Introduction

The problems of ecological environment mainly include air pollution, water pollution and soil pollution. The ecological environment problems are mainly caused by the unreasonable development and utilization of natural resources by human society. The core of eco-environmental problems is how to keep the balance between socio-economic development and the development and utilization of resources and environment, so as to realize the sustainable development of social economy. This is a major problem that we have been dealt with in China's social and economic development at the national and regional levels in the past 30 years of reform and opening up, and will continue to face in the coming decades. In other words, how to realize the coordinated development of ecological environment and social economy, and realize the sustainable development of social economy, is an important strategic issue that is inescapable by the society. The historical experience of developed countries shows that to realize the sustainable development of social economy, the sustainable development of ecological environment must be taken as the premise. Adhering to the coordinated development of social economy and ecological environment is a long-term national strategic policy that China must adhere to with the objective of sustainable development.

As the third longest river in the world, the Yangtze River Basin covers an area of more than 180,000 km$^2$ and is the largest river basin with the largest population in the world. The administrative division of the Yangtze River Economic Belt includes Shanghai, Jiangsu, Zhejiang, Anhui, Jiangxi, Hubei, Hunan, Chongqing, Sichuan, Guizhou and Yunnan, with a land area of more than 2.05 million square kilometers and a total population of more than 42.7% of the state in 2013, and the GDP exceeded

L. Sun (✉)
Institute of Applied Economics, Shanghai Academy of Social Sciences, Shanghai, China
e-mail: sunlin@sass.org.cn



X. Jing (ed.), *Development of the Yangtze River Economic Belt in China*, Urban Governance Practices in China,
https://doi.org/10.1007/978-981-16-1578-8_4

45.6% of the whole state in 2013. It is a super large economic belt across the eastern, central and western regions, including large-scale industrial aggregation and urban population clusters, and occupies a very important position in China's social and economic development. At the same time, as the largest river in China, the Yangtze River is the only "golden waterway" running through the east, middle and west of whole China. Its shipping ability is an important engine for the social and economic development of the Yangtze River Economic Belt.

In September 2014, the State Council issued the *Guidance on Promoting the Development of the Yangtze River Economic Belt Relying on the Golden Waterway*, which put forward the strategic objectives at the national level, that is to say, the Yangtze River Economic Belt will be built into a globally influential inland river economic belt, a coordinated development belt of interactive cooperation among the east, the central and the western regions, a comprehensively promoted internal and external opening-up belt along the Yangtze River and pioneering demonstration belt for the construction of ecological civilization. The construction of Yangtze River Economic Belt has become another important national strategy after coastal opening up and western development.

With the implementation of the national development strategy, there is no doubt that the Yangtze River Economic Belt will enter a new stage of rapid development. In the process of further promoting the development strategy of the Yangtze River Economic Belt by the state, due to the large-scale industrial transformation and upgrading and the further promotion of large-scale urbanization, the ecological environment pressure of the Yangtze River Economic Belt will be further intensified. The water and soil loss in the upper reaches of the Yangtze River aggravates the flood and drought in the basin and the discharge of industrial and domestic wastewater in the whole basin aggravates the water pollution of main stream and tributary of the Yangtze River. The degradation of ecological environment and the deterioration of environmental quality in the Yangtze River Basin will seriously restrict and affect the economic development of the Yangtze River Economic Belt.

The ecological environment of the Yangtze River Economic Belt is related to the interests of the whole region and the whole state. In the critical period of strengthening the construction of the Yangtze River Economic Belt and the "golden waterway" of the Yangtze River, it is required to deal with the relationship between economic development and ecological environment protection for the further development of the Yangtze River Economic Belt. Therefore, it is necessary to study how to avoid the transfer of pollution emission sources because of industry transfer and how to control the total amount of pollution emissions in the Yangtze River Basin. At the same time, it is necessary to study how to realize the restoration of the ecological environment system in the Yangtze River Basin and how to realize the comprehensive management, as well as how to establish the system construction of atmosphere, water resources, water ecological environment and soil protection. We will analyze the current situation of the ecological environment of the Yangtze River Economic Belt, comb the measures and effects of various provinces and cities in controlling water resources and environment, study and analyze the core problem to coordinated development of social economy and ecological environment at the provincial and national levels in this chapter by mainly combining the situation of the whole state and taking 9 provinces and 2 cities within the Yangtze River Economic Belt (i.e. the Yangtze River Economic Belt) as the object as well as focusing on the water resources in the Yangtze River Economic Belt.

# 2 Social and Economic Development and Ecological Environment Problems in the Yangtze River Economic Belt

## *2.1 Social and Economic Development of Yangtze River Economic Belt*

Over the past 30 years of reform and opening up, the population of the Yangtze River Economic Belt has increased dramatically and the scale of cities and market towns has been expanding just like other regions in China, large-scale manufacturing and heavy industrial enterprises have been gathering along the river, and the economic activities in the basin have become increasingly active day by day. It carried a big weight in the social economy of China (refer to Table 1).

The land area of the Yangtze River Economic Belt accounts for 21.23% of the state, but the permanent resident population accounted for 42.7%, GDP accounted for 45.6%, fiscal revenue accounted for 30.6%, fixed assets investment accounted for 40.4%, total retail sales of consumer goods accounted for 21.9%, new jobs accounted for 58.7%, and per capita GDP was 106.7% of the national average in 2013. The status or function of population size, GDP scale, fixed assets investment and absorption of employment is highly significant.

Within the Yangtze River Economic Belt, the social and economic development is extremely unbalanced. The social and economic development of the east, central and west regions has distinct characteristics. The eastern region of the Yangtze River Economic Belt is the most economically developed Yangtze River Delta region in China. The land area accounts for only 10.3% of the Yangtze River Economic Belt, but the permanent resident population accounted for 27.3%, GDP accounted for 45.6%, fiscal revenue accounted for 44.5%, fixed assets investment accounted for 34.3%, total retail sales of consumer goods accounted for 45.9%, new jobs accounted for 32.2%, and per capita GDP was 167.3% of the average of the Yangtze River Economic Belt in 2013. The eastern region has significant advantages in GDP scale, fiscal revenue, total retail sales of consumer goods and per capita GDP. On the basis of strong economic foundation, the eastern region is also advantageous over others for talent, capital, technology and information. At the same time, in order to adapt to the changes in the international economic environment and continuously improve the international competitiveness, the eastern region took the lead in accelerating the transformation of economic development mode and adjusting industrial structure as well as concentrating on the development of high-tech industry and modern service

**Table 1** Social and economic development of Yangtze River Economic Belt in 2013

| Provinces and cities | | Land area (10,000 km$^2$) | Permanent residence (10,000 people) | Per capita GDP (10,000 Yuan) | GDP (100 million) | Revenue (100 million yuan) | Fixed assets investment (100 million yuan) | Total retail sales of consumer goods (100 million yuan) | New jobs (10,000 people) |
|---|---|---|---|---|---|---|---|---|---|
| East | Shanghai | 0.63 | 2 415 | 9.01 | 21 602 | 4 109 | 5 648 | 8 019 | 60.1 |
| | Jiangsu | 10.26 | 7 939 | 7.45 | 59 162 | 6 568 | 35 983 | 20 656 | 81.6 |
| | Zhejiang | 10.2 | 5 498 | 6.83 | 37 568 | 6 908 | 20 194 | 15 138 | 104.3 |
| Total of east | | 21.09 | 15 852 | 7.46 | 118 332 | 17 585 | 61 825 | 43 813 | 246.0 |
| Central | Anhui | 13.97 | 6 030 | 3.16 | 19 039 | 3 365 | 18 251 | 6 481 | 67.5 |
| | Jiangxi | 16.7 | 4 522 | 3.17 | 14 339 | 2 357 | 12 866 | 4 551 | 54.1 |
| | Hunan | 21.18 | 6 691 | 3.66 | 24 502 | 3 307 | 18 381 | 8 940 | 80.1 |
| | Hubei | 18.59 | 5 799 | 4.25 | 24 668 | 3 565 | 20 177 | 10 465 | 72.9 |
| Total of central | | 70.44 | 23 042 | 3.58 | 82 548 | 12 594 | 69 675 | 30 437 | 274.6 |
| West | Sichuan | 48.14 | 8 107 | 3.24 | 26 261 | 2 784 | 21 049 | 10 355 | 93.5 |
| | Chongqing | 8.23 | 2 970 | 4.26 | 12 657 | 1 692 | 11 205 | 4 511 | 68.1 |
| | Yunnan | 38.33 | 4 687 | 2.5 | 11 721 | 2 975 | 9 622 | 4 036 | 31.6 |
| | Guizhou | 17.6 | 3 502 | 2.29 | 8 007 | 1 919 | 7 103 | 2 366 | 55.5 |
| Total of west | | 112.3 | 19 266 | 3.04 | 58 646 | 9 370 | 48 979 | 21 268 | 248.6 |

(continued)

**Table 1** (continued)

| Provinces and cities | Land area (10,000 km$^2$) | Permanent residence (10,000 people) | Per capita GDP (10,000 Yuan) | GDP (100 million) | Revenue (100 million yuan) | Fixed assets investment (100 million yuan) | Total retail sales of consumer goods (100 million yuan) | New jobs (10,000 people) |
|---|---|---|---|---|---|---|---|---|
| Total of Yangtze River Economic Belt | 203.83 | 58 160 | 4.46 | 259 526 | 39 549 | 180 479 | 95 518 | 769.2 |
| Whole state | 960 | 136 072 | 4.18 | 568 845 | 129 143 | 447 074 | 436 528 | 1 310 |
| Proportion of east (%) | 10.3 | 27.3 | 167.3 | 45.6 | 44.5 | 34.3 | 45.9 | 32.0 |
| Proportion of middle (%) | 34.6 | 39.6 | 80.3 | 31.8 | 31.8 | 38.6 | 31.9 | 35.7 |
| Proportion of west (%) | 55.1 | 33.1 | 68.2 | 22.6 | 23.7 | 27.1 | 22.3 | 32.3 |
| Proportion of Yangtze River Economic Belt to China (%) | 21.23 | 42.7 | 106.7 | 45.6 | 30.6 | 40.4 | 21.9 | 58.7 |

*Source China Statistical Yearbook of 2014*

industry, which will inevitably have the result that the traditional manufacturing industry will be gradually transferred to other regions, especially to the central and western regions of the Yangtze River Economic Belt.

The land area of the central region of the Yangtze River Economic Belt accounts for 34.6% of the total area. However, the permanent resident population accounted for 39.6%, GDP accounted for 31.8%, fiscal revenue accounted for 31.8%, fixed assets investment accounted for 38.6%, total retail sales of consumer goods accounted for 31.9%, new jobs accounted for 35.7%, and per capita GDP was only 80.3% of the average of the Yangtze River Economic Belt in 2013. The central region has relative advantages in population size, fixed asset investment and employment absorption, but it is below the average level of the Yangtze River Economic Belt in terms of GDP scale, fiscal revenue, total retail sales of consumer goods and per capita GDP. The land area of the western region accounts for 55.1% of the Yangtze River Economic belt. In 2013, the permanent resident population accounted for 33.1%, GDP accounted for 22.6%, fiscal revenue accounted for 23.7%, fixed assets investment accounted for 27.1%, total retail sales of consumer goods accounted for 22.3%, new jobs accounted for 32.3%, and per capita GDP was only 68.2% of the average of the Yangtze River Economic Belt. The western region plays an important role in population size and land area, but lags far behind the average level of the Yangtze River Economic Belt in terms of GDP scale, financial revenue, fixed asset investment and total retail sales of consumer goods.

Although the central and western regions of the Yangtze River Economic Belt lag behind the eastern region in many aspects, they have advantages in water resources, shipping, mineral resources and traditional industrial foundation. Heavy chemical industries such as steel, petrochemical, energy and building materials are developing rapidly. And in recent years, it is actively undertaking the transfer of related industries in the eastern coastal areas. On the one hand, the formation of this trend will bring about heavy industrialization in the middle and upper reaches of the Yangtze River Economic Belt; on the other hand, it will further aggravate the ecological environment pressure of the whole Yangtze River Basin. Meanwhile, due to the linkage of the ecological environment of the basin, the ecological environment pressure in the middle and upper reaches of the central and western regions will inevitably be transmitted to the eastern region of the lower reaches, which will have significant impact on the ecological environment.

Therefore, the social and economic development of the Yangtze River Economic Belt must consider the coordinated development with the ecological environment of the whole Yangtze River Basin and even the whole state, especially the relationship between social and economic development and ecological environment protection so that the transfer of pollution sources and pollutants caused by industrial transfer in the future can be avoided and contained.

## 2.2 *Water Pollution in the Yangtze River Economic Belt*

Enough attention shall be attracted to the problems of ecological environment in the Yangtze River Basin. The water environment of the Yangtze River Basin is becoming very severe, and the ecosystem is gradually being destroyed.

(I) **Current situation of water pollution in the Yangtze River in recent years**

With the development of social economy, the growth of population, the rapid development of industrial and agricultural production and urban construction in the Yangtze River Economic Belt, the discharge of waste water in the Yangtze River Basin is increasing year by year. The over standard rate of water quality in the provincial boundary of the Yangtze River Basin is rising. Water pollution in the basin, especially in the middle and lower reaches, has become a prominent problem to the protection of water resources in the Yangtze River.

The water pollution of the Yangtze River is mainly manifested in the following aspects: firstly, the pollution of the near-bank waters along the main stream of the Yangtze River has not been contained, which is threatening the safety of water in urban. Secondly, the pollution of tributaries is serious, and the river with over standard pollution is thousands of kilometers long. Thirdly, the lake eutrophication is still developing. The following is the basic situation of water pollution in the Yangtze River published in the *Bulletin on the State of the Environment in China* in recent years.

In 2009, there were 52 state-controlled sections in the main stream and 20 main tributaries of the Yangtze River, of which the water quality on 42 sections reached or was better than Class III, accounting for 80.8%. Among the 18 state-controlled sections in the main stream, the water quality of 17 sections reached or was better than Class III, and the water quality of Shanghai section is classified as IV; among the 34 state-controlled sections of main tributaries, the water quality of 25 sections reached or was better than that of class III, 4 sections with water quality of class IV or V, and 5 sections inferior to class V. The inferior class V sections are mainly concentrated in Chuhe River, Hengyang Changsha section of Xiangjiang River, Zhenjiang section of Beijing Hangzhou canal and outer Qinhuai River. The near-bank pollution belt commonly existed in sections of the main and tributaries of the Yangtze River. Among the 505 centralized drinking water sources in the region, the water quality of 450 water sources was up to the standard, and the main pollution indicators were ammonia nitrogen, iron, manganese, etc. There are 26 state-controlled points in Dongting Lake, Poyang Lake, East Lake, Xuanwu Lake, etc. in the region. The water quality of 6 points is class III, the water quality of 18 points is varying from IV to V, and the water quality of 2 points is inferior to class V. The main pollution indicators were total nitrogen, total phosphorus and permanganate indexes. Dongting Lake is at medium nutrient level, Poyang Lake and Xuanwu Lake are at light eutrophication, and East Lake is at medium eutrophication.

In 2010, among 105 state-controlled monitoring sections, the proportion of sections with class I–III, class IV, class V and inferior class V were 88.6%, 6.6%,

1.0% and 3.8% respectively. The water quality of the main stream of the Yangtze River is generally excellent. Compared with the previous year, there was no obvious change of the water quality. The water quality of the tributaries of the Yangtze River is generally good. Compared with the previous year, there was no obvious change of the water quality. Among the ten tributaries, the water quality of Yalong River, Minjiang River, Jialing River, Wujiang River, Yuanjiang River and Hanjiang River were the best, while the water quality of Dadu River, Tuojiang River, Xiangjiang River and Ganjiang River was good. However, the Meishan section of Minjiang River, Hengyang section of Xiangjiang River and Nanchang section of Ganjiang River were slightly polluted, and the main pollution index was ammonia nitrogen. The water quality of the provincial boundary reaches was excellent. In the 20 sections, the cross-section proportions of water quality class I–III and IV were 95.0% and 5.0%, respectively. There was no class V or inferior class V. Compared with the previous year, there was no obvious change of the water quality.

In 2011, among 94 state-controlled sections, the cross-section proportions of water quality class I–III, IV–V and inferior V were 80.9%, 13.8% and 5.3%, respectively. The water quality of the main stream of the Yangtze River was excellent. Among the 32 state-controlled sections, the cross-section proportions of water quality class I–III and IV were 96.9% and 3.1%, respectively. Compared with the previous year, there was no obvious change of the water quality. The tributaries of the Yangtze River were generally slightly polluted. The main pollution indexes were total phosphorus, ammonia nitrogen and chemical oxygen demand. Among the 62 state-controlled sections, the cross-section proportions of water quality I–III, IV–V and inferior V were 72.6%, 19.3% and 8.1%, respectively. Compared with the previous year, there was no obvious change of the water quality. Among them, the water quality of Yalong River, Hanjiang River and Jialing River are the best, Dadu River, Yuanjiang River, Xiangjiang River and Ganjiang River was good, Minjiang River and Tuojiang River were slightly polluted, and Wujiang River was heavily polluted. The water quality of the provincial boundary reaches was generally good. Among the 19 state-controlled sections, the cross-section proportions of water quality class I–III, IV and inferior V were 78.9%, 15.8% and 5.3%, respectively. Compared with the previous year, the proportion of water quality class I–III was decreased by 11.1% point, and the proportion of inferior class V was the same. The section along Wujiang River at the junction of Guizhou and Chongqing in Tongren, Guizhou was heavily polluted, and the main pollution index was total phosphorus.

In 2012, among the 160 state-controlled sections, the cross-section proportions of water quality class I–III, IV–V and inferior V were 86.2%, 9.4% and 4.4%, respectively. The water quality of the main stream of the Yangtze River was excellent. Among the 42 state-controlled sections, the cross-section proportions of water quality class I–III and class IV–V were 97.6% and 2.4%, respectively. The water quality of the tributaries of the Yangtze River was good. Among the 118 state-controlled sections, the cross-section proportions of water quality class I–III, IV–V and inferior V were 82.2%, 11.9% and 5.9%, respectively. Among the main tributaries of the Yangtze River, Tanglangchuan, Wujiang, Yunshui, Fuhe and Fuxi River were heavily polluted, outer Qinhuai River and Huangpu River are moderately polluted, Pudu

River, Minjiang River, Tuojiang River, Chuhe River, Baihe River, Tanghe River and Tangbai River were slightly polluted. The water quality of the provincial boundary section was good. The cross-section proportions of water quality class I–III, IV–V and inferior V 1% were 82.1%, 14.3% and 3.6%, respectively. The WanMu section of Wujiang River at the junction of Guizhou and Chongqing was heavily polluted, and the main pollution index was total phosphorus. According to the division of water resources, the cross-section proportions of water quality class I–III and inferior V were 79.0% and 8.6%, respectively.

In 2013, among the state-controlled sections, section with class I water quality accounted for 4.4%, with a year-on-year increase of 2.5% point; class II accounted for 51.0%, with a year-on-year increase of 0.4% point; class III accounted for 32.7%, with a year-on-year decrease of 4.2% point; class IV accounted for 6.9%, with a year-on-year increase of 0.6% point; class V accounted for 1.9%, with a year-on-year increase of 0.7% point; and inferior class V accounted for 3.1%, with flat year-on-year level. Compared with the previous year, the water quality of the Yangtze River Basin had no obvious change. The water quality of the state-controlled sections in the main stream of the Yangtze River was of class I–III, with a year-on-year increase of 4.9% point, accounting for 7.3% of the total sections; That of class I accounted 41.5%, with a year-on-year decrease of 3.7% point; that of class III accounted for 51.2%, with a year-on-year decrease of 1.2%. Compared with the previous year, the water quality of the main stream of the Yangtze River had no obvious change. Among the state-controlled sections in the tributaries of the Yangtze River, sections with class I water quality accounted for 3.4%, with a year-on-year increase of 1.7% points; that of class II accounted for 54.2%, with a year-on-year increase of 1.7% points; that of class III accounted for 26.3%, with a year-on-year decrease of 5.1% points; that of class IV accounted for 9.3%, with a year-on-year increase of 0.8% point; that of class V accounted for 2.6%, with a year-on-year increase of 0.9% point; and that of inferior class V accounted for 4.2%, with flat year-on-year level. Among the main tributaries, Tanglangchuan, Yunshui, Fuhe and Fuxi rivers were heavily polluted, and Minjiang, Tuojiang, Chuhe, outer Qinhuai River, Huangpu River, Huayuan River and Tangbai River were slightly polluted. The water quality of other tributaries was either excellent or good.

According to the bulletin data in recent years, the water quality of the Yangtze River Basin is basically stable, that is, there was no obvious improvement; the water quality of the main stream was sound, while the water pollution of the upstream tributaries was further aggravated. In addition, the situation announced in the environmental bulletin deviates from people's general feeling in the actual environment to some certain extent, and the improvement of water quality pollution in the Yangtze River Economic Zone is not so optimistic.

### (II) **Water pollution of the Yangtze River**

Water pollution in the Yangtze River Economic Zone involves wide range and large scale and in complex situation. Yin Weidong (2003) sorted out the main sources of water pollution in the Yangtze River, including non-point source, point source, mobile source, solid waste, etc.

The first is non-point source pollution. Soil erosion and farmland drainage are important factors affecting the overall water quality of the Yangtze River. Soil erosion brings pesticides, chemical fertilizers, nutrient elements in soil and some animal and plant humus into water body, which increases the concentration of suspended solids, BOD, COD and total phosphorus in water body. The second is point source pollution. With the rapid development of industrial and agricultural production in the Yangtze River Basin, the population and urban scale are expanding, and the surface water pollution is becoming more and more serious. The pollution discharge from the outlets along the Yangtze River is the fundamental reason for the near-bank pollution of the main stream and its large tributaries. With the further economic development of the Yangtze River Economic Belt, the sewage discharge of the whole basin was increased by 3%, and most of the sewage was directly discharged into the river without any treatment. The third is mobile source pollution. The total number of transport ships in the main stream of the Yangtze River is more than 100,000, most of which are not equipped with oil-water separation device and domestic sewage treatment device. Millions of tons of oily sewage, nearly one hundred million tons of domestic sewage and hundreds of millions tons of garbage are directly discharged into the Yangtze River every year, which constitutes the mobile pollution source that can not be ignored in the Yangtze River Basin. In addition, the continuous capsizing accidents of chemical transport vessels, a large number of sulfuric acid, cresol, kerosene, crude oil and other chemicals capsized into the river, further aggravating the water resources pollution of the Yangtze River. The fourth is solid waste pollution. Solid waste is a kind of solid residue which is discarded from various materials used in industrial manufacturing, construction, cooking, entertainment, agricultural production and other activities. As the untreated solid waste is washed by flood and leached by rain, all kinds of toxic substances can easily enter the water body and seriously pollute the water quality of the Yangtze River. The fifth is other pollutions. The dust and waste water discharged by industrial enterprises along the Yangtze River flow into the water body through direct falling or after rain washing. The surface runoff after rainfall carries pollutants from the atmosphere and soil into the water body, all of which will cause the pollution to the water quality of the Yangtze River.

### (III) **Sewage discharge scale in the Yangtze River Basin**

According to the *Annual Report on Environmental Statistics of 2012*, "the discharge of waste water in the Yangtze River Basin has exceeded 30 billion tons since 2007, which meant the sewage equivalent to the whole volume of Yellow River was discharged into the Yangtze River every year. The amount of waste water accepted by the Yangtze River Basin ranked the first among the seven major basins in China, accounting for nearly 40% of the national total, and the industrial wastewater discharge in the Yangtze River Delta alone accounted for more than 20% of the national total." During the 10 years from 2003 to 2012, the wastewater discharge of each region in the Yangtze River Economic Belt was on the rise on the whole, and the wastewater discharge in the lower reaches of the Yangtze River was significantly higher than that in the middle and upper reaches. At the same time, it shall be noted that the wastewater discharge in the middle and upper reaches of the Yangtze River has been increasing rapidly in recent years. According to the *Annual Report of Environmental Statistics of 2013*, "in recent years, due to the large inflow of water, the water quality of the mainstream of the Yangtze River was generally acceptable, but the pollution of urban river sections was relatively serious; the pollution of tributaries with relatively small flow was quite alarming. Taking the urban section of the Yangtze River mainstream as an example, the pollution zone along the shore has been expanding. In 1993, the polluted belt was 560 km long, and in 2003 it was 670 km, including more than 300 toxic pollutants. In terms of tributaries, the tributaries represented by the Taihu Lake Basin were eutrophicated, and the inferior class V water has long been existed."

Table 2 provides the basic situation of wastewater discharge, COD emission and ammonia nitrogen emission of provinces and cities in the Yangtze River Economic

**Table 2** Wastewater and pollutant discharge of Yangtze River Economic Belt in 2013

| Provinces and cities | | Total waste water discharge | | Total COD emission | | Total ammonia nitrogen emission | |
|---|---|---|---|---|---|---|---|
| | | 100 million tons | Proportion (%) | Ton | Proportion (%) | Ton | Proportion (%) |
| East | Shanghai | 222 963 | 7.41 | 235 624 | 2.75 | 45 755 | 4.31 |
| | Jiangsu | 594 359 | 19.74 | 1 148 888 | 13.39 | 147 429 | 13.90 |
| | Zhejiang | 419 120 | 13.92 | 755 113 | 8.80 | 107 489 | 10.13 |
| Total of east | | 1 236 442 | 41.06 | 2 139 625 | 24.94 | 300 673 | 28.34 |
| Central | Anhui | 266 234 | 8.84 | 902 684 | 10.52 | 103 328 | 9.74 |
| | Jiangxi | 207 138 | 6.88 | 734 470 | 8.56 | 88 827 | 8.37 |
| | Hunan | 307 227 | 10.20 | 1 249 012 | 14.56 | 157 704 | 14.87 |
| | Hubei | 294 054 | 9.77 | 1 058 215 | 12.34 | 124 856 | 11.77 |
| Total of central | | 1 074 653 | 35.69 | 3 944 381 | 45.98 | 474 715 | 44.75 |
| West | Sichuan | 307 648 | 10.22 | 1 231 965 | 14.36 | 137 036 | 12.92 |
| | Chongqing | 142 535 | 4.73 | 391 813 | 4.57 | 52 160 | 4.92 |
| | Yunnan | 156 583 | 5.20 | 542 227 | 6.32 | 58 049 | 5.47 |
| | Guizhou | 93 085 | 3.09 | 328 155 | 3.83 | 38 259 | 3.61 |
| Total of west | | 699 851 | 23.24 | 2 494 160 | 29.08 | 285 504 | 26.91 |
| Total of Yangtze River Economic Belt | | 3 010 946 | 43.30 | 8 578 166 | 36.46 | 1 060 892 | 43.19 |
| Whole state | | 6 954 433 | 100 | 23 527 201 | 100 | 2 456 553 | 100 |

*Note* The total proportion of the Yangtze River Economic Belt is the proportion to the whole State, and the rest is the proportion within the Yangtze River Economic Belt
*Source China Environmental Statistics Yearbook of 2014*

Belt in 2013. In terms of wastewater discharge, the proportion of Jiangsu Province was the largest in the Yangtze River Economic Belt and reached 19.74%. The discharge proportion of the eastern, central and western regions in the Yangtze River Economic Belt was 41.06%, 35.69% and 23.24% respectively, while the Yangtze River Economic Belt accounted for 43.30% of the national total. In terms of chemical oxygen demand (COD) emissions, the proportion of Hunan, Sichuan and Jiangsu ranked on the top and accounted for 14.56%, 14.36% and 13.39% of the Yangtze River Economic Belt, while the discharge of east, central and west regions accounted for 24.94%, 45.98% and 29.08% of the Yangtze River Economic Belt respectively, while the Yangtze River Economic Belt accounted for 36.36% of the national total. In terms of ammonia nitrogen emissions, the proportion of Hunan, Jiangsu and Sichuan ranked on the top and accounted for 14.87%, 13.9% and 12.92% of the Yangtze River Economic Belt, while the east, central and west regions accounted for 28.34%, 44.74% and 26.91% of the Yangtze River Economic Belt respectively, while the Yangtze River Economic Belt accounted for 43.19% of the national total. The proportion of wastewater discharge in the east, central and west regions was inversely related to the total COD and ammonia nitrogen emission, which indicated that the wastewater treatment status in the east region was better than that in the central and west regions.

The Yangtze River Basin, especially the middle and lower reaches of the Yangtze River Basin, is one of the basins with the highest population density, the largest economic activity intensity and the heaviest environmental pressure in China. The pollution of the lower reaches of the Yangtze River was more serious than that of the upper reaches, while that of the tributaries as more serious than that of the main stream. More than half of the lakes are in different degrees of eutrophication. Therefore, the level of urban sewage treatment in the Yangtze River Economic Belt needs to be further improved; various industrial parks, development zones and traditional industrial layout along the Yangtze River have structural pollution; high pollution industries such as chemical raw materials and chemical products manufacturing industry, paper and paper products industry, ferrous metal smelting and rolling processing industry, nonferrous metal smelting and rolling processing industry are too concentrated, therefore, it is necessary to make reasonable adjustment and strengthen governance in relevant provinces and cities. Agricultural pollution has a serious impact. According to the investigation, the total chemical oxygen demand, total phosphorus and total nitrogen entering Dongting Lake with agricultural source accounted for 51%, 86% and 65%, respectively. The flowing source pollution has great pressure on the water environment. The ship density in the waterway of the middle and lower reaches of the Yangtze River is high, and the transportation of dangerous goods is increasing year by year, which highlights the risk of water pollution accidents; due to the influence of water regime, water quality and human activities in the main stream of the Yangtze River and its main tributaries, the ecological security level of Poyang Lake, Dongting Lake and other large lakes has declined, and the overall water quality has been on the decline. However, the water quality of Taihu Lake, Dianchi Lake and Chaohu Lake, which are under the national governance, is so limited. In a word, the ecological deterioration of the Yangtze River

Basin is the result of the imbalance between the socio-economic development of the Yangtze River Economic Belt and the Yangtze River Basin and the ecological environment. How to carry out comprehensive and reasonable governance will directly affect the ecological environment security of the Yangtze River Basin and even that of the whole state.

## 3 Ecological Environment Governance of the Yangtze River Economic Belt

All problems of population structure, resources, energy and ecological environment will become the restricting factors in the process of medium and long-term economic development of China. The medium and long-term sustainable development can be realized only by overcoming the above constraints. The ecological environment of the Yangtze River Economic Belt is related to the interests of the whole region and the whole state. In the critical period of strengthening the construction of the Yangtze River Economic Belt and the "golden waterway" of the Yangtze River, the economic development and ecological environment protection shall be balanced for further development of the Yangtze River Economic Belt. In the "12th Five Year Plan", the state, provinces and cities have formulated major pollutant reduction and control objectives. The following will summarize the pollutant emission reduction objectives during the "12th Five Year Plan" and measures and achievements of water pollution control in the whole state, various provinces and cities in recent 2014.

### *3.1 Main Objectives of Water Pollution Prevention and Control in the Yangtze River Basin During the 12th Five Year Plan Period*

In 2012, the national "12th Five Year Plan" put forward the overall objective of energy conservation and emission reduction, and the relevant indicators were distributed to all provinces and cities in China step by step. China's overall objectives include: the energy consumption per 10000 yuan of GDP will be reduced to 0.869 tons of standard coal by 2015, 16% lower than that of 1034 tons of standard coal in 2010; during the 12th Five Year Plan, 670 million tons of standard coal was saved; in 2015, the total emission of chemical oxygen demand and sulfur dioxide was controlled at 23.476 million tons and 20.864 million tons, respectively, 8% less than the annual average in 2010; the total emissions of nitrogen oxides and nitrogen oxides were controlled at 2.38 million tons and 20.462 million tons, respectively, 10% lower than that in 2010. In 2015, the proportion of non-fossil energy in primary energy reached 11.4%, the water consumption per unit industrial added value was decreased by

30%, the resource output rate was increased by 15%, the comprehensive utilization rate of industrial solid waste reached 72%, and the urban sewage treatment rate and the harmless treatment rate of domestic garbage reached 85% and 80%, respectively, while the policy guidance of reasonable control of total energy consumption was followed. Under the unified deployment of the State Council, all the abovementioned indicators have been broken down to all provinces, municipalities and autonomous regions in China. The State Council requires all provinces, municipalities and autonomous regions to contain the excessive growth of high energy consumption and high pollution industries, make energy conservation and emission reduction as the focus of macro-control, as the breakthrough and important measures for adjusting the economic structure and changing the mode of growth. According to the requirements of the State Council, each province and autonomous region has formulated energy conservation and emission reduction objectives during the 12th Five Year Plan, issued relevant policies and measures, and put them into practice.

With regard to the Yangtze River Basin, the Ministry of Environmental Protection and the National Development and Reform Commission jointly issued a notice to require relevant ministries and municipalities to implement the *Water Pollution Prevention and Control Plan for the Middle and Lower Reaches of the Yangtze Ri*ver (2011–2015) in November 2011, hereinafter referred to as the *Plan*. The overall objectives put forward in the plan are: further optimization of industrial structure and layout, deepening of pollution control, continuous reduction of total discharge of water pollutants, further improvement of water environment management level, obvious achievements in heavy metal pollution control, stable quality of drinking water sources, stable and improved water environment quality, and eutrophication trend of critical lakes and reservoirs under control, the reduced eutrophication degree of the Yangtze River Estuary and adjacent sea areas, continuous improvement of environmental quality of the coastal waters, and gradually increasing the ecological security level of the river basin and estuarine coastal zone. The total control objective in terms of volume is: the total control objective in terms of volume for main pollutants in the basin and the provinces (districts and cities) within the basin shall be determined separately according to the National "12th Five Year Plan" Total Volume Control Plan for Main Pollutants, in combination with the overall demand for water environment quality improvement and opinions on limiting the total volume of pollutant discharge. Among them, the specific water quality objectives are: among the 48 assessment sections, the water quality of 15 sections shall reach class II, that of 20 sections shall reach class III, that for 7 shall reach class IV, and that of 6 shall reach class V. The water quality qualification rate of marine functional zones and coastal environmental functional zones shall reach 40% above, and the ecological security of coastal waters can be effectively guaranteed.

At the same time, the *Plan* also determined 837 specific backbone projects and investment of 45.981 billion yuan during the 12th Five Year Plan period. Among them, there are 343 industrial pollution prevention and control projects with an investment of 9.288 billion yuan; 284 selected construction projects for urban sewage treatment facilities (including pipe network improvement and sludge disposal), with an additional daily sewage treatment capacity of 8.9735 million tons and an investment of 20.746 billion yuan (including 175 projects under construction, with an additional daily sewage treatment capacity of 6.2865 million tons and an investment of 14.852 billion yuan), and 78 optional projects for urban sewage treatment facilities and equipment with a total of 3.4767 million tons sewage treatment capacity being added and an investment of 9.668 billion yuan; 210 projects for pollution prevention and control in key areas, with an investment of 15.947 billion yuan. If classification is carried out according to the control area: 260 projects in the Yangtze River mainstream control area with an investment of 15.817 billion yuan and with an estimated reduction of 227,000 tons of chemical oxygen demand and 28000 tons of ammonia nitrogen; 42 projects in the Yangtze River Estuary control area, with an investment of 5.189 billion yuan and estimated reduction of 51,000 tons of chemical oxygen demand and 9,000 tons of ammonia nitrogen; 196 projects in Dongting Lake control area, with an investment of 12.057 billion yuan and estimated reduction of 234,000 tons of chemical oxygen demand; in the control area of the middle and lower reaches of Hanjiang River, 119 projects with an investment of 5.873 billion yuan and estimated reduction of 99,000 tons of chemical oxygen demand and 11000 tons of ammonia nitrogen; 220 projects in Poyang Lake control area, with an investment of 7.045 billion yuan and estimated reduction of 146,000 tons of chemical oxygen demand and 17,000 tons of ammonia nitrogen.

## *3.2 Main Objectives of Water Pollution Prevention and Control in Provinces and Cities of the Yangtze River Economic Belt During the 12th Five Year Plan*

With the relevant indicators proposed in the national "12th Five Year Plan" being discomposed into all provinces, municipalities and autonomous regions, the overall objectives and specific constraint indicators of energy consumption per unit GDP, chemical oxygen demand, ammonia nitrogen, sulfur dioxide and total nitrogen oxides of each region during the 12th Five Year Plan period are formulated according to the requirements of the State Council. Table 3 shows the targets and indicators related to water pollution control during the 12th Five Year Plan in 9 provinces and 2 cities within the Yangtze River Economic Belt.

**Table 3** Main objectives of water pollution control in the Yangtze River Economic Belt during the 12th Five Year Plan

| Regions | Specific objectives |
|---|---|
| Shanghai | By 2015, the total amount of chemical oxygen demand, ammonia nitrogen, sulfur dioxide and nitrogen oxide in the city will be controlled within the national indicators, that is, 10.0, 12.9, 13.7 and 17.5% less than those in 2010. The ammonia nitrogen was included in the total *amount control index on the basis of chemical oxygen demand while considering the emission control of total nitrogen and total phosphorus*, and the total phosphorus and volatile organic compounds will be decreased further. In order to ensure the safety of drinking water and improve the water quality, efforts shall be made to control the total amount of water pollutants and comprehensively promote the treatment and protection of water environment. By 2015, the safety of drinking water will be basically guaranteed, and the qualification rate of centralized drinking water sources will reach 90% above; both the urban sewage treatment rate and the sludge treatment rate of sewage treatment plants will reach 85% above, the reduction rate of per capita domestic waste treatment capacity will be higher than 20%, and the harmless treatment rate of living garbage will be higher than 95% |
| Jiangsu | By 2015, the total emissions of chemical oxygen demand, ammonia nitrogen, sulfur dioxide and nitrogen oxides in the province will be controlled at 112,8000 tons, 140,400 tons, 925,000 tons and 1,214,000 tons respectively, which will be reduced by 11.9%, 12.9%, 14.8% and 17.5% respectively compared with 2010. We need to implement key projects for pollutant emission reduction, promote the implementation of urban sewage treatment projects, improve the urban sewage collection pipe network, improve the sewage collection rate, upgrade the existing facilities, strengthen nitrogen and phosphorus removal, and vigorously promote the sludge treatment and disposal of sewage treatment plants and the recycling of tail water. The water quality of centralized drinking water sources in cities, counties and towns will reach 100% and 95% respectively. The proportion of surface water quality inferior to class V will be 15%, and the proportion of surface water better than Class III will be more than 50% |
| Zhejiang | By 2015, the total emissions of chemical oxygen demand, ammonia nitrogen, sulfur dioxide and nitrogen oxides will be controlled at 746,000 tons, 103,600 tons, 593,000 tons and 699,000 tons respectively. The water consumption per 10,000 yuan of GDP will be decreased to 78 $m^3$, and the gross output value of unit construction land will be increased by 20% compared with 2010. The environmental quality of the whole province will be significantly improved, and the comprehensive index of ecological environment will be remained at the forefront of the state. The proportion of sections above province controlled level with water quality inferior to class V in the eight major water systems, canals and major lakes and reservoirs shall be controlled within 5%, and the proportion reaching or better than Class III will be more than 75%; the water quality of plain river network will be significantly improved; the water quality of centralized drinking water sources in cities above county level will be more than 90%; the water quality of coastal waters will be kept stable |

(continued)

**Table 3** (continued)

| Regions | Specific objectives |
|---|---|
| Anhui | By 2015, the total emissions of chemical oxygen demand, ammonia nitrogen, sulfur dioxide and nitrogen oxides in the whole province will be reduced by 7.2%, 9.9%, 6.1% and 9.8% respectively compared with 2010. The discharge of major pollutants will be effectively controlled, prominent environmental problems will be gradually solved, environmental quality in key areas and urban and rural areas will be improved, and the deterioration trend of ecological environment will be basically curbed. The total phosphorus emission in Chaohu Lake Basin will be decreased by 18.0% compared with that in 2010. The proportion of national control section (point position) inferior to class V water quality will be less than 20%, provincial control section (point) will be less than 10%; the proportion of state-controlled sections (point) with water quality better than Class III will be more than 40%, and province-controlled section (point position) will be more than 60%. The comprehensive control of water environment in Huaihe River Basin and Chaohu Lake Basin will achieve actual results. The water quality qualification rate of centralized drinking water sources will be more than 95% |
| Jiangxi | By 2015, the total emission of chemical oxygen demand in the whole province will be controlled at 732,000 tons, 5.8% lower than that in 2010; the total emission of ammonia nitrogen will be controlled at 85,200 tons, 9.8% lower than that in 2010; the total emission of sulfur dioxide will be controlled at 549,000 tons, 7.5% lower than that in 2010; and the total emission of nitrogen oxides will be controlled at 542,000 tons, 6.9% lower than that in 2010. The water quality of the monitored sections of the main river in the province is stabilized at about 82%; the qualification rate of water quality at the monitored points of Poyang Lake can reach 70%; the water quality qualification rate of the sections at the provincial and municipal boundaries can reach 80%. By 2015, the total amount of major pollutants discharged in the whole province will be effectively controlled, the quality of key river basins and regions will be maintained in good condition, the water quality of urban and rural drinking water sources will be improved, and important ecological functions will be achieved. The ecological functions of important ecological function reserves and nature reserves can be maintained with stability |
| Hubei | By 2015, the total emissions of chemical oxygen demand and ammonia nitrogen in the province will be controlled within 1,041,000 tons and 120,000 tons, respectively, 7.4% and 9.7% lower than that of 1,124,000 tons and 132,900 tons in 2010; the total emissions of sulfur dioxide and nitrogen oxides will be controlled within 637,000 tons and 586,000 tons, respectively, 8.3% and 7.2% lower than 695,000 tons and 631,000 tons in 2010. The proportion of province-controlled sections with class III will reach 86% to realize that the water in rivers can be drinkable, fish and shrimp can survive in the small rivers and streams, and the in inland lakes and rivers can be eliminated with odor and water can be restored transparency, so that safety of drinking water sources in urban and rural areas can be ensured, and the problem of drinking water safety in rural areas can be basically solved |

(continued)

**Table 3** (continued)

| Regions | Specific objectives |
|---|---|
| Hunan | By 2015, the total emissions of chemical oxygen demand and ammonia nitrogen in the province will be controlled within 1,244,000 tons and 152,900 tons, respectively, 7.2% and 9.8% lower than that of 1,341,000 tons and 169,500 tons in 2010; the total emissions of sulfur dioxide and nitrogen oxides will be controlled within 651,000 tons and 550,000 tons, respectively, 8.3% and 9.0% lower than 710,000 tons and 604,000 tons in 2010. The total amount of heavy metal lead emission will be controlled at 46.0 tons, 15% lower than 54.04 tons in 2010. The municipal sewage treatment rate will reach 85%, the qualification rate of water quality in province-controlled sections will reach 95% according to the functional area, and the water quality qualification rate of the Xiangjiang, Ziyuan, Yuanli trunk streams and the first-class tributaries will reach 95% |
| Chongqing | By 2015, the total emissions of chemical oxygen demand and ammonia nitrogen will be reduced by 7.2% and 8.8% respectively compared with those in 2010, and the total emissions of sulfur dioxide and nitrogen oxides will be reduced by 7.1% and 6.9% respectively. The water consumption per unit of industrial added value will be decreased by 30%, and the utilization rate of industrial solid waste will be increased steadily to 82%. On the premise that the upstream water quality of Yangtze River, Jialing River and Wujiang River meets the class II national surface water quality standard, the water quality of main control sections can generally meet the class II standard, the qualification rate of water environment functional area of the monitored section in secondary rivers will reach 85%, the water quality qualification rate of the urban centralized drinking water source area will reach 100%, and the main index qualification rate of the centralized drinking water source area in the construction town will be up to 95%. The environmental infrastructure will be basically improved. The centralized treatment rate of urban domestic sewage will reach 90%, the centralized treatment rate of urban domestic sewage will reach 75%, and the disposal rate of rural domestic sewage will reach 25%. The harmless disposal of sludge will be basically achieved |
| Sichuan | By 2015, the total emissions of chemical oxygen demand and ammonia nitrogen in the province will be controlled within 1,231,000 tons and 133,100 tons, respectively, 7.0% and 8.6% lower than 1,324,000 tons and 145,600 tons in 2010; the total emissions of sulfur dioxide and nitrogen oxides will be controlled within 844,000 tons and 577,000 tons, respectively, 9.0% and 6.9% lower than 927,000 tons and 620,000 tons in 2010. The proportion of state-controlled and province-controlled sections with water quality better than Class III will reach 85% and the proportion of water quality inferior to Class V will be controlled within 5%. Continue to focus on the strategic objective of building an ecological province and an ecological barrier in the upper reaches of the Yangtze River and strive to solve the problem of ecological degradation in critical areas |

(continued)

**Table 3** (continued)

| Regions | Specific objectives |
|---|---|
| Guizhou | By 2015, the total amount of chemical oxygen demand and sulfur dioxide emissions in the province will be controlled at 327,000 tons and 1,062,000 tons, respectively, 6.0% and 8.6% lower than 348,000 tons and 1,162,000 tons in 2010; the total emissions of ammonia nitrogen and nitrogen oxides will be controlled at 37,200 tons and 445,000 tons, respectively, 7.7% and 9.8% lower than 40,300 tons and 493,000 tons in 2010. The centralized treatment rate of urban domestic sewage will reach 95%, and the harmless treatment rate of municipal solid waste and feces will reach 90%. The proportion of state-controlled sections with surface water quality inferior to Class V is less than 20%. Gradually carry out pollution prevention and remediation of heavy metal contaminated sites and soil. The proportion of centralized drinking water sources in cities and towns with qualified water will be up to 90%, the qualification rate of centralized drinking water sources in central cities will be stabilized at 100%, and more than 80% in other cities and towns (county-level cities) |
| Yunnan | By 2015, the total chemical oxygen demand and sulfur dioxide emissions in the whole province will be controlled at 529,000 tons and 676,000 tons respectively, 6.2% lower than that of 564,000 tons and 704,000 tons in 2010. The total emissions of ammonia nitrogen and nitrogen oxides will be respectively controlled at 55,100 tons and 490,000 tons, 8.1% and 5.8% lower than the 60,000 tons and 520,000 tons in 2010. The water quality of six rivers and nine plateau lakes shall be further improved, and heavy metal pollution shall be effectively controlled. By 2015, on the whole, the inferior class V water bodies will be eliminated in nine plateau lakes, the emission of major pollutants will be reduced by more than 10%, and the main water environment quality indicators will be significantly improved. The qualification rate of water environmental function for state-controlled and province controlled sections of six major rivers in the province can be stabilized at more than 70%, and the proportion of state-controlled and province-controlled sections with water quality inferior to class V will be less than 20% |

*Source 12th Five Year Plan for Energy Conservation and Emission Reduction* of all provinces and cities

### *3.3 Main Measures and Effects of Water Pollution Control in Provinces and Cities in Yangtze River Economic Belt in 2014*

In 2014, certain effects have been achieved in 9 provinces and 2 cities in the Yangtze River Economic Belt for water pollution control through strengthening responsibility, supervision, formulating and adjusting support and guidance policies, and increasing investment in environmental protection. Since 9 provinces and 2 cities of the Yangtze River Economic Belt are located in the upper, middle and lower reaches of the Yangtze River Basin and the eastern, central and western regions, the measures for water pollution control in different regions represent different characteristics. According to the environmental status bulletins released by various localities, the main measures and achievements of water pollution control in provinces and cities of the Yangtze River Economic Belt in 2014 are summarized for eastern, central and western regions.

(I) **Main measures and effects of water pollution control in the eastern region of the Yangtze River Economic Belt**

1. Main measures and effects of water pollution control in Shanghai

In 2014, relying on the three-year environmental protection action plan, Shanghai steadily promoted the construction of emission reduction projects such as sewage treatment plants, industrial enterprises and agricultural sources, and accelerated the completion and operation of these projects to give full play to the benefits of emission reduction. Establishing the statistical data early warning mechanism to scientifically calculate the new increment and emission of pollutants; improve the construction of emission monitoring system, further implement the responsibility of enterprises and government supervision, standardize the internal self-monitoring, and increase the publicity of pollution source monitoring information; strengthen the construction of pollution reduction assessment system, and implement the system of daily inspection, regular assessment and notification of pollution reduction; strengthen and standardize the operation and management of emission reduction facilities, deepen the optimization and scheduling mechanism of sewage transportation, and constantly broaden the new road of management and emission reduction; continue to strengthen the inspection and guidance for key emission reduction enterprises through the preparation of on-site verification manual for emission reduction to ensure the efficient operation of pollution reduction facilities.

At the same time, in the past five years, the investment in environmental protection of the whole city has been increasing, accounting for about 3% of the GDP of the whole city. In 2014, the 70 billion yuan was invested in environmental protection. Among them, 27.179 billion yuan was invested in urban environmental infrastructure construction, 26.014 billion yuan in pollution source prevention and control, 529 million yuan in ecological protection and construction, 4.245 billion yuan in rural environmental protection, 456 million yuan in construction of environmental management capacity, 8.883 billion yuan in operation cost of environmental protection facilities, and 2.685 billion yuan in circular economy and other aspects.

In recent years, Shanghai has been increasing its efforts to cut and control pollution. Under the background of the continuous expansion of economic aggregate, water pollution control and protection have achieved certain results. Approved by the Ministry of Environmental Protection, the emissions of chemical oxygen demand, hydrogen and nitrogen, sulfur dioxide and nitrogen oxides in Shanghai are reduced by 4.78%, 2.57%, 12.81% and 12.52% respectively on the basis of 2013. The annual emission reduction targets are successfully completed, and the "12th Five Year" emission reduction targets as assigned by the state to Shanghai are completed one year ahead of the schedule.

In terms of water quality, the water quality of the backbone rivers in 2014 was basically the same compared with 2013; the environment quality of surface water continued to be improved, but the nitrogen and phosphorus pollution problem has become increasingly prominent, which has become one of the key factors limiting the further improvement of water environment quality in the city. In 2014, main water sections with water quality of class III accounted for 24.7%, that of class IV accounted for 16.9% and that of class V accounted for 9.1%, and that of inferior class V accounted for 49.3%. The main pollution indicators were ammonia nitrogen and total phosphorus; the permanganate index and average concentration of ammonia nitrogen in main rivers were 4.55 and 2.4 mg/L, which were 4.2 and 5% lower than those in 2013; the average concentration of total phosphorus was 0.313 mg/L, which was basically the same as that in 2013. The water quality of rivers in 2014 was improved compared with that in 2013. Among them, the water quality of 7 sections of the Yangtze River Estuary reached class III; compared with 2013, the water quality was slightly improved, and the concentration of hydrogen and nitrogen was decreased by 41.7%.

The system construction of environmental protection in Shanghai is also taking the lead in the country. In October 2014, the municipal government issued the *Guidance on Accelerating the Third-party Governance of Environment Pollution in the City*, and the Municipal Environmental Protection Bureau printed and issued the proposal of pilot works. The main contents include: focus on strengthening the responsibility of pollution control, strengthening the environmental supervision mechanism, formulating support and guidance policies, cultivating market players, promoting industry standardization and self-discipline, promoting and enforcing the implementation of third-party governance of environmental pollution, and promoting the market-oriented mechanism transformation from " those who created pollution shall clear it up "to "those who created pollution shall pay for the third governance". Since January 1, 2015, in order to further play the role of sewage charges in promoting pollution control and improve environmental quality, according to the national requirements and the needs of comprehensive deepening reform in Shanghai, the adjustment plan for the collection standard of sewage charges has been issued, and the sewage charge standard of four major pollutants, namely sulfur dioxide, nitrogen oxide, chemical oxygen demand and ammonia nitrogen are raised to 8, 9, 5 and 6 yuan/kg, and all five types of heavy metal pollutants including lead, mercury, chromium, cadmium and metal like arsenic in the sewage are fully implemented with charges; implement differentiated charging policies according to different emission concentration, total discharge amount and type of industry.

2. Main measures and effects of water pollution control in Jiangsu Province

In 2014, Jiangsu Province conscientiously implemented the 12th Five Year Plan for water pollution prevention and control of key national river basins, and taken a series of water pollution control measures. First of all, the prevention and control of water pollution in the Huaihe River and the Yangtze River shall be strengthened with the completion rate of 245 projects listed in the plan up to 70.6%. Organize the renovation of 12 key tributaries into the river. The assessment results of the pollution control in the Huai River and Yangtze River basins were excellent and ranked on the top of the state. Secondly, 1435 water pollutant reduction projects were completed, and the urban sewage treatment capacity was increased by 800,000 $m^3$/day, the trunk pipe network of 2,500 km for sewage collection was built, and the annual capacity of urban sewage treatment plants reached 3.83 billion cubic meters; thirdly, the investigation and evaluation of pollution sources involving heavy metal emissions in the whole province were carried out to further understand the discharge status of heavy metal pollutants, improve the prevention and control level for heavy metal, and seriously organize the implementation of national and provincial comprehensive prevention and control plans for heavy metal pollution, with the completion rate of key projects of 90.9% and 85.7% respectively; fourthly, completed a new round of comprehensive rectification of lead-acid batteries and renewable lead industry, shut down and eliminated 62 lead related enterprises in the province; fifthly, strengthened the special renovation efforts for environmental protection in coastal chemical industry parks, invested 5.85 billion yuan in the province, shut down 53 chemical enterprises, eliminated 86 chemical projects, renovated 199 enterprises by stopping the production, renovated 355 enterprises with time limit, and implemented "one pipeline for one enterprise" and exposed pipeline management for 281 enterprises, completed 1360 "three wastes" transformation projects, relocated 1,771 environmentally sensitive objects, and investigated and dealt with 192 cases of environmental violation; sixthly, strengthened the comprehensive improvement and ecological protection of the rural environment, comprehensively launched the pilot work of "covering and netting" comprehensive improvement of rural environmental in the whole province, built more than 200 sets of centralized sewage treatment facilities, more than 3000 sets of decentralized, micro power and power free sewage treatment facilities, and laid more than 3000 km of sewage pipe network.

In 2014, the total amount of waste water discharged in the province was 6.012 billion tons, and the total emissions of chemical oxygen demand, ammonia nitrogen, sulfur dioxide and nitrogen oxide were 1.1 million tons, 142,500 tons, 904,700 tons and 1.2326 million tons, respectively, which were 4.25%, 3.32%, 3.92% and 7.88% lower than those in 2013. The annual objectives are all over-fulfilled. The emission reduction tasks of chemical oxygen demand and sulfur dioxide in the 12th Five Year Plan were completed one year ahead of the schedule.

In 2014, the environmental quality of surface water in the whole province was slightly polluted. Among the 83 state-controlled sections listed in the national surface water environmental quality monitoring network, the sections with class III water quality accounted for 45.8%, that of class IV–V accounted for 53.0%, and that of inferior class V accounted for 1.2%. Compared with 2013, the proportion of sections to class III was almost the same, and the proportion of sections inferior to class V was decreased by 1.2% points. The average annual concentration of permanganate index in state-controlled section was 4.0 mg/L, which was 4.8% lower than that in 2013; the concentration of ammonia nitrogen was 0.51 mg/L, which was almost the same as that in 2013.

In 2014, the water quality of the main stream of the Yangtze River in Jiangsu Province was good, and the water quality of 10 monitored sections met the class III standard, and the water quality remained stable compared with 2013. The water quality of the main tributaries into the river was slightly polluted. Among the 45 controlled sections of 41 main tributaries, the sections of class III, IV–V and inferior class V accounted for 54.6%, 31.8% and 13.6%, respectively. The main pollutants affecting the water quality are ammonia nitrogen and total phosphorus. Compared with 2013, the proportion of sections at class III was decreased by 9.0% points, and the proportion of sections inferior to class V was increased by 4.5% points. In 2014, among the 9 sections for assessment and appraisal listed in the *National Water Pollution Prevention and Control Plan for the Middle and Lower Reaches of the Yangtze River (2011–2015)*, the annual average concentrations of 5 sections was up to the assessment targets, and 3 of the 4 sections satisfied the target requirements.

3. Main measures and effects of water pollution control in Zhejiang Province

Since 2014, Zhejiang Province has been carrying out the "Five-water Treatment" in the whole province, including sewage treatment, flood prevention, waterlogging water drainage, water supply protection and water saving. Water governance is regarded as an important content for deepening reform in an all-round way and reform project with key breakthroughs in Zhejiang Province. The "Five-water treatment" will be implemented step by step, with a timetable of three years, five years and seven years. Among them, outstanding problems have been solved in 2014–2016 and obvious results have been achieved; from 2014 to 2018, problems shall be basically solved and whole improvement shall be achieved; from 2014 to 2020, there shall be basically no problem and qualitative change can be achieved. In terms of specific measures, the first is to strengthen the construction of environmental infrastructure. In 2014, 61 new sewage treatment facilities in towns were added, 21 sewage treatment facilities were upgraded to grade A, 3130.7 km of urban sewage pipe network was added, and the sewage treatment capacity of cities above county level reached 9.401 million tons/day, and the sewage treatment rate was up to 89.1%. Secondly, industrial pollution control shall be thoroughly implemented. Since 2011, Zhejiang Province has carried out rectification and upgrading actions for heavy pollution and high energy consumption industries by focusing on six industries including lead-acid battery, electroplating, printing and dyeing, tanning and chemical industry. By 2014, more than 8500 heavily polluted enterprises in the province have been shut down and all straw pulp production lines and monosodium glutamate fermentation sections have been eliminated.

In 2014, the emissions of chemical oxygen demand, hydrogen nitrogen, sulfur dioxide and nitrogen oxides were reduced by 3.94%, 4.0%, 3.25% and 8.65% respectively on the basis of 2013, which successfully over-fulfilled the annual emission reduction targets. In 2014, the overall water quality of Zhejiang Province was basically good, but the pollution of plain river network was serious. The overall water quality of the main stream is basically good, and water quality of 63.8% of the sections reached or was better than Class III surface water standard. The proportion of class V and inferior class V has decreased by 2.3% points, which meant the water environment was improving. The water quality of the eight major water systems in Zhejiang Province was above the class III standard; the class I–III water quality of Qiantang River was 74.5%, which was 4.3% higher than that in 2013; the water quality of Wenzhou Aojiang River was class II to inferior class V. The water section with quality of class I–III of Ningbo Yongjiang River accounted for 50%. The Yongjiang River was slightly polluted. The Jinghang Canal and plain river network was still seriously polluted, and the water quality was mainly class IV–V and class III–inferior class V. In addition, the water quality of the lake was relatively poor, of which the water quality of West Lake was class III, that of Dongqian Lake was class IV, and that of Jianhu and Nanhu was class V. Most of the groundwater quality in Zhejiang Province was still in the natural state and has not been polluted.

(II) **Main measures and effects of water pollution control in the middle of Yangtze River Economic Belt**

1. Main measures and effects of water pollution control in Anhui Province

In 2014, Anhui Province has taken early warning, bulletin, and limited approval of EIA and so on focusing on the water pollution prevention in critical basins to effectively promote the implementation of the plan in accordance with the 12th Five Year Plan. Comprehensive environmental improvement was carried out for 8 rivers with serious pollution. By the end of 2014, 247 of the 346 projects listed in the plan in the Huaihe River Basin have been completed, 10 commissioned, 45 under construction, 34 in preliminary preparation, and 10 not started; among the 167 planning projects in Chaohu Basin, 76 have been completed, 17 commissioned, 53 under construction, 17 in preparation, and 4 not started; 70 of the 74 planning projects in the Yangtze River Basin have been completed, 2 under construction and 2 under preliminary preparation.

In the construction of urban sewage treatment facilities, 2,431 km of new sewage pipe network has been built and reconstructed; 16 urban sewage treatment plants have been built and expanded; 11 sewage treatment plants have been upgraded; 166 decentralized sewage treatment facilities in the industrial parks have been built. By the end of 2014, 118 urban sewage treatment plants had been put into operation, with a daily capacity of 5.0129 million tons, an average operating load over 95%, and a centralized treatment rate of urban sewage up to 90.19%.

In 2014, the total emission of chemical oxygen demand in the whole province was 885,600 tons, 1.90% lower than that in 2013. The total amount of ammonia nitrogen emission was 100,500 tons, 2.74% lower than that in 2013. The total emission of sulfur dioxide was 493,000 tons, 1.67% lower than that in 2013. The total emission of NOx was 807,300 tons, 6.53% lower than that in 2013. The total emission reduction targets for the year of chemical oxygen demand, ammonia nitrogen, sulfur dioxide and nitrogen oxides were all over-fulfilled.

In 2014, the water quality of the overall surface in the province was slightly polluted. Among 246 surface water monitoring sections (points), 67.9% of them are of class I-III, and 9.8% of them are inferior class V. Compared with 2013, there was no significant change in the overall water quality of the whole province, and the number of water quality sections (points) of class I to III and inferior to class V was almost remained stable.

The overall water quality of the Yangtze River Basin under the jurisdiction of the province is good. Among the 70 sections of 39 rivers monitored, 81.4% are of class I–III with excellent or good quality, and 1.4% are of inferior class V with severe pollution. The overall water quality of the main stream of the Yangtze River is excellent. Among the 20 sections, 15 sections are of class II and 5 sections are of class III. The overall water quality of the tributaries of the Yangtze River is good. Among the 38 tributaries monitored, the water quality of 21 tributaries is excellent, that of 7 is good, that of 5 is mild polluted, that of 4 is moderately polluted and that of 1 is severely polluted. Compared with 2013, the overall water quality of the Yangtze River Basin under the jurisdiction of the province has no obvious change, the proportion of sections with class I–III water quality has been decreased by 1.5% points, and the proportion of sections with inferior class V water quality has been remained unchanged.

In terms of water resources protection system, Anhui Province officially launched the provincial and cross city water environment ecological compensation mechanism along the Ta-pieh Mountains in 2014. At the same time, the pilot work of water environment ecological compensation of Xin'an River has been steadily promoted. By the end of 2014, the national and two provincial subsidies have reached 1.79 billion yuan with the investment for the pilot project of 6.07 billion yuan. The water quality of Xin'an River was under well control and kept excellent.

2. Main measures and effects of water pollution control in Jiangxi Province

In 2014, in order to realize the goal of "upgrading development, speeding up the well-off society, green rising, and rejuvenating Jiangxi Province through action", Jiangxi Province continuously strengthened environmental protection, and actively carried out water pollution reduction and control while maintaining sustainable and accelerated economic development. The first was to strengthen the environmental protection of drinking water sources, and to evaluate the environmental conditions of 138 centralized drinking water sources in 11 districts and cities of the province. The assessment results showed that the water quality qualification rate of 31 cities above prefecture level was 100%, and that of 107 cities below prefecture level was generally good, and the water quality qualification rate was 96%. Second was to continuously carry out the work of the *Water Pollution Prevention and Control Plan for the Middle and Lower Reaches of the Yangtze River* (2011–2015). In October 2014, the Ministry of Environmental Protection issued the *Notice on the Assessment Results of the Implementation of the Special Plan for Water Pollution Prevention and Control in Key River Basins in 2013*, which showed that all the eight sections assessed in Jiangxi Province were up to the standard, with the qualification rate of 100%, and the overall performance was good. A total of 2.03 billion yuan of environmental protection funds were invested in the province. 49 national emission reduction projects with letter of responsibility were completed with the investment of 8.15 billion yuan. 385 provincial key projects were fully completed with 3 billion yuan invested. 1173 km of pipeline network were newly built, reconstructed and maintained. The actual influent concentration of 79 urban sewage treatment plants was significantly increased compared with that of the previous year. Among them, the influent concentration of 41 sewage treatment plants was increased by 50%. The new sewage treatment capacity of 663,000 tons/day for the whole province was increased.

In 2014, the total amount of wastewater discharged in the province was 2082.89 million tons, an increase of 11.51 million tons or 0.56% over the previous year. The discharge of industrial wastewater was 648.56 million tons, a decrease of 33.74 million tons or 4.95% lower than the previous year; the discharge of industrial wastewater accounted for 31.14% of the total discharge. The discharge of urban domestic sewage was 1437.79 million tons, an increase of 44.62 million tons or 3.22% over the previous year, accounting for 68.69% of the total discharge. The emissions of chemical oxygen demand, ammonia nitrogen, sulfur dioxide and nitrogen oxides in the province were 720,100 tons, 86,000 tons, 534,400 tons and 540,100 tons, respectively, which were 1.96%, 3.20%, 4.18% and 5.31% lower than that of the previous year. The objective of annual emission reduction of the four pollutants has been already overfulfilled.

In 2014, the surface water quality of the whole province was good, and the water quality of important river sections has been improved steadily. The proportion of sections (points) of class I–III was 80.9%. Among them, the water quality of Xiuhe River and Dongjiang River was excellent, while that Ganjiang River, Fuhe River, Xinjiang River, Raohe River, Yangtze River, Yuanshui River and Pingshui River was good. The proportion of monitored points in lakes and reservoirs for class I–III was 60.0%. The water quality of Tuolin Lake and Xiannv Lake was excellent, and the water quality of Biyang Lake was slightly polluted with the main pollutants of total phosphorus and total ammonia.

3. Main measures and effects of water pollution control in Hubei Province

Located in the middle reaches of the Yangtze River, the water basin in Hubei Province is wide and the pollution control is difficult. In 2014, Hubei Province formulated the Regulations on *Prevention and Control of Water Pollution in Hubei Province*, which was implemented from July 1st of the same year. Local water pollutant discharge standards that are stricter than the national standards are formulated for environmentally sensitive areas, ecologically vulnerable areas and areas with insufficient water environment capacity and total water pollutant discharge control was implemented. In order to promote the water pollution governance of key river basins, the National Development and Reform Commission issued the investment plan within the central budget of Hubei Province in 2014, in which 14 water pollution control projects in Hubei Province have been launched with sewage treatment capacity of 6,700 tons/day and garbage treatment capacity of 296.5 tons/day as well as the total investment of 260 million yuan including the investment of 40 million yuan arranged in 2014.

In 2014, the proportion of sections up to class I–III of the main rivers in Hubei Province was 86.7%, with a year-on-year decrease of 0.3%. The proportion of sections with water quality inferior to class V was 5.1%, which remained unchanged on a year-on-year basis, and the overall water quality was stabilized in good condition. The water quality of the main stream of the Yangtze River and the main stream of the Han River was excellent, and the water quality of the tributaries of the Yangtze River and the Han River was generally good. The water quality of 75.0% of the main lakes and reservoirs met or was better than Class III, with a year-on-year decrease of 3.1%. The proportion of water basins with water quality inferior to class V was 3.1%, with a year-on-year decrease of 3.2%. The overall water quality was remained good.

Among the monitored sections of main rivers, 86.7% of the sections with good quality are satisfactory to class I–III, 8.2% with poor quality are satisfactory to class IV and V, and 5.1% are seriously polluted with water quality of inferior class V. The main pollution indicators of rivers are total phosphorus, chemical oxygen demand and five-day biochemical oxygen demand. Compared with 2013, the water quality of main rivers has been remained stable. Among the main lakes and reservoirs, 75.0% of the main lakes and reservoirs with good water quality are satisfactory to class I–III, 21.9% with poor quality to class IV and V, and 3.1% are seriously polluted with water quality of inferior class V. The main pollution indicators of lakes and reservoirs are chemical oxygen demand, five-day biochemical oxygen demand and total phosphorus. Compared with 2013, the water quality of main lakes and reservoirs has been remained stable. The water quality of the main stream of the Yangtze River is generally excellent. The water quality of all the 15 monitored sections is up to class II–III. The proportion of the sections meeting the functional zoning standard is 80.0%. The sections over standard are Wuxiakou (Chongqing-Hubei provincial boundary), Badong Huanglashi and Zigui Yinxingtuo. The over standard item is total phosphorus.

The overall water quality of the main stream of the Yangtze River has been improved compared with the same period of the previous year. The water quality of the main stream of Hanjiang River is excellent. The water quality of all the 20 monitored sections is up to the class I–II, and the qualification rate of water quality functional zone is 100%. The overall water quality of the main stream of Hanjiang River has been remained stable compared with the same period of the previous year. The water quality of the tributaries of the Yangtze River is generally good. Among the 87 monitored sections, 83.9% sections are of class I to III and 6.9% are inferior to class V. The proportion of sections with water quality meeting the functional zone standard is 75.9%, and the main over standard items are total phosphorus, chemical oxygen demand and ammonia nitrogen. Among the 83 comparable sections, the proportion of sections with water quality of class I–III is 83.1%, with a year-on-year decrease of 1.2% points. The proportion of sections with inferior class V is 7.2%, with a year-on-year increase of 1.2%. The overall water quality of the tributaries of the Yangtze River has been remained stable.

The water quality of the tributaries of Hanjiang River is generally good. Among the 36 monitored sections, 80.6% sections are of class II to III, and 5.6% are inferior class V. The sections with water quality meeting the functional zone standard accounted for 80.6%, and the main items over the standard are chemical oxygen demand, total phosphorus and ammonia nitrogen. The proportion of sections with water quality of class II–III has been remained unchanged year on year, and the proportion of sections inferior to class V is decreased by 2.7% points. There is no obvious change of the overall water quality of Hanjiang River tributaries.

The water quality of the main stream and tributaries in the Three Gorges Reservoir area is generally excellent. The water quality of 21 monitored sections all meet the class II–III standard. The proportion of water quality meeting the functional zone standard is 76.2%, and the main over standard items are total phosphorus and five day biochemical oxygen demand. There is no obvious change of water quality in the main stream and tributaries in the Three Gorges Reservoir area. The water quality of the main stream and tributaries in Danjiangkou Reservoir area is generally good. Among the 17 monitored sections, 76.5% sections are of class II–III, 5.9% of class V, and 17.6% of inferior class V. The proportion of water quality meeting the functional zone standard is 70.6%. The water quality of the main stream and tributaries of Danjiangkou Reservoir area has been remained stable compared with the same period of the previous year.

The water quality of the main lakes in Hubei Province is slightly polluted. Among the 20 waters of 16 province-controlled lakes, 60.0% of them are of class II to III, 35.0% are of class IV and 5.0% are inferior class V. The water quality qualification rate of the functional area is 50.0%, and the main over standard items are total phosphorus, chemical oxygen demand and five-day biochemical oxygen demand. Compared with 2013, the proportion of class II to class III is decreased by 5.0% points, and the proportion of inferior class V waters is decreased by 5.0% points, and the overall water quality of the lake has been remained stable. Among them, the water quality of Futou Lake, Liangzi Lake and Huanggai Lake is the best, the Changhu Jingmen waters was seriously polluted, and the water quality of Tangxun Lake and Houhu Lake has been declined. Among the 19 lakes which eutrophication can be evaluated, 12 is at medium nutrient level, 6 is at light eutrophication level and 1 is at medium eutrophication level.

4. Main measures and effects of water pollution control in Hunan Province

In 2014, Hunan Province vigorously promoted the "No. 1 key project" of the provincial government, and promoted the implementation of the "first three-year action plan" for the protection and governance of the Xiangjiang River. The provincial, municipal and county-level governments were cooperated and 1158 key projects were launched for industries along the banks, urban garbage, sewage and livestock breeding, with 1143 of them being completed and with a completion rate of 98.7%. Both the total number of projects and the completion rate of that year set a new record. At the same time, a multi-party coordination mechanism for key regional governance under the responsibility of the local government, led by the departments affiliated to the provincial government, and supported by multiple departments has been established. Significant progress has been made in the comprehensive renovation of the five key regions. The water quality of Xiangjiang River is on the trend of improvement through powerful pollution governance.

According to the accounting, in 2014, the chemical oxygen demand, ammonia nitrogen, sulfur dioxide and nitrogen oxides, the four major pollutants, included in the national assessment in Hunan Province were decreased by 1.6%, 2.1%, 2.7% and 6%, respectively, which meant all targets as directed by the state have been achieved and it has laid a good foundation to comprehensively complete the total emission reduction mission in the "12th Five Year plan".

Among the main rivers, among the 46 province-controlled sections in the main stream of Xiangjiang River, Zijiang River, Yuanjiang River and Lijiang River, there are 45 sections with water quality class I–III, accounting for 97.8%, and 1 section of class IV, accounting for 2.2%. The main pollution index was the total phosphorus. In the Xiangjiang River Basin, the water quality of the main stream is generally excellent. The water quality of 18 province-controlled sections of the main stream met or exceeded the class III standard. The concentration of heavy metals such as cadmium, mercury, arsenic, lead and hexavalent chromium meet the requirements of class II as specified in the *Environmental Quality Standard for Surface Water*. The average concentration of cadmium, arsenic and lead presented a downward trend, while the average concentration of mercury and hexavalent chromium was remained stable. Compared with the previous year, the proportion of sections with class I–III in the tributaries of Xiangjiang River was decreased by 4.8%, and the main pollution indexes were ammonia nitrogen, total phosphorus and chemical oxygen demand. In the Zijiang River Basin, the water quality of the main stream was generally excellent, and the water quality of 11 province-controlled sections in the main stream met or exceeded the class III standard. In the Yuanjiang River Basin, the water quality of the main stream is generally excellent. Among the 10 province-controlled sections in the main stream, there are 9 sections of class I–III, accounting for 90.0%, and 1 section of class IV, accounting for 10.0%. The main pollution index was total phosphorus. In the Lishui River Basin, the water quality of the main stream was generally excellent, and the water quality of the seven province-controlled sections of the main stream met or exceeded the class III standard. Among the 8 province-controlled sections in other basins, the water quality of 3 province-controlled sections in Hunan section of

Yangtze River, 4 province-controlled sections in Dongting Lake River and 1 province-controlled section in Wushui section of Beijiang River of Pearl River all met or was better than Class III, and water quality of other basins was basically stable.

In 2014, the Dongting Lake was slightly polluted, and the status was medium nutrient. Among the 11 province-controlled sections of Dongting Lake, 10 sections belonged to class IV, accounting for 90.9%; one section belonged to class V, accounting for 9.1%. The main pollutant was total phosphorus. Compared with the previous year, the water quality of Dongting Lake showed a downward trend, and the average concentration of total phosphorus, an indicator of nutrient status, was increased by 29.2%.

### (III) Main measures and effects of water pollution governance in the western region of the Yangtze River Economic Belt

1. Main measures and effects of water pollution governance in Chongqing

In 2014, in terms of industrial pollution prevention and control, it was focused on investigating the pollution sources of industrial enterprises in Chongqing. Together with the southwest supervision and inspection center of the Ministry of Environmental Protection and the Environmental Protection Department of Sichuan Province, environmental risk supervision of 29 cities, districts and counties in the Yangtze River Basin was carried out in Chongqing with more than 80000 pollution sources being checked and classified rectification has been implemented; the auditing for compulsory clean production of 91 industrial enterprises has been completed, 9 enterprises with potential pollution in the main urban area have been relocated, and total 175 enterprises with potential pollution risks in the main city have been relocated as well as 25 sewage treatment facilities in industrial parks have been built. Legislation investigation on pollution prevention and control of livestock and poultry breeding has been carried out and technical guidelines for pollution prevention and control of livestock and poultry breeding have been formulated. The special action on pollution prevention and control of livestock and poultry breeding as well as special supervision on environmental regulation of large-scale livestock and poultry farms have been taken. 141 farms in prohibited breeding areas have been shutdown, total emission reduction projects in 350 livestock and poultry breeding have been completed, and 825 large and medium-sized biogas projects for livestock and poultry breeding have been fulfilled.

In the aspect of lake, reservoir and river remediation, 25 lakes and reservoirs in the main urban area (urban function core area and expansion area) were completed, and the remediation effect of 22 secondary rivers in the main urban area was consolidated. More than 700 comprehensive governance projects were implemented. Phased results have been achieved for the pollution remediation of Taohua River, Qianjiang River, Binan River, Longxi River, Laixi River and other key secondary rivers; the pilot automatic monitoring points were established for water quality of Caiyun Lake and Qijiang River. More than 50 million yuan was launched for the cleaning and bleaching of the Three Gorges Reservoir area, and 180,000 tons of floating garbage and 73,000 tons of garbage in the fluctuating area were cleaned up.

In terms of domestic sewage treatment, six urban sewage treatment plants and 161 township sewage treatment plants were built or expanded. A total of 59 urban sewage treatment plants and 550 township sewage treatment plants have been built in the city. The design treatment capacity of domestic sewage has reached 3.65 million tons/day. The coverage rate of sewage treatment facilities in the whole city has reached 65.2%, the urban sewage treatment rate has reached 90%, and the township sewage treatment rate has reached 75%. A total of 1,327 rural centralized sewage treatment facilities have been built, and the rural domestic sewage treatment capacity has reached 95,000 tons/day. The specialized operation of sewage treatment facilities in 33 districts and counties (autonomous counties and economic development zones) has been promoted to continuously improve the operation and management on these facilities.

In 2014, the emission of chemical oxygen demand in Chongqing was 386,400 tons, including 53,300 tons from industrial sources, 212,700 tons from urban living sources, 700 tons from centralized treatment facilities, 119,700 tons from agricultural sources, and 51,300 tons from ammonia nitrogen in wastewater, which was composed of 3,400 tons from industrial sources, 35,400 tons from urban domestic sources and 300 tons from centralized treatment facilities and 12,200 tons from agricultural sources.

In 2014, the overall water quality of Chongqing section of the Yangtze River mainstream was excellent. Among the 15 monitored sections, the proportion of sections with class III water quality was 100%. The overall water quality of the tributaries of the Yangtze River was good. Among the 146 monitored sections of 79 rivers, the proportion of sections with class I–III, class IV, class V and inferior class V was 77.4%, 13.0%, 6.2% and 3.4% respectively, and 86.3% of the sections meet the function requirements of waters. The proportion of eutrophic sections in the backwater area of 36 primary tributaries was 44.4%. Among the 30 monitored sections in the Jialing River Basin, 73.3%, 10.0%, 10.0% and 6.7% of the sections were classified as I–III, class IV, class V and inferior class V, respectively. Among the 19 monitored sections in Wujiang River Basin, 78.9%, 10.5%, 5.3% and 5.3% of the sections were classified as I–III, class IV, class V and inferior class V, respectively. The water quality of centralized drinking water sources in the city was good, and the water quality qualification rate of centralized drinking water sources in 61 cities was up to 97.3%.

2. Main measures and effects of water pollution governance in Sichuan Province

In 2014, in terms of water pollution prevention and control in Sichuan Province, the first was to continuously consolidate the "Three Rivers" pollution control achievements, comprehensively check the key industrial enterprises along the Minjiang River, Tuojiang River and Jialing River Basin, and name the key enterprises for in-depth treatment; the second was to strengthen the treatment of black and odor River in urban areas. The environmental protection departments at all levels have carried out a comprehensive investigation on the black and odor rivers in their jurisdiction; the third was to actively promote the water pollution control of key small watersheds; the fourth was to strengthen the protection of drinking water sources. The *Regulations on the Protection and Management of Drinking Water Sources in Sichuan Province* shall be strictly followed, and the system of drinking water source protection zones shall be comprehensively implemented; the fifth was to promote the prevention and control of groundwater pollution. Some areas were selected to carry out the pilot work for groundwater environment restoration; the sixth was to further implement the withholding system of funds for water quality over the standard in key river basins, optimize and adjust the assessment sections, and gradually expand the scope of assessment. In order to promote the water pollution governance on key river basins, the central budget investment plan of Sichuan Province issued by the National Development and Reform Commission has included 17 water pollution treatment projects, with a sewage treatment capacity of 93,500 tons/day and a garbage treatment capacity of 1000 tons/day in 2014. The total investment of the project was 1.19 billion yuan including 700 million yuan arranged in 2014.

In 2014, the emissions of chemical oxygen demand, ammonia nitrogen, sulfur dioxide and nitrogen oxides in Sichuan Province were 121.63, 13.48, 79.64 and 58.54 million tons, respectively, with a year-on-year decrease of 1.27%, 1.66%, 2.49% and 6.23%, respectively. The annual emission reduction target directed by the state has been fulfilled. In 2014, the main stream of the Yangtze River, Jinsha River, Minjiang River, Tuojiang River and Jialing River in Sichuan Province was slightly polluted. The qualification rate of the main stream was 59.6%, with a year-on-year decrease of 17% points, and that of the tributaries was 67.4%, with no change over the same period of the previous year. 90 of the 139 province controlled sections have met the standard, with qualification rate of 64.8% and year-on-year decrease of 5.7%. The main pollution indexes were total phosphorus, ammonia nitrogen and chemical oxygen demand. The water quality qualification rate of the main stream of the Yangtze River, Jinsha River and Jialing River was 100%; the main stream of Minjiang River was slightly polluted, while the tributaries were moderately polluted. The main pollution indexes were total phosphorus, ammonia nitrogen and chemical oxygen demand. The main stream of Tuojiang River was slightly polluted and the tributaries were moderately polluted. The main pollution indexes were total phosphorus and ammonia nitrogen. At the same time, the water quality qualification rate of 9 lakes and reservoirs was 77.8%. The water quality of Panzhihua Ertan Reservoir, Qionghai Reservoir in Liangshanzhou and Shengzhong Reservoir in Nanchong was classified as II and the overall quality was excellent; the water quality of Dahong Lake in Guang'an, Heilongtan Reservoir in Meishan, Laoying Reservoir in Ziyang, Sancha Lake in Ziyang and Zipingpu Reservoir in Dujiangyan was classified as III and the overall quality was good; the water quality of Luban Reservoir in Mianyang was classified as IV due to the impact of total phosphorus and it was slightly polluted and failed to satisfy the specified category.

3. Main measures and effects of water pollution governance in Guizhou Province

In 2014, in terms of water pollution governance in Guizhou Province, on the one hand, it strengthened the environmental protection of drinking water sources. The *Technical*

*Specifications for Environmental Protection and Construction of Drinking Water Sources in Guizhou Province* have been prepared and issued, the *Special Inspection Work Plan for Environmental Protection of Centralized Drinking Water Sources above County Level in Guizhou Province* has been formulated and implemented, the division scheme of water source protection areas in 100 demonstration small towns has been revised and improved; and the comprehensive environmental improvement project of centralized drinking water source protection areas has been conscientiously organized and implemented in 2014. On the other hand, the prevention and control of water pollution in key river basins has been comprehensively promoted. The *Water Pollution Prevention and Control Plan for Three Gorges Reservoir and Its Upper Reaches, Ecological Compensation Measures for Chishui River Basin Water Pollution Prevention and Control, Qingshui River and Hongfeng Lake Ecological Compensation Mechanism* have been seriously organized and implemented and river chiefs system for environmental protection has been established in 8 basins including Wujiang River and Chishui River. The third was to strengthen the protection of sound lake ecological environment. The Annual Plan of Ecological Environment Protection Pilot Project of Hongfeng Lake and Baihua Lake in Guizhou Province (2014) has been organized and implemented. In 2012 and 2013, 17 projects for sound lake ecological environment were implemented; and the Fourth Joint Conference of Water Environment Protection in Wangfeng Lake Areas, i.e. Joint Law Enforcement and Inspection Work Program has been formulated and implemented. The fourth was to strengthen the system construction, strengthen the construction and operation management of automatic monitoring system, and steadily promote the release of self-monitoring and supervision data of the enterprise.

In 2014, a total of 34 key emission reduction projects in the province were included in the assessment of letter of responsibility, and all the national assessment of letter of responsibility has been completed. The four major pollutant emission reduction indicators and national assessment projects have satisfied the objectives of national assessment.

In 2014, the surface water quality of Guizhou Province was generally good. Among the 85 monitored sections of 44 rivers in the whole province, the environmental quality of surface water was mainly of class I–III, with 69 sections of class I–III, accounting for 81.2%, 6 sections of class IV and V, accounting for 7%, and 10 sections with inferior class V, accounting for 11.8%. Compared with 2013, the overall water quality had no obvious change in 2014, the proportion of sections with class I–III was decreased by 2.4% points, and the proportion of sections with inferior class V was decreased by 1% point. Among the three major water systems in the Yangtze River Basin, the water quality of Chishui River system was excellent, that of Yuan River system was good, and that of Wujiang River system was moderately polluted. A total of 31 monitoring sections are set up on 14 rivers of Wujiang River system. Among them, there were 12 main stream sections, 16 primary and 3 secondary tributary sections. The water quality was evaluated as moderate pollution, and the main pollution indicators were total phosphorus, ammonia nitrogen and chemical oxygen demand. There were 18 monitoring sections in Yuanjiang River system, including 16 main stream sections and 2 primary tributary sections. The water quality was evaluated as good. There were 10 monitoring sections in the Chishui-Qijiang River system including 7 main stream sections and 3 primary tributary sections, and the water quality was evaluated as excellent.

4. Main measures and effects of water pollution governance in Yunnan Province

Since the 12th Five Year Plan, Yunnan Province has further strengthened the prevention and control of water pollution in the upper reaches of the Three Gorges Reservoir area, and continued to promote the implementation of the 12th Five Year Plan. Firstly, it was necessary to do a good job in the early stage of the project and actively strive for financial support. It was continued to implement the "green channel" of administrative licensing for urban domestic sewage and garbage treatment projects involved in the "12th Five Year Plan" of the Three Gorges, and accelerate the implementation of the project. Second was to strengthen the water quality monitoring and dynamic analysis. Early warning shall be given to the areas where the water quality exceeds the control limit, and the relevant provinces and cities shall be urged to seek and rectify the existing problems in time to ensure that the water quality can be maintained stable and up to the standard. Third was to strengthen environmental supervision and assessment on important rivers, further optimize the distribution of water quality monitoring points, and urge industrial parks and industrial enterprises to implement the requirements of "zero discharge" of waste water through in-depth investigation on environmental risks in industrial enterprises within the basin. The fourth was to strengthen the basic work of the assessment of the 12th Five Year Plan of the Three Gorges Project. By the end of 2014, the water quality of each control section in the upper reaches of the Three Gorges Reservoir Area in Yunnan Province was generally good, and the water quality met the annual assessment requirements.

In 2014, the main rivers were slightly polluted and remained stable. The water quality of the cross-border sections of the main rivers of the six major water systems all met the water environment function requirements. Compared with 2013, the water quality of Erhai Lake in the nine plateau lakes was improved from class III to class II, and the water quality of other lakes was remained stable. In 2014, the monitoring results of water quality at 46 water sampling and monitoring points in 21 major cities in Yunnan Province showed that all 46 drinking water sources could meet the requirements for drinking water, with the qualification rate of 100%, 2.4% higher than that of the previous year. The centralized drinking water source protection was further strengthened.

The above summarizes the "12th Five Year Plan" objectives of water pollution prevention and control in nine provinces and two cities in the Yangtze River Economic Belt and presents the efforts made and results achieved by various regions to improve water pollution in 2014. It is not difficult to see that the nine provinces and two cities, which are located in the upper, middle and lower reaches of the Yangtze River Basin, maintained compulsory administrative ties with relevant ministries and agencies of the state in terms of planning, indicators, technical standards, funds and supervision, etc., and they mainly strive to implement water pollution reduction and control within their respective administrative regions, and only a few actions have been involved in the coordination or cooperation with neighboring provinces. Therefore, the water pollution control in each region was basically independent, and there was no collaborative and cooperative governance. This kind of independent relationship among administrative regions in the basin is not suitable for the externality of water pollution prevention and control and the particularity of the pollution in the basin. The prevention and control of water pollution and the protection of ecological environment are neither separable from the coordination or cooperation among the upper, the middle and the lower reaches, nor from the organization and coordination by cross regional coordination agencies beyond the regional interests.

## 4 Control and Coordinated Development of the Ecological Environment in the Yangtze River Economic Belt

Although some achievements have been made in water pollution control and prevention in all regions of Yangtze River Economic Belt, we can still see that the water pollution in some regions in the Yangtze River Basin was serious based on the water pollution situation in 2014 and the ecological environment system was confronting serious threatening, therefore the situation of water pollution control in the Yangtze River Basin was still not optimistic. The accumulated length of polluted belt along the main stream of the Yangtze River has exceeded 600 km, and the pollution of tributaries was more serious, and the eutrophication of lakes in the basin was prominent. Since the reform and opening up, provinces and cities along the Yangtze River have made great efforts to develop their economy, set up national, provincial and municipal development zones and chemical industrial parks with complex industrial types, diverse scales and grades, and put into operation a large number of high-polluting enterprises such as chemical manufacturing industry and paper industry. In recent years, the economically underdeveloped provinces in the middle and upper reaches of the Yangtze River began to take over the transfer of a large number of middle and low-end industries from the coastal areas in the east, which resulted in the influx of high-polluting and high-energy consumption industries into the middle and upper reaches of the Yangtze River, further aggravating the difficulty of water environment prevention and control in the Yangtze River Basin.

In order to achieve the fundamental improvement of the ecological environment in the Yangtze River Economic Belt, it is necessary to overcome so many difficulties and constraints existing in the process of water pollution prevention of Yangtze River and ecological environment governance in the Yangtze River Basin. Many of the constraints are caused by the insufficient coordination and cooperation mechanism between provinces and cities in the Yangtze River Economic Belt and the lack of trans-regional ecological environment coordination institutions. Therefore, first of all, it is necessary to establish a cooperation mechanism between provinces and cities in the Yangtze River Economic Belt in the aspects of water resources protection, water pollution prevention and control, and distribution of benefits from ecological environment protection in the long run. Secondly, it is necessary to establish a special institution for ecological environment protection in the Yangtze River Economic Belt to implement the national strategies related to the ecological environment governance in the Yangtze River Economic Belt.

## 4.1 Regional Cooperation in Ecological Environment Governance of Yangtze River Economic Belt

The *Guidance on Promoting the Development of the Yangtze River Economic Belt Relying on the Golden Waterway* issued by the State Council clearly pointed out that it was necessary to establish a mechanism for coordinated protection and control of ecological environment, and improve the joint prevention and control mechanism and early warning and emergency response system for environmental pollution in the Yangtze River. It was necessary to encourage and support provinces and cities along the Yangtze River to jointly set up the Yangtze River water environment protection and governance fund, and strengthen the joint governance of outstanding environmental problems. According to the principle of "whoever benefits from the development must pay the cost", the horizontal ecological compensation mechanism shall be explored in the upper, middle and lower reaches development areas, benefited areas and ecological protection areas, and the ecological compensation demonstration site shall be constructed relying on key ecological function areas. The trading of water rights, carbon emission rights and emission rights shall be promoted and the third-party treatment for environmental pollution shall be implemented.

Many ports and industrial cities along the Yangtze River and its tributaries are still in the initial process of industrialization. They are vigorously developing the steel, chemical industry, non-ferrous metals and other industries with high energy consumption, high pollution and high emission, which cause serious water pollution. The completion and operation of the Three Gorges Project has led to significant changes in the hydrological situation in the middle and lower reaches of the Yangtze River, posing a great challenge to the normal water supply and the maintenance of the relationship between the river and the lake. All these problems have caused serious impact on the ecological environment of the Yangtze River Economic Belt. In terms of ecological protection and environmental governance, the ecological environment in the upper reaches of the Yangtze River is fragile, and the ecological damage in the upper reaches of the Yangtze River can be easily transmitted to the middle and lower reaches to result in negative environmental externalities. Some people have studied the relationship between pollution emission and industrial development in 9 provinces and 2 cities in the Yangtze River Economic Belt. The results show that there is strong spatial externality of pollution emissions in different regions, which leads to the obvious spatial dependence of industrial development in all regions. The pollution emissions of all regions not only affect the local environmental quality and industrial development, but also influence the environmental quality and industrial development of neighboring provinces. In addition, the interactive effects caused by pollution emissions from different regions also impact the respective development of industries (Cui Muhua and Yin Lisong 2015).

Due to the relatively low level of economic development in the upper reaches of the Yangtze River and the lack of funds and policy support in environmental governance, local governments have the impulse to reduce the environmental access threshold in order to attract the investment. Establishing a reasonable transfer payment mechanism is one of the paths to prevent the creation of negative externalities of ecological environment. However, due to the high dependence on heavy chemical industry with high energy consumption, high pollution and high emission in the upstream underdeveloped areas, it is bound to face the trade-off between social and economic development and ecological environment protection. Although it is capable for the downstream developed areas to protect the ecological environment from further damage, there is no incentive to subsidize the regions taking over the industrial transfer. It is often difficult to reach an agreement on the cost sharing for trans-regional eco-environmental governance (Hou Xiaofei 2015).

At present, China's ecological compensation funds mainly come from financial transfer payments and special funds. Financial transfer payment is the main source of funds for ecological compensation. In the financial transfer payment for ecological compensation in China, there is an obvious pattern of "vertical funds more than horizontal funds". That is to say, in the financial transfer payment, the vertical transfer payment accounts for a larger proportion, especially the transfer payment from the central government to the local. In contrast, the horizontal transfer payment between administrative regions on the same level occurs just occasionally within the same province in the ecological compensation practice. The pilot project of trans-provincial ecological compensation in Xin'anjiang River Basin, which flows through Anhui Province and Zhejiang Province, was started in 2011. It was the pilot work for trans-provincial ecological compensation and was smoothly developed between Anhui and Zhejiang provinces only under the organization and coordination of the Ministry of Finance, the Ministry of Environmental Protection and other central departments. However, the payment conditions for Zhejiang Province to cash in 100 million yuan of compensation funds was triggered only until 2014 when the water quality of exit boundary section of Xin'anjiang River met the standard and it was the first time for China to make horizontal transfer payment for ecological compensation (Wang Shuhua 2014).

Due to the great pressure of ecological protection in the Yangtze River Basin, trans-regional ecological compensation mechanism has not yet been established. Liu Yang et al. (2015) put forward specific policy suggestions, including "establishing a legal ecological compensation mechanism", "promoting communication and cooperation between the two parties of ecological compensation", "exploring diversified ways and means for ecological compensation", "improving the formulation of ecological compensation standards" and "strengthening the performance evaluation of ecological compensation". There is no doubt that the establishment and implementation of ecological compensation mechanism shall be guaranteed by corresponding laws and regulations; the ecological compensation mechanism in basin involves the interests relationship between the upstream and downstream, and between multiple departments and it is necessary to establish relevant exchange and cooperation platform for comprehensive consultation; the government led mechanism often causes great financial pressure on the central or local governments, so the financing channels of compensation funds shall be actively broadened by making full use of marketing means and various social investments shall be encouraged; on the basis of cost-benefit analysis, the range value of ecological compensation standard shall be determined, so as to improve the research method of ecological compensation standard and support the implementation of ecological compensation policy; in order to enhance the effectiveness and long-term implementation of ecological compensation policy, it is necessary to evaluate the water environment performance on regular basis.

There are many complementary relations among the provinces and cities in the Yangtze River Economic Belt, including those in the east, central and west provinces in terms of industrial structure, capital and technology. In the ecological environment, especially the water resources pollution and control in the Yangtze River Basin, that how to use economic means to adjust the basin ecological governance and regional interests relations has become the focus of attention. That is, how to establish an effective ecological compensation mechanism in the Yangtze River Basin, adjust the interests relationship between the upper and lower reaches of the Yangtze River by adjusting the fiscal and tax relations, and form a close cooperation system for the development and protection of the Yangtze River Basin so as to realize the sustainable development of the Yangtze River Basin.

## 4.2 Ecological Environment Governance of Yangtze River Economic Belt Based on National Strategy

The *Guidance on Promoting the Development of the Yangtze River Economic Belt Relying on the Golden Waterway* issued by the State Council pointed out: "the rivers and lakes shall be in harmony and ecology with civilization. It was necessary to establish and improve the strictest ecological environment protection and water resources management system, strengthen the supervision and comprehensive management of the ecological environment in the whole Yangtze River Basin, respect the laws of nature and river evolution, coordinate the relationship between rivers and lakes, the upper, middle and lower reaches, and the relationship between mainstream and tributaries, protect and improve the ecological service function of the basin, as well as promote the green cycle and low-carbon development of the basin".

In the seventh part of the *Guidance*, it is proposed that "the Yangtze River water resources shall be effectively protected and utilized. The strictest water resources management system shall be implemented and the red line for the development and utilization of water resources and the red line for water use efficiency in the Yangtze River shall be defined. It is necessary to strengthen the unified regulation of water resources in the river basin, ensure the safety of water for life, production and ecology, and strictly control and govern the water pollution of the Yangtze River. It is necessary to clarify the pollution receiving red line in water function area, improve the supervision and management system of water function area, scientifically check and verify the pollution receiving capacity in the basin, and strictly control the total amount of sewage discharged into rivers (lakes). Substantially reduce the emission of chemical oxygen demand and ammonia nitrogen, and strengthen the control on pollutants such as total phosphorus and total nitrogen".

In order to achieve the above objectives of ecological environment in the Yangtze River Economic Belt, regional coordinated development institutions based on national strategy are indispensable. According to the current reality, the governments along the Yangtze River are still in the state of self-governance in terms of pollution prevention and control. The coordination and cooperation system and mechanism of the Yangtze River Economic Belt are not perfect, and joint force of governance cannot be formed. Ecological and environmental protection itself is a systematic project, which needs the division and cooperation of multiple departments and fields. If all regions act at their own free will and respective responsibility, it will be difficult to form the joint force and achieve the expected objectives of environmental protection. The division of regional administration and the cross functions resulted in the impossibility of unified management in the basin. The current basin management institutions, Yangtze River Water Resources Commission and the Taihu Lake Basin Authority have single and limited authorities and cannot effectively undertake the responsibilities of comprehensive coordination, supervision and management.

The ecological environment of the Yangtze River Economic Belt shall be considered as a systematic project at the national level and to the height of national strategy. However, the lack of trans-regional authority in the Yangtze River Economic Belt will bring a series of problems. For example, the trans-regional problems such as reasonable industrial layout and adjustment of ecological environment in the Yangtze River Economic Belt and the implementation of inter-regional ecological compensation mechanism cannot be solved. At present, the most important is to realize the coordinated development of social economy and ecological environment among different regions of the Yangtze River Economic Belt through the top-level design. In order to make the top-level design of the ecological environment of the Yangtze River Economic Belt and make a detailed and perfect master plan, a special institution superior to provinces and cities must be set up and it must be a powerful institution to manage and formulate special laws and regulations for unified coordination and management. The National Development and Reform Commission, the Ministry of Finance, the Ministry of Environmental Protection and other relevant central ministries and commissions, together with the local governments of provinces and cities along the Yangtze River, can establish the "Yangtze River Economic Belt Ecological Environment Committee" in the primary state and regularly organize ministerial coordination and joint meeting to fully discuss the trans-provincial ecological and environmental issues of the Yangtze River Economic Belt. It is necessary for the state to innovate the system mechanism from the height of coordinated development strategy of the Yangtze River Economic Belt, and improve the sustainable development of the trans-provincial ecological environment of the Yangtze River Economic Belt and the mutually beneficial linkage development of the upper, middle and lower reaches through authoritative and national institutional arrangements.

China's economic development is still in the stage of total industrialization, and the total economic volume will continue to grow at a rate of about 7%. The Yangtze River Economic Belt accounts for more than 40% of China's total economic volume and will continue to expand. Therefore, the industrial and domestic discharge in the middle and upper reaches of the Yangtze River will continue to increase in the short period of time. The ecological environment of the Yangtze River Economic Belt will continue to face great pressure, and it is still difficult to change the local deterioration of the ecological environment. At the same time, the restoration of ecological environment is a long term and systematic project. The reduction of pollutant emissions depends on the long-term strategic economic restructuring at the macro level, the industrial restructuring at the regional level and the innovation and promotion of energy-saving and emission reduction technologies at the industrial level. In order to control the sewage discharge in the Yangtze River Economic Belt, reduce the harmful pollutants in the sewage, and continuously improve the ecological environment of the Yangtze River Basin, it is necessary to promote and implement their respective strategic measures at the national, regional and industrial levels at the same time.

From the national level, it is necessary to set up a trans-regional authority in the Yangtze River Economic Belt as soon as possible, carry out the top-level design of ecological environment governance and restoration in the Yangtze River Economic Belt, and conduct the pilot work for the ecological environment compensation mechanism in the Yangtze River Economic Belt Basin; at the regional level, the provinces and cities in the Yangtze River Economic Belt shall accelerate the transformation and upgrading of industrial structure according to different development stages. The high energy consumption and high emission enterprises shall be reduced, and the discharge of sewage and harmful pollutants shall be decreased. At the industrial level, there is still great potential to improve the technical level of energy conservation and emission reduction. It is necessary to speed up the promotion and popularization of sewage treatment technologies and products, and reduce pollutant emissions from the technical level. At the level of social consciousness, it requires to strengthen the propaganda of consciousness for ecological environment protection in the whole society.

# Integrated Development of Regional Finance in the Yangtze River Economic Belt

**Yan Zhang**

In 2013, the "two belts and one road" strategy was proposed in China with the Yangtze River Economic Belt, the Silk Road Economic Belt and the 21st century Maritime Silk Road as the core. During the 13th Five Year Plan and even in a long subsequent development stage as well as in the process of implementing the national strategy of "two belts and one road" and the regional integration in depth development, the financial cooperation and financial integration of the Yangtze River Economic Belt will continue to be strengthened.

## 1 Connotation of Financial Integration

### *1.1 Concept Discrimination*

Financial integration means that the same steps and measures are taken in the regional financial system for the financial institutions, financial policies and financial operation by taking the financial center as the leading factor and the operation rules of regional market economy as the basis. The objective of coordinated intervention, management and regulation of financial operation can be achieved with the operation efficiency being improved through mutual coordination, cooperation and interaction, so that the coordinated development of regional economy and society can be achieved to reach the ultimate goal of regional economic integration and stable financial development (Ding Wenli 2009).

There is a close relationship between financial cooperation and financial integration. Under the condition of market economy, the division of work and cooperation

Y. Zhang (✉)
Institute of Applied Economics, Shanghai Academy of Social Sciences, Shanghai, China
e-mail: zhangyan@sass.org.cn



X. Jing (ed.), *Development of the Yangtze River Economic Belt in China*, Urban Governance Practices in China,
https://doi.org/10.1007/978-981-16-1578-8_5

among economic entities become a very common phenomenon. Through opening financial control and strengthening financial policy coordination among regions, financial industry activities can be relatively freely carried out among regions, and the elements of financial industry can be redistributed and combined among regions, so as to realize the mutual integration of regional financial systems. However, as an important part of financial integration, financial cooperation is only the manifestation of the initial stage of financial integration, and is the behavior of different active principals in financial industry. Financial integration is the process or state of gradual integration and unification of two or more active principals in financial industry.

Financial integration includes not only the financial integration between states, but also that among regions within a state. Global integration is the highest goal of financial integration, which includes the integration of global financial market, capital flow, financial institutions, currency, financial coordination and supervision. However, it takes the whole world as the object of integration, and a better financial foundation and a long-term running process are required. There is still a long way to go for its realization. The implementation conditions of regional financial integration are relatively easy to be realized. For example, due to the strong internal cohesion formed on the basis of long-term economic and trade integration in Europe, the financial integration has been initially realized in this region.

Financial integration can be separated into two levels: ① integration of financial activities. It refers to that various barriers and obstacles in the regional financial system need to be eliminated as far as possible. In business activities, various trading instruments, trading markets, capital prices, settlement and exchange, and currency types tend to be consistent or have great convergence, which is mainly reflected in the integration of financial markets, institutions, instruments and even currencies. ② financial system integration. It refers to the integration and fixation of financial activities through contractual legal provisions and certain organizational forms to constitute a number of systems that must be observed. This is a higher level of integration, the process is more tortuous and complex because it is necessary to transfer or even waive the interests of regional economy and financial entities.

## *1.2 Dynamic Mechanism*

Financial resources can be divided into three levels (Bai Qinxian 1998), including basic core financial resources, i.e. monetary funds in a broad sense, which run through the whole process of financial activities; substantive financial resources at the intermediate level, which refer to the financial organization system and financial instrument system, and those are the means to realize various functions of financing; and the overall functional high-level financial resources, including financial system and relevant laws and regulations, standards, practices and consciousness, which has functions of regulation, restriction, encouragement and feedback. The elements of various levels of financial resources are closely related with functional relations by mutual coupling.

Pareto improvement of financial efficiency is the functional mechanism of financial integration and spatial allocation of financial resources in specific regional space. On the one hand, with the help of financial regional movement, the regional financial industrial structure can be adjusted and the rational structure and balanced allocation of financial elements at all levels can be promoted. Thus, the scale of transactions can be expanded and the increasing scale economic returns of financial industry can be obtained. On the other hand, the cost (including transaction cost, friction cost, etc.) for supply and demand transaction-adjustment of financial resources under financial integration needs to be minimized. It is required to reduce the uncertainty of financial information exchange, technology diffusion and innovation process, and minimize the cost of learning, information, governance and innovation.

Financial integration is the result of regional difference and regional movement of financial resource endowment. The development of financial industry in different regions is unbalanced, asynchronous and in different growth stages. The difference of financial industry growth among regions, that is, the spatial gradient of financial industry, is the direct cause to form the financial industry radiation (or diffusion) and then to promote the financial integration. Due to the joint effects of specific regional conditions, historical and accidental factors, accumulation effect and path dependence, the financial industry aggregation effect in financial centers is very strong in the geographical space with effective scale. Through continuous absorption of financial resources, the scale expansion of regional financial industry and the improvement of financial industry efficiency, the advanced growth stage of financial industry will be gradually achieved. The financial center can direct the financial resources to the surrounding financial growth poles and financial fulcrum, and drive the development through its diffusion effect.

Financial integration is also the result of continuous cooperation and coordination of regional financial industry management system. Both the "formal constraints" such as financial system, policies, regulations, standards and practices and the "informal constraints" such as financial consciousness, financial culture and professional ethics form the management system of the financial industry. No barrier in capital control and other legal, regulatory and institutional aspect will exist for the complete financial integration. Investors are free to carry out the portfolio and can make immediate adjustments. However, the financial industry management system often has strong regional characteristics, so it is necessary to strengthen the coordination and cooperation between regional financial industry systems, so that the ability of the whole financial regional system to withstand and digest financial turbulence can be improved and the development of financial integration in depth can be promoted.

### *1.3 Spatial Organization Structure*

The spatial structure of financial integration, also known as financial regional system, refers to the spatial arrangement and combination of financial center, financial hinterland and financial network system. Financial hinterland is composed of multiple financial growth poles and financial fulcrum around the financial center and is the coverage of financial core radiation. Any change in the three elements of financial regional system will lead to simple or complex structure, expanded or contracted regional scope and scale, and improved or declined function and grade. According to the scale or gradation of financial centers, financial regional system has hierarchy, including senior financial regional system, secondary financial regional system, primary financial regional system and potential financial regional system. At the same time, the boundaries of financial regional systems at different levels overlap with each other to construct the multidimensional financial regional system.

The financial center has strong external correlation of financial industry and is the top level city in the financial regional system. Its aggregation effect has been weakened, but its diffusion effect shall be gradually increased. However, the financial growth pole is different and it is the priority choice of financial center to expand outward, and then it will spread from the financial growth pole to the financial fulcrum. The hierarchical radiation of financial centers is not equidistant and uniform, but in leaps and bounds. Generally speaking, the radiation transmission power of financial center decreases with the increase of distance. However, the financial growth pole with better transportation area, more developed communication technology and better financial industry foundation can effectively overcome the resistance of natural distance and will become the first choice for financial center radiation.

The financial service network presents itself in space a composite spatial system of nodes and axes. Generally speaking, financial center is the initiator of radiation, the financial hinterland (composed of many financial growth poles and financial fulcrum around the financial center) is the specific partner to receive radiation, and the financial network system is the channel to carry the radiation, that is, only through airport, transportation corridor, energy source and information network can the regional transmission, circulation, allocation and combination of financial resources be realized. British scholar Dow divided the evolution of banking spatial system into six stages. ① Financial intermediaries serving the local community; ② the reputation of operators brought market expansion, but it was still limited to the local community; ③ the banking system developed to the whole state; ④ expansion to overseas based on the domestic market; ⑤ compete with nonbanking financial institutions on the national market; ⑥ deregulation brought international competition and eventually led to the concentration of related activities in financial center. The process can be summarized as follows: the banking system starts from the stage of local or regional banks, and forms regional and national financial centers through the decentralization stage of national banks and the concentration of financial activities in special locations, and then reach the stage of international development and stage of concentration to international financial centers.

# 2 Development Trend of Financial Industry in the Yangtze River Economic Belt

## *2.1 Development Trend of Banking Industry*

### (I) Deposit business

In 2014, the balance of domestic and foreign currency deposits of financial institutions in China was 117.4 trillion yuan, and the balance of domestic and foreign currency deposits of financial institutions in the Yangtze River Economic Belt was 48.6 trillion yuan in the same period, accounting for 41.4% of the whole state. Since 2010, the proportion of domestic and foreign currency deposits of financial institutions in the Yangtze River Economic Belt has been increasing slowly from 40.8% in 2010 to 41.4% in 2014 with an increase of 0.6%.

In 2014, the balance of domestic and foreign currency deposits of financial institutions in China was increased by 9.6% year-on-year, and the balance of domestic and foreign currency deposits of financial institutions in the Yangtze River Economic Belt was increased by 9.7%, 0.1% point higher than that of the whole state. Since 2010, the growth rate of domestic and foreign currency deposits of financial institutions in the Yangtze River Economic Belt has been decreased significantly, from 20.8% in 2010 to 9.7% in 2014 with a decline of 10.1%.

In 2014, the balance of unit deposits and savings deposits in China accounted for 50.4% and 41.7% respectively, and the balances of unit deposits and savings deposits in the Yangtze River Economic Belt accounted for 51.4% and 41.6% respectively. In 2014, the proportion of unit deposits and savings deposits in the Yangtze River Economic Belt accounted for 42.2% and 41.2% of the whole state, respectively, which were 0.2% and 1.4% higher than that in 2010 (refer to Table 1).

### (II) Loan business

In 2014, the balance of domestic and foreign currency loans of financial institutions in China was 86.8 trillion yuan, and that of financial institutions in the Yangtze River Economic Belt was 36.2 trillion yuan, accounting for 41.8% of the whole state. Since 2010, the proportion of domestic and foreign currency loans of financial institutions in the Yangtze River Economic Belt has been decreased from 42.8% in 2010 to 41.8% in 2014 with a decline of 1% point.

In 2014, the balance of domestic and foreign currency loans of financial institutions in China was increased by 13.3% year-on-year. In the same period, the balance of domestic and foreign currency loans of financial institutions in the Yangtze River Economic Belt was increased by 12.6% year-on-year, and the growth rate was 0.7% points lower than that of the whole state. Since 2010, the growth rate of domestic and foreign currency loans of financial institutions in the Yangtze River Economic Belt has been gradually decreased from 20.1% in 2010 to 12.6% in 2014 with a decline of 7.5%.

**Table 1** Balance of domestic and foreign currency deposits of financial institutions in the Yangtze River Economic Belt and proportion to the whole state

| Year | Category | Balance of various deposits (trillion yuan) | Year on year growth (%) | Proportion of unit deposit (%) | Proportion of savings deposits (%) |
|---|---|---|---|---|---|
| 2010 | Yangtze River Economic Belt | 29.9 | 20.8 | 35.5 | 40.9 |
| | Whole state | 73.3 | 19.8 | 34.5 | 41.9 |
| | Proportion of Yangtze River Economic Belt | 40.8 | – | 42.0 | 39.8 |
| 2011 | Yangtze River Economic Belt | 34.0 | 13.9 | 52.9 | 41.2 |
| | Whole state | 82.7 | 12.7 | 51.2 | 42.0 |
| | Proportion of Yangtze River Economic Belt | 41.2 | | 42.6 | 40.4 |
| 2012 | Yangtze River Economic Belt | 38.9 | 14.4 | 52.4 | 42.1 |
| | Whole state | 94.3 | 14.1 | 50.8 | 42.8 |
| | Proportion of Yangtze River Economic Belt | 41.3 | – | 42.7 | 40.6 |
| 2013 | Yangtze River Economic Belt | 44.3 | 13.7 | 51.9 | 41.7 |
| | Whole state | 107.1 | 13.5 | 50.6 | 42.2 |
| | Proportion of Yangtze River Economic Belt | 41.3 | – | 42.4 | 40.9 |
| 2014 | Yangtze River Economic Belt | 48.6 | 9.7 | 51.4 | 41.6 |
| | Whole state | 117.4 | 9.6 | 50.4 | 41.7 |
| | Proportion of Yangtze River Economic Belt | 41.4 | – | 42.2 | 41.2 |

*Data source* Regional financial operation report of provinces and cities in 2010 and 2014

In 2014, the proportions of short-term, medium and long-term loans of financial institutions in China accounted for 38.8% and 54.4% of the total loans, respectively. In the same period, the proportions of short-term, medium and long-term loans in the Yangtze River Economic Belt accounted for 38.6% and 56.3% respectively. In 2014, the proportions of short-term, medium and long-term loans in the Yangtze River Economic Belt accounted for 41.5% and 43.2% of the total, respectively, which was decreased by 4.4% points and increased by 1.3% points compared with that of 2010 (refer to Table 2).

**Table 2** Balance of domestic and foreign currency deposits of financial institutions in the Yangtze River Economic Belt and proportion to the whole state

| Year | Category | Balance of various loans (trillion yuan) | Year on year growth (%) | Proportion of short term loans (%) | Proportion of medium and long term loans (%) |
|---|---|---|---|---|---|
| 2010 | Yangtze River Economic Belt | 21.8 | 20.1 | 36.1 | 58.6 |
| | Whole state | 50.9 | 19.6 | 33.6 | 59.9 |
| | Proportion of Yangtze River Economic Belt | 42.8 | – | 45.9 | 41.9 |
| 2011 | Yangtze River Economic Belt | 24.9 | 14.2 | 39.6 | 57.0 |
| | Whole state | 58.2 | 14.3 | 37.4 | 57.4 |
| | Proportion of Yangtze River Economic Belt | 42.8 | – | 45.3 | 42.5 |
| 2012 | Yangtze River Economic Belt | 28.5 | 14.5 | 41.4 | 54.4 |
| | Whole state | 67.3 | 15.6 | 39.9 | 54.1 |
| | Proportion of Yangtze River Economic Belt | 42.4 | – | 44.0 | 42.6 |
| 2013 | Yangtze River Economic Belt | 32.2 | 13.0 | 41.4 | 54.4 |
| | Whole state | 76.6 | 13.9 | 40.7 | 53.5 |
| | Proportion of Yangtze River Economic Belt | 42.0 | – | 42.8 | 42.7 |
| 2014 | Yangtze River Economic Belt | 36.2 | 12.6 | 38.6 | 56.3 |
| | Whole state | 86.8 | 13.3 | 38.8 | 54.4 |
| | Proportion of Yangtze River Economic Belt | 41.8 | – | 41.5 | 43.2 |

*Data source* Regional financial operation report of provinces and cities in 2010–2014

(III) **Comparison between provinces and between cities**

1. Deposit business

Among the provinces and cities in the Yangtze River Economic Belt in 2014, the deposit scale in Jiangsu Province was the largest, accounting for 20% of the Yangtze River Economic Belt, while that of Guizhou Province was the smallest, accounting for 3.2% of the Yangtze River Economic Belt. From the perspective of growth rate, the deposit growth rate of provinces and cities in the upper and middle reaches of the Yangtze River was higher, where the deposit growth of Guizhou Province was the fastest with a year-on-year growth rate of 15.1%; the growth rate of loans in provinces and cities in the lower reaches of the Yangtze River is lower, where the deposit growth rate of Shanghai was the lowest, with a year-on-year growth of 6.7%. From the perspective of deposit structure, the proportion of unit deposits in Shanghai was the highest, accounting for 59.8% of the total deposits; the proportion of unit deposits in Hunan Province was the lowest, accounting for 40.8% of the total deposits. The proportion of savings deposits in Hunan Province was the highest, accounting for 54.4% of the total deposits; whilst the proportion of savings deposits in Shanghai was the lowest, accounting for 29.8% of the total deposits (refer to Table 3).

2. Loan business

In 2014, the loan scale in Jiangsu Province was the largest, accounting for 20% of the Yangtze River Economic Belt, and that in Guizhou Province was the smallest, accounting for 3.4% of the Yangtze River Economic Belt. From the perspective of growth rate, the loan growth rate of provinces and cities in the upper and middle reaches of the Yangtze River was higher, where the growth of Guizhou Province was the fastest, with a year-on-year growth rate of 22.5%; the loan growth of provinces

**Table 3** Balance and proportion of domestic and foreign currency deposits of financial institutions in provinces and cities of the Yangtze River Economic Belt in 2014

| City | Domestic and foreign currency deposits of financial institutions | | | Proportion of savings deposits (%) | Proportion of unit deposit (%) |
|---|---|---|---|---|---|
| | Balance (trillion yuan) | Year on year growth (%) | Proportion in the Yangtze River Economic Belt (%) | | |
| Shanghai | 7.4 | 6.7 | 15.2 | 29.8 | 59.8 |
| Jiangxu | 9.7 | 9.8 | 20.0 | 38.0 | 56.5 |
| Zhejiang | 7.9 | 7.5 | 16.3 | 39.3 | 52.5 |
| Anhui | 3.0 | 11.7 | 6.2 | 48.6 | 46.1 |
| Jiangxi | 2.2 | 11.1 | 4.5 | 49.8 | 44.5 |
| Hubei | 3.6 | 10.9 | 7.5 | 47.5 | 43.9 |
| Hunan | 3.0 | 12.6 | 6.2 | 54.4 | 40.8 |
| Chongqing | 2.5 | 10.4 | 5.2 | 42.9 | 53.3 |
| Sichuan | 5.4 | 12.1 | 11.1 | 47.1 | 44.9 |
| Guizhou | 1.5 | 15.1 | 3.2 | 43.3 | 51.6 |
| Yunnan | 2.3 | 8.2 | 4.6 | 43.2 | 51.7 |
| Yangtze River Economic Belt | 48.6 | 9.7 | 100.0 | 41.6 | 51.4 |

*Data source* Regional financial operation report of provinces and cities in 2014

**Table 4** Balance and proportion of domestic and foreign currency loans of financial institutions in provinces and cities of the Yangtze River Economic Belt in 2014

| City | Domestic and foreign currency loans of financial institutions | | | Proportion of short term loans (%) | Proportion of medium and long term loans (%) |
|---|---|---|---|---|---|
| | Balance (trillion yuan) | Year on year growth (%) | Proportion in the Yangtze River Economic Belt (%) | | |
| Shanghai | 4.8 | 8.0 | 13.2 | 28.0 | 59.4 |
| Jiangsu | 7.2 | 11.7 | 20.0 | 43.3 | 51.5 |
| Zhejiang | 7.1 | 9.2 | 19.7 | 56.4 | 39.6 |
| Anhui | 2.3 | 15.6 | 6.3 | 34.9 | 59.2 |
| Jiangxi | 1.6 | 19.7 | 4.3 | 42.2 | 54.9 |
| Hubei | 2.5 | 15.6 | 7.0 | 34.1 | 61.4 |
| Hunan | 2.1 | 13.9 | 5.7 | 29.2 | 68.9 |
| Chongqing | 2.1 | 14.6 | 5.7 | 28.6 | 66.5 |
| Sichuan | 3.5 | 14.7 | 9.6 | 31.6 | 66.2 |
| Guizhou | 1.2 | 22.5 | 3.4 | 22.8 | 75.6 |
| Yunnan | 1.8 | 13.9 | 5.1 | 31.4 | 65.0 |
| Yangtze River Economic Belt | 36.2 | 12.6 | 100.0 | 38.6 | 56.3 |

*Data source* Regional financial operation report of provinces and cities in 2014

and cities in the lower reaches of the Yangtze River was slower, where the loan growth rate of Shanghai was the lowest, with a year-on-year growth of 8%. From the perspective of loan structure, the proportion of medium and long-term loans in Guizhou Province was the highest, accounting for 75.6% of the total, while the proportion of short-term loans was the lowest, accounting for 22.8% of the total. The proportion of medium and long-term loans in Zhejiang Province was the lowest, accounting for 39.6% of the total, and the proportion of short-term loans was the highest, accounting for 56.4% of the total (refer to Table 4).

## 2.2 *Development Trend of Securities Industry*

At the end of 2014, there were 1,179 listed companies in the Yangtze River Economic Belt, an increase of 51 companies over the previous year and an increase of 252 over 2010. The amount of stock financing was 269.68 billion yuan, an increase of 109.13 billion yuan over the previous year and a decrease of 221.07 billion yuan compared with 2010. Among them, the financing amount of A share was 264.91 billion yuan, an increase of 122.83 billion yuan over the previous year, and a decrease of 92.74

**Table 5** Development of securities industry in Yangtze River Economic Belt (Unit: 100 million yuan)

| Year | Number of listed companies at the end of the year (enterprise) | Stock financing | | | Domestic bond financing |
|---|---|---|---|---|---|
| | | A share financing | H share financing | Total | |
| 2010 | 927 | 3 576.5 | 404.0 | 4 907.5 | 3 934.8 |
| 2011 | 1 069 | 3 105.2 | 161.9 | 3 267.1 | 5 366.2 |
| 2012 | 1 132 | 1 337.9 | 504.9 | 1 842.8 | 9 545.8 |
| 2013 | 1 128 | 1 420.8 | 184.7 | 1 605.5 | 9 279.8 |
| 2014 | 1 179 | 2 649.1 | 47.7 | 2 696.8 | 14 462.5 |

*Data source* Regional financial operation report of provinces and cities in 2010–2014

billion yuan compared with 2010; the financing amount of H shares was 4.77 billion yuan, an decrease of 13.7 billion yuan compared with the previous year, and decrease of 35.63 billion yuan compared with 2010. 1446.25 billion yuan was raised by the domestic bond market, an increase of 518.27 billion yuan over the previous year, and a sharp rise over 2010 with an increase of 1052.77 billion yuan (Table 5).

The number of listed companies in Zhejiang Province was the largest, 266 in total, accounting for 22.6% of the Yangtze River Economic Belt; whilst that in Guizhou Province was the least with only 21 companies, accounting for 1.8% of the Yangtze River Economic Belt. The amount of stock financing in Zhejiang Province was the largest, accounting for 23.9% of the Yangtze River Economic Belt; whilst that of Jiangxi Province was the lowest with 3.33 billion yuan, accounting for 1.2% of the Yangtze River Economic Belt. The amount of bond financing in Jiangsu Province was the largest, accounting for 28.2% of the Yangtze River Economic Belt; whilst that in Guizhou Province was the least, accounting for 3.4% of the Yangtze River Economic Belt (refer to Table 6).

## 2.3 Development Trend of Insurance Industry

In 2014, the premium income of the national insurance industry was 2,023.48 billion yuan, and that of the Yangtze River Economic Belt was 824.61 billion yuan, accounting for 40.8% of the national total. Since 2010, the proportion of premium income of the Yangtze River Economic Belt to that of the state has been decreased slightly from 41% in 2010 to 40.8% in 2014, with a decrease of 0.2% point.

In 2014, the premium income of the national insurance industry was increased by 17.5% year-on-year, while that of the Yangtze River Economic Belt was increased by 17.2%, 0.3% points lower than the national growth rate. Since 2010, the growth rate of insurance premium income in the Yangtze River Economic Belt has been

**Table 6** Development of securities industry in provinces and cities of Yangtze River Economic Belt

| Regions | Listed companies at the end of the year | | Amount of stock financing | | Domestic bond financing | |
|---|---|---|---|---|---|---|
| | Quantity (enterprises) | Proportion (%) | Amount (100 million yuan) | Proportion (%) | Amount (100 million yuan) | Proportion (%) |
| Shanghai | 204 | 17.3 | 291.0 | 10.8 | 695.0 | 4.8 |
| Jiangsu | 254 | 21.5 | 366.4 | 13.6 | 4 075.3 | 28.2 |
| Zhejiang | 266 | 22.6 | 644.0 | 23.9 | 2 274.0 | 15.7 |
| Anhui | 80 | 6.8 | 185.1 | 6.9 | 1 550.9 | 10.7 |
| Jiangxi | 32 | 2.7 | 33.3 | 1.2 | 547.1 | 3.8 |
| Hubei | 86 | 7.3 | 146.2 | 5.4 | 707.0 | 4.9 |
| Hunan | 75 | 6.4 | 313.0 | 11.6 | 721.6 | 5.0 |
| Chongqing | 40 | 3.4 | 195.6 | 7.3 | 1 084.3 | 7.5 |
| Sichuan | 92 | 7.8 | 387.2 | 14.4 | 1 377.6 | 9.5 |
| Guizhou | 21 | 1.8 | 64.5 | 2.4 | 495.6 | 3.4 |
| Yunnan | 29 | 2.5 | 70.5 | 2.6 | 934.1 | 6.5 |
| Yangtze River Economic Belt | 1 179 | 100.0 | 2 696.8 | 100.0 | 14 462.5 | 100.0 |

*Data source* Regional financial operation report of provinces and cities in 2014

gradually decreased from 30% in 2010 to 17.2% in 2014, with a decrease of 12.8% points.

In 2014, the proportion of the national property insurance premium and life insurance premium income to the premium income was 35.6% and 64.4%, respectively. During the same period, the proportion of property insurance premium and life insurance premium income in the Yangtze River Economic Belt was 38.6% and 61.4%, respectively, which were 3% points higher and 3% points lower than the national level. From 2010 to 2014, the proportion of property insurance premium income in the Yangtze River Economic Belt was increased by 10.9% points, and the personal insurance premium income was decreased by 10.9% points. In 2014, the property insurance premium income and life insurance premium income of the Yangtze River Economic Belt accounted for 44.2% and 38.8% of the national total, respectively. These two items of proportion were increased by 1.9% points and decreased by 1.7% points respectively compared with 2010 (refer to Table 7).

Among the provinces and cities in the Yangtze River Economic Belt, the insurance premium income scale of Jiangsu province was the largest in 2014, amounting to 168.38 billion yuan and accounting for 20.4% of the Yangtze River Economic Belt; the insurance premium income scale of Guizhou province was the smallest,

**Table 7** Premium income and expenditure of insurance industry in the Yangtze River Economic Belt and proportion to the state

| Year | Category | Premium income (100 million yuan) | Year on year growth (%) | Proportion of property insurance premium (%) | Proportion of life insurance premium (%) | Premium expenditure (100 million yuan) |
|---|---|---|---|---|---|---|
| 2010 | Yangtze River Economic Belt | 5 956.3 | 30.0 | 27.7 | 72.3 | 1 309.7 |
| | Whole state | 14 528.0 | 30.4 | 26.8 | 73.2 | 3 200.4 |
| | Proportion of Yangtze River Economic Belt | 41.0 | – | 42.3 | 40.5 | 40.9 |
| 2011 | Yangtze River Economic Belt | 5 973.4 | 0.3 | 33.0 | 67.1 | 1 643.6 |
| | Whole state | 14 339.3 | −1.3 | 32.2 | 67.8 | 3 929.4 |
| | Proportion of Yangtze River Economic Belt | 41.7 | – | 42.6 | 41.2 | 41.8 |
| 2012 | Yangtze River Economic Belt | 6 402.0 | 7.2 | 35.4 | 64.6 | 1 982.7 |
| | Whole state | 15 487.9 | 8.0 | 34.4 | 65.6 | 4 716.3 |
| | Proportion of Yangtze River Economic Belt | 41.3 | – | 42.5 | 40.7 | 42.0 |
| 2013 | Yangtze River Economic Belt | 7 050.7 | 10.1 | 37.9 | 62.1 | 2 636.6 |
| | Whole state | 17 222.2 | 11.2 | 36.1 | 63.9 | 6 212.9 |
| | Proportion of Yangtze River Economic Belt | 40.9 | – | 43.0 | 39.8 | 42.4 |

(continued)

**Table 7** (continued)

| Year | Category | Premium income (100 million yuan) | Year on year growth (%) | Proportion of property insurance premium (%) | Proportion of life insurance premium (%) | Premium expenditure (100 million yuan) |
|---|---|---|---|---|---|---|
| 2014 | Yangtze River Economic Belt | 8 246.1 | 17.2 | 38.6 | 61.4 | 3 069.4 |
| | Whole state | 20 234.8 | 17.5 | 35.6 | 64.4 | 7 216.2 |
| | Proportion of Yangtze River Economic Belt | 40.8 | – | 44.2 | 38.8 | 42.5 |

*Data source* Regional financial operation report of provinces and cities in 2010–2014

amounting to 21.31 billion yuan and accounting for 2.6% of the Yangtze River Economic Belt. From the perspective of premium income structure, most income for provinces and cities sourced from personal insurance, of which the proportion of personal insurance income in Hubei was the highest, accounting for 68.7% and the proportion of property insurance income was the lowest, accounting for 31.3%; the proportion of personal insurance income in Guizhou Province was the lowest, accounting for 47.2% and the proportion of property insurance income was the highest, accounting for 52.8% (refer to Table 8).

# 3 Financial Center Construction of the Yangtze River Economic Belt

## *3.1 Development Plan of Financial Centers in Major Cities*

According to the *Construction Plan of Shanghai International Financial Center* during the "12th Five-Year Plan" issued by the National Development and Reform Commission in January 2012, and in accordance with the strategic objective of "basically completed the construction of an international financial center compatible with China's economic strength and the international status of RMB" by 2020, it is necessary to aim at the world's first-class international financial center, comprehensively expand financial service functions, accelerate the improvement of financial innovation capabilities, continuously strengthen the international connotation and global influence of Shanghai's financial market, and strive to basically establish Shanghai as the global center for RMB product innovation, trading, pricing and clearing house by 2015.

**Table 8** Premium income of insurance industry in various provinces and cities of the Yangtze River Economic Belt and proportion to the state

| Regions | Premium income | | Property insurance | | Personal insurance | |
|---|---|---|---|---|---|---|
| | Amount (100 million yuan) | Proportion in the Yangtze River Economic Belt (%) | Amount (100 million yuan) | Proportion to premium income (%) | Amount (100 million yuan) | Proportion to premium income (%) |
| Shanghai | 987.0 | 12.0 | 343.0 | 34.8 | 644.0 | 65.2 |
| Jiangsu | 1 683.8 | 20.4 | 606.3 | 36.0 | 1 077.5 | 64.0 |
| Zhejiang | 1 258.0 | 15.3 | 602.0 | 47.9 | 656.1 | 52.2 |
| Anhui | 572.0 | 6.9 | 241.0 | 42.1 | 331.0 | 57.9 |
| Jiangxi | 400.4 | 4.9 | 138.8 | 34.7 | 261.6 | 65.3 |
| Hubei | 700.2 | 8.5 | 219.4 | 31.3 | 480.9 | 68.7 |
| Hunan | 587.7 | 7.1 | 211.3 | 36.0 | 376.5 | 64.1 |
| Chongqing | 407.3 | 4.9 | 138.9 | 34.1 | 268.4 | 65.9 |
| Sichuan | 1 060.6 | 12.9 | 395.5 | 37.3 | 665.2 | 62.7 |
| Guizhou | 213.1 | 2.6 | 112.4 | 52.7 | 100.6 | 47.2 |
| Yunnan | 376.0 | 4.6 | 177.3 | 47.2 | 198.7 | 52.8 |
| Yangtze River Economic Belt | 8 246.1 | 100.0 | 3 185.9 | 38.6 | 5 060.5 | 61.4 |

*Source* Regional financial operation report of various provinces and cities in 2014

The Overall Plan for the Construction of Wuhan Regional Financial Center (2014–2030) was issued by Wuhan in April 2015. Efforts shall be exerted to build the regional financial center in Central China and a national professional financial center focusing on science and technology finance as well as national financial backstage service base by 2020; A gathering area for diversified financial institutions oriented to serve the real economy, the financial innovation pilot zone with the characteristics of element market and the financial innovation pilot zone with Internet finance as the precursor shall be constituted to innovate and develop the green finance, consumer finance, logistics finance and shipping finance with the target that the added value of the financial industry can reach 200 billion yuan. By 2030, it is planned to build a national financial center with national professional financial center as the breakthrough point, and form a national financial center matching with the national central city-Wuhan. In the future, Wuhan Equity Custody Trading Center shall further play its role to expand the scope of services, attract non-listed small and medium-sized joint stock enterprises in Central China to handle the businesses of equity registration, equity pledge financing, equity transfer, etc. in Wuhan Equity Custody Trading Center, and promote Wuhan regional trading center to become the investment and financing service platform for small and medium-sized enterprises in central China. It was proposed in the plan that the listed resources of the urban agglomeration in the middle reaches of the Yangtze River and the central region shall be fully integrated and the merger and reorganization of listed companies shall be advanced.

In June 2012, the Fourth Party Congress of Chongqing clarified the goal of Chongqing to build a financial center in the upper reaches of the Yangtze River. At the financial work conference of Chongqing on 11 February 2015, the mayor Huang Qifan pointed out that efforts shall be made in Chongqing to promote the construction of the financial center in the upper reaches of the Yangtze River from the following aspects. One is to vigorously develop various financial institutions and further expand the scale of the financial industry; second is to work hard so that the ratio between loan balance and GDP can be up to 2:1 to further improve the ratio of deposit to loan and continuously enhance the aggregation and radiation function of financial industry in Chongqing; third is to set the target that the proportion of the financial industry to GDP can exceed 9% by 2017 and 10% by 2020; forth is the financial service function could be enhanced continuously, and the financial "full license" could be obtained as far as possible; fifth is to achieve the reasonable financing ratio of 45:35:20 for banks, direct financing market and non-bank financial institutions; sixth is to keep the non-performing asset rate of various financial institutions to be relatively low; seventh is to continuously improve the national economic securitization rate with the target of 100% by 2020; eighth is to make great efforts for the construction of financial element market system; ninth is to expand the financial opening to the outside world and actively develop offshore financial settlement, cross-border RMB settlement, credit card settlement, third party payment settlement, bonded logistics settlement and other businesses.

On 25 September 2014, the State Council issued the *Guidance on Promoting the Development of the Yangtze River Economic Belt Relying on the Golden Waterway*. In terms of financial cooperation and innovation, the *Guidance* proposed to promote qualified private capital to initiate the establishment of small and medium-sized financial institutions such as private banks in the middle and upper reaches. Guide the qualified innovative, entrepreneurial and growing SMEs in the region to list on the national equities exchange and quotations system for equity financing, debt financing and asset restructuring. Explore and innovate financial products, encourage the development of financial leasing services, and support the standardization of ship models in the Yangtze River. Large port and shipping enterprises shall be encouraged to integrate coastal ports and shipping resources with capital as the bond. Policy financial institutions shall be encouraged to increase support for the construction of comprehensive transportation system along the river.

## 3.2 *Analysis on the Competitiveness of Regional Financial Centers*

(I) **Indicator system**

The factors affecting the competitiveness of financial centers can be divided into 3 categories: demand factor, supply factor and environmental factor (refer to Table 9). The demand factors mainly include the economic scale, the level of economic development, the degree of economic opening-up, and the living standards of the residents; the supply factors include the financial scale and the financial depth; the environmental factors include the location, government finance, technological innovation, traffic conditions, etc. These 3 factors together constitute the indicator system of competitiveness of financial center.

(II) **Data description and empirical method**

We will take 11 provincial capital cities or municipalities directly under the central government in the Yangtze River Economic Belt as the research objects to evaluate their financial competitiveness according to the above 3 categories of evaluation indicators. There are 3 level-1 indicators, including demand factor, supply factor and environmental factor; there are 8 level-2 indicators, including economic development level, economic opening up, investment, financial scale, financial development level, government finance, and technology innovation indicators. There are 16 level-3 indicators, namely GDP, industrial added value, fixed asset investment proportion, per capita GDP, per capita disposable income of urban residents, foreign

**Table 9** Indicator system of competitiveness of financial center

| Level 1 indicators | Level 2 indicators | Level 3 indicators |
|---|---|---|
| Demand factors | Economic scale | GDP, industrial added value and proportion of fixed assets investment |
| | Level of economic development | Per capita GDP and per capita disposable income of urban residents |
| | Economic opening up | Dependence on foreign trade, FDI |
| Supply factors | Financial scale | Deposits from financial institutions, loans from financial institutions and premium income |
| | Financial development level | Financial depth and insurance depth |
| Environmental factors | Government finance | Fiscal revenue |
| | Technical innovation | Authorized amount of patent application and transaction amount of technology contract |
| | Infrastructure | Revenue from telecommunication services |

trade dependence, FDI, deposits in financial institutions, loans from financial institutions, premium income, financial depth, insurance depth, financial income, number of patent applications granted, technical contract turnover, and telecommunications business income. The financial depth is the ratio between the sum of deposits and loans of financial institutions and GDP in the same period, and the insurance depth is the ratio between premium income and GDP in the same period. The empirical analysis will be mainly carried out in factor analysis, and the data were collected in 2014. The data were collected from the statistical bulletin of each city in 2014.

The factor analysis and cluster analysis will be used to evaluate the financial competitiveness of each city. According to the requirements of factor analysis, firstly, the evaluation matrix shall be established. 16 columns and 11 lines of evaluation matrix will be established with indicator variables and data of 11 cities to analyze the correlation of variables in the matrix to verify the significance of factor analysis. As the units of each index variable are not in uniform, and the variance of individual variable is large, the specific standard method is used to standardize the value to Z score in order to avoid excessive impact on factor load. The original data are carried out with non-dimensional processing. After the transformation, the average value is zero and the standard deviation is 1.

1. Factor analysis model

$$\begin{cases} Z_1 = a_{11}F_1 + a_{12}F_2 + \cdots + a_{1p}F_p + c_1U_1 \\ Z_2 = a_{12}F_1 + a_{22}F_2 + \cdots + a_{2p}F_p + c_2U_2 \\ \ldots \\ Z_m = a_{m1}F_1 + a_{m2}F_2 + \cdots + a_{mp}F_p + c_mU_m \end{cases}$$

by introducing the matrix marker:

$$X = \begin{pmatrix} X_1 \\ X_2 \\ \vdots \\ X_p \end{pmatrix} \quad A = \begin{pmatrix} a_{11}, & a_{12}, & \cdots & a_{m1} \\ a_{12}, & a_{22}, & \cdots & a_{m2} \\ \cdots & \cdots & \cdots\cdots \\ a_{1p}, & a_{2p}, & \cdots & a_{mp} \end{pmatrix} \quad F = \begin{pmatrix} F_1 \\ F_2 \\ \vdots \\ F_p \end{pmatrix} \quad U = \begin{pmatrix} U_1 \\ U_2 \\ \vdots \\ U_p \end{pmatrix}$$

the equation can be abbreviated as:

$$\underset{(m\times 1)}{Z} = \underset{m\times p}{A} \cdot \underset{p\times 1}{F} + \underset{m\times m}{C} \cdot \underset{m\times 1}{U}$$

and it meet:

(1) $P \le m$.
(2) $COV(F, U) = 0$(That is $F$ is not related to $U$).
(3) $E(F) = 0$ $COV(F) = \mathrm{I_p}$, that is $F_1, \ldots, F_p$ are not related and variances are 1 and average values are 0.

(4) $E(U) = 0$ $COV(U) = I_m$, that is $U_1, \ldots, U_m$ are not related and all of them are standardized variables. It is assumed that $Z_1, \ldots, Z_m$ are standardized but not independent.

Where, $A$ is called factor load matrix, and its element $a_{ij}$ represents the load of No. $Z_i$ variable on the $F_j$ which is the No. $j$ factor and referred to as factor load for short. If $Z_i$ is regarded as a vector of p dimensional factor space, $a_{ij}$ represents the projection of $Z_i$ on the coordinate axis $F_j$.

The steps of factor analysis are as follows:

(1) Input the original data, calculate the sample mean and variance, and carry out standardization processing.
(2) Find sample correlation coefficient matrix $R = (r_{ij})_{p \times p}$.
(3) Finding the characteristic root of correlation coefficient matrix $\lambda_i(\lambda_1, \lambda_2, \ldots, \lambda_p > 0)$ and the corresponding orthonormal eigenvectors.
(4) Determine the number of common factors.
(5) Calculate the common variance of common factors.
(6) Rotate the load matrix to better explain the common factors.
(7) Make a professional interpretation of public factors.

2. Cluster analysis

The function of cluster analysis is to establish a classification method, by which a batch of samples or variables are classified according to their relative degree in nature. There are many types of distance, among which Euclidean distance is the most widely used in cluster analysis, and its expression is as follows:

$$d_{ij} = \sqrt{\sum_{k=1}^{m} (X_{ik} - X_{jk})^2}$$

where $X_{ik}$ represents the observation value of the No. $k$ indicator of No. $i$ sample, $X_{jk}$ represents the observation value of No. $k$ indicator of No. $j$ sample, and $d_{ij}$ is the Euclidean distance between No. $i$ sample and No. $j$ sample. The smaller the DIJ, the closer the properties between No. $i$ and No. $j$ samples, and the samples with similar properties can be included in one category.

When the distance between samples is determined, the samples shall be classified. There are many classification methods, among which the hierarchical clustering method is the most widely used method in cluster analysis. Firstly, each of the n samples is classified into one category, and then the 2 classes with the minimum distance can be combined into one category each time. After the combination, the distance between categories shall be recalculated, and this process continues until all the samples are included in one category. The classification results can be drawn into an intuitional cluster spectrum.

The steps of hierarchical clustering method for cluster analysis are as follows:

(1) Determine the indicators of the samples to be classified.
(2) Collect data.
(3) To carry out transformation (such as standardizing or normalizing) of data.
(4) Each sample is classified into its own category, i.e. n samples will be classified into n categories.
(5) The distance between each category is calculated to obtain a distance symmetric matrix, and the 2 categories closest to each other are combined into one category.
(6) After combination, if the number of categories is greater than 1, then recalculate the distance between categories and continue for combination until all samples are classified as one category.
(7) The last step is to draw the hierarchical diagram, and different classification results are obtained according to different classification standards or different classification principles.

Rotate the above data for 25 times by Quartmax (max forth power) by SPSS17.0 software, so that each element in the factor load matrix could be polarized as far as possible, so as to explain the practical significance of common factors. According to the principle that the extracted number of factor depends on the variance contribution of common factors to the original variables, and the greater the variance contribution, the more important the common factors will become, and the higher the degree of the description for the studied regional characteristics will be. When the characteristic value of the factors on the top list of importance is greater than 1, and the cumulative variance contribution rate reaches or exceeds 85%, these factors can represent the original multiple variables to reflect the comprehensive characteristics of the studied region.

### (III) Empirical results

By solving the characteristic equation of the correlation matrix, 11 unit characteristic vectors are obtained. The results show that 3 factors can be selected as the main factors for analysis. The total variance explained and the factor load matrix after rotation are shown in Table 10.

Through the analysis of the factor load matrix after rotation, the 2 principal components are explained as follows: common factor 1 has relatively large load on 12 indicators, namely GDP, fixed assets ratio, industrial added value, deposits in financial institutions, loans from financial institutions, premium income, fiscal income, foreign trade dependence, FDI, total revenue of telecommunications business, patent authorization volume and technical contract turnover. From the perspective of the significance represented by the indicators, they mainly reflect the economic scale and innovation, and can be regarded as the scale and environmental factors of the financial center with a contribution rate of 70.03%. Common factor 2 has relatively large load on the two indicators of financial depth and insurance depth. From the perspective of the significance represented by the indicators, they mainly reflect the

**Table 10** Analysis of variance contribution

| Components | Initial eigenvalues | | | Extract sum of squares loading | | | Rotate sum of squares loading | | |
|---|---|---|---|---|---|---|---|---|---|
| | Total | % of variance | Accumulated % | Total | % of variance | Accumulated % | Total | % of variance | Accumulated % |
| 1 | 11.574 | 72.338 | 72.338 | 11.574 | 72.338 | 72.338 | 11.206 | 70.035 | 70.035 |
| 2 | 1.881 | 11.756 | 84.094 | 1.881 | 11.756 | 84.094 | 1.998 | 12.487 | 82.522 |
| 3 | 1.692 | 10.573 | 94.667 | 1.692 | 10.573 | 94.667 | 1.943 | 12.145 | 94.667 |

**Table 11** Load matrix of principal factor after rotation

| Variable | F1 | F2 | F3 |
|---|---|---|---|
| GDP | 0.988 | −0.099 | 0.053 |
| Fixed assets proportion | −0.748 | −0.235 | −0.590 |
| Industrial added value | 0.945 | −0.244 | 0.092 |
| Deposits in financial institutions | 0.973 | 0.187 | 0.100 |
| Loans from financial institutions | 0.973 | 0.165 | 0.128 |
| Premium income | 0.981 | 0.172 | 0.051 |
| Financial revenue | 0.978 | 0.013 | −0.029 |
| Foreign trade dependence | 0.902 | 0.310 | 0.067 |
| FDI | 0.976 | −0.005 | −0.077 |
| Per capita GDP | 0.263 | −0.208 | 0.935 |
| Financial depth | 0.313 | 0.927 | 0.013 |
| Insurance depth | 0.385 | 0.860 | −0.053 |
| Disposable income of residents | 0.555 | 0.187 | 0.795 |
| Total revenue of telecommunication service | 0.970 | −0.044 | −0.141 |
| Number of patents granted | 0.924 | 0.047 | −0.057 |
| Turnover of technical contract | 0.883 | −0.060 | 0.100 |

level of financial development and can be regarded as the financial development level factor of the financial center with a contribution rate of 12.49%. Common factor 3 has a relatively large load on two indicators, namely GDP per capita and disposable income of residents. From the perspective of the significance represented by the indicators, they mainly reflect the level of economic development and can be regarded as the economic development factor of the financial center with contribution rate of 12.15% (refer to Table 11).

(IV) **Scores on factor and sorting**

The scores F1, F2 and F3 of the 3 common factors are obtained by regression method, and then the 3 scores on factor after rotation are weighted and summed with their variance contribution rate as the weight to obtain the scores of comprehensive factor, i.e. $F = (F1 \times 70.03 + F2 \times 12.49 + F3 \times 12.15)/94.67$. According to the scores of comprehensive factor, the sorting of the financial competitiveness of each city is shown in Table 12.

(V) **Cluster analysis**

Scores on factor are obtained by factor analysis. Hierarchical clustering method is used to carry out cluster analysis of 16 cities, and the results show that they can be divided into three categories. Among them, the first category is directed only to Shanghai, the reason of which is the leading financial competitiveness score and leading position of Shanghai in the financial center system of the Yangtze River

**Table 12** Competitiveness scores of financial centers in various cities

| City | F1 | F2 | F3 | F |
|---|---|---|---|---|
| Shanghai | 2.62 | 0.52 | 0.23 | 2.04 |
| Nanjing | −0.14 | 0.29 | 1.32 | 0.10 |
| Hangzhou | −0.11 | 0.61 | 1.43 | 0.18 |
| Hefei | −0.55 | −0.74 | −0.56 | −0.58 |
| Nanchang | −0.81 | −0.20 | −0.26 | −0.66 |
| Wuhan | 0.08 | −1.25 | 0.39 | −0.06 |
| Changsha | −0.40 | −1.42 | 1.07 | −0.35 |
| Chongqing | 0.68 | −1.11 | −1.83 | 0.12 |
| Chengdu | 0.29 | 1.05 | −0.56 | 0.28 |
| Guiyang | −0.93 | 0.83 | −0.78 | −0.68 |
| Kunming | −0.74 | 1.43 | −0.44 | −0.42 |

Economic Belt. The second category of financial centers includes 5 cities. Most of the competitiveness scores of the five cities are between 0 and 1, while the financial competitiveness score of Wuhan is slightly lower than 0. The third category includes 5 cities, namely Changsha, Kunming, Hefei, Nanchang and Guiyang. The competitiveness score of these cities is negative, of which the financial competitiveness score of Changsha is higher and that of Guiyang is the lowest (refer to Fig. 1 and Table 13).

From the perspective of the three common factors and in terms of scale and environmental factor (F1) of financial centers, scores of Shanghai, Chongqing, Chengdu and Wuhan are significantly higher than those in other cities, which indicates that the financial development scale of these financial center cities is relatively large, and the economic and financial development environment is relatively good. In terms

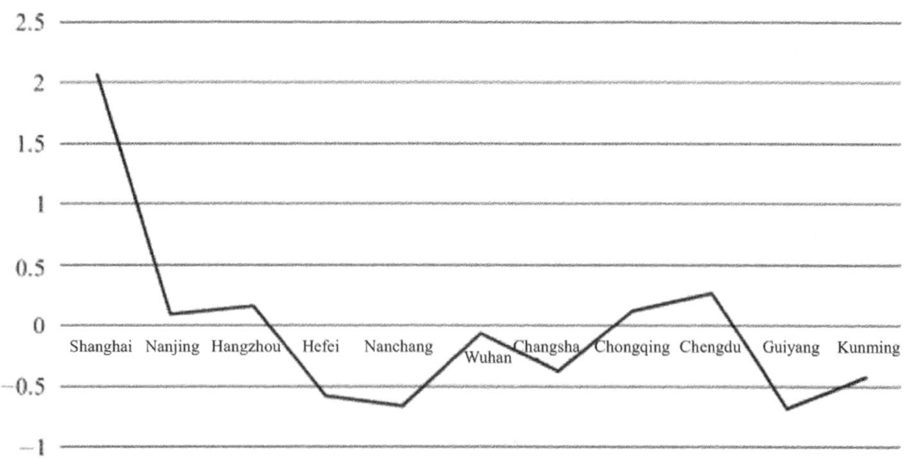


**Fig. 1** Financial competitiveness score of cities in Yangtze River Economic Belt

**Table 13** Cluster analysis results

| Cluster | Quantity | City |
|---|---|---|
| Category 1 | 1 | Shanghai |
| Category 2 | 5 | Chengdu, Chongqing, Hangzhou, Nanjing, Wuhan |
| Category 3 | 5 | Changsha, Kunming, Hefei, Nanchang, Guiyang |

of financial development level factor (F2) of financial centers, scores of Kunming, Chengdu, Guiyang, Shanghai, Hangzhou and Nanjing are relatively high, which indicates that these cities are relatively better in terms of financial development rate relative to economic scale. In terms of the economic development factor (F3) of the financial center, scores of Hangzhou, Nanjing, Changsha, Wuhan and Shanghai are high, which indicates that these cities are in the leading position in terms of economic development. In general, among the cities with high scores in financial competitiveness, all 3 common factors of Shanghai are positive, indicating that the competitiveness of the financial center is advanced in all aspects; Nanjing and Hangzhou are the leaders in financial development and economic development, but are weak in financial scale and financial environment; the score of Chongqing is high in financial scale and financial environment, however, it is relatively backward in terms of financial development and economic development; Chengdu is the most advanced in terms of financial development, but relatively backward in terms of economic development; the score of Wuhan is higher in terms of financial scale, financial environment and economic development, but relatively backward in terms of financial development.

# 4 Division and Cooperation of Financial Industry in the Yangtze River Economic Belt

## *4.1 Division of Work in Financial Industry*

In 2012, the location quotient of financial industry in the Yangtze River Economic Belt was 1.14, 0.14 higher than that in 2005, and the degree of specialization was higher than the national level. Among them, the specialization level of the financial industry in the lower reaches of the Yangtze River was the highest, followed by the upper reaches of the Yangtze River; the financial industry specialization level in the middle reaches of the Yangtze River was relatively low (lower than the national level).

In 2012, there were six provinces and cities with higher level of specialization (with location quotient greater than 1) in financial industry, and they were Shanghai, Chongqing, Zhejiang, Sichuan, Jiangsu and Yunnan with the level from high to low. There were five provinces and cities with lower specialization (location quotient less than 1), and they were Anhui, Hubei, Jiangxi, Hunan and Guizhou. Compared with

**Table 14** Variation of location quotient of financial industry in Yangtze River Economic Belt

| Region | Year 2005 | Year 2012 | Variation |
|---|---|---|---|
| Shanghai | 1.60 | 1.62 | 0.02 |
| Jiangsu | 0.95 | 1.07 | 0.13 |
| Zhejiang | 1.37 | 1.42 | 0.05 |
| Anhui | 0.56 | 0.88 | 0.32 |
| Jiangxi | 0.54 | 0.74 | 0.20 |
| Hubei | 0.53 | 0.85 | 0.32 |
| Hunan | 0.51 | 0.54 | 0.03 |
| Chongqing | 0.75 | 1.64 | 0.89 |
| Sichuan | 1.01 | 1.27 | 0.26 |
| Guizhou | 0.99 | 0.90 | −0.09 |
| Yunnan | 1.05 | 1.03 | −0.02 |
| Upper reaches of Yangtze River | 0.96 | 1.24 | 0.28 |
| Middle reaches of Yangtze River | 0.53 | 0.74 | 0.21 |
| Lower reaches of Yangtze River | 1.27 | 1.31 | 0.04 |
| Yangtze River Economic Belt | 1.00 | 1.14 | 0.14 |

*Data sources Statistical Yearbook of China's Tertiary Industry of 2013* and *Statistical Yearbook of China's Tertiary Industry of 2006*

2005, the location quotients of Chongqing, Hubei, Anhui, Sichuan and Jiangsu have been increased significantly in 2012 (refer to Table 14).

Among the six provinces and cities with high level of financial industry specialization in 2012, the specialization of financial industry in Shanghai and Chongqing was the highest. From the perspective of geographical location, the two places are located in the upper and lower reaches of the Yangtze River Economic Belt and constitutes the relatively high point of financial development or financial agglomeration. However, Jiangxi and Hunan in the middle reaches of the Yangtze River had a relatively low financial specialization. Both of them are located in the middle reaches of the Yangtze River, and constitutes a relatively low point of financial development. Therefore, giving full play to the advantages of higher level of financial specialization of the central cities in the upper and lower reaches of the Yangtze River, especially those of Shanghai and Chongqing, can effectively radiate and drive the financial and economic development and promote the financial integration of the Yangtze River Economic Belt.

## *4.2 Regional Capital Circulation*

In 2014, the cumulative transaction of China's inter-bank market was 302.4 trillion yuan, with a year-on-year increase of 28.5% and an increase of 39.2% points over the previous year. In terms of regions, the transaction volume in the eastern, central, western and northeast regions was increased by 24.0, 38.3, 37.8 and 26.8% year-on-year. In terms of provinces and cities, the total transaction volume of Beijing, Guangdong, Shanghai, Jiangsu and Zhejiang exceeded 70% of the national total; Shaanxi, Hunan and Henan ranked among the top three provinces in terms of transaction volume growth, with a year-on-year growth of 164.6%, 92.0% and 76.0% respectively.

As a whole, it showed a trend of flowing from Beijing to other provinces and cities (see Table 15). In 2014, the net capital financing in Beijing was 77.0 trillion yuan, with a year-on-year increase of 34.6 trillion yuan and Beijing was the region with the highest capital outflow. Guangdong, Jiangsu, Shanghai, Shandong and Jilin were ranked the top five in terms of net financing, with a total of 45.1 trillion yuan. Compared with the previous year, Heilongjiang, Guizhou and Hunan have changed from net outflow to net inflow; Yunnan, Tianjin, Hainan and Tibet have changed from net inflow to net outflow.

From the perspective of the Yangtze River Economic Belt, Jiangsu and Shanghai have a large scale of net capital inflow in the money market, which were 13.5 trillion yuan and 7.7 trillion yuan respectively. Hubei, Anhui, Sichuan, Zhejiang and Jiangxi also had a certain scale of net capital inflow between 1 trillion yuan and 4 trillion yuan. The net inflow scale in Chongqing, Hunan and Guizhou was relatively small

**Table 15** Net capital inflow (outflow) of money market in 2014 (Unit: trillion yuan)

| Province (city) | Net in (+)/net out (−) | Province (city) | Net in (+)/net out (−) |
|---|---|---|---|
| Guangdong | 14 | Ningxia | 0.8 |
| Jiangsu | 13.5 | Chongqing | 0.6 |
| Shanghai | 7.7 | Hunan | 0.5 |
| Shandong | 5.5 | Guizhou | 0.5 |
| Jilin | 4.5 | Gansu | 0.3 |
| Liaoning | 4.2 | Heilongjiang | 0.1 |
| Shanxi | 4.1 | Hebei | 0 |
| Fujian | 3.4 | Qinghai | 0 |
| Hubei | 3.3 | Tianjin | 0 |
| Anhui | 3.2 | Tibet | −0.1 |
| Sichuan | 1.9 | Hainan | −0.1 |
| Guangxi | 1.6 | Shanxi | −0.1 |
| Zhejiang | 1.3 | Yunnan | −0.4 |
| Inner Mongolia | 1.2 | Xinjiang | −0.6 |
| Jiangxi | 1.1 | Beijing | −77 |
| Henan | 0.8 | | |

*Source* China Regional Financial Operation Report in 2014

and was less than 1 trillion yuan. Yunnan had a net capital outflow of 0.4 trillion yuan on the money market. It is worth paying the attention that the net capital outflow of Hunan has changed from the net outflow of the previous year to net inflow, and the growth rate of transaction volume was ranked the second in China, which indicated that the money market transactions in Hunan Province was relatively active in 2014, and the demand for funds was on the rise.

## *4.3 Progress of Financial Cooperation in the Yangtze River Economic Belt*

In recent years, the financial cooperation and regional integration of the Yangtze River Economic Belt have achieved win-win results, and the regional financial cooperation has been substantially promoted with remarkable achievements.

(I) **The institutional arrangement and organizational framework of regional financial cooperation have been initially established**

At the sub-regional level, the institutional framework of regional financial cooperation between the Yangtze River Delta region and the middle reaches of the Yangtze River city cluster has initially taken shape. In November 2007, the governments of Shanghai, Jiangsu Province and Zhejiang Province and the People's Bank of China jointly signed the *Framework Agreement on Promoting Coordinated Financial Development and Supporting Regional Economic Integration in the Yangtze River Delta Region* in Shanghai. Since 2008, Shanghai, Jiangsu and Zhejiang jointly has been held the Yangtze River Delta financial forum every year. In the first half of 2012, the branches of the People's Bank of China in Jiangxi, Hubei and Hunan provinces jointly put forward the idea of *Financial Cooperation and Co-construction Zone for City Cluster in the Middle Reaches of the Yangtze River*, and issued the *Guidance on Financial Support for the Development of City Cluster in the Middle Reaches of the Yangtze River* in August of the same year. In 2013, Wuling Mountain, Wumeng Mountain and other poverty alleviation and development financial service linkage and coordination mechanism was established. Based on this mechanism, relevant branches of the People's Bank of China in the region actively promoted the financial cooperation with neighboring provinces. At the regional level, the first Yangtze River Economic Belt financial forum was held in Wuhan on October 25, 2014. The governments of 9 provinces and 2 cities in the Yangtze River Economic Belt have considered the in-depth regional financial cooperation as an important subject, and jointly explored the ways to accelerate financial innovation and cooperation in the Yangtze River Economic Belt, including regional opening of financial market, large regional circulation of financial elements, large regional cooperation of financial ecology, and realization of linkage development of regional economy and finance.

### (II) The trans-regional allocation of financial resources and the trans-regional operation of financial institutions have increased significantly, and the efficiency has been continuously improved

Under the direction of Shanghai Banking Regulatory Bureau, the banking financial institutions in Shanghai actively provided financial support to the relevant construction projects in the Yangtze River Economic Belt. As of the end of March 2015, the loan balance of major commercial banks used to support the Yangtze River Economic Belt reached 311.38 billion yuan, accounting for 6.3% of the loan balance, with an increase of 29.79 billion yuan or 10.6% over the beginning of the year, and the growth rate exceeded the growth rate of loans by 7.1% points. Bank credit is mainly used to support the construction of the comprehensive three-dimensional transportation corridor of the Yangtze River Economic Belt, innovation driven and industrial transformation and upgrading, economic and trade cooperation and development, and improvement of the function of the Yangtze River golden waterway.

In 2010, Hankou Bank set up a branch in Chongqing, making substantial progress in regional financial cooperation in the middle reaches of the Yangtze River. In 2015, the *Special Plan for the Reform and Innovation of Science and Technology Finance in Wuhan City Circle* proposed to study the feasibility to establish branches of legal person financial institutions in Hubei, Hunan and Jiangxi in the economic compact zone of the middle reaches of the Yangtze River. At the same time, it was proposed in the plan to promote the integration of financial credit market, note market, payment and settlement, financial information service and factor allocation market in Wuhan city circle.

By the end of 2014, there were 187, 186 and 202 provincial branches of banking legal person financial institutions, securities companies and insurance companies in other provinces and cities of the Yangtze River Economic Belt, respectively, with an increase of 13.3%, 22.4% and 3.6% compared with the end of 2012. 21 city commercial banks in Jiangsu, Shanghai, Zhejiang, Hubei, Guizhou, Jiangxi, Chongqing and Sichuan signed strategic cooperation agreements for universal deposit and cash withdrawal. The rapid development of regional off-site loan business has become an important part to satisfy the fund demand of regional economic development. By the end of 2014, the inflow balance of ecdemic loans from financial institutions in the region was at total of 1,421.7 billion yuan, an increase of 50.4% over the end of 2012. Capital market cooperation has developed in depth, and the influence of regional equity market has extended to other provinces. By the end of 2014, 71 enterprises in 11 provinces and cities had been attracted to be lsited. Securities companies in Shanghai and other places have provided banking services for investment such as listing guidance, package financing plan, merger and reorganization, etc.

### (III) Financial infrastructure such as bill system, payment and settlement develops towards integration

In terms of regional bill market integration, branches of the People's Bank of China in Shanghai, Jiangsu, Zhejiang and Anhui jointly issued a document to announce that the discount of commercial acceptance bills accepted or held by enterprises listed in the key promotion list in three provinces and one city can be processed in priority in all outlets of commercial banks within the three provinces and one city, and the People's Bank of China shall give priority to rediscount commercial acceptance bills to promote the extensive use of commercial acceptance bill in three provinces and one city. In terms of payment and settlement integration, the bulk electronic payment system (BEPS) has been successfully launched in three provinces and one city in East China, the check image exchange business has been widely used in the Yangtze River Delta region, and the construction of bank card acceptance environment has been constantly optimized. In December 2012, Hubei and Hunan branches of the People's Bank of China took advantage of the proximity of Longshan and Laifeng counties in Hunan Province to jointly carry out county financial cooperation pilot projects, and issued the *Implementation Plan for the Integration of Individual Payment and Settlement Business in Longfeng Demonstration Zone.*

There are still some problems and obstacles in the process of regional financial cooperation in the Yangtze River Economic Belt. First is the planning and coordination mechanism of regional financial cooperation needs to be strengthened. Administrative barriers hindered the free circulation of regional financial resources. There were not so many high-level regional financial cooperation. Regional financial cooperation happened mainly at the sub-regional level, and the cooperation was relatively scattered, and was lack of systematic and operational institutional arrangements. Second is the regional financial cooperation is not balanced. The regional financial cooperation in the middle and lower reaches of the Yangtze River has made more achievements, but the regional financial cooperation in the upper reaches of the Yangtze River still lay in its infancy. Third is the function of financial center city needs to be further strengthened. The reasonable and effective division of work has not been implemented in the Yangtze River Economic Belt, and the radiation and driving force from core cities have not provided enough power for the regional financial cooperation of the whole Yangtze River Economic Belt. It is necessary to further promote the aggregation of financial industry towards core cities, and constantly enhance the influence and radiation of financial center cities. Fourth is no strong financial cooperation platform is available. The Yangtze River Economic Belt spans nine provinces and two cities with a space span of more than 2000 km. With the continuous infiltration of regional economy, regional financial risks were gradually exposed. However, the information sharing between financial institutions and regulatory agencies in the region is still insufficient. When financial institutions carry out trans-provincial business, financial institutions are facing the problems of difficult management and lack of means for risk management, both of which increases the cost of regional financial cooperation.

# 5 Countermeasures and Suggestions to Promote the Financial Integration of the Yangtze River Economic Belt

In a long development phase in the future, the economic and social development of the Yangtze River Economic Belt will be accelerated, which requires a large amount of investment. As for the financial cooperation in the Yangtze River Economic Belt, the following financial needs shall be supported. First is to vigorously support the central infrastructure construction. Under the context of Yangtze River Economic Belt strategy, to realize "the belt and road initiative" interconnection infrastructure; including the Yangtze River "golden waterway" governance and large projects of ports and terminals along the river as well as the construction of comprehensive three-dimensional channel. Second is to vigorously support the undertaking and transfer of industries in the central and western regions. The demonstration area of industrial transfer shall be built to guide the gradient transfer of industries in the lower reaches of the Yangtze River from east to west, including steel, automobile, electrical equipment and other traditional industrial projects. Third is to continuously and vigorously support the development of small and micro enterprises and rural urbanization. Fourth is to vigorously support entrepreneurial and innovative enterprises and to promote the development of strategic emerging industries including intelligent manufacturing, energy conservation and environmental protection, new energy vehicles, and modern service industries such as tourism, pension and health care system.

## *5.1 Promote the Cooperation and Innovation of Financial Institutions*

### (I) **Promote the intensive development and global operation of financial institutions**

It is necessary to promote the change from the extensive development mode of emphasizing speed over quality and emphasizing scale over structure in the past and to focus on the efficiency, constantly optimize business processes and organizational structure, realize the optimized allocation of various business elements, and improve the operational efficiency. Accelerate the pace of financial innovation, steadily promote the comprehensive operation of financial institutions, and provide customers with all-round and diversified financial services. Through the establishment of branches, the establishment of agency relationship or merger and acquisition of foreign financial institutions, to promote the transnational operation of financial institutions, cultivate world-class transnational financial institutions, and realize the global development of financial industry.

### (II) Strengthen the cooperation among regional financial institutions

Promote financial enterprises to set up regional headquarters and branches in surrounding cities, and encourage domestic and foreign financial institutions to set up branches in the middle and upper reaches of the Yangtze River. Promote horizontal cooperation among regional financial institutions, encourage financial institutions along the Yangtze River to carry out joint loans and regional credit granting, and support large-scale projects and infrastructure construction in the region, as well as the industrial development of connectivity in the region. Promote the financial institutions of various provinces and cities in the Yangtze River Economic Belt to develop comprehensive financing such as loans and settlement in different locations, promote the circulation of funds from areas with abundant funds to areas lacking of funds, reduce financing costs and improve financing efficiency. Encourage cooperation among banking institutions and among banking, securities and insurance industries to jointly provide compound financial services.

### (III) Attach importance to the development of small and medium sized financial institutions

We shall attach importance to the development of regional joint-stock commercial banks with the advantages of property right structure, low transaction cost, information advantage, flexible operation and strong adaptability, so as to serve high-tech industries and private growth enterprises and to further promote the financial industry cluster development of the Yangtze River Economic Belt.

### (IV) Set up new financial institutions to serve the construction of Yangtze River Economic Belt

In order to meet the huge capital demand of the construction of the Yangtze River Economic Belt, financial organizations, like the Yangtze River Development Bank, are specialized in the infrastructure construction and economic development of the Yangtze River Economic Belt. The Yangtze River Development Bank shall be set up under the leadership of Shanghai. Financial institutions in all provinces and cities shall provide capital stock. The proportion of equity can be determined according to the financial scale of the provinces and cities in the Yangtze River Economic Belt, and the voting rights and the appointment of directors and senior executives can be decided accordingly. The Yangtze River Development Bank shall establish a new organization and management system and actively carry out product innovation, business innovation, service innovation, process innovation, channel innovation, management innovation, and business model innovation to provide better financial services for the economic and social development of the Yangtze River Economic Belt.

### 5.2 *Promote the Opening and Innovation of Financial Market and Encourage the Trans-Regional Circulation of Funds*

The importance shall be attached to direct financing and the construction of financial markets, promote the opening of financial markets to the outside world, and serve the development of financial cooperation in the Yangtze River Economic Belt.

(I) **Speed up the development of direct financing in the Yangtze River Economic Belt**

Make full use of bond, stock, fund and other financial markets to provide multi-level financing products and services according to the characteristics of the project. Encourage more enterprises in the Yangtze River Economic Belt, especially those in the middle reaches of the Yangtze River, to raise funds through the capital market in Shanghai to meet the long-term capital needs for infrastructure construction; take the advantages of the capital market to carry out mergers and acquisitions, and promote industrial upgrading and transformation; guide various venture capital funds, venture capital funds and private equity funds in Shanghai to support more small and micro enterprises in the Yangtze River Economic Belt and scientific and technological innovation. The Yangtze River Investment Fund can be set up to be as a direct financing channel to provide financial support for the development of emerging industries and venture capital in the region. The infrastructure shall be built in the form of financial leasing to provide public services so that the investment and financing needs of infrastructure construction in the Yangtze River Economic Belt can be satisfied.

(II) **Promote the financial opening up of the Yangtze River Economic Belt**

The channel to connect the Yangtze River Economic Belt and foreign financial markets can be established through the Shanghai Free Trade Zone. On the one hand, low-cost capital will be introduced, and various offshore financing means in Shanghai will be used to provide offshore loans and issue offshore bonds to traders, logistics providers and producers in the region, so as to reduce the financial operation cost. On the other hand, it is necessary to find suitable investment channels for the funds in the Yangtze River Economic Zone, and to invest in deposits, bonds, equity, funds and other financial instruments in the international financial market through the international financial institutions in the free trade zone of Shanghai. It is required to guide financial institutions in the Yangtze River Economic Belt to strengthen trans-regional cooperation, promote the use of RMB in foreign-related economic activities, and increase the proportion of RMB cross-border two-way investment in the Yangtze River Economic Belt. Financial institutions are encouraged to issue RMB overseas loans to support enterprises in the Yangtze River Economic Belt to "going out".

**(III) Actively develop trans-regional property rights trading markets and support trans-regional asset restructuring**

To promote the development and growth of regional enterprises to make better use of the securities market, it is not only limited to listed financing, but also it is necessary to promote the enterprises to use the securities market to carry out reorganization, merger and acquisition as well as the vertical or horizontal integration of capital and resources. Promote the cooperation of property rights exchanges in various provinces and cities, develop a unified and perfect regional property rights trading mechanism, gradually form a unified regional property rights trading market, and promote the adjustment and optimization of regional economic structure. Promote the asset restructuring of state-owned enterprises, realize the reasonable flow and optimal allocation of state-owned property rights, attract private and mixed capital to enter the market, and develop the mixed ownership economy through the regional property rights trading market; further facilitate the property rights trading and investment as well as financing activities of small and medium-sized enterprises and high-tech enterprises in the region.

## *5.3 Promote the Further Improvement of Financial Cooperation Mechanism*

**(I) Establish and improve the mechanism of cooperation and consultation**

In order to break the regional blockade, it is necessary to establish the corresponding cooperation mechanism through the consultation and communication between the financial departments and even the competent government departments. Regularly plan high-level finance meetings and forums, strengthen the awareness of regional collaborative development, and promote the financial element market and financial institutions to provide satisfactory financial services to all regions. Further improve the sense of social responsibility of the financial industry and give full play to the role of finance in transforming the development mode, build harmonious society and promote people's livelihood. Give full play to the role of local financial service office and actively discuss financial cooperation in credit cooperation, mixed operation cooperation, financial infrastructure and information sharing.

**(II) Strengthen the cooperation of financial supervision departments in the field of regional financial policy**

The Shanghai headquarters of the People's Bank of China shall, together with the Nanjing Branch, Wuhan Branch, Chengdu Branch and Chongqing Business Management Department of the People's Bank of China, strengthen their coordination and cooperation in financial policies and play its important role in transmitting monetary policy and supporting local economic development. Take the advantages of the dynamic adjustment mechanism of differential reserves, refinancing, rediscount, medium-term lending facilities and other policy instruments to provide effective total credit support for the implementation of the strategy. Strengthen the coordination of credit policy with monetary policy, industrial policy, fiscal policy and regional policy, actively meet the financial needs of industrial clusters in the Yangtze River Economic Belt, and promote industrial transformation and upgrading. Explore the effective integration of policy finance, development finance and commercial finance, and promote the establishment of diversified and sustainable investment and financing mechanism. Establish and improve the regional financial supervision coordination and anti-money laundering cooperation mechanism to ensure regional financial stability. According to the characteristics of financial risk transmission, it is aimed to explore the financial supervision policies under the financial cooperation, and formulate perfect policies and measures to prevent cross regional financial risks. Strengthen the communication and consultation of financial regulatory policies, and conduct joint supervision on trans-regional institutions and funds. Local regulatory authorities shall jointly carry out the investigation and disposal of anti-money laundering to prevent regional money laundering risk.

### (III) Promote coordination and cooperation among financial centers

There can be several financial centers in a country or region, but there shall be reasonable division of work and clear positioning among financial centers. For example, New York is the capital market center and the clearing center of dollar trading in the United States, Chicago is the center of derivatives market; another example is that Luxembourg, Edinburgh and Berlin are the world fund management centers, and Frankfurt is the European monetary policy center and derivatives trading center. Therefore, for general cities, the development of financial centers needs to seek professional development according to their comparative advantages in economic development and industrial structure. For example, as the first scientific and technological financial reform and innovation pilot area in China, the construction of Wuhan Financial Center can give full play to the characteristics of science and technology finance and can be developed into a professional financial center.

Promote the cooperation and coordination of financial centers in the Yangtze River Delta, the middle reaches of the Yangtze River and Chengdu Chongqing Economic Zone. The central cities of the three megalopolis in the Yangtze River Economic Belt, including Shanghai, Wuhan and Chongqing, shall be clear about the division of work and functional orientation of financial central cities through communication and consultation. Through the gathering of functional financial institutions headquarters and the reasonable layout of financial branches, the positive externalities and cumulative circular causal effect of financial center network can be enhanced, and the ability of integrating financial resources can be improved so that a closer financial connection between each other can be formed and developed into a financial center with different characteristics and at different levels.

## 5.4 *Build Financial Transaction and Information Platform to Promote the Integration of Financial Infrastructure*

(I) **Build regional trading platform**

Build regional e-bill trading center to form a unified trading platform integrating bill trading, custody, clearing, inquiry and other functions. Standardize the circulation and transaction of commercial bills, and provide information disclosure and related services. Carry out bank card and related equipment, software design and technology research and development by taking the advantages of the rapid development of information industry, bank card EMV migration, e-commerce innovation and other opportunities and take the lead in completing the industrial upgrading and build the complete bank card industry chain.

(II) **Build a unified credit system and improve credit service system**

Bring the functions of the People's Bank of China into full play in managing the credit reference industry, improve the functions of the credit reference system, and expand the scope of information collection; integrate the enterprise and personal credit information in the government information platform into the credit reference system; transform the joint credit reporting system led by the industrial and commercial sectors into the market-oriented operation, form the complementarity between financial credit reporting institutions and commercial credit reporting institutions, and cultivate and support the credit reference agencies such as local rating, credit investigation, credit management consultation and commercial account collection to improve the credit information service system.

(III) **Develop information processing system of financial center**

Knowledge and information are the key factors affecting the financial industry aggregation. The knowledge and information attributes of financial products or financial business links determine the tendency of aggregation or decentralization. The four links of information processing system of financial center—information collection, transfer, transmission and accumulation, need to be strengthened. The perfect international financial information system shall be established in Shanghai and effective connection with Chongqing, Wuhan and other regional financial centers shall be built to form an important financial information source in the Yangtze River Economic Belt. Give full play to the role of regional financial industry association, strengthen the communication and consultation of financial industry association, gradually improve the standards of financial information, and promote the information accumulation, information transmission and information exchange of financial institutions.

(IV) **Promote the outsourcing of financial services along the Yangtze River**

With the development of information technology and financial intensification, in order to reduce the cost of rent and labor, the world financial center often moves the financial backstage business, such as data processing, to the financial center cities in developing countries. The Yangtze River Economic Belt with good information infrastructure and professional talents is one of the best options. The financial center cities in the Yangtze River Economic Belt shall actively develop the service outsourcing business of the backstage business of international financial institutions, vigorously develop the information infrastructure (mobile Internet and cloud computing, etc.), increase the introduction and cultivation of financial talents, and improve the social credit reporting system, so as to actively undertake the outsourcing of international financial services.

In order to develop financial service outsourcing in the Yangtze River Economic Belt, international well-known outsourcing providers shall be introduced, such as Reuters financial services and Indian software outsourcing giant Tata consulting, etc., as well as domestic well-known financial service outsourcing enterprises, such as Vanceinfo, Digital China, iSoftStone etc. Shanghai shall expand the outsourcing of financial services from the Yangtze River Delta to the Yangtze River Economic Belt, and cultivate a number of local outsourcing contractors with international competitiveness. Outsource a number of financial services which are relying on information technology to get rid of the constraints of geographical space to cities along the Yangtze River Economic Belt, such as financial settlement, data processing and backup. Shanghai shall further integrate all the platform resources of the outsourcing industrial belt of the Yangtze River Economic Belt, covering technology, market, intellectual property, talent, policy consultation, etc., and establish a full chain public service platform covering the outsourcing industry chain of the Yangtze River Delta.

# Coordinated Development of Ports in the Yangtze River Economic Belt

**Xiaojuan Wang**

## 1 Introduction

Relying on the "golden waterway" to build the Yangtze River Economic Belt was raised to national strategy by the top-level decision-making and deployment. At present, with the official launch of the national strategy for the construction of the Yangtze River Economic Belt, the "golden waterway" of the Yangtze River has been entrusted with the new mission of connecting the east and the west, connecting the river and the sea, and it is ushering its real golden period. The Yangtze River's freight volume has ranked the first in the world's inland rivers, but there are still contradiction between the large-scale ships and the insufficient navigable capacity of the waterway and problem of the tense port working surface; the contradiction between the low level of water logistics service and the growing high-quality logistics service; the contradiction between the increasing freight volume of the upstream and downstream and the insufficient passing capacity of the Three Gorges shiplock. In the new development period, the critical points are how to solve the current constraints on the function of the "golden waterway", to solve the problems existing in the Yangtze River, such as the poor channel conditions in some sections of the Yangtze River, the insufficient carrying capacity of the Three Gorges dam area, large scale ships, the low degree of standardization, the insufficient role of port comprehensive hub, the stable and uncertain security situation, and the weak ability of industry transformation and upgrading as well as insufficient capability for sustainable development. It has become an important topic to promote the construction of the Yangtze River Economic Belt by improving the function of the golden waterway of the Yangtze River and promoting the radiation effect of the port on the regional economy.

X. Wang (✉)
Institute of Applied Economics, Shanghai Academy of Social Sciences, Shanghai, China
e-mail: wangxiaojuan@sass.org.cn



X. Jing (ed.), *Development of the Yangtze River Economic Belt in China*, Urban Governance Practices in China,
https://doi.org/10.1007/978-981-16-1578-8_6

The study evolves closely around the contradictions and bottlenecks in the construction of the "golden waterway" of the Yangtze River, borrows the experience of river basin economic development abroad and experience of inland rivers and coastal port development. On the basis of in-depth field research, the latest theory and trend of shipping development have been used. Based on the linkage among upper reaches, middle reaches and lower reaches, that how to grasp the development trend of world shipping by promoting port cooperation, improving navigation conditions and ship type standardization construction was studied. It is necessary to adhere to the simultaneous operation of development and protection, enhance the function of "golden waterway" of the Yangtze River, and promote the modernization of shipping on Yangtze River.

## 2 Development Status of Ports in the Yangtze River Economic Belt

The Yangtze River originates from the Tuotuo River in the southwest of Geladandong Snow Mountain, the main peak of Tanggula Mountains on the Qinghai Tibet Plateau, flows through 11 provinces, cities and autonomous regions including Qinghai, Tibet, Yunnan, Sichuan, Chongqing, Hubei, Hunan, Jiangxi, Anhui, Jiangsu and Shanghai and finally flows into the East China Sea in Shanghai with a total length of 6300 km. It is ranked the third in the world for inland rivers following the Amazon and the Nile and it is with the basin area of more than 18 thousand square kilometers and accounts for about one fifth of the total area of China. It is the longest river in China. The basin area of the main waterway of the Yangtze River is large and terrain is so complicated. The basic navigation conditions and capabilities in the upper, middle and lower reaches are so different. According to the hydrological and geographical characteristics of the river, the upper, middle and lower reaches of the Yangtze River are divided into the upper reaches of Yichang, the middle reaches from Yichang to Hukou and the lower reaches below the Hukou. According to the characteristics of waterway maintenance and management, the upper, middle and lower reaches of the Yangtze River are divided into the upper reaches waterway of Yangtze River (above Yichang), the middle reaches waterway of the Yangtze River from Yichang to Hankou, and the lower reaches waterway of the Yangtze River from Hankou to Changjiang Estuary.

## *2.1 Development of Ports Along the Yangtze River Economic Belt*

### (I) Transport capacity of the Yangtze River trunk stream

At present, the 2808 km waterway of the Yangtze River trunk stream has fully reached the standard of level 3 or above. The minimum maintenance standard of the Yangtze River waterway below Wuhan reaches the national first class waterway standard; the minimum maintenance standard of the waterway from Wuhan to Chongqing reaches the national level II or above; the minimum maintenance depth of the waterway from Chongqing to Yibin reaches the national level III or above.

Port operation is the wind vane of the economic situation. The shipping on Yangtze River plays a significant role in supporting and guaranteeing the economic and social development along the Yangtze River. The steady growth of cargo throughput along the Yangtze River is inseparable from the economic development of the hinterland. The annual amount of passing cargo of the Yangtze River ranked first in the world's inland rivers for 10 consecutive years since 2005 when it won its first place for the first time. However, in recent years, due to both external and domestic demand, the growth rate of port throughput in China has generally been narrowed, the growth rate of cargo throughput of ports along the Yangtze River has also slowed down significantly, and the overstock of iron ore, coal and other resource products has become severe.

1. Cargo throughput

From 2011 to 2014, 1.66 billion tons, 1.8 billion tons, 1.92 billion tons and 2.06 billion tons of goods were respectively completed in the Yangtze River trunk stream. In 2014, the cargo throughput of the Yangtze River trunk stream was increased by 7.3% year-on-year. From 2011 to 2014, the cargo throughput of ports above the scale of the Yangtze River trunk stream was 1.58 billion tons, 1.75 billion tons, 1.86 billion tons and 1.99 billion tons respectively, with the throughput increasing year by year and with the year-on-year growth of 7.2% in 2014.

2. Foreign trade throughput

China's foreign trade has entered a new normal with medium and low speed growth. Due to weak foreign demand and trade barriers as well as the sluggish export, many export enterprises along the Yangtze River are facing the serious situation. Although the foreign trade throughput of the Yangtze River trunk stream shows an increasing curve, the growth rate is obviously slowing down. From 2011 to 2014, the ports above the Yangtze River trunk stream completed 195 million, 230 million, 249 million and 263 million tons of foreign trade cargo throughput respectively, with the year-on-year growth of 5.2% in 2014.

**Table 1** Transport capacity of the Yangtze River trunk stream (2011–2014)

| Year | Amount of passing cargo (100 million tons) | Cargo throughput (100 million tons) | Foreign trade cargo throughput (100 million tons) | Container throughput (TEU) |
|---|---|---|---|---|
| 2011 | 16.6 | 15.8 | 1.95 | 1 119.3 |
| 2012 | 18 | 17.5 | 2.3 | 1 240.7 |
| 2013 | 19.2 | 18.6 | 2.49 | 1 357 |
| 2014 | 20.6 | 19.9 | 2.63 | 1 259.5 |
| Total | 74.4 | 71.8 | 9.37 | 4 976.5 |

*Note* Both cargo throughput and foreign trade cargo throughput are the completed amount by ports above designated scale in the same year
*Source* Original information on the website of the Ministry of Transport

3. Container throughput

In recent years, affected by the slowdown of world economy and trade growth, the weak demand of major economies and the rapid growth of labor costs in domestic, the growth of container throughput in most ports has slowed down at various degrees. After years of continuous growth, the container throughput of the Yangtze River trunk waterway reached an inflection point in 2014, with only 12.955 million TEU being completed in the whole year with the year-on-year decrease of 4.5%. The container throughput growth was rising in 2011–2013. From 2011 to 2013, the container throughput was 11.193 million TEU, 12.407 million TEU and 13.57 million TEU respectively, with an increase of 23.2%, 10.9% and 9.1% respectively over the same period of the last year (refer to Table 1).

(II) **Completion of various cargoes along the Yangtze River trunk stream**

From the perspective of classification, most bulk cargoes have maintained growth since 2011 (refer to Table 2). From 2011 to 2014, the cargoes with increasing throughput include: light industrial and pharmaceutical products, mining and construction materials, grain, wood, coal and products, non-metallic ores, chemical raw materials and products, mechanical equipment and electrical appliances, metal products, fertilizers and pesticides, and non-ferrous metals, respectively, with the increase of 38%, 55%, 209%, 35%, 15%, 2%, 17%, 6%, 9%, 44% and 14% respectively compared with 2011. The types of goods with declined throughput include agricultural, forestry, animal husbandry and fishery products, cement, salt, coal and products, oil and gas products, and steel, with the decrease of 51%, 37%, 7%, 1%, 20% and 10% respectively compared with 2011 (refer to Table 2).

(III) **Port development along the Yangtze River**

1. Development of main ports along the Yangtze River

(1) Cargo throughput of major ports. From the perspective of cargo throughput, except Yichang and Anqing, the cargo throughput of other ports in the Yangtze River Economic Belt has shown a relatively gentle growth since 2011,

**Table 2** Completion of various goods along the Yangtze River (Unit: 10,000 tons)

| Type of goods | 2014 | 2013 | 2012 | 2011 |
|---|---|---|---|---|
| Agriculture, forestry, animal husbandry and fishery products | 201.13 | 236.7 | 602.75 | 407.3 |
| Light industry and pharmaceutical products | 622.84 | 624.52 | 615.46 | 451.62 |
| Mine construction materials | 3 677.34 | 3 149.02 | 2 926.7 | 2 365.92 |
| Cement | 522.38 | 949.55 | 982.86 | 822.84 |
| Foodstuff | 1 811.12 | 1 255.69 | 692.65 | 585.49 |
| Salt | 177.95 | 215.54 | 222.39 | 191.55 |
| Others | 10 793.25 | 9 820.57 | 9 133.92 | 7 999.18 |
| Wood | 1157.83 | 1 147.54 | 1 062.58 | 1010.01 |
| Coal and products | 13 896.93 | 15 583.29 | 14 452.18 | 14 085.5 |
| Nonmetallic ore | 2 718.20 | 2 847.48 | 2 724.53 | 2 659.46 |
| Chemical raw materials and products | 2 051.93 | 1 735.45 | 1 753.87 | 1 750.13 |
| Machinery, equipment, electrical appliances | 281.88 | 261.05 | 260.53 | 265.08 |
| Metal ore | 18 992.54 | 18 118.22 | 16 845.13 | 17 440.39 |
| Oil, gas and products | 2 295.80 | 2 676.88 | 2 747.66 | 2 852.32 |
| Chemical fertilizer and pesticide | 1 096.53 | 764.51 | 648.47 | 763.93 |
| Nonferrous Metals | 21.19 | 25.80 | 15.00 | 18.58 |
| Steel | 2 760.39 | 2 697.03 | 2 380.66 | 3 076.81 |

*Sources* ① Qian Zhiwu, Wang Jiao: *Production and Operation of Major Port Enterprises along the Yangtze River in 2012, China Ports*, issue No. 2, 2013
② Wang Jiao: *Operation and Prospect of Major Port Enterprises along the Yangtze River in 2014, China Ports*, issue No. 2, 2015

among which the growth rate of Jiujiang Port was the highest. From January to November 2014, the cargo throughput had been increased by 104.63% compared with the same period in 2011; the cargo throughput of Yichang Port from January to November 2014 had been decreased by 18.9% compared with that in 2011. From the perspective of internal structure, the port development level of the Yangtze River Economic Belt had obvious gradient characteristics. The economic development gradient declined from the east to the west, and the cargo throughput of the ports between the upstream, middle and lower reaches was quite different (refer to Table 3). The port cargo throughput was concentrated in the downstream ports. From January to November 2014, the port cargo throughput in the lower reaches accounted for 81.45% of the total of the Yangtze River Economic Belt, while that of the middle reaches and the upper reaches of the Yangtze River Economic Belt accounted for 9.5% and 9.05% respectively.

(2) Container throughput of major ports. From the perspective of container throughput of major ports, the container throughput of other ports in the Yangtze River Economic Belt except Jiangyin and Suzhou has shown an

**Table 3** Cargo throughput of main ports along the Yangtze River trunk stream (Unit: 10,000 tons)

| Port | Month 1–11 of 2014 | Month 1–11 of 2013 | Month 1–11 of 2012 | Month 1–11 of 2011 |
|---|---|---|---|---|
| Yibin | 1 304 | 1 050 | 1 121 | 1 064 |
| Luzhou | 2 803 | 2 446 | 2 159 | 1 930 |
| Chongqing | 13 327 | 12 304 | 11 302 | 10 353 |
| Yichang | 562 | 494 | 629 | 693 |
| Jingzhou | 731 | 657 | 556 | 462 |
| Wuhan | 7 570 | 7 134 | 7 012 | 7 005 |
| Huangshi | 2 185 | 1 935 | 1 682 | 1 659 |
| Jiujiang | 7 252 | 5 473 | 4 460 | 3 544 |
| Anqing | 2 686 | 2 645 | 2 909 | 2 758 |
| Chizhou | 3 890 | 3 517 | 3 193 | 2 830 |
| Tongling | 6 391 | 5 379 | 5 006 | 4 241 |
| Wuhu | 9 934 | 8 322 | 7 554 | 6 777 |
| Ma'anshan | 7 241 | 6 788 | 6 221 | 4 780 |
| Nanjing | 19 073 | 18 440 | 17 257 | 15 956 |
| Zhenjiang | 12 086 | 12 997 | 12 328 | 10 524 |
| Jiangming | 11 355 | 11 582 | 11 881 | 11 757 |
| Suzhou | 43 331 | 41 843 | 39 111 | 34 723 |
| Yangzhou | 7 049 | 5 560 | 4 332 | 3 950 |
| Taizhou | 14 318 | 13 854 | 11 809 | 10 878 |
| Nantong | 19 572 | 18 416 | 16 895 | 15 859 |

*Source* China Ports, 2014–2011, issue No. 12

increasing trend since 2011. Among them, the growth rate of Yibin Port was the highest and had been increased by 1496.4% from January to November 2014 compared with the same period in 2011; the container throughput of Jiangyin Port from January to November 2014 had been decreased by 53.4% compared with that in 2011. From the perspective of internal structure, container throughput also has obvious gradient characteristics. From the east to the west, the economic development gradient decreased, and the port container throughput between the upstream, middle and downstream regions varied greatly (refer to Table 4). The port container throughput was concentrated in the downstream ports. From January to November 2014, the port container throughput in the downstream region accounted for 77.57% of the total of the Yangtze River Economic Belt, while that of the middle and upper reaches of the Yangtze River Economic Belt accounted for only 11.21% and 11.22% respectively.

(3) Foreign trade cargo throughput of major ports. From the perspective of foreign trade cargo throughput of major ports, since 2011, except Jiangyin, the foreign

**Table 4** Container throughput of main ports along the Yangtze River trunk stream (Unit: 1,000 TEU)

| Port | Month 1–11 of 2014 | Month 1–11 of 2013 | Month 1–11 of 2012 | Month 1–11 of 2011 |
|---|---|---|---|---|
| Yibin | 113 | 56.6 | 22.6 | 7.2 |
| Luzhou | 284.7 | 164 | 113.7 | 90.6 |
| Chongqing | 931.6 | 837.1 | 717.3 | 628.5 |
| Yichang | 111.1 | 91.9 | 68.9 | 54.5 |
| Jingzhou | 87.3 | 86.1 | 65.8 | 58.1 |
| Wuhan | 909 | 773 | 700.4 | 654.5 |
| Huangshi | 22.8 | 21.1 | 20.9 | 19.2 |
| Jiujiang | 199.00 | 176.6 | 145.8 | 125.4 |
| Anqing | 40.10 | 32.2 | 23.2 | 16.2 |
| Chizhou | 12.00 | 10.2 | 8.5 | 7.5 |
| Tongling | 24.60 | 19.2 | 8.2 | 9.5 |
| Wuhu | 356.90 | 258.8 | 232.3 | 198.7 |
| Ma'anshan | 96.40 | 66.8 | 81.5 | 73.5 |
| Nanjing | 2 497.40 | 2 408.6 | 2 082.1 | 1 663.1 |
| Zhenjiang | 346.30 | 345 | 350.7 | 337.6 |
| Jiangming | 475.50 | 1 102.9 | 1 053.1 | 1 020.7 |
| Suzhou | 4 033 | 4 881.6 | 5 251.5 | 4 202.6 |
| Yangzhou | 496.00 | 457.4 | 362.1 | 364.7 |
| Taizhou | 176.80 | 159.6 | 121 | 109.1 |
| Nantong | 640.40 | 539.6 | 460.1 | 498.9 |

*Source* China Ports, 2014–2011, issue No. 12

trade cargo throughput of other ports in the Yangtze River Economic Belt has shown an increasing trend, of which the growth rate of Luzhou Port was the highest, with an increase of 137.04% from January to November 2014 compared with the same period in 2011; the foreign trade throughput of Jiangyin Port from January to November 2014 had been decreased by 2.24% compared with that in 2011. From the perspective of internal structure, the gradient characteristics of foreign trade throughput were more obvious. The gradient of economic development from east to West decreases, and the foreign trade throughput of upstream, middle and lower reaches differed greatly (refer to Table 5). The foreign trade throughput of ports was mainly concentrated in the downstream ports. From January to November 2014, the foreign trade throughput of the downstream regions accounted for 92.68% of the total of the Yangtze River Economic Belt, while the middle reaches and upper reaches only accounted for 5.17% and 2.15% respectively.

**Table 5** Foreign trade throughput of main ports along the Yangtze River trunk stream (Unit: 10, 000 tons)

| Port | Month 1–11 of 2014 | Month 1–11 of 2013 | Month 1–11 of 2012 | Month 1–11 of 2011 |
|---|---|---|---|---|
| Yibin | – | – | – | – |
| Luzhou | 64 | 45 | 32 | 27 |
| Chongqing | 470 | 412 | 378 | 319 |
| Yichang | 55 | 45 | 37 | 27 |
| Jingzhou | 38 | 40 | 30 | 26 |
| Wuhan | 645 | 537 | 454 | 381 |
| Huangshi | 371 | 298 | 243 | 219 |
| Jiujiang | 178 | 170 | 130 | 116 |
| Anqing | 21 | 20 | 14 | 10 |
| Chizhou | 20 | 20 | 15 | 19 |
| Tongling | 37 | 28 | 17 | 17 |
| Wuhu | 200 | 171 | 142 | 150 |
| Ma'anshan | 86 | 59 | 59 | 58 |
| Nanjing | 1 800 | 2 027 | 1 626 | 964 |
| Zhenjiang | 2 186 | 2 459 | 1 933 | 1 727 |
| Jiangming | 1 223 | 1 361 | 1 276 | 1 251 |
| Suzhou | 11 130 | 10 071 | 9 566 | 9 021 |
| Yangzhou | 564 | 354 | 365 | 326 |
| Taizhou | 1 481 | 1 071 | 993 | 891 |
| Nantong | 4 302 | 3 996 | 3 482 | 2 735 |

*Source* China Ports, 2014–2011, issue No. 12

## 2.2 Development of Major Coastal Ports in the Yangtze River Economic Belt

In recent years, under the stimulation of the goal of establishing the maritime power, implementing the national marine strategy and China (Shanghai) pilot Free Trade Zone, the cargo throughput of ports above designated scale in China has reached 11.2 billion tons, with a year-on-year increase of 4.8%, and the completed throughput was 3.5 billion tons, with an increase of 5.9% and the growth rate dropped by 3.8% points compared with the same period of last year; domestic trade reached 7.7 billion tons, with an increase of 4.3% and the growth rate dropped by 4.3% points compared the same period of the last year. The container throughput of ports above designated scale reached 200 million TEUs, with a year-on-year increase of 6.1% and the growth rate dropped by 1% compared with the same period of the last year.

The coastal ports in the Yangtze River Economic Belt are concentrated in the lower Yangtze River Delta, including Shanghai Port, Ningbo Zhoushan Port and

Lianyungang Port. Coastal ports play a particularly important role in the construction of the Yangtze River Economic Belt. In the long run, with the continuous promotion of the Yangtze River waterway regulation, the modernization of Inland River Maritime Service and shipping information management, the standardization of inland river ships and the increase of average tonnage, as well as the cultivation of river sea intermodal transportation and river sea direct transportation, combined waterway and railway transport and combined waterway and road transport, as the first channel in the Yangtze River Economic Belt, the role of the Yangtze River will be more important. With the development strategy of Yangtze River Economic Belt and the construction of free trade pilot zone, higher requirements are put forward for coastal ports, and there will be significant strategic opportunities for the development of coastal port groups.

1. Port cargo throughput

From January to November 2014, the three major coastal ports had completed a total cargo throughput of 1598.69 million tons. The cargo throughput of ports above designated scale accounted for 31.7% of the national total compared with the same period in 2013 (refer to Table 6). However, it continued to maintain a particularly important position in economic and port shipping development in China. From January to November 2014, the cargo throughput growth of Ningbo Zhoushan Port and Lianyungang Port had been increased compared with the previous year, while Shanghai Port presented negative growth. In 2014, the cargo throughput was 614.06 million tons, with a decrease of 1.92% compared with 2013. In addition, according to the list of top 10 cargo throughput ports, the throughput of Ningbo Zhoushan Port exceeded 800 million tons in 2013, and reached 873 million tons in 2014, with a growth rate of 7.86%. Not only was the cargo throughput ranked the first in the world and the total amount is huge, but also the growth rate performed excellent with the strong growth momentum.

**Table 6** Cargo throughput of coastal ports in major areas of Yangtze River Economic Belt (Unit: 10,000 tons)

| Region | Month 1–11 of 2014 | Month 1–11 of 2013 | Month 1–11 of 2012 | Month 1–11 of 2011 |
|---|---|---|---|---|
| Shanghai Port | 61 406 | 62 606 | 58 332 | 57 021 |
| Lianyun Port | 18 065 | 17 399 | 15 929 | 14 484 |
| Ningbo Zhoushan Port | 80 398 | 74 927 | 68 348 | 64 104 |
| Total | 159 869 | 154 932 | 142 609 | 135 609 |
| Whole state | 1 022 690 | 974 935 | 890 960 | 832 452 |
| Proportion in China (%) | 15.63 | 15.89 | 16.01 | 16.29 |

*Source* Website of the Ministry of Transport of China

According to the data, the cargo throughput of Ningbo Zhoushan Port surpassed Shanghai port for the first time in 2012 by more than 8 million tons and was ranked the first in both China and the world. In 2014, Ningbo Zhoushan Port accumulated strength by opening up new routes, new hinterland and improving port collection and distribution. The gap between Ningbo Zhoushan Port and Shanghai Port expanded from 34 million tons in 2013 to 118 million tons, occupying the first place in China and even the world in terms of total amount and growth rate. Under the influence of industrial adjustment and industrial relocation, the proportion of bulk cargo in Shanghai Port such as coal and iron ore has declined year by year. In addition, the recovery of international trade is slow, and the container throughput has not been improved significantly. The port throughput has been decreased by 267% ~ 755 million tons on year-on-year basis.

With its geographical location at the mouth of the Yangtze River and the economic position of Shanghai as the national trade center, Shanghai Port became the leader of the Yangtze River waterway. In recent years, Shanghai Port Group has continued to implement the "Yangtze River Strategy" to strengthen the integration of port berths and shipping routes. However, considering that the development of deep water shoreline resources of Shanghai Port has become saturated, and the pressure of traffic organization and pollution prevention caused by huge logistics is increasing, so it is urgent for other ports to share the logistics pressure of Shanghai Port. To give full play to Ningbo Zhoushan Port, the world's largest comprehensive port, the fifth largest container port, and the largest sea-rail intermodal port in the south, we can take its advantages of rich deep water shoreline resources and huge logistics carrying capacity. At present, it has been formally put on the agenda to accelerate the construction of Ningbo Zhoushan river-sea intermodal transport center and to establish a large northward channel.

2. Foreign trade cargo throughput

From the perspective of foreign trade cargo throughput (see Table 7), in 2014, due to the continuous decline in the growth rate of foreign trade import and export, the growth rate of foreign trade cargo throughput of coastal ports in the Yangtze River Economic Belt showed an obvious downward trend. From January to November 2014, the total foreign trade cargo throughput of the three coastal ports reached 839.26 million tons, a year-on-year increase of 5.21%, accounting for a slight decrease of 25.91% over the same period of the last year.

3. Port container throughput

According to the ranking data, the top 10 container throughput ports in China in 2014 were Shanghai Port, Shenzhen Port, Ningbo Zhoushan Port, Qingdao Port, Guangzhou Port, Tianjin Port, Dalian Port, Xiamen Port, Yingkou Port and Lianyungang Port in sequence. The ranking order of the top 10 container ports in China mainland in 2014 did not change much compared with that in 2013, and the order of the top 8 container ports was completely consistent with that of the previous year (refer to Table 8). Yingkou Port jumped from the 11th in 2013 to the 9th in

**Table 7** Cargo throughput of ports above designated scale in Yangtze River Delta

| Region | Foreign trade cargo throughput | Port proportion (%) | | Proportion in China (%) | |
|---|---|---|---|---|---|
| | 10,000 tons | Month 1–11 of 2014 | Month 1–11 of 2013 | Month 1–11 of 2014 | Month 1–11 of 2013 |
| Shanghai Port | 35 094 | 41.82 | 43.38 | 10.80 | 11.3 |
| Lianyun Port | 10 202 | 12.16 | 12.20 | 3.10 | 3.2 |
| Ningbo Zhoushan Port | 38 630 | 46.03 | 44.42 | 11.90 | 11.6 |
| Total | 83 926 | 100.0 | 100.0 | 25.91 | 26.16 |
| Whole state | 323 927 | – | – | 100.0 | 100.0 |

*Source* Website of the Ministry of Transport of China

**Table 8** Port container throughput in 2014 (Unit: 10,000 TEU)

| Ranking in 2014 | Ranking in 2013 | Port | 2014 | Growth rate (%) | 2013 | Growth rate (%) |
|---|---|---|---|---|---|---|
| 1 | 1 | Shanghai Port | 3 528.50 | 4.96 | 3 361.70 | 3.34 |
| 2 | 2 | Shenzhen Port | 2 403.00 | 3.23 | 2 327.90 | 1.47 |
| 3 | 3 | Ningbo-Zhoushan Port | 1 945.00 | 12.10 | 1 735.07 | 7.27 |
| 4 | 4 | Qingdao Port | 1 662.44 | 7.10 | 1 552.2 | 7.03 |
| 5 | 5 | Guangzhou Port | 1 616.00 | 5.54 | 1 531.10 | 5.25 |
| 6 | 6 | Tianjin Port | 1 405.00 | 7.98 | 1301.20 | 5.76 |
| 7 | 7 | Dalian Port | 1 012.76 | 1.12 | 1 001.50 | 24.19 |
| 8 | 8 | Xiamen Port | 857.24 | 7.05 | 800.80 | 11.19 |
| 9 | 11 | Yingkou Port | 576.82 | 8.81 | 530.10 | 9.28 |
| 10 | 9 | Lianyungang Port | 500.54 | −8.79 | 548.80 | 9.32 |
| 11 | 10 | Suzhou Port | 445.00 | −16.12 | 530.50 | −9.52 |
| 12 | 12 | Foshan Port | 287.26 | 4.46 | 275.00 | 3.11 |
| 13 | 17 | Humen Port | 283.60 | 49.82 | 189.29 | 36.25 |
| 14 | 13 | Nanjing Port | 276.00 | 3.41 | 266.90 | 15.94 |
| 15 | 15 | Rizhao Port | 242.00 | 19.39 | 202.70 | 15.89 |
| 16 | 14 | Yantai Port | 236.12 | 9.82 | 215.00 | 16.22 |
| 17 | 16 | Fuzhou Port | 223.94 | 13.22 | 197.80 | 8.38 |
| 18 | 18 | Quanzhou Port | 188.45 | 10.79 | 170.10 | 0.24 |
| 19 | 19 | Dandong Port | 167.00 | 10.74 | 150.80 | 24.80 |
| 20 | 20 | Zhongshan Port | 135.70 | 2.80 | 132.00 | 6.45 |

2014. Affected by this, Lianyungang Port and Suzhou Port, which ranked 9th and 10th in 2013, respectively had one place down in 2014. Suzhou Port ranked 11th in 2014 and was not listed in the top 10. This also showed that top 10 container ports in China were all occupied by coastal ports. In 2014, there were 10 ports with container throughput of more than 5 million TEU in mainland China. Among the top ten container ports in China, there were 7 ports with more than 10 million TEU with the same number as in 2013, namely, Shanghai Port, Shenzhen Port, Ningbo Zhoushan Port, Qingdao Port, Guangzhou Port, Tianjin Port and Dalian Port. After the container throughput of Dalian Port exceeded 10 million TEU for the first time in 2013 by reaching 10.015 million TEU, 10.132 million TEU was completed in 2014, and firmly held the position in the list of ports above ten million TEU.

The container throughput of the coastal ports in the Yangtze River Economic Belt has achieved and maintained a steady growth. In 2014, the container throughput of the coastal ports in the Yangtze River Economic Belt reached 59.7404 million TEU, with a year-on-year increase of 5.81%. In 2014, Shanghai Port completed 35.285 million TEU and was ranked first in the list, and also ranked first in both China and the world. Lianyungang Port achieved 5.05 million TEU of container throughput due to the huge drop of 8.8% growth rate in 2014. Ningbo Zhoushan Port completed 19.449 million TEU in the whole year, which was only about 500,000 TEU lower than the standard of 20 million TEU.

## 3 International Experience of Coordinated Port Development

It is the common experience of many developed countries in the process of modernization to start from the coastal areas and go back inland, then to the deep hinterland. As the modern economic development and international trade development are inseparable, and bulk trade is often inseparable with ocean and coastal shipping, coastal ports, as the bulk trade distribution centers, often play as the pivot in economic development. The coastal cities with good ports have a strong radiation effect on the inland. The radiation generally expands along the important traffic trunk lines to the deep hinterland. The inland river shipping has the characteristics of large traffic volume, low cost and well connection with the hinterland of the river basin, which leads to its unique advantages in conducting radiation and provides various market conditions and various elements for the gradient development of the economy.

A series of measures were carried out in the Rhine River in Europe and Tokyo Bay in Japan by promoting the comprehensive development and utilization of water resources, establishing the comprehensive management organization for unified development, establishing the waterway network with unified standards, direct approaching between trunk and branches, communication between river and sea, large-scale centralized development in short period of time, full application of advanced technology, and promotion of modern development of water transportation so that the river management was promoted and the regional economy development was driven. The experience of port development in developed countries can be taken as the reference for the construction of the "golden waterway" of the Yangtze River and the coordinated development of ports in the Yangtze River Basin.

## *3.1 Experience from the Rhine River Basin in Europe*

The main experience of the development of the Rhine River basin includes the first is the development of sound shipping network. The comprehensive management of the river waterways was carried out, and inland river shipping was vigorously developed by improving the waterway level; at the same time, the inland road, railway, pipeline transportation and other logistics transportation modes were connected with shipping, and a three-dimensional transportation network system was established. Second is the port city linkage to develop the "point–line–area" basin economy. A perfect logistics and shipping network system can help to build a gathering area of industries and talents, thus to promote the formation of the economic belt along the river, and finally structure the "point–line–area" spatial development pattern with the core port city as the radiation point, the riverside economic belt as the development line, and the basin economic zone as the development plane. Third is the simultaneous regulation and development. The ecological environment protection shall be paid enough attention. Various measures are combined and a unified basin management organization was established for the development of the Rhine River Basin, the corresponding laws and regulations were formulated and perfected, and the ecological environment protection was integrated into the development strategy, so that equal attention can be paid to the technical, social, economic and ecological elements.

## *3.2 Integration of New York New Jersey Port*

The experience of the coordinated development of New York New Jersey Port can be summarized as two in one, which means the committee management and landlord port operation. New York Port and New Jersey Port were originally two independent ports, which belonged to the states of New York and New Jersey respectively. In history, the argument between two ports about the ownership of some neighboring areas has never stopped. For the better development of the two ports, the New York and New Jersey governments jointly established the New York and New Jersey Port Authority on April 30, 1921. It covers an area of about 1500 square miles, centered on the statue of liberty in New York, with a radius of 25 miles. It was divided into two port areas, New York and New Jersey. The port authority was officially named (Port Authority of New York and New Jersey) in 1972 to show the characteristics of the joint formation of the two states. After more than 80 years of development, New York New Jersey Port has become the largest port on the east coast of the United States by 2005, with a cargo throughput of 125 million tons and a container throughput of 5.26 million TEU.

There are many things to learn from the integration of New Jersey Port in New York, among which the most important is its unique management system and flexible management system. From the perspective of management system, the New York New Jersey Port Authority is a self-sufficient public institution in finance. It has no tax support from any state or local authority, and has no authority to levy any tax. The port authority mainly relies on the income from users of its facilities to maintain its management and operation. The port authority is governed by the management committee, which is composed of 12 members. Six governors from each state are appointed as the members with the approval of the State Senate. The management board appoints an executive director to implement the policies and be responsible for the daily management. Under this unique management system, the New York New Jersey Port Authority, as a public organization, is not built on the basis of traditional bureaucratic system, but more like an enterprise. It has the greatest autonomy in a certain scope of authority and can independently determine how the port shall develop. Therefore, it is very efficient in policy formulation and implementation.

### *3.3 Integration of Tokyo Bay Port Group in Japan*

The experience of coordinated development of Tokyo Bay Port Group in Japan can be summarized as follows: government guidance, division of work and cooperation, dislocation development and complementary advantages. In 1951, the Japanese government enacted the "harbor law", which strengthened the government's rights in the overall planning. It stipulated that the central government (the Ministry of transport) should formulate a five-year plan for the development of ports in the whole country, and determine the quantity, scale and policy of port development in the whole country. As early as 1967, the Port Bureau of Japan's Ministry of transport put forward the proposal of "the basic concept of the Tokyo Bay harbor plan". It is suggested that the seven ports in the region, including Tokyo port, Chiba port, Kawasaki port, Yokohama port, Yokosuka port, Kisaradzu port and Funabashi port, be integrated into an organic group with different division of work to form a "wide area harbor". The implementation of this concept has solved the problem of port competition in Tokyo Bay and transformed the competition of each port into an overall joint force. After years of development, Tokyo Bay Port Group has more and more formed a distinct function division system. Each main port undertakes different functions according to its own foundation and characteristics, and forms a combination on the basis of division of work and cooperation and complementary advantages. Although the operation still maintains its own independence, it forms a whole in the external competition, jointly soliciting goods and publicizing the whole. In this way, the six ports have formed a multi-functional complex, making full use of resources and enhancing competitiveness.

## 4 External Environment for Coordinated Development of Ports in the Yangtze River Economic Belt

### *4.1 International Environment*

From 2000 to 2007, the world economy has maintained a relatively high growth trend. In August 2007, the U.S. subprime mortgage crisis broke out, the world economic growth rate fell to 2.8% in 2008, and the economic growth rate was negative in 2009. From 2010 to 2013, the world economic growth has been on a slide, and the world economy has maintained a weak growth. The complexity of the world economic situation also has an impact on world trade volume. From 1999 to 2008, the export volume and import volume of world trade were kept with certain increase every year, but the world trade showed negative growth in 2009, and the growth rate of export and import in 2012 was almost zero, and the growth of world trade was not optimistic.

Like the current world economy, the development of port transportation industry has entered a new round of adjustment. At present, the global economic growth is slowing down and the international trade is decreasing, which has caused serious negative impact on the development of port transportation industry both at home and abroad. From the perspective of future trade volume in China, the *2030 China Shipping Development Outlook* released by Shanghai International Shipping Research Center in 2015 put forward that China will remain as the world's largest cargo trading country in 2030, and will dominate the shipping trade of global container. By 2030, China's international shipping volume is expected to reach 6.2 billion tons, accounting for 17% of the global shipping volume. Among them, the demand for iron ore and coal in dry bulk transportation will significantly slow down, the import of grain and oil will grow rapidly, and the total volume of import and export cargo by international container on sea will exceed 200 million TEU.

The change of world economic structure, especially under the expectation of a new round of complicated and changeable trade situation, a new pattern of maritime trade routes will be formed. The growth of maritime transport volume among Asian countries and regions will be accelerated, and position of China in maritime trade will be gradually improved. In this process, the port group of Yangtze River Economic Belt, which undertakes more than one third of the national cargo throughput, will embrace more opportunities and confront more competitions.

### *4.2 Domestic Environment*

From the perspective of domestic environment, China will move from the middle and late stage of industrialization to the later stage of industrialization in the next 15 years, and the goal of building a moderately prosperous society in an all-round way and doubling national income shall be realized within this 15 years. China's economic development will enter the "shifting period" of growth rate, the "pain period" of structural adjustment and the "digestion period" of early stimulus policies, and a new normal with 7% economic growth will be formed. Structural upgrading will become the main feature of economic development. The investment and export-oriented economy will gradually transit to the consumption oriented economy, and gradually change from material consumption to service-oriented consumption. The industrial structure will be adjusted rapidly, and will be upgraded from "manufacturing workshop" to "service aircraft carrier" through the transformation and upgrading of the industry driven by informatization. The implementation of the new concept of regional development strategy will be accelerated, and the molding of all-round development pattern of simultaneous development of river and sea and interaction between east and west will be expedited.

(I) **Opening wider to the outside world and implementing the "The Belt and Road Initiative" strategy**

Promoting "The Belt and Road Initiative" strategy is not only the need for China to expand and deepen its opening up, but also the need to strengthen mutually beneficial cooperation with Asia, Europe, Africa and the rest of the world. The "The Belt and Road Initiative" will build a new round of opening up "one body two wings", while speeding up the opening up to the west while enhancing the opening level to the east to boost the edge of the inland border areas to the forefront of the opening up. The Belt and Road Initiative strategy includes not only the free trade agreement in the traditional sense, but also the Greater Mekong cooperation, the economic corridor, the transnational transportation line and the financial cooperation. For such an important logistics node, the port will usher the rare development opportunity. According to "The Belt and Road Initiative" vision plan, 16 ports including Shanghai, Tianjin, Ningbo-Zhoushan, etc. were defined as the "Maritime Strategic Fulcrum for Shanghai". The allocation of trade and production elements along the line will be optimized in The Belt and Road Initiative strategy by relying on the interconnection of infrastructure along the line. It will speed up the interconnection of various transportation modes such as highways, railways, civil aviation and transportation on sea. Therefore, how to seize the opportunity to promote the coordinated development of the port and to realize the transformation and upgrading of the ports in the Yangtze River Economic Belt is the need to dock "The Belt and Road Initiative" strategy.

(II) **The construction of the Yangtze River Economic Belt has become a new choice for China's regional development by linking the east, the middle and the west**

In recent years, great changes have taken place in some basic conditions supporting China's regional economic development, which are mainly manifested in the cumulative effect of the long-term continuous investment in large-scale for transportation and communication infrastructure, especially the formation of high-speed railway network and the formation of river-sea intermodal transport network. The traditional relatively static regional development pattern in China has been changed, so it makes the rapid circulation of element resources between different regions possible, which greatly shortened the space-time distance between different regions, thus to provide basic conditions for reshaping the pattern of regional development, especially promoting the linkage development between regions. In this context, since the 18th National Congress of the Communist Party of China, the new generation of central leadership has rapidly formed a new vision and layout for China's economic development, and put forward the strategic concept of promoting the construction of the Yangtze River Economic Belt by relying on the "golden waterway" of the Yangtze River. With the river basin as the link, the coastal area as the driving force, the hinterland as the focus, the east and the west are linked together with gradient advancement and common development. It marks that China's national regional strategic choice has entered a new stage since the reform and opening up, that is, great importance starts to be given on the linkage effect between different regions and the overall development.

The river to sea transportation can be realized by the Yangtze River "golden waterway" construction and the future port throughput will present growth trend. According to the *2030 China Shipping Development Outlook*, the shipping demand of the Yangtze River in 2030 will reach nearly 3.8 billion tons. The Yangtze River will become the main channel for resource allocation in the east, middle and west, and the volume of container and liquefied natural gas will be increase at least four times compared with the present. For a long time, the hinterland of the Yangtze River has always been a battleground for the ports in the lower reaches of the Yangtze River. The cargo from the Yangtze River accounts for the majority of Shanghai Port, and the water-water container transfer has reached 45.7%. With the promotion of the strategy of the Yangtze River Economic Belt and in order to cope with the increase of throughput in the future, it is necessary to have the coordinated development of ports. Within the scope of coordinated port planning along the Yangtze River Economic Belt, the phenomenon of disordered and crowded ports can be solved.

### (III) The policy effect of free trade zone promotes the optimization and upgrading of ports in the Yangtze River Economic Belt

Shanghai Port is the estuary of the "golden waterway" of the Yangtze River, and it is the key point to realize direct river-sea connection. The establishment of Shanghai free trade zone provides favorable conditions for Shanghai Port development to find the new growth point. On the one hand, the FTZ will further promote the upgrading of the whole foreign trade and processing industry in the lower reaches, deepen the integration process of trade and finance, so as to promote the regional institutional innovation, and force the hinterland cities to create a better financial policy environment and ecological environment as well as obtain new development opportunities. On the other hand, a free trade zone with convenient investment and trade, free currency exchange, efficient and convenient supervision, and standardized legal environment will help Shanghai Port to truly realize the transformation from "within the border and custom" to "inside the border and outside the custom" and vigorously promote the development of intermediary trade so that it can play more active role in the process of global resource allocation. In recent years, the trend of large-scale ship development and the fierce competition of surrounding ports make it have to face its own development bottleneck. To enlarge the effect of the free trade zone, the ports in the lower reaches are required to actively cooperate with the surrounding ports.

## 5 Constraints on Coordinated Development of Ports in the Yangtze River Economic Belt

The construction of the "golden waterway" of the Yangtze River is the basic condition of the national strategy for the Yangtze River Economic Belt. Although the construction of the "golden waterway" has made great achievements in recent years and the navigation capacity has been greatly improved, there are still some bottlenecks in the Yangtze River Navigation, such as poor channel conditions in some sections of the Yangtze River, the insufficient carrying capacity of the Three Gorges dam area, the large-scale ship and low degree of standardization, and the role of port comprehensive hub being not fully played, stable but uncertain security situation, as well as weak industrial transformation and upgrading and weak sustainable development capacity, which have affected the port development and the driving and radiating function of ports on regional economy.

### *5.1 Navigation Potential of Yangtze River to Be Improved*

This is the primary problem that must be solved to promote port cooperation in the Yangtze River Economic Belt. At present, the Yangtze River shipping develops rapidly, but the quality of development is not good enough, and the benefits of port and shipping enterprises are not well enough. Compared with the new requirements of supporting the growth of the Yangtze River Economic Belt and the development of urbanization, industrialization, informatization and agricultural modernization, there is still a big gap.

(I) **Insufficient transit capacity of the Yangtze River**

It is mainly manifested in the saturation of the capacity of the Three Gorges shiplock in the upper reaches, the bottleneck of the waterway conditions in the middle reaches of Jingjiang River, and the clearance height of the lower reaches represented by the Nanjing Yangtze River Bridge. In addition, the governance over the whole segment system is not enough, and the channel development and maintenance capacity is insufficient.

1. Saturated capacity of Three Gorges shiplock

At present, the transportation through the dam of the Three Gorges is mainly by the shiplock, being supplemented by dam crossing on highway. The annual capacity of two-way shiplock for the Three Gorges dam is designed to be 100 million tons, and dam crossing by highway is mainly carried out by the highway in the south of the river. According to the relevant statistical data of the Three Gorges navigation administration, the cargo volume through the lock exceeded 100 million tons in 2011 but it was decreased in 2012. However, the freight volume of the lock exceeded 100 million tons again in 2013, breaking through the design capacity of the Three Gorges shiplock. According to the preliminary research of the Yangtze River Navigation Administration Bureau and the Comprehensive Transportation Research Institute of the National Development and Reform Commission, the freight volume of the upper reaches of the Yangtze River will reach 150 million tons around 2014, but Chongqing alone will have a total industrial output value of 2 trillion yuan in 2015, which will generate 180 million tons of water transportation. With the increase of transportation demand in the future, the transportation capacity through the shiplock will become the bottleneck of transportation through the dam. Therefore, effective measures shall be taken to improve the transportation capacity.

2. Bottleneck of channel in Jingjiang section of middle reaches

The water depth of channel for the middle reaches is obviously lower than that of the upper and lower reaches. Especially in the dry season, the appearance of multiple bends, narrow and shallow shoal and other navigation obstructing nodes in the middle reaches of the Yangtze River make it difficult to maintain the channel. The maintenance scale and standard are low and lagging far behind the maintenance standard of the channel in the lower reaches of the Yangtze River. However, with the obvious trend of large-scale ships in the lower reaches of the Yangtze River and the Three Gorges Reservoir area, the channel conditions in the middle reaches are becoming increasingly unbearable. The channel in the middle reaches of the Yangtze River plays an important role in connecting the upper and lower reaches. If the middle reaches is smooth, the Yangtze River will be smooth. The obstruction of the middle reaches has seriously restricted the overall benefits of the "golden waterway" of the Yangtze River.

3. The problem of clearance height in the lower reaches as represented by Nanjing Yangtze River Bridge

Nanjing Yangtze River Bridge, built in 1968, is the first highway railway bridge in China. With the development of the "golden waterway" of the Yangtze River, the contradiction between Nanjing Yangtze River Bridge and Yangtze River shipping is deepening. Because the clearance height of the bridge is only 24 m, 10,000 ton ships cannot go up along the river. A large number of transportation materials must be transshipped in Nanjing, which wastes a lot of financial and human resources, and affects the transportation efficiency of the Yangtze River "golden waterway". The buildings crossing the river (such as bridges) have also become one of the biggest bottlenecks to prevent the Yangtze River Navigation from turning into the "golden waterway".

Since then, the clearance of the newly-built Wuhu, Tongling, Anqing and other Yangtze River bridges also referred to the clearance height of Nanjing Yangtze River Bridge by mistake. Taking the impact on Anhui Province as an example, the 213 km deep-water channel from Nanjing to Tongling, which can be used for 10,000 ton class ocean ships, has not been fully utilized. Anhui Province cannot open direct foreign trade routes, and a large number of transportation materials must be transshipped in Nanjing. The lack of effective development of port economy and opening to the outside world has also seriously restricted the overall development of Anhui economy.

### (II) **Small scale of coastal ports**

The ports along the Yangtze River are small in scale, single in function, unreasonable in structure and unsuitable in collecting and distributing systems. Most of the ports are limited to traditional loading and unloading business and transit business. The construction capacity of wharf is relatively surplus, and the homogenization competition is intensified. With the decentralization of national port administrative authority to local governments, the enthusiasm of local governments to develop ports is unprecedented. The government pursued the political achievements only but failed to fully implement the profound connotation of the scientific outlook on development, which resulted in serious duplication of construction, aggravation of homogeneous competition, low investment efficiency of port enterprises and serious waste of resources.

The funds for wharf construction are insufficient. This is the bottleneck restricting the development of the port. The Yangtze River port needs a lot of investment to adjust its structure and to upgrade. However, the Yangtze River port enterprises have very low profit, so it is far from satisfying the needs of enterprise development by relying on their own capital capacity. Moreover, the loan interest rate remains high, the enterprise financing is becoming more difficult and the financing cost is getting higher.

### (III) **Port software construction is generally lagging behind**

In the Yangtze River Economic Belt, especially in the lower reaches of the Yangtze River, ports are often continuously developed in patches, and the utilization rate of coastline is quite high. However, other departments, such as material and industrial departments, have such problems as scattered distribution and long shoreline occupation, which lead to the phenomenon of more occupation and less use, shallow use of deep water, private use of public land, and vicious development. As a result, the hardware and software of each port cannot form the situation of complementary advantages and reasonable division of work, which reduces the overall utilization efficiency. Most of the ports and shipping enterprises are state-owned enterprises with weak market service consciousness. The efficiency of port loading and unloading as well as customs clearance cannot compete with that of international ports. The ship owners, cargo owners, shipping agents, freight forwarders and port and shipping enterprises are not getting along well with each other.

In addition, compared with developed countries, most ports are still backward in their understanding of the functions of information systems, and have not placed them at the height of enterprise development strategy, business process reengineering and decision-making research. The international advanced concepts of shipping automation and intelligence have not been fully reflected in the shipping market of the Yangtze River Economic Belt. There is no innovation system and mechanism in shipping technology innovation, and the investment in research and development is very limited.

(IV) **Unreasonable port charges**

The purpose to collect the port construction fee is for the port infrastructure construction, but after the subject of collection is changed, 80% of the current port construction fee is handed over to the state, and the other 20% is fed back to the local government. The part to the local government has not been used for the construction of port infrastructure, which has violated the original purpose of levying this charge. In addition, the collection standard of port construction fee is very high, which greatly increases the burden of cargo owners. The original intention of levying harbor dues on cargo is to solve the problem of capital sources of port infrastructure, but now it has completely become administrative fees.

## *5.2 Problems in Cooperation Between Ports*

(I) **The customs clearance system in the Yangtze River Basin needs to be improved**

At present, the General Administration of Customs (GAC) has 12 agencies directly under the GAC, such as Wuhan Customs in 11 provinces and cities along the Yangtze River. There are still many restrictions on trans-regional declaration, and the related procedures are complicated and at high cost. For example, although the customs agencies in Hubei are under the jurisdiction of Wuhan Customs, their business is relatively independent and there are similar problems. For example, goods are shipped from Yichang and Xiangyang to Wuhan for export, customs transfer procedures must be handled.

At present, Shanghai Customs has established a regional customs clearance cooperation mechanism with all customs directly under the GAC, so as to realize the full coverage of regional customs clearance reform. At the same time, Shanghai port has played an active role as a hub port to build a domestic support base for local export enterprises. In recent years, Shanghai Customs has steadily promoted the pilot of tax refund policy at the port of departure, strengthened the contact with the customs of Wuhan and Qingdao, followed up the implementation and made timely evaluation. According to the relevant information of the GAC, as of 2014, the GAC has established customs clearance cooperation mechanism for the Yangtze River Delta region, Shanghai and six provinces in Central China, Sichuan, Chongqing and Shanghai. According to the laws of market and logistics, it is necessary to promote the regional customs clearance reform of 11 provinces and cities in the Yangtze River Economic Belt in the future and strive to realize the integration of different customs along the Yangtze River.

(II) **Lack of trans-regional cooperation mechanism between ports**

The improvement of the layout of the Yangtze River port system and the formation of a good competition and cooperation relationship between the ports are the basic guarantee for the Yangtze River ports to act their functions. The construction of Shanghai International Shipping Center will directly promote the development of ports along the Yangtze River in Jiangsu Province, and further strengthen the advantages of ports along the Yangtze River in Anhui Province. Other areas of the Yangtze River will gradually form a port group with Wuhan as the center in the middle reaches and Chongqing as the center in the upper reaches. The layout of the Yangtze River port system will continue to be improved, and its functions will continue to be expanded. However, no matter in terms of economic strength, market environment, business philosophy and management technology, there is a big gap between the ports in the middle and upper reaches of the Yangtze River and the ports in the lower reaches of the Yangtze River Delta. There is no cooperation mechanism between the ports and the top-level design to promote the cooperation between ports. On the one hand, due to the fierce market competition, some ports in the lower reaches of Yangtze River Delta continue to explore the middle and upper reaches of the market, and on the one hand, the ports in upper and middle reaches need to seek funds and technology to develop and strengthen themselves. At present, the demand for cooperation and alliance between ports in all upper, middle and lower reaches of the Yangtze River is constantly strengthening. It is urgent to establish a formal coordination and communication mechanism to increase the exchange and cooperation between ports in the Yangtze River.

Because of the above problems, the shipping potential of the Yangtze River has not been brought into full play, and the role of the "golden waterway" of the Yangtze River as a major traffic artery running through the eastern, central and western regions of China has also been affected. The proportion of senior channel is not high, the obstruction problem of middle and upper reaches channel is prominent, and the efficient collection and distribution system has not been formed yet. The connections of various modes of transportation are not smooth, and the effective connection of railway to waterway, road to waterway and air to railway has not been realized yet. At the same time, the Yangtze River Economic Belt is still lack of institutions that can effectively coordinate the actions of the whole basin. As a result, the problem for unified planning and construction of new railway lines, airports, ports and other major infrastructure have not been solved. The trans-regional transport of the "golden waterway" of the Yangtze River is far from the requirements of economic development. There are few large-scale multilateral joint investment projects, and it is difficult to carry out the inter-city industrial division of work. The regional ecological cooperation mechanism has been failed to be constructed.

# 6 Countermeasures and Suggestions for Promoting Coordinated Development of Ports

It is a long-term strategy to enhance the "golden waterway" function of the Yangtze River and promote the coordinated development of ports in the Yangtze River Economic Belt. According to the *Guidance* of the State Council on the construction of the Yangtze River Economic Belt and the *Comprehensive Three-dimensional Transportation Corridor Planning of the Yangtze River Economic Belt (2014–2020)*, various places along the Yangtze River Economic Belt have issued several *Implementation Opinions* and *Action Plans* on promoting and participating in the construction of the Yangtze River Economic Belt, and put forward the strategic objectives and strategic ideas for port development. However, to promote the coordinated development of ports in the basin and to coordinate and balance the interests between ports, it is necessary to jump out of the limitations of regional space and put forward policy ideas at the operation level.

## *6.1 Establish a Collaborative Mechanism Led by Port Enterprises*

### (I) Give full play to the role of trade associations

The trade association is composed by the enterprises which are the main body of the market because of their own profit tendency. Once the industry association becomes an independent non-governmental organization, it can protect the interests of the industry externally, form a self-discipline mechanism internally, and prevent the disordered competition of enterprises. At present, China Port Association at both national level and port association at local level have been established. The main task of China Port Association is to perform the functions of industry service, industry coordination and industry self-discipline at the national level. China Port Association has also established a single industry branch such as port container branch, road transportation branch, port cruise branch, and the Yangtze River port branch based on the Yangtze River system. However, the port association at regional level based on the port group has not yet been established. The access to trans-regional port service, coordination and self-discipline is beyond the grasp of port associations at the local level, such as Shanghai Port Association, Zhejiang Port Association and

Jiangsu Port Association. However, port associations at the regional level can break through administrative barriers and administrative blockades to become the lubricant for cooperation between ports.

The higher-level intergovernmental coordination and cooperation platform has not been established in the Yangtze River Economic Belt yet. Learning from the successful experience of European ports organizations, the port shipping association of the Yangtze River Economic Belt shall be established as soon as possible, and the port coordination shall be given the priority. Special groups shall be set up in the aspects of port planning and construction, port market supervision, port safety and environmental protection, port information and training, etc. to promote the integration of transportation costs, tax and fee standards, customs clearance procedures, market management, administrative law enforcement, and policy system. At the same time, a more effective project promotion mechanism, evaluation mechanism and reward and punishment mechanism shall also be established to accelerate the realization of interconnection of market information sharing and data query, monitoring information exchange, information application and management information approval in the Yangtze River Economic Belt, and resource allocation and shipping market regulation shall be strengthened to avoid vicious competition.

To establish the regional port and shipping association of the Yangtze River Economic Belt, it is necessary to ensure the independence of the association in terms of personnel, capital and operation at first. The industry association is neither the agency assigned by the government, nor an organization for retired government officials to exert their balanced heat. In the operation of the association, it shall be independent from the government management department. The association is the spokesman of the members to maintain communication with the government rather than the medium for the government to transmit policy information to its members. Secondly, the relationship between the regional port shipping association and the national and local port shipping association shall be well handled. The regional port shipping association can be either reorganized from the local port shipping association or established independently.

(II) **Establish the leading position of port enterprises**

Enterprises are the main body of market competition, resource allocation and port system cooperation. The real regional port coordinated development can only be realized through the extensive cooperation of port enterprises. Port enterprises are mainly divided into three types: port enterprise groups in various ports, state-owned enterprises with trans-regional investment in port business, foreign professional wharf investors and wharf operators affiliated to shipping companies. Among these three types of enterprises, port groups and large domestic state-owned enterprises are more likely to be affected by the government. It is required to further develop market mechanism and interest mechanism, take enterprises as the main body and take capital as the link, with the project as the carrier, so that the new model of cross industry and cross regional port operation can be established and the capital operation, investment in other places, cooperative operation, and even merger or organizing enterprise alliances shall be encouraged. At the same time, all kinds of capital outside the region shall be encouraged for the port construction and operation of the Yangtze River Economic Belt.

### (III) Weaken the port management function of the government

It establish the administrative system in which ports are directly managed by local governments and separated from administrative enterprises in the Port Law, which came into effect on January 1, 2004. The core of the system is the separation of government from enterprises and multiple enterprises operation. One port with one authority to carry out unified management and it clearly stipulates the management authorities and responsibilities of transportation and port administration departments of governments at all levels and it reflects that government departments shall mainly perform the functions of overall planning, policy regulation, information guidance, organization and coordination, service providing, and inspection and supervision. As an independent market subject, port enterprises operate independently according to law and compete fairly according to market rules. However, after the port management is localized, the competition between the ports becomes more and more fierce. The essence of the competition is the competition between port cities, which reflects the interest demands of each port city. Under the influence of the current administrative organization structure and the evaluation mechanism of local government officials, local governments all pursue the maximization of monopoly interests within the scope of administrative divisions, which leads to the prominent influence of government in port development. This development trend with local interests as the leading factor and with the will of the government will undoubtedly affect the realization of the overall interests of the ports in the Yangtze River Economic Belt. At the same time, port groups dominated by state-owned capital are still the main force of ports in various regions. The management of these port groups, including some listed port groups, are still appointed by the local government. The status of ports as the main body of the market is affected, and the goal of maximizing the overall interests of the port service area cannot be truly guaranteed. The local government shall transform from a development oriented government to a service-oriented government and shall strictly limit its behavior to the aspects of formulating port cooperation terms and supervision, creating the good institutional environment for port development, and providing stable and guaranteed public goods and services for the society. The government shall position itself as the main body of coordination rather than the micro economic subject and shall withdraw itself from port competition in order to ensure the autonomy of port operation. Its function in the port cooperation of Yangtze River Delta is to create a relaxed, standardized and fair market environment through legislation.

## *6.2 Enhance the Function of the Golden Waterway of the Yangtze River*

**(I) Enhance the navigation capacity of the Yangtze River**

Due to the natural conditions of the trunk channel of the Yangtze River, there are some shoals that hinder the navigation, as a result that the navigation scale of some sections is reduced, and the navigation capability of the Yangtze River trunk line is greatly weakened. Therefore, it is necessary to carry out comprehensive and systematic regulation and construction of the trunk channel of the Yangtze River, and constantly strengthen the construction of production facilities in the channel to ensure the smooth and orderly navigation; it is necessary to speed up the optimization of ship operation organization and further promote the process of large-scale and standardization of ships; it is necessary to strengthen the information intelligent management of the trunk channel of the Yangtze River to improve the level of shipping development. In accordance with the construction policy to "deepen the lower reaches, smooth the middle reaches, extend the upper reaches and connect the tributaries", we will focus on promoting the construction and maintenance of 12.5 m deep-water channel of Nanjing downstream, the demonstration and approval of "645" project in Yi'an section, the construction of waterway regulation projects in Jingjiang river section, reef blasting regulation project in the channel at the tail of the reservoir, and upgrading of upper reaches waterway of Chongqing. We shall actively coordinate the work of new channel in the early stage, and strongly support the construction of tributaries to accelerate the formation of high level channel network with interconnected trunk and tributaries and radiation to the basin. It is necessary to construct the key informatization projects such as the Yangtze River trunk line digital waterway, promote the construction of comprehensive service information platform for various transportation modes, and continuously improve the shipping intelligence of Yangtze River.

**(II) Overall planning and rational distribution of the Yangtze River shoreline resources development and utilization**

The development and utilization of shoreline resources involves multiple sectors, such as maritime affairs, port-shipping, transportation, water conservancy, land, channel and environmental protection. The functions of the departments are intersecting with each other, and there is no unified planning available. The management of shoreline resources is in the state of mutual evasiveness and absence of supervision. The states, cities and even provinces along the river are fighting independently in their own battle and it is difficult to coordinate with each other. Therefore, it is necessary to investigate the resources along the Yangtze River shoreline, work out the overall plan for the development and utilization of resources, and make overall plans for the development and utilization of resources along the Yangtze River. All provinces and cities shall also formulate their own overall plans for the development and utilization of shoreline resources in accordance with the master plan, scientifically plan and demonstrate the layout of industries, cities and towns, water source protection, coastal ecological protection, public ports and shoreline facilities, so as to guide the rational development and efficient utilization of shoreline resources, direct the development of port shoreline to gather at public terminals and core ports, and improve the function of core ports as well as to expand the radiation capacity of the port and improve the efficiency of intensive use of resources so that the core port can truly become the engine to drive industrial progress and regional development.

### *6.3 Develop Shipping Service Industry and Enhance Port Competitiveness*

The core of ports in Yangtze River Economic Belt is three shipping centers, namely Shanghai International Shipping Center, Wuhan Shipping Center and Chongqing Shipping Center. At present, the construction of Shanghai International Shipping Center has achieved a critical stage of transformation and upgrading. According to the radiation space and actual capacity, the international shipping center can be classified into global and regional types, and according to the service, it can be separated into cargo type (such as Singapore) and service type (such as London). From the perspective of long-term development, Shanghai International Shipping Center will still take port function rather than shipping function as the core, however it is an urgent need to improve the information and transaction function of shipping service and market transaction in order to realize the combination of tangible logistics pattern and intangible trade service such as trade transaction, information transmission, capital operation, financial service and technology development, then to control and influence the goal of the global industry and shipping market.

In the future, with the 12.5-m deep-water channel of the Yangtze River extending to Nanjing Port, it is necessary to further optimize the functional layout of regional ports, strengthen the cooperation among the three major shipping centers, strengthen the integration of regional inland river and offshore shipping resources, and enhance the domestic trade service function of the port. In the process of supporting the development of China's coastal ports and ports along the Yangtze River, a cluster of shipping service industries has been formed, including international finance, international trade, production and processing, technical exchange, shipping information, ship trading, shipping insurance, and maritime legal services.

In addition, a unified platform for resource information exchange shall be established for all ports in the Yangtze River Economic Belt and the integration and sharing shall be realized to form effective channels for connection, communication and cooperation. The port logistics information and dynamics can be timely communicated through the sharing of customer information, so that the dependence and integrity between ports can be improved. The interconnection of management information system can be realized through improving the collection and distribution system to form a comprehensive and efficient transportation network. The overall competitiveness and service quality of the port group can be improved through the construction of a win-win port collection and distribution system based on the extension of the industrial chain. All ports within the group shall actively cooperate, learn from each other and communicate with each other, give full play to the policy effect and enhance the aggregation and radiation function of ports; the cost can be reduced and customer can be satisfied through technical cooperation to effectively improve the management level and management ability of ports in the Yangtze River Delta region and enhance the technical level of ports.

# Industrial Division of Work and Cooperation in the Yangtze River Economic Belt

**Fuzhuo Fan**

In the process of industrial development in the Yangtze River Economic Belt, industrial competition is the normal, but not all of regional economic development. The win-win result can be achieved only by cooperating in competition and competing in cooperation. Through the cooperation and division of work, the member regions of the Yangtze River Economic Belt will build their own advantageous industries and products into specialized production, and realize the complementary advantages through the unified market. The production cost will be reduced to result in significant economic benefits. In recent years, the research on the Yangtze River Economic Belt has attracted extensive attention of the academic community, and the research literatures have emerged increasingly. Zhao Lin et al. (2013), Xu Changle (2014), Li Xuesong et al. (2015) and Zou Lin (2015) respectively studied the development of Yangtze River Economic Belt from different perspectives. On the basis of relevant research, it is supposed to make a statistical description and analysis of the industrial division of work in the Yangtze River Economic Belt over a long time span.

## 1 Measurement Method

The F-series measurement indicators constructed by Fan Fuzhuo (2007, 2009) are selected in this chapter to measure the industrial division of work in the Yangtze River Economic Belt. The reason is that, in the sense of methodology, compared with other measurement indicators, the F-series measurement indicators have unique advantages, and the unification between regional path analysis and industry path analysis system in the research of regional division of work. In this way, the industrial

F. Fan (✉)
Institute of Applied Economics, Shanghai Academy of Social Sciences, Shanghai, China
e-mail: ffz@sass.org.cn

 
X. Jing (ed.), *Development of the Yangtze River Economic Belt in China*, Urban Governance Practices in China,
https://doi.org/10.1007/978-981-16-1578-8_7

division of work in the Yangtze River Economic Belt can be discussed in two ways. One is from the perspective of region to analyze the industries with the highest specialization intensity, the industries with the highest specialization status and their changes, analyze the specialization level and its changes of each member region, and then grasp the variation tendency of industrial division of work in the Yangtze River Economic Belt on the whole. The other is from the perspective of industry to analyze the member regions with the highest localization intensity and the member regions with the highest localization force, analyze the localization level and its changes of each subdivision industry, and then grasp the variation tendency of industrial division of work in the Yangtze River Economic Belt.

The meaning of some symbols is simply explained. $m$ represents the number of member regions in the Yangtze River Economic Belt, and $i$ represents one of the regions, then $i = 1, 2, \ldots, m$. $n$ represents the number of sub industries included in the industrial economic system, and $j$ represents one of the sub industries, then $j = 1, 2, \ldots, n$. In this paper, $s_{ij}$ is used to represent the share of the output value of industry $j$ in the region $i$ in the total industrial output value of the same region; $s'_{ij}$ is the share of the output value of industry $j$ in the total industrial output value of the Yangtze River Economic Belt; $s'_{ij}$ is the share of the output value of industry $j$ in region $i$ in the output value of industry $j$ of the Yangtze River Economic Belt, and $s'_i$ is the share of the total industrial output value of region $i$ in the total industrial output value of the Yangtze River Economic Belt; Normalize the scale of the member regions of the Yangtze River Economic Belt to 1, and use $s*j$ to represent the share of the total industrial output value of industry $j$ in the total industrial output value of the Yangtze River Economic Belt; normalize the scale of each sub industry to 1, and use the $s_i'^*$ to represent the share of the total industrial output value of region $i$ in the total industrial output value of the Yangtze River Economic Belt.

## 1.1 Regional Path

Look at the measurement method of regional path at first. These measurement methods contain two assumptions: 1. for the Yangtze River economic belt, it is assumed that it is in a closed economic state, and there is no external economic connection; 2. it is assumed that the demand structure of each region in the Yangtze River Economic Belt for various industries is consistent. When these two assumptions (not considering the transportation cost) are combined, the regional trade will happen when there are differences in the industrial output structure between regions.

If $\Gamma RC_{ij}$ is used to represent the specialization intensity measured by location quotient, then:

$$\Gamma RC_{ij} = s_{ij}/s_j \quad (1)$$

If the specialization intensity is greater than 1, it indicates that there is specialization advantage in industry $j$ for region $i$; otherwise, if the specialization intensity is less than 1, it indicates that there is no specialization advantage in industry *j* for region *i*.

If $prc_{ij}$ is used to represent the professional status of industry *j* in region *i*, then:

$$prc_{ij} = \frac{2(s_{ij} - s_j)}{\sum_{j=1}^{n}(|s_{ij} - s_j|)} \quad (2)$$

The value range of specialization status is $[-1, 1]$. When the specialization status is greater than 0, the higher is the specialization grade, the more important the industry *j* *will be* in the export of region *i*; conversely, the lower the specialization grade, the less important of industry *j* will be in the export of region *i*. When the specialization status is less than 0, the higher is the specialization grade, the more important the industry *j* will be in the import of region *i*; on the contrary, the smaller is the specialization grade, the less important the industry *j* will be in the region *i*.

If $FRC_i$ is used to represent the specialization coefficient of region *i*, which reflects the relative scale of interregional trade with other regions of the Yangtze River Economic Belt and then:

$$FRC_i = \frac{1}{2}\sum_{j=1}^{n}|s_{ij} - s_j| \quad (3)$$

From the perspective of regional path, $FRC_{mn}$ is used to represent the regional division coefficient, which reflects the relative scale of interregional trade in the Yangtze River Economic Belt and then:

$$FRC_{mn} = \frac{1}{2}\sum_{i=1}^{m}\left(s_i'\sum_{j=1}^{n}|s_{ij} - s_j|\right) \quad (4)$$

Formula (4) shows that the regional division coefficient is the weighted average of the specialization coefficient of the member regions within the Yangtze River Economic Belt.

$FRC_i^*$ is used to represent the structural difference coefficient of region *i*, which reflects the relative scale of interregional trade between region *i* and other regions when the scale of each region is normalized to 1 and then:

$$FRC_i^* = \frac{1}{2}\sum_{j=1}^{n}|s_{ij} - s_j^*| \quad (5)$$

$FRC_{mn}^*$ is used to represent the structural difference coefficient of industry, which reflects the relative scale of interregional trade in the Yangtze River Economic Belt when the scale of each region is normalized to 1 and then:

$$FRC_{mn}^{*} = \frac{1}{2m}\sum_{i=1}^{m}\sum_{j=1}^{n}\left|s_{ij} - s_{j}^{*}\right| \tag{6}$$

## 1.2 Industry Path

Then look at the measurement method of industry path. The hypothesis of closed economy and consistent demand structure in different regions are expressed by the regional path. The two hypotheses can be expressed by industry path as follows: one is the isolated system hypothesis, that is to assume that the industrial economic system has no economic connection with other economic systems (such as the primary industry, construction industry, tertiary industry, etc.); the second is the uniform spatial distribution, which means the spatial distribution is uniform for each industry of the industrial economic system from the perspective of consumption.

The intensity of localization is used to reflect the structural attribute of regional division of work, which is represented by $\Gamma II_{ij}$ and then:

$$\Gamma II_{ij} = s_{ij}' / s_{i}' \tag{7}$$

Obviously, formula (1) and formula (7) are equivalent. If the localization intensity is greater than 1, it indicates that industry $j$ has localization advantage in region $i$; conversely, if the localization intensity is less than 1, it indicates that industry $j$ has no localization advantage in region $i$.

For the scale attribute of regional division of work, from the perspective of industry path, the consideration will be mainly focused on the influence caused by the difference of relative scale of different regions (in the spatial distribution of total industrial output value of the Yangtze River Economic Belt, the relative scale of different regions is quite different). For an industry, the relative scale factor of region is introduced, and "localization force" is used to measure the relative size of localization scale in different regions. $pii_{ij}$ is used to represent the localization power of industry $j$ in region $i$.

$$pii_{ij} = \frac{2\left(s_{ij}' - s_{i}'\right)}{\sum_{i=1}^{m}\left(\left|s_{ij}' - s_{i}'\right|\right)} \tag{8}$$

The value range of localization force is [−1, 1]. When the localization force is greater than 0, the greater the localization force is, the more important the position of industry $j$ will be in region $i$ for export; conversely, the smaller the localization force is, the less important the position of industry $j$ will be in region $i$ for export. When the localization force is less than 0, the greater the localization force is, the more important the position of industry $j$ will be in region $i$ for import; conversely, the smaller the localization force is, the less important the position of industry *j* will be in region *i* for import.

$FII_j$ is used to represent the localization coefficient of industry *j*, which reflects the relative scale of inter industry trade in this industry and then:

$$FII_j = \frac{1}{2}\sum_{i=1}^{m}\left|s'_{ij} - s'_i\right| \tag{9}$$

From the perspective of industry path, $FII_{mn}$ is used to represent the regional division coefficient which reflects the relative scale of inter industry trade in the Yangtze River Economic Belt and then:

$$FII_{mn} = \frac{1}{2}\sum_{j=1}^{n}\left(s_j\sum_{i=1}^{m}\left|s'_{ij} - s'_i\right|\right) \tag{10}$$

Formula (4) and formula (10) are equivalent. This shows that the regional division coefficient is not only the weighted average of the specialization coefficient of each region, but also the weighted average of the localization coefficient of each industry.

$FRC_j^*$ is used to represent the distribution difference coefficient of industry *j*, which reflects the relative scale of inter industry trade between industry *j* and other industries when the scale of each industry is normalized to 1 and then:

$$FII_j^* = \frac{1}{2}\sum_{i=1}^{m}\left|s'_{ij} - s'^*_i\right| \tag{11}$$

The $FII_{mn}^*$ is used to represent the coefficient of spatial distribution difference, which reflects the relative scale of inter industry trade in the Yangtze River Economic Belt when the scale of each industry is normalized to 1 and then:

$$FII_{mn}^* = \frac{1}{2n}\sum_{j=1}^{n}\sum_{i=1}^{m}\left|s'_{ij} - s'^*_i\right| \tag{12}$$

The two hypotheses based on regional path are equivalent to those based on the industry path. Therefore, some concepts (measurement method) based on regional path and some (measurement method) based on industry path have symmetrical connection (or even equivalent). As a result, in the sense of methodology, the unification of regional path analysis and industry path analysis system can be realized.

# 2 Specialization of Member Regions in the Yangtze River Economic Belt

First of all, the data used in this chapter are briefly explained. Since the reform and opening up, China has adjusted and revised the classification standards of national economic sectors for many times. The latest national standard is the *Classification of National Economic Sectors* (GB/T 4754-2011) promulgated and implemented since 2011. According to different versions of industry classification standards, the industry classification is slightly different. In order to discuss the industrial division of work in the Yangtze River Economic Belt, it is necessary to merge and process the data provided by different versions of national industry classification standards, so that the comparability of comparative analysis between different years can be improved. From the perspective of regional path, the data of Chongqing is included into Sichuan, so the regional samples are taken from 10 member regions; from the perspective of industry path, the industry samples involve 32 subdivided industries, and the data of sub industry of total industrial output value are adopted. In addition, although the statistical caliber of industry is different in years, because the difference of industry distribution and spatial distribution in Yangtze River Economic Belt will be mainly discussed in this chapter, the impact of change of statistical caliber on the analysis conclusion will be relatively limited.

From the perspective of regional path, the industrial division of work in the Yangtze River Economic Belt under the assumption of closed economy and consistent demand structure in different regions.

## *2.1 Specialization Intensity*

According to the analysis in the first section, we can find out which industries have the advantages of specialization and which industries have the disadvantages by using the specialization intensity. Table 1 lists the top 8 industries with the highest specialization intensity among the member regions of the Yangtze River Economic Belt in 1985. It can be found that for a member region, the specialization intensity of different industries is varying. For example, in Jiangsu Province, the specialization intensity of computer, communication and other electronic equipment manufacturing industry was 1.53 in 1985, ranking the first, while that of rubber and plastic products industry was 1.10, ranking the eighth. Another example is Yunnan. In 1985, the specialization intensity of tobacco products industry reached 6.09, ranking the first, while the specialization intensity of chemical raw materials and chemical products manufacturing industry was 1.23, ranking the eighth. This shows that the specialization advantages of different industries are varying for a region. Jiangsu has higher specialization advantages over rubber and plastic products in computer, communication and other electronic equipment manufacturing industries, while Yunnan's advantages in tobacco products industry are over those in chemical raw materials and

**Table 1** Top 8 industries with the highest specialization intensity in the member regions of the Yangtze River Economic Belt in 1985

| Region | Top 8 industries with specialization intensity |
|---|---|
| Shanghai | Chemical fiber (2.61), cultural and educational supplies (2.58), gas production (2.04), instrumentation (1.62), computer (1.45), ferrous metals processing (1.41), electrical machinery (1.35), textile and clothing (1.34) |
| Jiangsu | Computer (1.53), textile industry (1.42), non-metallic mining (1.28), non-metallic products (1.22), and instrumentation (1.14), chemical fiber (1.12), machinery equipment (1.11), rubber and plastics (1.10) |
| Zhejiang | Wine and beverage (1.75), non-metallic mining (1.61), electrical machinery (1.54), rubber and plastics (1.48), leather products (1.47), textile industry (1.36), instrumentation (1.25), paper industry (1.24) |
| Anhui | Coal mining (3.06), tobacco products (2.26), petroleum processing (1.92), food processing (1.59), wine and beverage (1.50), power generation (1.49), non-metallic mining (1.43), gas production (1.39) |
| Jiangxi | Coal mining (2.74), wood processing (2.51), other industries (1.96), power generation (1.54), pharmaceutical production (1.50), furniture manufacturing (1.45), transportation (1.39), food processing (1.33) |
| Hubei | Transportation (2.39), oil exploitation (2.37), petroleum processing (1.91), ferrous metals processing (1.67), water production (1.50), furniture manufacturing (1.47), non-metallic mining (1.22), printing industry (1.21) |
| Hunan | Ferrous metals mining and dressing (2.71), coal mining (2.19), petroleum processing (1.88), other industries (1.82), tobacco products (1.70), paper industry (1.64), non-metallic mining (1.55), wine and beverage (1.33) |
| Sichuan | Oil mining (5.23), ferrous metals mining (3.46), coal mining (1.82), food processing (1.64), wine and beverage (1.53), paper industry (1.36), ferrous metals processing (1.33), power generation (1.32) |
| Guizhou | Tobacco products (4.93), coal mining (2.96), wine and beverage (2.10), power generation (2.02), ferrous metals mining and dressing (1.79), computer (1.35), other industries (1.33), gas production (1.22) |
| Yunnan | Tobacco products (6.09), other industries (2.53), coal mining (1.57), power generation (1.52), wine and beverage (1.51), wood processing (1.33), food processing (1.32), chemical raw materials (1.23) |

chemical products manufacturing industries. For different member regions, it can be found that there are differences in specialization intensity among the top 8 industries. In terms of the average of the specialization intensity of the eight industries, that of Guizhou, Sichuan and Yunnan is relatively large, say 2.21, 2.21 and 2.14, respectively, ranking in the top three, while that of Jiangsu, Zhejiang and Hubei is smaller, say 1.24, 1.46 and 1.72 respectively, ranking the last three. This shows that there are differences in the situation of specialization in different member regions; however, the level of specialization in different member regions is not clear from the information provided in Table 1. It can also be found that for different member regions, industries with professional advantages are different. In general, although different member regions have the advantages of specialization in a certain field, the scale of the advantage is often different. For example, from the information provided in

Table 1, Jiangxi and Hubei have the advantages of specialization in the transportation equipment manufacturing industry with the corresponding specialization intensity of 1.39 and 2.39 respectively. From Table 1, it is difficult to find two member regions with the same specialization advantage industries. This shows that there is a certain degree of division of work in the organization and production of industrial products among different member regions, and the level of division of work needs to be further analyzed.

Table 2 lists the top 8 industries with the highest specialization intensity in the member regions of the Yangtze River Economic Belt in 2013. Similarly, for a member region, the professional advantages of different industries are varying. For example, the petroleum processing, coking and nuclear fuel processing industries in Shanghai have a greater specialization advantage (the specialization intensity is 2.46), while the

**Table 2** Top 8 industries with specialization intensity in member regions of Yangtze River Economic Belt in 2013

| Region | Top 8 industries with specialization intensity |
|---|---|
| Shanghai | Petroleum processing (2.46), transportation (2.05), computer (2.02), tobacco products (2.01), furniture manufacturing (1.44), cultural and educational supplies (1.40), machinery equipment (1.35), gas production (1.24) |
| Jiangsu | Instrumentation (2.01), chemical fiber (1.55), computer (1.53), electrical machinery (1.39), wood processing (1.27), chemical raw materials (1.27), textile and clothing (1.26), metal products (1.24) |
| Zhejiang | Chemical fiber (2.95), leather products (2.45), textile industry (2.25), furniture manufacturing (2.11), cultural and educational supplies (1.92), rubber and plastics (1.76), textile and clothing (1.63), paper industry (1.57) |
| Anhui | Ferrous metals mining (2.53), coal mining (2.06), printing industry (1.55), electrical machinery (1.55), food processing (1.55), wood processing (1.48), power generation (1.46), rubber and plastics (1.39) |
| Jiangxi | Other industries (3.39), non-metallic products (1.79), cultural and educational supplies (1.71), textile and clothing (1.69), leather products (1.66), ferrous metals mining (1.60), pharmaceutical production (1.59), printing industry (1.50) |
| Hubei | Petroleum exploitation (4.17), non-metallic mining (2.50), ferrous metals mining (2.22), food processing (2.13), wine and beverage (1.87), transportation (1.68), non-metallic products (1.43), ferrous metals processing (1.22) |
| Hunan | Non-metallic mining (2.03), coal mining (2.00), tobacco products (1.79), other industries (1.79), wood processing (1.70), food processing (1.68), non-metallic products (1.59), printing industry (1.54) |
| Sichuan | Petroleum exploitation (4.82), wine and beverage (2.88), ferrous metals mining (2.16), coal mining (1.92), gas production (1.80), furniture manufacturing (1.64), non-metallic mining (1.62), transportation (1.55) |
| Guizhou | Coal mining (13.44), wine and beverage (4.11), tobacco products (3.22), power generation (3.16), non-metallic mining (2.93), pharmaceutical production (1.74), non-metallic products (1.64), wood processing (1.22) |
| Yunnan | Tobacco products (10.73), coal mining (4.21), ferrous metals mining (4.03), other industries (2.89), power generation (2.48), non-metallic mining (2.04), ferrous metals processing (1.70), water production (1.25) |

specialization advantage of gas production and supply industry is relatively smaller (the specialization intensity is 1.24). Another example is Guizhou, where the specialization advantage of coal mining, washing and dressing industry (the specialization intensity is as high as 13.44) is over that of wood processing and wood, bamboo, rattan, palm and grass products (the specialization intensity is 1.22). For different member regions, there are differences in the specialization intensity of eight industries with greater specialization advantages. By comparing the average of specialization intensity of eight industries in member regions, it is found the average of Guizhou, Yunnan and Sichuan is higher, say 3.93, 3.67 and 2.30 respectively, ranking in the top three, while that of Jiangsu, Anhui and Shanghai is relatively lower, say 1.44, 1.70 and 1.75, respectively, ranking the last three. This shows that in 2013, there are differences in the specialization level of member regions of the Yangtze River Economic Belt; for how much of this difference, it is difficult to make a clear answer only based on the information provided by the specialization intensity. Similarly, for different member regions, the industries with professional advantages are also varying. For example, comparing Shanghai with Sichuan, it can be found that among the top 8 industries in terms of specialization intensity, only three industries are the same, namely transportation equipment manufacturing industry, furniture manufacturing industry and gas production and supply industry. Even so, the specialization intensity is also different. The specialization intensity of the three industries in Shanghai is 2.05, 1.44 and 1.24, and that of Sichuan is 1.55, 1.64 and 1.80 respectively. The advantages of specialization are different, so are the positions. Transportation equipment manufacturing industry ranks the second in Shanghai and the eighth in Sichuan. This shows that in 2013, there was a certain degree of division of work in the organization and production of industrial products among different member regions in the Yangtze River Economic Belt. The level of division of work needs to be further analyzed.

Comparing Table 1 with Table 2, it is easy to find two pieces of valuable information. Firstly, for one member region, the top eight industries in terms of specialization intensity have changed greatly or slightly in two years. For example, compared with 1985, the chemical fiber manufacturing industry, instrumentation manufacturing industry, ferrous metal smelting and rolling processing industry, electrical machinery and appliance manufacturing industry, textile and clothing industry, clothing industry exited from the top 8 in 2013, and were replaced by petroleum processing, coking and nuclear fuel processing industry, transportation equipment manufacturing industry, tobacco products industry, furniture manufacturing industry and machinery manufacturing industry. As for the manufacturing of cultural, educational, industrial, sports and entertainment products, gas production and supply, and computer, communication as well as other electronic equipment manufacturing industries, the changes are mainly reflected in the changes of the scale for professional advantages. Secondly, for one member region, the average of specialization intensity of the top eight industries has changed. In comparison, among the 10 member regions of the Yangtze River Economic Belt, the average of 7 member regions has been increased, and that of Guizhou, Yunnan and Zhejiang has been increased by 1.72, 1.53 and 0.62 respectively; that of Anhui, Hunan and Shanghai have been decreased by 0.13, 0.09 and

0.05 respectively. Does this mean that compared with 1985, the level of specialization in 7 regions was increased in 2013, while that in 3 regions was decreased in 2013? Obviously, further analysis and discussion are required.

## 2.2 Specialization Status

From the perspective of regional path, the specialization intensity mainly reflects whether an industry in a member region has the specialization advantage; on this basis, the specialization status integrates the relative scale factor of the industry (from the industry distribution of the total industrial output value of the Yangtze River Economic Belt, the relative scale of different industries is varying), and reflects the relative importance of an industry in a member region from the perspective of interregional trade. Table 3 lists the top 8 industries in the Yangtze River Economic Belt in 1985. It is not difficult to find that for a member region, the relative importance of different industries is significantly different. For example, in Shanghai, the specialization status of machinery and equipment manufacturing industry was 0.17, and that of metal products industry was 0.05; that is, under the assumption of closed economy and consistent demand structure in different regions, the share of machinery and equipment manufacturing industry in the export of Shanghai was 17%, while that of metal products industry was 5%. Another example is Jiangsu, where the specialization status of textile industry was 0.50, and that of metal products industry was 0.02; that is, under the assumption of closed economy and consistent demand structure in different regions, textile industry accounted for 50% of export in Jiangsu, while metal products industry only accounted for 2%. For different member regions, there were differences in the top 8 industries of the specialization status. For example, compared with Shanghai, ferrous metal smelting and rolling industry, chemical fiber manufacturing industry, cultural and educational supplies, industrial beauty, sports and entertainment products manufacturing industry have existed from the top 8 of specialization status in Jiangsu, and were replaced by non-metallic mineral products industry, chemical raw materials and chemical products manufacturing industry, and rubber and plastic products industry. As for the five industries which all entered the top eight specialization status of Shanghai and Jiangsu, the size and/or ranking of their specialization status in the two regions are also different. For example, the specialization status of machinery and equipment manufacturing industry in Shanghai is 0.17, ranking the first, and that in Jiangsu is 0.10, ranking the third.

Table 4 lists the top 8 industries in the Yangtze River Economic Belt in 2013. Similarly, it can be found that for one member region, the specialization status of different industries is quite varying. For example, the transportation equipment manufacturing industry, computer, communication and other electronic equipment manufacturing industry, petroleum processing, coking and nuclear fuel processing industry, mechanical equipment manufacturing industry, tobacco product industry, cultural and educational, industrial beauty, sports and entertainment products industry, rubber and plastic products industry and furniture manufacturing industry ranked in the top

**Table 3** Top 8 industries with specialization status in member regions of the Yangtze River Economic Belt in 1985

| Region | Top 8 industries with specialization status |
|---|---|
| Shanghai | Mechanical equipment (0.17), ferrous metals processing (0.16), chemical fiber (0.12), electrical machinery (0.09), computer (0.09), textile industry (0.08), cultural and educational supplies (0.06), metal products (0.05) |
| Jiangsu | Textile industry (0.50), computer (0.14), machinery and equipment (0.10), non-metallic products (0.09), chemical raw materials (0.04), electrical machinery (0.03), rubber and plastics (0.03), metal products (0.02) |
| Zhejiang | Textile industry (0.37), electrical machinery (0.17), rubber and plastics (0.11), wine and beverage (0.10), non-metallic products (0.07), textile and clothing (0.03), leather products (0.03), paper industry (0.03) |
| Anhui | Food processing (0.28), tobacco products (0.21), coal mining (0.16), petroleum processing (0.10), non-metallic products (0.08), power generation (0.08), wine and beverage (0.05), non-metallic mining (0.01) |
| Jiangxi | Other industries (0.29), food processing (0.15), coal mining (0.13), transportation (0.10), non-metallic products (0.09), power generation (0.08), wood processing (0.05), pharmaceutical production (0.04) |
| Hubei | Transportation (0.42), ferrous metals processing (0.28), petroleum processing (0.12), textile industry (0.06), petroleum exploitation (0.04), textile and clothing (0.03), furniture manufacturing (0.02), non-metallic products (0.02) |
| Hunan | Other industries (0.25), chemical raw materials (0.12), tobacco products (0.11), petroleum processing (0.10), coal mining (0.09), non-metallic products (0.08), paper industry (0.06), transportation (0.05) |
| Sichuan | Food processing (0.34), ferrous metals processing (0.13), oil mining (0.12), coal mining (0.07), coal mining (0.34), wine and beverage (0.07), power generation (0.06), transportation (0.04), mechanical equipment (0.04) |
| Guizhou | Tobacco products (0.45), power generation (0.11), coal mining (0.10), machinery and equipment (0.10), wine and beverage (0.08), other industries (0.07), computer (0.04), ferrous metals processing (0.04) |
| Yunnan | Tobacco products (0.48), other industries (0.27), food processing (0.09), chemical raw materials (0.05), power generation (0.05), wine and beverage (0.03), coal mining (0.02), printing industry (0.01) |

8; under the assumption of closed economy and consistent demand structure in different regions, transportation equipment manufacturing industry accounted for 34% of foreign export trade, while furniture manufacturing industry only accounted for 1%. Another example is Hubei, where the food processing and manufacturing industry, transportation equipment manufacturing industry, non-metallic mineral products industry, wine, beverage and refined tea manufacturing industry, ferrous metal smelting and rolling processing industry, textile industry, non-metallic mineral mining and dressing industry and ferrous metal mining and processing industry ranked in the top 8; under the assumption of closed economy and consistent demand structure in different regions, food processing and manufacturing industry accounted for 33% of the export trade, while the mining and dressing industry of ferrous metals accounted for 3%. For different member regions, the top eight industries were also

**Table 4** Top 8 industries with specialization status in member regions of Yangtze River Economic Belt in 2013

| Region | Top 8 industries with specialization status |
|---|---|
| Shanghai | Transportation (0.34), computer (0.33), petroleum processing (0.13), machinery and equipment (0.11), tobacco products (0.05), cultural and educational supplies (0.02), rubber and plastics (0.01), furniture manufacturing (0.01) |
| Jiangsu | Computer (0.27), electrical machinery (0.19), chemical raw materials (0.14), ferrous metals processing (0.08), instrumentation (0.07), mechanical equipment (0.05), metal products (0.05), chemical fiber (0.04) |
| Zhejiang | Textile industry (0.26), chemical fiber (0.13), rubber and plastics (0.09), power generation (0.09), textile clothing (0.07), leather products (0.07), electrical machinery (0.06), mechanical equipment (0.05) |
| Anhui | Electrical machinery (0.26), food processing (0.19), power generation (0.14), coal mining (0.08), other industries (0.08), non-metallic products (0.07), rubber plastics (0.06), ferrous metals mining and processing (0.05) |
| Jiangxi | Other industries (0.57), non-metallic products (0.15), textile and clothing (0.06), food processing (0.06), pharmaceutical production (0.05), cultural and educational supplies (0.03), leather products (0.03), printing industry (0.01) |
| Hubei | Food processing (0.33), transportation (0.29), non-metallic products (0.10), wine and beverage (0.08), ferrous metals processing (0.07), textile industry (0.04), non-metallic mining (0.04), ferrous metals mining (0.03) |
| Hunan | Other industries (0.22), machinery equipment (0.20), food processing (0.19), non-metallic products (0.13), coal mining (0.06), tobacco products (0.05), wood processing (0.04), paper industry (0.03) |
| Sichuan | Transportation (0.25), wine and beverage (0.18), computer (0.15), food processing (0.12), non-metallic products (0.08), coal mining (0.06), ferrous metals mining (0.03), pharmaceutical production (0.02) |
| Guizhou | Coal mining (0.38), power generation (0.25), wine and beverage (0.13), tobacco products (0.07), non-metallic products (0.07), pharmaceutical production (0.04), ferrous metals processing (0.03), non-metallic mining (0.02) |
| Yunnan | Tobacco products (0.30), other industries (0.25), power generation (0.17), ferrous metals processing (0.10), coal mining (0.01), ferrous metals mining and dressing (0.03), food processing (0.02), non-metallic mining (0.01) |

different in specialization status. For example, in the top 8 industries of Shanghai and Hubei, only the transportation equipment manufacturing industry overlapped, while the other seven industries were different. In fact, it also reflected the division of work and cooperation in the organization and production of industrial products among different member regions in the Yangtze River Economic Belt. Only in this sense, compared with the intensity of specialization, the information provided by specialization status is more limited.

Comparing Table 3 with Table 4, we can find important information, that is, for one member region, the top 8 industries with specialization status have been changed in 2013 compared with 1985. For example, in Shanghai, compared with 1985, ferrous metal smelting and pressing industry, chemical fiber manufacturing industry, electrical machinery and equipment manufacturing industry, textile industry and metal products industry exited from the top 8 specialization status in 2013, and were replaced by transportation equipment manufacturing industry, petroleum processing, coking and nuclear fuel processing industry, tobacco products industry, rubber and plastic products industry and furniture manufacturing industry. For the three industries overlapped in two years, the specialization status was also different. The specialization status of machinery and equipment manufacturing industry in the two years was 0.17 and 0.11 respectively; the specialization status of computer, communication and other electronic equipment manufacturing industry in the two years was 0.09 and 0.33 respectively; the specialization status of culture and education, arts and crafts, sports and entertainment products manufacturing industry in the two years was 0.06 and 0.02 respectively. Another example is Sichuan. Compared with 1985, four of the top eight industries with specialization status were overlapped and four have been changed.

Next, we compare the top 8 industries in terms of specialization intensity with the top 8 industries in terms of specialization status. Let's look at the situation of 1985 at first. Comparing Table 1 with Table 3, it can be found that for one member region, compared with the top 8 industries in terms of specialization intensity, the industries with the top 8 specialization status were different. Take Shanghai as an example, compared with the top 8 industries in terms of specialization intensity, the gas production and supply industry, instrumentation manufacturing industry, computer, communication and other electronic equipment manufacturing industry, textile and clothing industry have exited from the top 8 in terms of specialization status, and were replaced by mechanical equipment manufacturing industry, computer, communication and other electronic equipment manufacturing industry, textile industry and metal products industry. Let's look at the situation in 2013 now. A similar situation can be found by comparing Table 2 with Table 4. For example, in Sichuan, compared with the top 8 industries in terms of specialization intensity, the petroleum processing, coking and nuclear fuel processing industry, gas production and supply industry, furniture manufacturing industry and non-metallic mining and dressing industry have exited from the top 8 in terms of specialization status, and were replaced by computer, communication and other electronic equipment manufacturing industry, food processing and manufacturing industry, non-metallic mineral products industry and pharmaceutical production industry.

What causes this change? It is mainly caused by the differences in the relative scale of different industries in the industry distribution of the total industrial output value in the Yangtze River Economic Belt. In the Yangtze River Economic Belt, in 1985, the textile industry, machinery equipment manufacturing industry, food processing and manufacturing industry and chemical raw materials as well as chemical products manufacturing industry ranked in the top four, accounting for 14.6%, 11.2%, 8.3% and 6.6% respectively, and the concentration ratio of the four industries was 40.7%; In 2013, the chemical raw materials and chemical products manufacturing industry, transportation equipment manufacturing industry, computer, communication and other electronic equipment manufacturing industry and mechanical equipment manufacturing industry ranked in the top four, accounting for 8.8%, 8.5%, 8.4%

and 8.3% respectively, and the concentration ratio of the four industries was 34.0%, 6.7% lower than that in 1985.

Because of the differences in the relative scale of different industries, if the specialization intensity of two industries in one region of the Yangtze River Economic Belt is the same (and greater than 1.00), it is inevitable that the industry with relatively large scale will have comparatively higher specialization status, while the relatively small scale industry will have comparatively lower specialization status. The result is that, for one member region, although the specialization intensity of some industries is small (but greater than 1.00), because the industry occupies a large share in the industry distribution of the total industrial output value of the Yangtze River Economic Belt, its specialization ranking in this member region will be higher than that of the specialization intensity. Of course, the change of this kind of ranking also has certain restrictions or regularity. Comparatively speaking, if the specialization intensity is greater than 1, the specialization status must be greater than 0, while for the industry with specialization intensity less than 1, the specialization status must be less than 0. To some extent, this correspondence restricts the ranking change of these two.

## 2.3 Regional Specialization Coefficient and Regional Structure Difference Coefficient

After analyzing the strength and status of specialization, a comparative analysis is carried out in this paper on the specialization coefficient and structural difference coefficient of the member regions of the Yangtze River Economic Belt. Let's first look at the specialization coefficient of the member regions of the Yangtze River Economic Belt. From Table 5, it is not difficult to find that the specialization coefficients of different member regions in the Yangtze River Economic Belt were quite different in 1985 and 2013. In 1985, the specialization level of Yunnan, Guizhou and Jiangxi was relatively high, with the regional specialization coefficients of 0.3127, 0.2557 and 0.1848 respectively, ranking in the top three; Jiangsu, Zhejiang and Hubei had a lower level of specialization, with the regional specialization coefficients of 0.1222, 0.1415 and 0.1516, respectively, ranking in the last three. In 2013, the specialization level of Yunnan, Guizhou and Shanghai was relatively high, with the regional specialization coefficients of 0.4408, 0.4323 and 0.2597, ranking in the top three; Jiangsu, Anhui and Sichuan had a lower level of specialization, with the regional specialization coefficients of 0.1632, 0.1668 and 0.1885, respectively, ranking in the last three. By comparing the specialization level of the member regions of the Yangtze River Economic Belt in the two years, it is not difficult to find that the specialization level of other member regions has been increased to varying degrees except for Anhui which has a slight decrease of 6.0%. Among them, Guizhou, Shanghai and Zhejiang have greatly improved their specialization level by 69.1%, 57.6% and 42.2% respectively, ranking in the top three. Compared with the previous analysis, it shows

**Table 5** Specialization coefficient and structural difference coefficient of member regions in the Yangtze River Economic Belt in 1985 and 2013

| Region | Regional specialization coefficient | | | Regional structural difference coefficient | | | Overestimated (%) | |
|---|---|---|---|---|---|---|---|---|
| | 1985 | 2013 | Variation (%) | 1985 | 2013 | Variation (%) | 1985 | 2013 |
| Shanghai | 0.164 8 | 0.259 7 | 57.6 | 0.236 1 | 0.299 9 | 27.0 | 43.2 | 15.5 |
| Jiangsu | 0.122 2 | 0.163 2 | 33.5 | 0.187 7 | 0.256 5 | 36.7 | 53.6 | 57.2 |
| Zhejiang | 0.141 5 | 0.201 3 | 42.2 | 0.187 7 | 0.256 9 | 36.9 | 32.6 | 27.6 |
| Anhui | 0.177 5 | 0.166 8 | −6.0 | 0.122 7 | 0.147 0 | 19.8 | −30.9 | −11.9 |
| Jiangxi | 0.184 8 | 0.242 5 | 31.2 | 0.148 1 | 0.225 1 | 52.0 | −19.9 | −7.2 |
| Hubei | 0.150 6 | 0.198 4 | 31.8 | 0.181 8 | 0.202 2 | 11.3 | 20.7 | 1.9 |
| Hunan | 0.180 1 | 0.209 4 | 16.2 | 0.123 0 | 0.163 2 | 32.7 | −31.7 | −22.0 |
| Sichuan | 0.157 9 | 0.188 5 | 19.4 | 0.140 7 | 0.174 5 | 24.0 | −10.9 | −7.5 |
| Guizhou | 0.255 7 | 0.432 3 | 69.1 | 0.211 8 | 0.359 3 | 69.6 | −17.1 | −16.9 |
| Yunnan | 0.312 7 | 0.440 8 | 41.0 | 0.245 6 | 0.350 3 | 42.6 | −21.5 | −20.5 |
| Yangtze River Economic Belt | 0.160 2 | 0.202 3 | 26.3 | 0.178 5 | 0.243 5 | 36.4 | 11.4 | 20.4 |

*Note* The so-called "variation" refers to the deviation degree of regional specialization coefficient or regional structure difference coefficient in 2013 from those in 1985; the so-called "overestimated" refers to the deviation degree of regional structure difference coefficient relative to regional specialization coefficient

that there is a certain degree of risk to use the tendency of the average change of one region specialization intensity to judge the trend of the change of specialization level for a region. As a comprehensive response to the change of specialization coefficient of each member region, the industrial division coefficient of the Yangtze River Economic Belt has been increased from 0.1602 in 1985 to 0.2023 in 2013, with an increase of 26.3%.

Then look at the structural difference coefficient of the member regions in the Yangtze River Economic Belt. It can also be found that there are some differences between different member regions in 1985 and 2013. In 1985, the coefficient of structural difference of Yunnan, Shanghai and Guizhou was greater, namely 0.2456, 0.2361 and 0.2118, respectively, ranking the top three; the coefficient of structural difference of Anhui, Hunan and Sichuan was smaller, namely 0.1227, 0.1230 and 0.1407, respectively, ranking the last three. In 2013, the coefficient of structural difference of Guizhou, Yunnan and Shanghai was larger, namely 0.3593, 0.3503 and 0.2999, respectively, ranking in the top three; the coefficient of structural difference of Anhui, Hunan and Sichuan was smaller, namely 0.1470, 0.1632 and 0.1745, respectively, ranking the last three. Comparing the two years, we can find that compared with 1985, the coefficient of structural difference of the 10 member regions in the

Yangtze River Economic Belt has been increased to varying degrees. Among them, the coefficient of structural difference of Guizhou, Jiangxi and Yunnan has increased by a large margin, namely 69.6%, 52.0% and 42.6% respectively, while that of Hubei, Anhui and Sichuan has increased by a small margin, namely 11.3%, 19.8% and 24.0% respectively. As a comprehensive response to the variation of structural difference coefficient of each member region, the industrial structure difference coefficient of the Yangtze River Economic Belt has been increased from 0.1785 in 1985 to 0.2435 in 2013, with an increase rate of 36.4% and 10.1% points over the industrial division coefficient.

## *2.4 Industrial Division Coefficient and Industrial Structure Difference Coefficient*

As can be seen from Table 6, compared with 1985, the coefficient of industrial division of work and the coefficient of industrial structure difference in the Yangtze River Economic Belt have been greatly improved in 2013; however, in the past 30 years, the tendency of variation needs to be further analyzed. Table 6 lists the industrial division coefficient, industrial structure difference coefficient and spatial distribution difference coefficient of the Yangtze River Economic Belt from 1985 to 2013. Judging from the industrial division coefficient of the Yangtze River Economic Belt, it shows a trend of "decline—rise–decline". In 1985, it was 0.1602, and it was decreased to 0.1574 in 1988; then, after a long-term climbing up, it reached the maximum value of 0.2179 in 2004, increased by 36.0% compared with 1985; then, it showed a trend of slow decline and it was 0.2023 in 2013 with the increase rate being narrowed by 9.7% points compared with 2004. The variation tendency of industrial division coefficient shows that the level of industrial division of the Yangtze River Economic Belt has been greatly improved from the middle and late period of 1980 to 2004. In the past 10 years, the level of industrial division has declined to a certain extent instead of increasing. From the difference coefficient of industrial structure of the Yangtze River Economic Belt, the development trend was different and presented the trend of "rise—relatively high fluctuation", which shows the trend of industrial structure alienation among the member regions in the Yangtze River Economic Belt. It started from 0.1785 in 1985 and climbed up to 0.2522 in 2004, 41.3% higher than that in 1985; after that, it kept the development trend at fluctuation trend and at a relatively high level, with the highest of 0.2600 in 2010 and 0.2435 in 2013.

It shall be noted that while discussing the regional industrial division of work in the Yangtze River Economic Belt, the influence of the relative scale of the region shall not be ignored. In addition to the fact that the variation tendency of industrial division coefficient and industrial structure difference coefficient is not completely synchronous, it will lead to overestimation of the level for regional division of work. For the industrial division of work in the Yangtze River Economic Belt, if we ignore

**Table 6** Industrial division coefficient, industrial structure difference coefficient and spatial distribution difference coefficient of Yangtze River Economic Belt from 1985 to 2013

| Year | Industrial division coefficient | Coefficient of industrial structure difference | | Coefficient of spatial distribution difference | |
|---|---|---|---|---|---|
| | | Value | Overestimated (%) | Value | Overestimated (%) |
| 1985 | 0.160 2 | 0.178 5 | 11.4 | 0.204 5 | 27.7 |
| 1986 | 0.157 6 | 0.175 2 | 11.2 | 0.202 2 | 28.3 |
| 1987 | 0.158 4 | 0.175 8 | 10.9 | 0.200 4 | 26.4 |
| 1988 | 0.157 4 | 0.180 9 | 14.9 | 0.202 2 | 28.5 |
| 1989 | 0.158 4 | 0.182 7 | 15.3 | 0.200 2 | 26.3 |
| 1990 | 0.166 4 | 0.187 0 | 12.4 | 0.203 0 | 22.0 |
| 1991 | 0.170 3 | 0.196 5 | 15.4 | 0.209 5 | 23.0 |
| 1992 | 0.169 3 | 0.192 0 | 13.4 | 0.205 9 | 21.6 |
| 1993 | 0.179 4 | 0.199 0 | 10.9 | 0.212 1 | 18.2 |
| 1994 | 0.185 0 | 0.214 7 | 16.1 | 0.220 3 | 19.1 |
| 1995 | 0.180 2 | 0.212 4 | 17.9 | 0.219 0 | 21.6 |
| 1996 | 0.186 6 | 0.221 5 | 18.7 | 0.226 6 | 21.4 |
| 1997 | 0.191 0 | 0.225 7 | 18.1 | 0.228 8 | 19.8 |
| 1998 | 0.192 5 | 0.237 4 | 23.3 | 0.231 4 | 20.2 |
| 1999 | 0.197 6 | 0.239 2 | 21.1 | 0.234 0 | 18.5 |
| 2000 | 0.193 4 | 0.238 2 | 23.2 | 0.229 3 | 18.6 |
| 2001 | 0.195 2 | 0.236 6 | 21.2 | 0.234 5 | 20.1 |
| 2002 | 0.201 6 | 0.243 6 | 20.8 | 0.235 8 | 17.0 |
| 2003 | 0.208 1 | 0.248 1 | 19.2 | 0.242 8 | 16.6 |
| 2004 | 0.217 9 | 0.252 2 | 15.7 | 0.249 0 | 14.2 |
| 2005 | 0.210 8 | 0.242 0 | 14.8 | 0.252 0 | 19.5 |
| 2006 | 0.209 5 | 0.246 4 | 17.6 | 0.258 3 | 23.3 |
| 2007 | 0.209 7 | 0.247 7 | 18.1 | 0.256 7 | 22.4 |
| 2008 | 0.207 9 | 0.246 7 | 18.7 | 0.259 0 | 24.6 |
| 2009 | 0.202 8 | 0.242 1 | 19.4 | 0.256 1 | 26.3 |
| 2010 | 0.206 8 | 0.260 0 | 25.8 | 0.258 7 | 25.1 |
| 2011 | 0.204 8 | 0.245 4 | 19.8 | 0.248 2 | 21.2 |
| 2012 | 0.202 6 | 0.243 8 | 20.4 | 0.248 7 | 22.8 |
| 2013 | 0.202 3 | 0.243 5 | 20.4 | 0.252 8 | 25.0 |

*Note* The so-called "overestimated" refers to the deviation degree between the coefficient of industrial structure difference or the coefficient of spatial distribution difference from the coefficient of industrial division of work the regional relative scale factor and apply the coefficient of industrial structure difference for discussion, we will overestimate the level of industrial division of work in the Yangtze River Economic Belt, and the degree of overestimation varies from 10.9% (1987) to 25.8% (2010). If we compare the specialization coefficient and structural difference coefficient of the member regions in the Yangtze River Economic Belt, we can deeply understand the differences between the two. In 1985, among the 10 member regions in the Yangtze River Economic Belt, the structural difference coefficient of four regions was higher than its specialization coefficient. Among them, it was overestimated by 53.6%, 43.2% and 32.6% respectively in Jiangsu, Shanghai and Zhejiang, and the structural difference coefficient of six member regions was lower than their specialization coefficient. Among them, it was underestimated by 31.7%, 30.9% and 21.5% respectively in Hunan, Anhui and Yunnan, ranking the top three. As a comprehensive response, the industrial structure of the Yangtze River was 11.4% higher than the industrial structure. In 2013, among the 10 member regions in the Yangtze River Economic Belt, the structural difference coefficient of four regions is higher than its specialization coefficient. Among them, it is overestimated by 57.2%, 27.6% and 15.5% respectively in Jiangsu, Zhejiang and Shanghai; the structural difference coefficient of six member regions was lower than their specialization coefficient. Among them, it was underestimated by 22.0%, 20.5% and 16.9%, respectively in Hunan, Yunnan and Guizhou, ranking the top three. As a comprehensive response, the industrial structure difference coefficient of the Yangtze River economic belt was 20.4% higher than the industrial division coefficient. This shows that if we ignore the relative scale factor of the region and compare the specialization level of different member regions in the Yangtze River Economic Belt by using the regional structure difference coefficient, it will be easy to lead a wrong judgment.

## 3 Localization of Industries in the Yangtze River Economic Belt

On the basis of discussing the industrial division of work in the Yangtze River Economic Belt from the regional path, symmetrically, the industrial division of work in the Yangtze River Economic Belt will be explored in this section under the assumption of isolated system and consistent spatial distribution of various industries along the industry path.

### *3.1 Localization Intensity*

According to the analysis in the Sect. 1, we can find out which member regions of an industrial industry have either localization advantages or localization disadvantages. Table 7 lists the top four member regions in terms of localization intensity of

**Table 7** Top four member regions of the Yangtze River Economic Belt in 1985

| Industry | Top four member regions in terms of localization intensity |
|---|---|
| Coal mining, washing and dressing industry | Anhui (3.06), Guizhou (2.96), Jiangxi (2.74), Hunan (2.19) |
| Oil and gas exploitation | Sichuan (5.23), Hubei (2.37), Jiangsu (0.43), Guizhou (0.15) |
| Mining and dressing of ferrous metals | Sichuan (3.46), Hunan (2.71), Guizhou (1.79), Anhui (1.35) |
| Non-metallic ore mining and dressing industry | Zhejiang (1.61), Hunan (1.55), Anhui (1.43), Jiangsu (1.28) |
| Food processing and manufacturing industry | Sichuan (1.64), Anhui (1.59), Jiangxi (1.33), Yunnan (1.32) |
| Wine, beverage and refined tea manufacturing industry | Guizhou (2.10), Zhejiang (1.75), Sichuan (1.53), Yunnan (1.51) |
| Tobacco products industry | Yunnan (6.09), Guizhou (4.93), Anhui (2.26), Hunan (1.70) |
| Textile industry | Jiangsu (1.41), Zhejiang (1.36), Shanghai (1.09), Hubei (1.06) |
| Textile, clothing and garment industry | Shanghai (1.34), Zhejiang (1.21), Hubei (1.18), Jiangsu (0.95) |
| Leather, fur, feather and its products and footwear industry | Zhejiang (1.47), Hunan (1.22), Jiangsu (1.03), Sichuan (1.01) |
| Wood processing and wood, bamboo, rattan, palm, grass products industry | Jiangxi (2.51), Yunnan (1.33), Anhui (1.20), Sichuan (1.10) |
| Furniture manufacturing industry | Hubei (1.47), Jiangxi (1.45), Zhejiang (1.18), Yunnan (1.14) |
| Paper and paper products industry | Hunan (1.64), Sichuan (1.36), Jiangxi (1.27), Zhejiang (1.24) |
| Printing and recording media reproduction | Sichuan (1.29), Yunnan (1.23), Hubei (1.21), Hunan (1.01) |
| Culture and education, arts and crafts, sports and entertainment products manufacturing industry | Shanghai (2.58), Zhejiang (0.99), Jiangsu (0.82), Hunan (0.48) |
| Petroleum processing, coking and nuclear fuel processing industries | Anhui (1.92), Hubei (1.91), Hunan (1.88), Jiangxi (1.09) |
| Chemical raw materials and chemical products manufacturing industry | Hunan (1.33), Yunnan (1.23), Sichuan (1.09), Jiangsu (1.08) |
| Pharmaceutical production industry | Jiangxi (1.50), Shanghai (1.22), Sichuan (1.12), Hubei (0.98) |
| Chemical fiber manufacturing industry | Shanghai (2.61), Jiangsu (1.12), Zhejiang (0.71), Jiangxi (0.71) |
| Rubber and plastic products industry | Zhejiang (1.48), Shanghai (1.17), Jiangsu (1.10), Guizhou (0.88) |

(continued)

**Table 7** (continued)

| Industry | Top four member regions in terms of localization intensity |
|---|---|
| Non-metallic mineral products industry | Jiangxi (1.31), Hunan (1.27), Anhui (1.26), Jiangsu (1.22) |
| Ferrous metal smelting and rolling industry | Hubei (1.67), Shanghai (1.41), Sichuan (1.33), Guizhou (1.15) |
| Metal products industry | Shanghai (1.32), Zhejiang (1.14), Jiangsu (1.09), Hubei (0.90) |
| Machinery equipment manufacturing industry | Shanghai (1.25), Guizhou (1.22), Jiangsu (1.11), Sichuan (1.06) |
| Transportation equipment manufacturing industry | Hubei (2.39), Jiangxi (1.39), Hunan (1.20), Sichuan (1.15) |
| Electrical machinery and apparatus manufacturing industry | Zhejiang (1.54), Shanghai (1.35), Jiangsu (1.09), Hunan (0.88) |
| Computer, communication and other electronic equipment manufacturing industry | Jiangsu (1.53), Shanghai (1.45), Guizhou (1.35), Jiangxi (0.96) |
| Instrumentation manufacturing industry | Shanghai (1.62), Zhejiang (1.25), Jiangsu (1.14), Sichuan (0.95) |
| Production and supply of electricity and heat | Guizhou (2.02), Jiangxi (1.54), Yunnan (1.52), Anhui (1.49) |
| Gas production and supply industry | Shanghai (2.04), Anhui (1.39), Guizhou (1.22), Jiangsu (0.98) |
| Water production and supply industry | Hubei (1.50), Jiangxi (1.31), Hunan (1.25), Anhui (1.04) |
| Other industries | Yunnan (2.53), Jiangxi (1.96), Hunan (1.82), Guizhou (1.33) |

industrial subdivisions in the Yangtze River Economic Belt in 1985. It is not difficult to find that there are large or small differences in the localization intensity of different member regions for an industrial subdivision industry. For example, in the tobacco products industry, the localization intensity of Yunnan is 6.09, ranking the first, and the localization intensity of Hunan is 1.70, ranking the fourth; the localization advantages of Yunnan and Hunan are quite different. Another example is cultural and educational supplies, arts and crafts, sports and entertainment supplies, the localization intensity of Shanghai was 2.58, ranking the first, while that of Hunan was 0.48, ranking the fourth; in fact, except that the localization intensity of Shanghai was greater than 1, the localization intensity of all other member regions was less than 1, indicating that the industry was localization disadvantageous in all member regions except Shanghai. According to the information provided in Table 7, the localization advantages difference of some sub industries in different member regions are either quite large or relatively small. For different sub industries, we can find that the intensity of localization is also different among the four member regions with the highest localization intensity. In terms of the average of localization intensity of the top four member regions, the average of tobacco products industry, coal mining, washing and dressing industry and ferrous metal mining and processing industry was relatively large, which was 3.74, 2.74 and 2.33, respectively, ranking the top three; the average of metal products industry, rubber and plastic products industry and machinery equipment manufacturing industry was small, which was 1.11, 1.16 and 1.16, respectively, ranking the bottom three. However, we cannot judge the localization level of different sub industries only based on this. From the perspective of the top four member regions with higher localization intensity of different sub industries, it is difficult to find two completely consistent sub industries. For one member region, the localization intensity of different sub industries in the region is also different. This shows that the organization and production of products in different industries are varying to some extent in spatial distribution; however, the level of industrial division of work in the Yangtze River Economic Belt needs to be further discussed and elaborated.

Table 8 lists the top four member regions in the Yangtze River Economic Belt in 2013. It is also easy to find that for a sub industry, the localization intensity of different member regions is varying. For example, in coal mining, washing and dressing industry, the localization intensity of Guizhou was as high as 13.44, ranking the first, while that of Hunan was 2.00, ranking the fourth, indicating that the localization advantages of the industry were quite different between Guizhou and Hunan. Another example is the chemical raw materials and chemical products manufacturing industry. The localization intensity of Jiangsu was as high as 1.27, ranking the first, while that of Hunan was 0.95, ranking the fourth, which indicated that the localization advantages (or disadvantages) of this industry were relatively lower compared with Jiangsu and Hunan. For different sub industries, from the average of localization intensity of the top four member regions, the average of coal mining washing and dressing industry, tobacco product industry and tobacco product industry were 5.43, 4.44 and 2.74, respectively, ranking in the top three; the average of chemical raw materials and chemical products manufacturing, metal products industry and instrumentation manufacturing industry were 1.05, 1.10 and 1.11, respectively, ranking in the bottom three. Of course, it is not possible to judge the localization level of a subdivision industry only according to the average of localization intensity. This judgment will be verified in the following analysis. Furthermore, by comparing the top four regions in terms of localizations intensity of different industries, we can find that there are differences among different sub industries. This difference shows that, on the whole, there is a certain degree of division of work in the organization and production of industrial products in China. The level of division of work needs to be further analyzed and discussed.

Comparing Table 7 with Table 8, two pieces of important information can be found. Firstly, for a specific sub industry, the four member regions with the higher localization intensity have been changed from 1985 to 2013. For example, in the chemical fiber manufacturing industry, compared with 1985, Shanghai exited from the top four in terms of localization intensity in 2013, and was replaced by Sichuan; as for the other three member regions, the localization intensity of Jiangsu and Zhejiang was increased from 1.12 to 1.55, that of Zhejiang Province was increased from 0.71

**Table 8** Top four member regions in terms of localization intensity in Yangtze River Economic Belt in 2013

| Industry | Top four member regions in terms of localization intensity |
|---|---|
| Coal mining, washing and dressing industry | Guizhou (13.44), Yunnan (4.21), Anhui (2.06), Hunan (2.00) |
| Oil and gas exploitation | Sichuan (4.82), Hubei (4.17), Shanghai (0.62), Guizhou (0.00) |
| Mining and dressing of ferrous metals | Yunnan (4.03), Anhui (2.53), Hubei (2.22), Sichuan (2.16) |
| Non-metallic ore mining and dressing industry | Guizhou (2.93), Hubei (2.50), Yunnan (2.04), Hunan (2.03) |
| Food processing and manufacturing industry | Hubei (2.13), Hunan (1.68), Anhui (1.55), Sichuan (1.38) |
| Wine, beverage and refined tea manufacturing industry | Guizhou (4.11), Sichuan (2.88), Hubei (1.87), Yunnan (1.12) |
| Tobacco products industry | Yunnan (10.73), Guizhou (3.22), Shanghai (2.01), Hunan (1.79) |
| Textile industry | Zhejiang (2.25), Hubei (1.20), Jiangsu (1.17), Jiangxi (0.72) |
| Textile, clothing and garment industry | Jiangxi (1.69), Zhejiang (1.63), Jiangsu (1.26), Anhui (0.95) |
| Leather, fur, feather and its products and footwear industry | Zhejiang (2.45), Jiangxi (1.66), Hunan (1.07), Anhui (1.02) |
| Wood processing and wood, bamboo, rattan, palm, grass products industry | Hunan (1.70), Anhui (1.48), Jiangsu (1.27), Jiangxi (1.23) |
| Furniture manufacturing industry | Zhejiang (2.11), Sichuan (1.64), Shanghai (1.44), Hunan (1.26) |
| Paper and paper products industry | Zhejiang (1.57), Hunan (1.51), Sichuan (1.10), Hubei (0.98) |
| Printing and recording media reproduction | Anhui (1.55), Hunan (1.54), Jiangxi (1.50), Sichuan (1.13) |
| Culture and education, arts and crafts, sports and entertainment products manufacturing industry | Zhejiang (1.92), Jiangxi (1.71), Shanghai (1.40), Jiangsu (1.00) |
| Petroleum processing, coking and nuclear fuel processing industries | Shanghai (2.46), Zhejiang (1.25), Yunnan (1.23), Hunan (1.17) |
| Chemical raw materials and chemical products manufacturing industry | Jiangsu (1.27), Zhejiang (1.02), Hubei (0.98), Hunan (0.95) |
| Pharmaceutical production industry | Guizhou (1.74), Jiangxi (1.59), Sichuan (1.22), Yunnan (1.18) |
| Chemical fiber manufacturing industry | Zhejiang (2.95), Jiangsu (1.55), Sichuan (0.25), Jiangxi (0.20) |
| Rubber and plastic products industry | Zhejiang (1.76), Anhui (1.39), Shanghai (1.11), Hubei (0.98) |

(continued)

**Table 8** (continued)

| Industry | Top four member regions in terms of localization intensity |
|---|---|
| Non-metallic mineral products industry | Jiangxi (1.79), Guizhou (1.64), Hunan (1.59), Hubei (1.43) |
| Ferrous metal smelting and rolling industry | Yunnan (1.70), Hubei (1.22), Jiangsu (1.21), Guizhou (1.20) |
| Metal products industry | Jiangsu (1.24), Zhejiang (1.17), Anhui (1.02), Hubei (0.98) |
| Machinery equipment manufacturing industry | Hunan (1.51), Shanghai (1.35), Zhejiang (1.12), Jiangsu (1.10) |
| Transportation equipment manufacturing industry | Shanghai (2.05), Hubei (1.68), Sichuan (1.56), Jiangsu (0.83) |
| Electrical machinery and apparatus manufacturing industry | Anhui (1.55), Jiangsu (1.39), Zhejiang (1.16), Jiangxi (1.01) |
| Computer, communication and other electronic equipment manufacturing industry | Shanghai (2.02), Jiangsu (1.53), Sichuan (1.34), Hunan (0.56) |
| Instrumentation manufacturing industry | Jiangsu (2.01), Zhejiang (0.95), Shanghai (0.86), Hunan (0.62) |
| Production and supply of electricity and heat | Guizhou (3.16), Yunnan (2.48), Anhui (1.46), Zhejiang (1.36) |
| Gas production and supply industry | Sichuan (1.80), Zhejiang (1.31), Shanghai (1.24), Guizhou (1.07) |
| Water production and supply industry | Sichuan (1.49), Zhejiang (1.47), Yunnan (1.25), Hunan (1.20) |
| Other industries | Jiangxi (3.39), Yunnan (2.89), Hunan (1.79), Anhui (1.22) |

to 2.95, and that of Jiangxi province was further increased from 0.71 to 2.95 by a large margin. Secondly, for a specific sub industry, the average of localization intensity of the four member regions has been changed to a certain extent from 1985 to 2013. Compared with 1985, the average of localization intensity in 22 of the 32 sub industries was increased in 2013. Among them, the average of coal mining and washing industry, non-metallic mineral mining and dressing industry and wine, beverage and refined tea manufacturing industry was increased by 2.69, 0.91 and 0.78 respectively, ranking in the top three; the average of 10 industries was decreased. Among them, the average of petroleum processing, coking and nuclear fuel processing industries, instrumentation manufacturing industry and chemical raw material and chemical products manufacturing industry was decreased more than other industries by 0.17, 0.13 and 0.13 respectively, ranking in the top three. Based on this, we can conclude that compared with 1985, the localization level of 22 industries was increased and the localization level of 10 industries was decreased in 2013. The reliability of this conclusion needs to be discussed and verified later.

### 3.2 Localization Forces

From the perspective of industry, the localization intensity mainly reflects whether a sub industry has localization advantages in this member region in the Yangtze River Economic Belt; on this basis, the localization force integrates the relative scale factor of the member regions (from the spatial distribution of the total industrial output value of the Yangtze River Economic Belt, the relative scale of different member regions is quite varying) and it reflects the relative importance of different member regions to an industry from the perspective of inter industry trade.

Let's take a look at the top four member regions of the Yangtze River Economic Belt in 1985 (refer to Table 9). It is easy to find that for a sub industry, the localization forces of different member regions were varying. For example, as for the culture and education, arts and crafts, sports and entertainment products manufacturing industry, the localization force of Shanghai was as high as 1.00, ranking the first, while that of Jiangxi was—0.07, ranking the fourth. This shows that Shanghai almost occupies the share of the export trade between this industry and other industries. Another example is the transportation equipment manufacturing industry. The localization force of Hubei was 0.75, ranking the first, while that of Hunan was 0.07, ranking the fourth. It shows that in the trade between this industry and other industries, Hubei occupied 75% of the export trade, while Hunan only occupied 7%. For different sub industries, it can be found that the localization force is different from the top four member regions. For example, comparing the chemical raw materials and chemical products manufacturing industry with the pharmaceutical production industry, only Sichuan and Shanghai were overlapped; moreover, the localization forces of these two member regions in the two sub industries were also different. To some extent, this difference also shows that, on the whole, there is a certain degree of division of work in the organization and production of industrial products in the Yangtze River Economic Belt.

Let's look at the top four member regions in the Yangtze River Economic Belt in 2013 (refer to Table 9). It can also be found that for an industry, the localization forces in different regions are varying. For example, in the electrical machinery and equipment manufacturing industry, the localization force of Jiangsu was as high as 0.65, ranking the first, while that of Jiangxi was only 0.00, ranking the fourth. It shows that in the trade between this industry and other industries, Jiangsu accounted for 65% of the export trade, while the share of Jiangxi can be ignored. Another example is the instrumentation manufacturing industry. The localization force of Jiangsu was as high as 1.00, ranking the first, while that of Guizhou was only −0.05, ranking the fourth. It shows that Jiangsu occupied the whole share of export trade in the trade between this industry and other industries, while other member regions in the Yangtze River Economic Belt were all places of trade import. For different sub industries, the localization force is different among the top four member regions. For example, comparing the rubber and plastic products industry with the non-metallic mineral products industry, only the localization force of Hubei Province overlapped, and there were obvious differences in the localization forces of Hubei Province in

**Table 9** Top four member regions in the Yangtze River Economic Belt in 1985 in terms of localization force

| Industry | Top four member regions in terms of localization forces |
|---|---|
| Coal mining, washing and dressing industry | Anhui (0.28), Sichuan (0.23), Hunan (0.19), Jiangxi (0.16) |
| Oil and gas exploitation | Sichuan (0.78), Hubei (0.22), Guizhou (−0.03), Yunnan (−0.05) |
| Mining and dressing of ferrous metals | Sichuan (0.64), Hunan (0.26), Anhui (0.05), Guizhou (0.04) |
| Non-metallic ore mining and dressing industry | Zhejiang (0.30), Jiangsu (0.27), Hunan (0.18), Anhui (0.11) |
| Food processing and manufacturing industry | Sichuan (0.56), Anhui (0.26), Jiangxi (0.09), Yunnan (0.08) |
| Wine, beverage and refined tea manufacturing industry | Zhejiang (0.34), Sichuan (0.27), Anhui (0.12), Guizhou (0.10) |
| Tobacco products industry | Yunnan (0.43), Guizhou (0.23), Anhui (0.20), Hunan (0.13) |
| Textile industry | Jiangsu (0.58), Zhejiang (0.26), Shanghai (0.12), Hubei (0.04) |
| Textile, clothing and garment industry | Shanghai (0.62), Zhejiang (0.21), Hubei (0.17), Guizhou (−0.07) |
| Leather, fur, feather and its products and footwear industry | Zhejiang (0.70), Hunan (0.21), Jiangsu (0.07), Sichuan (0.02) |
| Wood processing and wood, bamboo, rattan, palm, grass products industry | Jiangxi (0.57), Anhui (0.12), Sichuan (0.11), Yunnan (0.10) |
| Furniture manufacturing industry | Hubei (0.49), Zhejiang (0.20), Jiangxi (0.18), Jiangsu (0.06) |
| Paper and paper products industry | Hunan (0.35), Sichuan (0.33), Zhejiang (0.20), Jiangxi (0.08) |
| Printing and recording media reproduction | Sichuan (0.53), Hubei (0.35), Yunnan (0.11), Hunan (0.01) |
| Culture and education, arts and crafts, sports and entertainment products manufacturing industry | Shanghai (1.00), Zhejiang (0.00), Guizhou (−0.05), Jiangxi (−0.07) |
| Petroleum processing, coking and nuclear fuel processing industries | Hubei (0.44), Hunan (0.28), Anhui (0.25), Jiangxi (0.02) |
| Chemical raw materials and chemical products manufacturing industry | Hunan (0.35), Jiangsu (0.24), Sichuan (0.17), Shanghai (0.13) |
| Pharmaceutical production industry | Shanghai (0.56), Jiangxi (0.26), Sichuan (0.18), Hubei (−0.03) |
| Chemical fiber manufacturing industry | Shanghai (0.92), Jiangsu (0.08), Jiangxi (−0.03), Guizhou (−0.06) |
| Rubber and plastic products industry | Zhejiang (0.48), Shanghai (0.32), Jiangsu (0.20), Guizhou (−0.02) |

(continued)

**Table 9** (continued)

| Industry | Top four member regions in terms of localization forces |
|---|---|
| Non-metallic mineral products industry | Jiangsu (0.39), Zhejiang (0.17), Hunan (0.16), Anhui (0.13) |
| Ferrous metal smelting and rolling industry | Shanghai (0.41), Hubei (0.35), Sichuan (0.20), Jiangxi (0.02) |
| Metal products industry | Shanghai (0.65), Jiangsu (0.20), Zhejiang (0.15), Yunnan (−0.05) |
| Machinery equipment manufacturing industry | Shanghai (0.59), Jiangsu (0.27), Sichuan (0.08), Guizhou (0.06) |
| Transportation equipment manufacturing industry | Hubei (0.75), Sichuan (0.09), Jiangxi (0.08), Hunan (0.07) |
| Electrical machinery and apparatus manufacturing industry | Shanghai (0.47), Zhejiang (0.40), Jiangsu (0.13), Hunan (−0.06) |
| Computer, communication and other electronic equipment manufacturing industry | Jiangsu (0.53), Shanghai (0.43), Guizhou (0.04), Jiangxi (−0.01) |
| Instrumentation manufacturing industry | Shanghai (0.69), Jiangsu (0.16), Zhejiang (0.15), Sichuan (−0.03) |
| Production and supply of electricity and heat | Sichuan (0.25), Anhui (0.19), Guizhou (0.15), Hunan (0.15) |
| Gas production and supply industry | Shanghai (0.88), Anhui (0.10), Guizhou (0.02), Jiangsu (−0.02) |
| Water production and supply industry | Hubei (0.62), Hunan (0.21), Jiangxi (0.15), Anhui (0.03) |
| Other industries | Hunan (0.38), Yunnan (0.32), Jiangxi (0.25), Guizhou (0.05) |

the two industries. In fact, it is difficult to find such two sub industries from Table 10, that is, the two sub industries with completely consistent specialization force among the top four member regions. This difference also shows that, on the whole, there is a certain degree of division of work in the organization and production of industrial products in the Yangtze River Economic Belt.

Comparing the two years, we can find that for a sub industry, compared with 1985, the top four member regions in terms of localization forces have been changed in 2013. For example, in the transportation equipment manufacturing industry, compared with 1985, Jiangxi and Hunan exited from the top four in 2013 and were replaced by Shanghai and Guizhou; as for the other two member regions, the localization force of Hubei was decreased from 0.75 in 1985 to 0.30 in 2013, and the ranking dropped from the first to the third, while the localization force of Sichuan was increased from 0.09 to 0.32 with ranking remained at the second. Another example is the computer manufacturing industry, communication and other electronic equipment manufacturing industry. Compared with 1985, Jiangxi exited from the top four in 2013 and was replaced by Sichuan; as for the other three member regions, the

**Table 10** Top four member regions in the Yangtze River Economic Belt in 2013 in terms of localization force in industries

| Industry | Top four member regions in terms of localization forces |
|---|---|
| Coal mining, washing and dressing industry | Guizhou (0.40), Sichuan (0.19), Anhui (0.14), Yunnan (0.13) |
| Oil and gas exploitation | Sichuan (0.61), Hubei (0.39), Guizhou (−0.03), Yunnan (−0.03) |
| Mining and dressing of ferrous metals | Sichuan (0.28), Anhui (0.24), Hubei (0.23), Yunnan (0.15) |
| Non-metallic ore mining and dressing industry | Hubei (0.37), Hunan (0.21), Sichuan (0.20), Guizhou (0.10) |
| Food processing and manufacturing industry | Hubei (0.39), Hunan (0.20), Sichuan (0.18), Anhui (0.16) |
| Wine, beverage and refined tea manufacturing industry | Sichuan (0.61), Hubei (0.22), Guizhou (0.16), Yunnan (0.01) |
| Tobacco products industry | Yunnan (0.57), Shanghai (0.18), Hunan (0.15), Guizhou (0.10) |
| Textile industry | Zhejiang (0.72), Jiangsu (0.21), Hubei (0.07), Jiangxi (−0.06) |
| Textile, clothing and garment industry | Zhejiang (0.44), Jiangsu (0.38), Jiangxi (0.19), Anhui (−0.02) |
| Leather, fur, feather and its products and footwear industry | Zhejiang (0.83), Jiangxi (0.15), Hunan (0.02), Anhui (0.00) |
| Wood processing and wood, bamboo, rattan, palm, grass products industry | Jiangsu (0.44), Hunan (0.28), Anhui (0.20), Jiangxi (0.07) |
| Furniture manufacturing industry | Zhejiang (0.55), Sichuan (0.26), Shanghai (0.11), Hunan (0.07) |
| Paper and paper products industry | Zhejiang (0.62), Hunan (0.29), Sichuan (0.09), Hubei (−0.01) |
| Printing and recording media reproduction | Anhui (0.32), Hunan (0.31), Jiangxi (0.21), Sichuan (0.11) |
| Culture and education, arts and crafts, sports and entertainment products manufacturing industry | Zhejiang (0.66), Jiangxi (0.20), Shanghai (0.15), Jiangsu (0.00) |
| Petroleum processing, coking and nuclear fuel processing industries | Shanghai (0.67), Zhejiang (0.22), Hunan (0.08), Yunnan (0.03) |
| Chemical raw materials and chemical products manufacturing industry | Jiangsu (0.97), Zhejiang (0.03), Guizhou (−0.02), Yunnan (−0.02) |
| Pharmaceutical production industry | Jiangxi (0.42), Sichuan (0.32), Guizhou (0.17), Yunnan (0.05) |
| Chemical fiber manufacturing industry | Zhejiang (0.62), Jiangsu (0.38), Guizhou (−0.04), Yunnan (−0.05) |

(continued)

**Table 10** (continued)

| Industry | Top four member regions in terms of localization forces |
|---|---|
| Rubber and plastic products industry | Zhejiang (0.74), Anhui (0.20), Shanghai (0.05), Hubei (−0.01) |
| Non-metallic mineral products industry | Jiangxi (0.22), Hunan (0.22), Sichuan (0.20), Hubei (0.19) |
| Ferrous metal smelting and rolling industry | Jiangsu (0.62), Hubei (0.19), Yunnan (0.16), Guizhou (0.04) |
| Metal products industry | Jiangsu (0.74), Zhejiang (0.24), Anhui (0.02), Hubei (−0.02) |
| Machinery equipment manufacturing industry | Hunan (0.34), Jiangsu (0.27), Shanghai (0.22), Zhejiang (0.15) |
| Transportation equipment manufacturing industry | Shanghai (0.38), Sichuan (0.32), Hubei (0.30), Guizhou (−0.06) |
| Electrical machinery and apparatus manufacturing industry | Jiangsu (0.65), Anhui (0.23), Zhejiang (0.12), Jiangxi (0.00) |
| Computer, communication and other electronic equipment manufacturing industry | Jiangsu (0.59), Shanghai (0.27), Sichuan (0.14), Guizhou (−0.06) |
| Instrumentation manufacturing industry | Jiangsu (1.00), Zhejiang (−0.03), Shanghai (−0.03), Guizhou (−0.05) |
| Production and supply of electricity and heat | Zhejiang (0.31), Guizhou (0.24), Anhui (0.21), Yunnan (0.21) |
| Gas production and supply industry | Sichuan (0.60), Zhejiang (0.28), Shanghai (0.11), Guizhou (0.01) |
| Water production and supply industry | Zhejiang (0.44), Sichuan (0.37), Hunan (0.09), Shanghai (0.04) |
| Other industries | Jiangxi (0.53), Hunan (0.23), Yunnan (0.17), Anhui (0.07) |

localization force of Jiangsu was increased from 0.53 to 0.59 with ranking remained at the first; the localization force of Shanghai was decreased from 0.43 to 0.27, with ranking remained at the second; and the localization force of Guizhou was decreased from 0.04 to −0.06, and it was changed from place of export to import with ranking changed from the third to the fourth. To some extent, this change shows that the situation of industrial division of work in the Yangtze River Economic Belt has been changed either greatly or slightly in 2013 compared with 1985.

Compare the top four member regions in terms of localization intensity with the top four member regions in terms of localization force. Let's look at the comparison result in 1985. It can be found that for an industry, compared with the top four member regions in terms of localization intensity, the top four member regions in terms of localization force have been changed greatly or slightly. For example, in the chemical raw materials and chemical products manufacturing industry, compared with the top four member regions in terms of localization intensity, Yunnan has exited from the top four localization force and was replaced by Shanghai; as for the other three regions, the ranking of Hunan and Sichuan has not been changed, while the ranking of Jiangsu has risen from No. 4 to No. 2. Then let's look at the comparison result in 2013. It can also be found that for one sub industry, compared with the top four member regions in terms of localization intensity, the top four member regions in terms of localization force have been changed to a certain extent. Take the computer, communication and other electronic equipment manufacturing industry as an example, comparing with the top four member regions in terms of localization intensity, Hunan Province has exited from the top four in terms of localization force and was replaced by Guizhou Province; as for the other three regions, Jiangsu Province has risen from the second to the first, Shanghai has slipped from the first to the second, and ranking of Sichuan has remained unchanged.

What causes this difference? In the spatial distribution of the total industrial output value of the Yangtze River Economic Belt, the relative scale of different member regions is varying. It can be seen from Table 11 that in the spatial distribution of the total industrial output value of the Yangtze River Economic Belt in 1985, the total industrial output value of Jiangsu, Shanghai and Sichuan was relatively large and accounted for 21.7%, 20.7% and 12.4% respectively of the total industrial output value of the Yangtze River Economic Belt, ranking in the top three; the scale of the total industrial output value of Guizhou, Yunnan and Jiangxi was relatively small and accounted for 2.3%, 3.3% and 4.1% respectively of the total the industrial output value of the Yangtze River Economic Belt, ranking in the bottom three. In 2013, the industrial output value of Jiangsu, Zhejiang and Sichuan was relatively large and accounted for 31.3%, 14.7% and 11.9% respectively of the total industrial output

**Table 11** Scale and spatial distribution of total industrial output value of the Yangtze River Economic Belt in 1985 and 2013

| Industry | Scale (100 million yuan) | | Distribution (%) | | |
|---|---|---|---|---|---|
| | 1985 | 2013 | 1985 | 2013 | Variation |
| Shanghai | 825.2 | 32 088.9 | 20.7 | 7.5 | −13.3 |
| Jiangsu | 862.5 | 134 648.9 | 21.7 | 31.3 | 9.7 |
| Zhejiang | 446.6 | 62 980.3 | 11.2 | 14.7 | 3.4 |
| Anhui | 244.7 | 33 756.8 | 6.2 | 7.9 | 1.7 |
| Jiangxi | 163.8 | 24 676.9 | 4.1 | 5.7 | 1.6 |
| Hubei | 433.0 | 39 209.0 | 10.9 | 9.1 | −1.8 |
| Hunan | 288.3 | 32 843.2 | 7.2 | 7.6 | 0.4 |
| Sichuan | 492.0 | 51 114.0 | 12.4 | 11.9 | −0.5 |
| Guizhou | 91.0 | 8 074.6 | 2.3 | 1.9 | −0.4 |
| Yunnan | 131.4 | 10 289.1 | 3.3 | 2.4 | −0.9 |
| Yangtze River Economic Belt | 3 978.6 | 429 681.6 | 100.0 | 100.0 | 16.8 |

*Note* The so-called "variation" refers to the deviation degree of the share of the member regions of the Yangtze River Economic Belt in 2013 compared with that in 1985

value of the Yangtze River Economic Belt in the spatial distribution of the total industrial output value of the Yangtze River Economic Belt, ranking in the top three; the industrial output value of Guizhou, Yunnan and Jiangxi was relatively small and accounted for 1.9%, 2.4% and 5.7% respectively of the total industrial output value of the Yangtze River Economic Belt, ranking in the bottom three. Compared with 1985, the spatial distribution of the total industrial output value of the Yangtze River Economic Belt has been changed in 2013: among the 10 member regions, the relative scale of five member regions has been increased. Among them, the relative scale of Jiangsu, Zhejiang and Anhui was increased by 9.7, 3.4 and 1.7% points respectively, ranking in the top three; the relative scale of five member regions was decreased. Among them, the relative scale of Shanghai, Hubei and Yunnan was decreased by 13.3, 1.8 and 0.9% points respectively, ranking in the top three. As a result, compared with 1985, the spatial distribution of the total industrial output value of the Yangtze River Economic Belt was changed by 16.8%.

Because of the differences in the relative scale of different member regions in the Yangtze River Economic Belt, if the localization intensity of a sub industry in two member regions is the same (and greater than 1.00), it is inevitable that the member region with larger relative scale has higher localization force, while the localization force was relatively lower for member region with small scale. The result is that, for a sub industry, although the localization intensity of some member regions is small (but greater than 1.00), due to their large share in the spatial distribution of the total industrial output value of the Yangtze River Economic Belt, the localization force ranking of the member region is higher than that of the localization intensity. Of course, the change of this kind of ranking also has certain restrictions, or regularity. Comparatively speaking, the localization force must be greater than 0 in the member regions with localization intensity greater than 1, while the localization force must be less than 0 in the member regions with localization intensity less than 1. As a result, compared with the ranking of localization intensity, the change of the ranking of localization force is confined to a certain range.

### *3.3 The Localization Coefficient and the Distribution Difference Coefficient of Industry*

From the perspective of industry path, after discussing the localization intensity and localization force, the localization coefficient and distribution difference coefficient of industrial sub industries in the Yangtze River Economic Belt in 1985 and 2013 are analyzed (refer to Table 12). Let's first look at the comparison of localization coefficients of industries. It is easy to see that the localization coefficients of different sub industries are obviously different in 1985 and 2013. In 1985, the localization coefficients of petroleum and natural gas exploitation, ferrous metal mining and dressing, and coal mining and washing were 0.6714, 0.4731 and 0.4497, respectively, ranking in the top three; the localization coefficients of printing and recording

**Table 12** Localization coefficient and distribution difference coefficient of industries in 1985 and 2013

| Total | Localization coefficient of industry | | | Distribution difference coefficient of industries | | | Overestimated (%) | |
|---|---|---|---|---|---|---|---|---|
| | 1985 | 2013 | Variation (%) | 1985 | 2013 | Variation (%) | 1985 | 2013 |
| Coal mining, washing and dressing industry | 0.449 7 | 0.579 5 | 28.9 | 0.419 3 | 0.539 4 | 28.6 | −6.8 | −6.9 |
| Oil and gas exploitation industry | 0.6714 | 0.743 6 | 10.8 | 0.651 2 | 0.713 5 | 9.6 | −3.0 | −4.0 |
| Mining and dressing of ferrous metals | 0.473 1 | 0.491 4 | 3.9 | 0.444 9 | 0.450 0 | 1.1 | −6.0 | −8.4 |
| Non-metallic ore mining and dressing industry | 0.228 9 | 0.369 3 | 61.3 | 0.247 0 | 0.321 7 | 30.2 | 7.9 | −12.9 |
| Food processing and manufacturing industry | 0.141 8 | 0.261 0 | 84.0 | 0.130 1 | 0.223 7 | 71.9 | −8.3 | −14.3 |
| Wine, beverage and refined tea manufacturing industry | 0.245 5 | 0.364 3 | 48.4 | 0.222 9 | 0.325 0 | 45.8 | −9.2 | −10.8 |
| Tobacco products industry | 0.386 2 | 0.410 4 | 6.2 | 0.378 8 | 0.403 9 | 6.6 | −1.9 | −1.6 |
| Textile industry | 0.157 8 | 0.255 0 | 61.6 | 0.188 2 | 0.284 8 | 51.3 | 19.3 | 11.7 |
| Textile and garment industry | 0.114 8 | 0.212 7 | 85.3 | 0.135 3 | 0.249 5 | 84.4 | 17.8 | 17.3 |
| Leather, fur, feather and its products and footwear industry | 0.075 5 | 0.257 5 | 241.0 | 0.095 8 | 0.240 0 | 150.5 | 26.9 | −6.8 |
| Wood processing and wood, bamboo, rattan, palm, grass products industry | 0.108 6 | 0.193 4 | 78.0 | 0.098 1 | 0.235 0 | 139.7 | −9.7 | 21.6 |

(continued)

**Table 12** (continued)

| Total | Localization coefficient of industry | | | Distribution difference coefficient of industries | | | Overestimated (%) | |
|---|---|---|---|---|---|---|---|---|
| | 1985 | 2013 | Variation (%) | 1985 | 2013 | Variation (%) | 1985 | 2013 |
| Furniture manufacturing industry | 0.104 3 | 0.296 6 | 184.3 | 0.126 9 | 0.267 2 | 110.7 | 21.6 | −9.9 |
| Paper and paper products industry | 0.134 3 | 0.134 8 | 0.4 | 0.109 6 | 0.106 3 | −3.0 | −18.4 | −211 |
| Printing and recording media reproduction industry | 0.066 8 | 0.135 2 | 102.5 | 0.046 6 | 0.114 7 | 146.0 | −30.2 | −15.2 |
| Culture and education, arts and crafts, sports and entertainment products manufacturing industry | 0.327 8 | 0.206 0 | −37.2 | 0.335 3 | 0.253 2 | −24.5 | 2.3 | 22.9 |
| Petroleum processing, coking and nuclear fuel processing industries | 0.224 5 | 0.163 8 | −27.1 | 0.221 2 | 0.151 8 | −31.3 | −1.5 | −7.3 |
| Chemical raw materials and chemical products manufacturing industry | 0.067 8 | 0 086 2 | 27.2 | 0.076 7 | 0.139 1 | 81.3 | 13.2 | 61.4 |
| Pharmaceutical manufacturing industry | 0.080 1 | 0.080 1 | 0.0 | 0.080 0 | 0.082 5 | 3.1 | −0.2 | 2.9 |
| Chemical fiber manufacturing industry | 0.360 0 | 0.457 1 | 27.0 | 0.384 2 | 0.494 1 | 28.6 | 6.7 | 8.1 |

(continued)

**Table 12** (continued)

| Total | Localization coefficient of industry | | | Distribution difference coefficient of industries | | | Overestimated (%) | |
|---|---|---|---|---|---|---|---|---|
| | 1985 | 2013 | Variation (%) | 1985 | 2013 | Variation (%) | 1985 | 2013 |
| Rubber and plastic products industry | 0.110 6 | 0.150 6 | 36.1 | 0.140 4 | 0.147 7 | 5.2 | 26.9 | −1.9 |
| Non-metallic mineral products industry | 0.122 0 | 0.201 4 | 65.2 | 0 139 4 | 0.160 7 | 15.3 | 14.3 | −20.2 |
| Ferrous metal smelting and rolling industry | 0.207 1 | 0.106 8 | −48.4 | 0.185 9 | 0.139 0 | −25.2 | −10.2 | 30.2 |
| Metal products industry | 0.100 7 | 0.101 5 | 0.8 | 0.130 5 | 0.141 7 | 8.6 | 29.6 | 39.6 |
| Machinery equipment manufacturing industry | 0.087 5 | 0.116 1 | 32.7 | 0.103 7 | 0.159 7 | 54.0 | 18.5 | 37.5 |
| Transportation equipment manufacturing industry | 0.201 6 | 0.206 9 | 2.6 | 0.176 5 | 0.187 5 | 6.2 | −12.5 | −9.4 |
| Electrical machinery and apparatus manufacturing industry | 0.151 9 | 0.189 1 | 24.6 | 0.181 6 | 0.225 6 | 24.2 | 19.6 | 19.3 |
| Computer, communication and other electronic equipment manufacturing industry | 0.217 0 | 0 284 1 | 31.0 | 0.240 4 | 0.322 2 | 34.0 | 10.8 | 13.4 |
| Instrumentation manufacturing industry | 0.186 1 | 0.316 5 | 70.1 | 0.215 9 | 0.366 7 | 69.9 | 16.0 | 15.9 |

(continued)

**Table 12** (continued)

| Total | Localization coefficient of industry | | | Distribution difference coefficient of industries | | | Overestimated (%) | |
|---|---|---|---|---|---|---|---|---|
| | 1985 | 2013 | Variation (%) | 1985 | 2013 | Variation (%) | 1985 | 2013 |
| Production and supply of electricity and heat | 0.156 9 | 0.171 3 | 9.1 | 0.127 2 | 0.138 2 | 8.7 | −19.0 | −19.3 |
| Gas production and supply | 0.244 6 | 0.159 3 | −34.9 | 0.261 1 | 0.132 6 | −49.2 | 6.7 | −16.8 |
| Water production and supply | 0.088 1 | 0.158 8 | 80.2 | 0.099 7 | 0.122 0 | 22.4 | 13.1 | −23.2 |
| Other industries | 0.157 4 | 0.261 0 | 65.8 | 0.150 7 | 0.248 9 | 65.1 | −4.2 | −4.6 |
| Total | 0.160 2 | 0.202 3 | 26.3 | 0.204 5 | 0.252 8 | 23.6 | 27.7 | 25.0 |

*Note* The so-called “variation” refers to the deviation degree of the localization coefficient of the industry or the distribution difference coefficient of the industry relative to 1985; the so-called “overestimation” refers to the deviation degree of the distribution difference coefficient of the industry with respect to the localization coefficient of the industry media reproduction industry, chemical raw materials and chemical products manufacturing industry, leather, fur, feather and their products and footwear industry were smaller, namely, 0.0668, 0.0678 and 0.0755, respectively, ranking in the last three. In 2013, the localization coefficients of oil and gas exploitation, coal mining and washing industry and ferrous metal mining and dressing industry were relatively large, namely 0.7436, 0.5795 and 0.4914, respectively, ranking in the top three; the localization coefficients of pharmaceutical production, chemical raw materials and chemical products manufacturing and metal products industry were smaller, namely 0.0801, 0.0862 and 0.1015 respectively, ranking in the bottom three. By comparing the localization coefficient of sub industries in 1985 and 2013, it can be found that the localization coefficient of 28 sub industries among 32 has been improved. Among them, the scale of leather, fur, feather and their products, footwear industry, furniture manufacturing industry and printing and recording media reproduction industry was increased by 241.0%, 184.3% and 102.5% respectively, ranking in the top three; The results showed that the localization coefficient of the four industries, including ferrous metal smelting and rolling industry, culture and education, arts and crafts, sports and entertainment products manufacturing industry, gas production and supply industry and oil processing industry, and coking and nuclear fuel processing industry, were reduced by 48.4%, 37.2%, 34.9% and 27.1%, respectively. Here, we can use the average of localization intensity to judge the variation tendency of industry localization level. The verification conclusion is that there is a large deviation and it is not so reliable. As a comprehensive response to the change of localization coefficient of each sub industry, the industrial division coefficient of the Yangtze River Economic Belt was increased from 0.1602 in 1985 to 0.2023 in 2013, with the amplitude of 26.3%.

Let's look at the comparison of distribution difference coefficients of industries. It can be found that whether in 1985 or 2013, there were large or small differences between different sub industries. In 1985, the distribution difference coefficients of petroleum and natural gas mining, ferrous metal mining and dressing, and coal mining and washing industry were 0.6512, 0.4449 and 0.4449, respectively, ranking in the top three; the distribution difference coefficients of printing and recording media reproduction industry, chemical raw materials and chemical products manufacturing industry and pharmaceutical production industry were 0.0466, 0.0767 and 0.0800, respectively, ranking in the last three. In 2013, the distribution difference coefficients of oil and gas exploitation, coal mining and washing industry and chemical fiber manufacturing industry were 0.7135, 0.5394 and 0.4941, respectively, ranking in the top three; the distribution difference coefficients of pharmaceutical production, paper and paper products industry and printing and recording media replication industry were 0.0825, 0.1063 and 0.1147, respectively, ranking in the bottom three. Comparing the distribution difference coefficient of the two years, it can be found that, compared with 1985, the distribution difference coefficient of 27 out of 32 industries was increased in 2013. Among them, the amplitude in leather, fur, feather and their products and footwear industry, printing and recording media reproduction industry, wood processing and wood, bamboo, rattan, palm, grass products and furniture manufacturing industries was increased by more than 100%, namely 150.5%,

146.0%, 139.7% and 110.7%, respectively, ranking in the top four; the distribution difference coefficient of five industries was decreased. Among them, the gas production and supply industry, petroleum processing, coking and nuclear fuel processing industry, and ferrous metal smelting and rolling industry was decreased by 49.2%, 31.3% and 25.2%, respectively, ranking in the top three. As a comprehensive response to the change of distribution difference coefficient of each sub industry, the spatial distribution difference coefficient of industry in Yangtze River Economic Belt was increased from 0.2045 in 1985 to 0.2528 in 2013, with the amplitude of 23.6%.

### *3.4 Industrial Division Coefficient and Spatial Distribution Difference Coefficient*

For the variation tendency of industrial division coefficient in the Yangtze River Economic Belt, the analysis has been carried out in the previous context, here we will mainly focus on the discussion of the spatial distribution difference coefficient. The difference coefficient of industrial spatial distribution in the Yangtze River Economic Belt showed a trend of decreasing first and then rising from 0.2045 in 1985 to 0.2528 in 2013, with an increase of 23.6%. If we ignore the relative scale factor of industries and use the coefficient of spatial distribution difference to discuss the industrial division of work in the Yangtze River Economic Belt, the level of industrial division of work in the Yangtze River Economic Belt was overestimated from 14.2% (2004) to 28.5% (1988). The comparison between the localization coefficient of industry and the distribution difference coefficient of industry is helpful to deepen the understanding of this problem. In 1985, among 32 industries, the coefficient of distribution difference of 17 industries was higher than the localization coefficient of industries. Among them, the metal products industry, rubber and plastic products industry, leather, fur, feather and their products and footwear industry were overestimated by 29.6%, 26.9% and 26.9% respectively, ranking in the top three; The distribution difference coefficient of 15 industries was lower than the localization coefficient of industries. The printing and recording media reproduction industry, power and heat production and supply industry, and paper and paper products industry were underestimated by 30.2%, 19.0% and 18.4%, respectively, ranking in the bottom three. In 2013, among the 32 industries, the distribution difference coefficient of 13 industries was higher than the localization coefficient of industries. Among them, the chemical raw materials and chemical products manufacturing industry, metal products industry and mechanical equipment manufacturing industry were overestimated by 61.4%, 39.6% and 37.5% respectively, ranking in the top three in terms of overestimation; the distribution difference coefficient of 19 industries was lower than the localization coefficient of industries; the water production and supply industry, paper and paper products industry and non-metallic mineral products industry were underestimated by 23.2%, 21.1% and 20.2% respectively, ranking in the top three in terms of underestimation. This difference shows that if we ignore the relative scale factor of industries and use the distribution difference coefficient of industries to compare the localization level of different sub industries in the Yangtze River Economic Belt, it is bound to make a wrong judgment.

## 4 Conclusion

The measurement method developed by Fan Fuzhuo (2007, 2009) was applied in this chapter to analyze the industrial division of work in the Yangtze River Economic Belt over a long time span. From the perspective of regional path, it is found in this chapter that for a member region of the Yangtze River Economic Belt, the specialization intensity and status of different industries are varying, and the difference changes with the passage of time; for different member regions, the regional specialization coefficients are different, and since the middle and late 1980s, the specialization coefficient of most regions has been improved more or less. From the perspective of industry path, for an industrial industry in the Yangtze River Economic Belt, the localization intensity and localization coefficient of different member regions are varying, and this difference changes with the passage of time; for different industrial industries, the difference of industry localization coefficient was relatively large, and since the middle and late 1980s, the localization coefficient of most industries has been improved more or less. The general conclusion is that compared with the middle and late 1980s, the level of division of work in the Yangtze River Economic Belt has been greatly improved. If we ignore the relative scale factors of regions or industries and use the coefficient of industrial structure difference or spatial distribution difference to discuss the industrial division of work in the Yangtze River Economic Belt, the level of industrial division of work in the Yangtze River Economic Belt will be overestimated.

# References


1. *China Environmental Statistics Bulletin,* Ministry of Environmental Protection of 2014.
2. *China Environmental Statistics Yearbook* of 2014 [M]. China Statistics Press, 2014.
3. *Environmental Status Bulletin* by environment protection bureau (department) of all provinces and cities in 2014.
4. Walder, A.G., Luo, T., & Wang, D. (2013). Social Stratification in Transitional Economies: Property Rights and the Structure of Markets. Theory and Society. Advance online publication. https://doi.org/10.1007/s11186-013-9203-2.
5. Yunxiang yan, Food Safety and Social Risk in Contemporary China, The Journal of Asian Studies Vol. 71, No. 3 (August) 2012.
6. Chunhui Chen. Research on the linkage development of manufacturing industry and logistics industry in Fujian Province Based on grey correlation [J]. Chinese market, 2012(2).
7. Shaozhi Chen, Haichuan Zhou. Connotation, orientation and implementation path of forestry ecological civilization construction [J]. Academic Journal of Zhongzhou, 2014(7).
8. Tao Chen. Dynamic evaluation of economic sustainable development capacity of Yangtze River Economic Belt [J]. The World of Survey and Research, 2015(7).
9. Sheng Cheng, Junbiao Zhang. Steady state and chaos analysis of dynamic evolution process of industrial clusters [J]. Academic Monthly, 2007(10).
10. Yan Cheng. Research on the linkage development of logistics industry in Yangtze River Economic Belt [D]. Shanghai: Doctoral Dissertation of East China Normal University, 2013.
11. Muhua Cui. Pollution emission and scenario planning of Yangtze River Economic Belt [J]. Academics, 2015(4).
12. Jun Ding. The ports along the Yangtze River in Jiangsu and Shanghai are most affected by the use of river sea direct vessels [N]. 21st Century Business Herald, 2014-06-20.
13. Fuzhuo Fan. Measurement of regional specialization [J]. Economic Research Journal, 2007(9).
14. Fuzhuo Fan. Measurement of regional division of work in China: method and empiriacal study [M]. Shanghai: Shanghai Academy of Social Sciences Press, 2009.
15. Songhai Fang, Weinong Wang, Hanquan Huang. Research on increasing the income of farmers and expanding rural consumption [J]. Journal of Management World, 2011(5).
16. Jianxiong, Guo. From Malthus trap to endogenous growth: re-understanding of the relationship between industrialization and agricultural development [J]. Journal of Renmin University of China, 2014(6).
17. Xiaofei Hou. Challenges and Countermeasures for the integrated development of the Yangtze River Economic Belt [J]. Regional Economic Review, 2015(5).
18. Ming Hu. Research on the synergistic development effect of producer services and agriculture in China [J]. Issues in Agricultural Economy, 2013(12).
19. Qinghua Huang, Zhibo Zhou, Han Liu. Industrial structure evolution and policy orientation of the Yangtze River Economic Belt [J]. Economic Theory and Business Management, 2014(4).




X. Jing (ed.), *Development of the Yangtze River Economic Belt in China*, Urban Governance Practices in China,
https://doi.org/10.1007/978-981-16-1578-8

20. Feifei Ji, Wen Chen. Research progress of financial center spatial system and its enlightenment to Yangtze River Delta integration [J]. Economic Geography, 2013(2).
21. Jianhua Jiang, Chengjun Liu, Gang Liu, Yiming Wang. Spatial pattern and evolution of regional information industry in China [J]. Forum on Science and Technology in China, 2014(2).
22. Xing Jin, Ying Gao. Empirical analysis of regional agricultural industrial structure in Jiangsu Province [J]. Nanjing Journal of Social Sciences, 2014(7).
23. Xuejun Jin, Lintian. Financial geography: new developments of geography in foreign countries [J]. Economic Geography, 2004(24).
24. Xueqing Jing. An empirical study on the linkage development of Shanghai service industry and Yangtze River Delta economy [J]. Journal of Nantong University, 2012(3).
25. Xueqing Jing et al. Industrial transformation and structural development of Yangtze River Economic Belt [M]. Shanghai: Shanghai Academy of Social Sciences Press, 2015.
26. Chunyan Li, Chuanhao Wen. Theory and Practice Exploration of Win-win Cooperation of Yangtze River Economic Belt—View Summary of Academic Seminar on "Yangtze River Economic Belt Summit Forum" [J]. China Industrial Economics, 2015(2).
27. Genfan Li. The Natural Productive Forces and Study on the Agricultural History (Part I): What Way to Cognize the Natural Productive Forces [J]. Agricultural History of China, 2014(2).
28. Genfan Li. The Natural Productive Forces and Study on the Agricultural History (Part III): The Natural Productive Forces and the Natural Productivity in Agriculture [J]. Agricultural History of China, 2014(4).
29. Xiaojian Li. Financial Geography Theory and China's Financial Geography Research [J] Economic Geography, 2006(6).
30. Xuesong Li, Bowen Sun. Density, Distance, Segmentation and Regional Market Integration—Demonstration from Yangtze River Economic Belt [J]. Macroeconomics, 2015(6).
31. Zhen Li, Mingyuan Liu. Benefit Compensation Mechanism and System Construction of Regional Economic Cooperation [J]. Social Sciences in Nanjing, 2012(8).
32. Minshu Lin, Mingyuan Liu. Benefit Sharing and Compensation Mechanism in Regional Economic Cooperation [J]. Finance& Economics, 2012(5).
33. Sifeng Liu, Tianbang Guo. Grey System Theory and Its Application [M]. Kaifeng: Henan University Press, 1991.
34. Weiliu. Analysis of Regional Economic Differences in the Yangtze River Economic Belt [J]. Resources and Environment in the Yangtze Basin, 2006(2).
35. Xiaoling Liu. The Development Pattern of Yangtze River Container, River and Sea Intermodal Transport Needs to be Optimized [J]. 中国港口, 2015(8).
36. Liuyang, Jun Bi. Sustainable Development Strategy of Yangtze River Economic Belt from the Perspective of Ecological Compensation [J]. China Development, 2015(1).
37. Jun Lu. Review on the Linkage Development of Logistics Industry and Manufacturing Industry [J]. Economic Forum, 2013(11).
38. Feng Luo, Qi Li. Enlightenment and Reflection of EU Integration on the Coordinated Development of Yangtze River Delta [J]. Journal of Chinese Academy of Governance, 2010(3).
39. Yonggang Pan. Some Thoughts and Suggestions on the Joint Development of Port Groups in the Yangtze River Delta [J]. Communication Shipping, 2014(10).
40. Zhiwu Qian, Jiao Wang. The Production of Main Port Enterprises along the Yangtze River was Improving in Stability in 2013 [J]. China Ports, 2014(2).
41. Jiuwen Sun, Aimin Li. Research on the Overall Pattern of Regional Development of "Overall Dispersion with Concentrated Advantages" Based on New Economic Geography [J]. Economic Perspectives, 2012(5).
42. Weibin Tang et al. The Amount of Pollution in the Yangtze River and its Tributaries is still rising rapidly [N]. Economic Information Daily, 2014-12-08.
43. Ning Wang, Changlin Ye, Shukai Cai. Interaction and Coordinated Development of Agricultural Policy and Environmental Policy [J]. Soft Science, 2010(1).
44. Bo Wang. Research on the linkage development of manufacturing industry and regional logistics in Liaoning Province [J]. Science and Technology Information, 2012(33).

45. Guomin Wang. Risk Management and Prevention System Construction of Agricultural Natural Disasters [J]. Social Science Research, 2007(4).
46. Jianhong Wang. Division of Main Port Functions of Tokyo Bay Port Group in Japan and Its Enlightenment [J]. China Harbour Engineering, 2008(2).
47. Jiao Wang. Experience and Prospect of major port enterprises along the Yangtze River in 2014 [J]. ChinaPorts, 2015(2).
48. Liehui Wang, Boke Mao. Comparison and selection of port group institutional cooperation modes and Its Enlightenment to Yangtze River Delta [J]. Social Sciences, 2010(6).
49. Maolin Wang, Leiming Feng et al. Grey Comprehensive Correlation Analysis on the Linkage Development of Manufacturing Industry and Logistics Industry in Tianjin [J]. Logistics Technology, 2013(12).
50. Mingzhi Wang, Kezhao. Analysis of Port Economic Operation and Situation in the Yangtze River Delta Region in 2014 [J]. Shipping Management, 2015(4).
51. Shuhua Wang. Construction of Cross Provincial Ecological Compensation Mechanism in Yangtze River Economic Belt [J]. Reform, 2014(6).
52. Jian Wei. Synchronization of Four Modernizations and Improvement of Urbanization Quality [J]. Academic Monthly, 2013(5).
53. Chuanqing Wu, Xu Dong. Evaluation of Sustainable Development Ability of Yangtze River Economic Belt [J]. Luojia Management Review, 2014(1).
54. Qun Wu. Research on the Linkage Development of Logistics Industry and Manufacturing Industry in Jiangxi Province [J]. Jiangxi Social Sciences, 2013(6).
55. Shaohong Wu, Jikun Huang, Yanhua Liu, Jiangbo Gao, Jun Yang, Wentao Wang, Yunhe Yin, Hao Luan, Wanlu Dong. Pros and Cons of Climate Change on China [J]. China Population. Resources and Environment, 2014(1).
56. Jiquan Xiang. Equalization of Basic Public Services: Policy Objectives and Institutional Guarantee [J]. Journal of Central China Normal University (Humanities and Social Sciences), 2008(1).
57. Li Xiao. Research on the Relationship Between Consumption Structure and Income of Rural Residents in China [J]. Journal of Agricultural Economics, 2012(11).
58. Changle Xu. Industrial Division of Work and Cooperation in the Construction of Yangtze River Economic Belt [J]. Reform, 2014(6).
59. Yinan Xu. Research on the Development of Regional Financial Cooperation in the Yangtze River Delta [J]. Statistical Theory and Practice, 2010(2).
60. Gang Yang, Mengyu Yang. Spatial Correlation Effect of Agricultural TFP in China: An Empirical Study Based on Static and Dynamic Spatial Panel Models [J]. Economic Geography, 2013(11).
61. Ruihua Yao et al. Current Situation of Water Environment in the Middle and Lower Reaches of the Yangtze River and Countermeasures for Pollution Control [J]. Yangtze River, 2014(1).
62. Jingzhong Ye, Miao An. Theoretical Origin and Practical Reflection of Modern Agricultural Development Model [J]. Guizhou Social Sciences, 2010(10).
63. Sen Ye. Research on Regional Industrial Linkage–Taking IC industry linkage between Pudong New Area and Yangtze River Delta as an Example [D]. Shanghai: Doctoral Dissertation of East China Normal University, 2009.
64. Weidong Yin. Current situation and Legal Countermeasures of Water Pollution Control in Yangtze River [J]. China Water Resources, 2003(6).
65. Qingwen Yu. Glorious Course and Great Achievement–50 Years Development of China's Information Industry [D]. http://www.ccnews.com.cn. 1999 年 10 月。
66. Taofang Yu, Feng Zhen, Hong Wu. The Regional Structure of the Yangtze River Economic Belt. From the Perspective of "Core Periphery" [J]. Urban Planning Forum, 2007(3).
67. Guang Zeng, Ji Zhou. Calculation and Analysis of the Index of China's Strong Industrial Provinces Based on Factor Analysis and Cluster Analysis [J]. Journal of Industrial Technological Economics, 2015(10).
68. Chewei Zhang, Dewen Wang. The fundamental change of the nature of farmers' income—Investigation on the Change of Farmers' Income Structure and Growth in Different Regions [J]. China Rural Survey, 2004(1).

69. Fengchao Zhang. Research on Financial Regional System [M]. Beijing: People's Publishing House, 2006.
70. Houming Zhang, Jianping Zeng. Ideas and Suggestions on Coordinated Development of Regional New Generation Information Technology Industry [EB/OL]. China Economic News, 4th Dec., 2014.
71. Houming Zhang, Shilei Liu. Thoughts and Suggestions on Promoting Orderly Transfer of Electronic Information Industry [EB/OL]. China Economic News, 11th April, 2014.
72. Peigang Zhang. Agricultural modernization Volume I [M]. Wuhan: Huazhong University of Science and Technology Press, 2002.
73. Qinwen Zhang, Xuemeng Wang. Grey System Analysis of Rural Economy – Model, Method and Application [M]. Beijing: Academic Journal Press, 1989.
74. Feng Zhao, Xiaochuan Xing, Huixuan Li. A Review of the Research on Urban and Rural Labor Mobility: Theory and Empirical Study in China [J]. China Population. Resources and Environment, 2015(4).
75. Lin Zhao, Tignying Xu, Changle Xu. Time and Space Analysis of Economic Evolution of Yangtze River Economic Belt [J]. Resources and Environment in River Basin, 2013(7).
76. China Statistical Yearbook of 2014 compiled by the Bureau of Statistics of the People's Republic of China [M]. Beijing: China Statistics Press, Year 2014.
77. Cheng Zhou. An Introduction to the Law of Solving Difficulties in Agriculture [J]. Chinese Rural Economy, 2010(3).
78. Changzheng Zhu. Grey Correlation Analysis on the Linkage Development of Manufacturing Industry and Logistics Industry in Shaanxi Province [J]. Enterprise Economy, 2011(8).
79. Hang Zhu. A study on the financial integration between the two sides of the Taiwan Strait [D]. Tianjin: Doctoral Dissertation of Nankai University, 2013.
80. Lin Zou, Gang Zeng, Xianzhong Cao, Siyu Chen. Spatial Characteristics of Economic Network of Yangtze River Economic Belt [J]. Economic Geography, 2015(6).

The manufacturer's authorised representative in the EU is Springer Nature Customer Service Centre GmbH, Europaplatz 3, 69115 Heidelberg, Germany. If you have any concerns regarding our products, please contact ProductSafety@springernature.com

Printed and bound by CPI Group (UK) Ltd, Croydon, CR0 4YY
30/09/2026
02225290-0008